# Arms
# and the
# Enlisted
# Woman

# Arms
# and the
# Enlisted
# Woman

## JUDITH
## HICKS
## STIEHM

 Temple University Press ■ Philadelphia

Temple University Press, Philadelphia 19122
Copyright © 1989 by Judith Hicks Stiehm
All rights reserved
Published 1989
Printed in the United States of America

Library of Congress Cataloging-in-Publication Data
Stiehm, Judith.
    Arms and the enlisted woman.
    Bibliography: p. 306
    Includes index.
    1. United States—Armed Forces—Women.   I. Title.
UB418.W65S75    1988       355'.0088042
87-33645
ISBN 0-87722-565-6 (alk. paper)

# Contents

# Acknowledgments

A grant from the Russell Sage Foundation provided an invaluable research leave. Alida Brill, then a Sage program officer, was especially supportive. Many other individuals provided generous assistance, advice, and admonition. Among them were the following:

| | | |
|---|---|---|
| Jerry Anderson | Patricia Gormley | Patricia Murphy |
| Shirley Bach | Heidi Hartman | Patricia Murray |
| Lois Banner | Cynthia Hilyard | Barbara Nyce |
| Chris Batjer | William Hogan, Jr. | Lough O'Daly |
| Carolyn Becraft | Anne Hoiberg | Diane Ordes |
| Sue Berryman | Jeanne Holm | Matthew Price |
| Martin Binkin | Jim Hosek | Gail Reals |
| Grace Blancett | Richard Hunter | Robin Romans |
| Kathy Byerly | Mark Kann | Rebecca Salokar |
| D'Ann Campbell | Karen Keesling | Georgia Sandler |
| Sue Canfield | Catherine Kelliher | Joel Savelle |
| Sandra Carey | Nora Kinzer | Tom Scilia |
| Beth Coye | Faris Kirkland | Mady Segal |
| Joan Creelan | Jean Klick | Frances Shea |
| Roma Danysh | Kathryn Knudsen | Natalie Stewart-Smith |
| Lois DeFleur | Lawrence Korb | Alan Terl |
| Linda De Pauw | Cecile Landrum | Patricia Thomas |
| C. M. Devilbiss | Sharon Lord | Dean Tice |
| Zahava Doering | John Lovell | Victoria Watkins |
| Mark Eitelberg | Chris Lowe | June Willenz |
| Cynthia Enloe | Mary Mayer | Ruth Woidyla |
| Jennifer Frutig | Bettie Morden | Ann Wright |
| Robert Goldich | Charles Moskos | Henry Zubkoff |
| Nancy Goldman | | |

Chapter 2, "The Generations of Enlisted Women," appeared in *Signs* 2, no. 1 (1985); a revision of Chapter 3, "Backlash and Freeze," appeared in conference proceedings titled *Women in the United States Armed Forces: Progress and Barriers in the 1980s*, edited by Nancy H. Loring, 1984; and a version of Chapter 9, "Biology, Sex, and the Family," appeared in *Women, Biology and Public Policy*, edited by Virginia Sapiro for Sage Publications, 1985.

# Arms and the Enlisted Woman

# Introduction

This book is about America's most unknown soldiers—enlisted women in the Army, Air Force, Navy, and Marines. It is also about the making of policies concerning enlisted women. Above all, it is an effort to explain why those policies so often appear to fly in the face of both logic and evidence.

I hope that those who are serving and who have served as enlisted women will like this book—that they will find it fair, authentic, and meaningful.

I know some readers will not like it. Some of my feminist friends will find it militaristic, flawed by a "me tooism" that insists upon women's being allowed to do the forbidden without reflecting upon what the forbidden is. (In this case, of course, it is consenting and preparing to kill people.) Some of my military friends will not like it either. They will deplore what they see as my valuing of equity over effectiveness; they will find my disregard of experience reckless; and they will believe that my assumption that women can contribute to the nation's defense in the same ways as men misplaces the burden of proof.

Anticipating these responses, I should like to be explicit about why I have written this book, what it contains, and why I believe its implications are profound.

## WHY I HAVE WRITTEN THIS BOOK

Why do some people sacrifice their lives for others? Why do some people feel justified in taking the lives of others?

I have previously explored these questions by examining the thinking of both participants in organizations committed to nonviolence and U.S. military officers. As a political theorist, I do this by immersing myself in what has been said and written. I attempt to uncover unstated assumptions and to grasp the internal coherence of my subjects' views, with particular attention to apparent illogic and to departures from evidence. I try to understand the meaning of beliefs and statements in their context. Having done this, I ask myself, "Of what is this an instance?" or, "What is the meaning of these beliefs and statements *in general?*"

My work is not grounded in a particular political, sociological, or psychological theory. It does not follow a prescribed methodology. It draws upon and uses personal narratives, field interviews, historical exposition, analyses of others' data, and the reading of minutes and memos. I have used this approach in two other volumes, *Nonviolent Power* and *Bring Me Men and Women: Mandated Change at the U.S. Air Force Academy.*

I wrote *Nonviolent Power* energized by the events of the late 1950s and early 1960s and by a touch of pride in ancestors who had participated in the Underground Railroad. In it I sought to outline several theories of nonviolence underpinning the rhetoric and work of leaders and organizations in the U.S. civil rights and antiwar movements. *Nonviolent Power* was addressed, though, to the vast majority of Americans who will never practice or punish nonviolent resistance, but whose judgment in the form of "public opinion" will almost certainly determine the winner of any nonviolent struggle. I noted with particular interest the uneasy shift of public opinion when Martin Luther King, Jr., first suggested that nonviolent action might be appropriate in the northern and urban parts of the United States, and, later, when he indicated that it might be well to consider U.S. participation in the world arena (especially in Vietnam) in light of the principles so applauded when directed against rural, southern sheriffs.

American ambivalence about King's Nobel Peace Prize forced me to recognize that few Americans are serious about nonviolence. Some deem it an admirable way for the weak to protest against domestic injustice, but the powerful tend not to protest but simply to write (or rewrite) the law. Thus, in the domestic arena the powerful do not resort to "naked" violence, but to the "legitimate" violence known as law and its enforcement. Further, in the international context "security" tends to be sufficient justification for any violent act (legal or illegal) authorized by the President or Congress.

The contrast between women's energetic participation in the civil rights and antiwar movements and their near exclusion from both law enforcement and the military led me to reflect that men in our culture are trained to expect private and governmental, legal and illegal violence, and that they consider violence an appropriate counter to violence. American women, on the other hand, are likely to abhor violence, and to believe that they can or should be exempted from using it *and* from having it used on them. Few are reluctant, however, to ask men to use violence on their behalf—for example, to arrest, try, and imprison a rapist.

Further, although I was personally attracted by and to nonviolent action, and did my best to describe and explain its tenets, it was not, finally, persuasive to me. I believed that if it is possible to offer protection to innocent others, one is compelled to do so. Sacrifice of my own life for a principle was comprehensible; permitting the slaughter of persons I had the capacity to protect was not. In this respect I imagine that my thinking is in accord with the views of professional military personnel.

Accordingly, I made my next project a study of "violent thought"—the assumptions and understandings of those explicitly committed to the use of socially sanctioned, legitimate violence. Military and police personnel accept the capacity and willingness to use violence as part of their profession. They train for, plan, and execute acts of violence, and they are honored and rewarded for doing so. Because those who choose life-taking, life-risking, and sometimes life-sacrificing occupations are not often philosophers, my problem was to find a probe to tap their *weltanschauung*, to reveal their assumptions.

Congress provided an answer in 1975 when it directed that the U.S. military academies accept women. This mandated change created precisely the right circumstances for an exploration of military thought.* The academies had to assess their every principle and activity to determine whether they were intrinsically "military" or merely "manly." Those which were "military" had to be preserved regardless of women's displeasure and/or inexperience; those which were only "manly" were liable to challenge and change.

*Bring Me Men and Women* describes in detail the integration of women into the Air Force Academy. This account (made possible by the Academy's generous cooperation) is *not* about the women cadets. I assumed the women to be normal and, therefore, not especially interesting. The objects of my curiosity and investigation were the male officers who were discomfited by, yet made and implemented, an integration policy mandated by Congress. My goal was to understand how the staff understood and justified their role, which they refer to as "the profession of arms."

In a concluding essay on women and combat, I asked whether men's monopoly on the role of warrior undermines women's claim to be full citizens, and whether that monopoly is necessary to the preservation of the role. Many Air Force officers believe as strongly as Army and Marine officers that women should not serve in combat. Yet arguments based on physical strength, "cohesion," and "rightness" are surely more compelling when the scenario is ground combat than when it is air combat. The latter is conducted by a small number of highly trained officers using expensive and sophisticated equipment. When beliefs are intensely held in the face of common sense or experience, one suspects that something

*Another but more painful set of "right circumstances" derives from the loss of a war.

important is at stake, even if that something is neither obvious nor articulated. In pursuit of that something, I turned my attention to the source of so much anxiety for military men—military women, and, in particular, enlisted women. My assumption was that the fundamental is best sought in the ordinary, and that women Academy graduates and other women officers can be assimilated or accommodated as members of an elite rather than as women. The real test for the military, then, is the use (and the reasons offered for the use) of low-visibility enlisted women.

CONTENTS

When I asked enlisted women what they would most like to have civilians know about them, the answer often was a variation of "Tell them we are normal." When I asked civilians if they had ever seen a soldier in a maternity uniform, the answer often was suspicious silence. "Are you kidding?" was the implicit response.

The story that needs to be told about enlisted women goes far beyond affirming the ordinariness of the women who join the military for education, opportunity, and travel, just as men do. It goes beyond providing pictures that establish that there are indeed women soldiers, sailors, airmen, as female members of the Air Force are called, and marines, and beyond the portrayal of basic training, for basic does not serve the same initiation function for women that it serves for men. A group of women go through basic training together, and their supervising cadre contains some women. Thus, it is only at her first assignment that a woman is likely to encounter a nearly all-male and sometimes hostile environment. It then becomes clear just how isolated many military women are, just how limited are the resources available to them, and just how much sexual pressure can be exerted on them. Moreover, it is only in the "real" military that women begin to understand their permanent minority status and the boundaries set on their participation.

Part I of this book, The American Enlisted Woman, offers an overview of her experience that draws on hundreds of individual and group conversations with enlisted women serving all over the world and covering a period of some six years. (An autobiographical narrative by a six-year Air Force veteran supplements their testimonies; see Appendix A.) Chapter 2 analyzes how rapid and externally determined policy changes affected military women of different "generations"—that is, women who held different ranks and were of different ages when a specific change occurred (such as permitting pregnant women to stay in service). Finally, we will look at a period (lasting from 1980 to 1982) of "backlash" against the changes that had marked the previous decade. Not a reversal, but a steady state, was the result of that backlash.

The subject of Part II, Making Policy for Enlisted Women, could fill volumes. To provide both specificity and generality, I have focused on the period from 1972 to 1986 and on a single service when discussing particular topics. This section begins with a review of what is known about military opinions of military women. The good news is that military women are proud of themselves and their work; the bad news is that they are not so well regarded by their male peers, even though objective measures suggest that women do about as well as men. Furthermore, much military opinion holds that women are not discriminated against, but are actually favored!

The Navy is the focus of the chapter that discusses changes made in women's military role through litigation and legislation. This is not the usual way to change military policy, since both the courts and Congress tend to leave things military to the military.

In policy debates on women in the military reference is frequently made to "studies" that "prove" a particular point. Such research is the subject of Chapter 6. Some of these studies are quick, dirty, and non-professional; others are meticulously conducted by social scientists. One needs to know which is which. Unfortunately, military men and women alike are now tired of "research on women." Some are simply weary of the disproportionate attention given a small percentage of personnel; many women are tired of being treated as "specimens," and also of the implication that there is something deficient, mysterious, or at least irregular about them.

The Air Force is highlighted in the bottom-line chapter on how military personnel systems operate, and how the services determine the number of women they "access." That figure places a ceiling on the number of women who can serve in the military, yet it is *never* referred to as a quota.

Part III, Meta-Influences on Policies, explores factors that are fundamental, but difficult to measure or to show as directly causal. Chapter 8 examines the views of the American public as documented in survey data going back to 1940. Some of these data cast doubt on the congruence of the views of the American public, the military, and Congress. This is true in part because traditional views of biology, sex, and family (Chapter 9) are compatible with military service for men, but not with military service for women. Chapter 10 argues that myths necessary to the pursuit of war are difficult to sustain in the presence of women. The need to believe the unbelievable, then, leads to continued tension about enlisted women, as well as to a tendency to ignore them, thus contributing to their "unknown" state.

### IMPLICATIONS

There are now more than 200,000 women in uniform. These semi-permanent, minority invaders of a male institution fill a variety of nontraditional jobs—jobs that are not so dominated by women in the civilian sector that the military *must* recruit women or leave the jobs unfilled (as would be the case, for instance, with nursing). Even if these women continue to be seen as substitutes for unavailable men—that is, as "better-than-nothings"—in today's military they are substitutes not for men who have been sent to the front, but for men who have chosen to remain at home. If mobilization and/or a draft should occur, a cadre of senior, trained, professional women will already be in place—something that has never been true before.

Perhaps most important, though, women who wear uniforms are counterexamples: living disproof of widely held (and perhaps essential) beliefs about the military. An impulse to minimize the resulting dissonance, would explain the recurring attempts to minimize the number of military women and the roles they play. That is, the need to minimize evidence counter to central military beliefs, rather than any objective need, may account for the military's uneasy accommodation of its token women.

In this volume three such beliefs are identified. One is that war is manly. The second is that protectors protect. The third is that any soldier is substitutable for any other. These beliefs are widely shared, deeply held, and greatly resistant to disproof or "demythologizing." This suggests that they are functional even if not logical. People *want* to believe them.

So what? What does this knowledge contribute to our understanding of our most lethal institution? What does it mean for policymaking?

First, planners should consider "normalizing" the military: bringing the ratio of women up to the 40 to 60 percent range. Second, they should think about reserving the slots now open to women for women, instead of trying to guarantee equal access to these while reserving other slots for men only. This would guarantee more overall equity and permit a fuller utilization of talent. Third, they should consider giving women their own functional corps. Essentially this occurs with nursing now. But why not give women tanks, missiles, and supplies as well? Or give women the Air Force. Women are now eligible for most Air Force slots—just add the opportunity to fly in combat and let women have that service *in toto*.

The theoretical implications of this study are more radical—that is, fundamental. First, it suggests that the leaders most dangerous to our health may be not the military but civilians. Military personnel repeat and use military myths, but they also know the reality of military practice, and their military advice is rooted in that knowledge. On the other hand, civilians without military experience may be prone to take military myths and rhetoric literally. Thus, civilians, not the military, may be more likely to propel the nation into unwise action.

Second, this study suggests that the "Man Problem" really exists.

Again, many military experts and leaders continue to base grave reservations about the expanded role of women in the military on the assumed negative effect of their presence on cohesion, combat effectiveness, and "long-term national survival." (The latter refers to decreased national fertility due to female casualties and male demoralization.) Interestingly, these reservations derive not from doubts about women's capacities, but from doubts about the effect of women's presence on men.

Since women cannot know what it is like in their absence, it is hard to estimate just how disruptive their presence is. Clearly, however, it alters the military if service is no longer a way to demonstrate manhood. It alters the assumptions of military incentive systems to have mother–soldiers. It alters our thinking when we conceptualize men as armed and women as unilaterally disarmed—yet surviving, perhaps even thriving. It alters our view of the military as a "fair" institution and a source of opportunity when we realize that it is currently an even better deal for women than men because it provides equal pay for comparable work, numerous benefits, and still exempts women from combat.

Perhaps the most important thing about enlisted women, though, is simply that they exist. By existing they continuously challenge and confound basic beliefs about the military. This makes it more likely that both the military and civilians will think carefully about the nature of this institution that has a potential not only to guard but also to threaten the nation.

# PART I

The
American
Enlisted
Woman

# 1

# Overview:
# The Most
# Unknown
# Soldiers

Enlisted personnel rarely emerge as individuals. When they do, it is almost inevitably because of heroic acts of combat. Because enlisted women are relatively few and new, because they are not assigned to combat, and because ambivalence about their role continues, they are both individually and collectively an unknown quantity. In Appendix A a veteran of the U.S. Air Force tells her own story. This concrete and particular account (virtually unedited) tells the story of one woman in one service at a specific moment. The airman tells how she came to enlist. She also describes her basic training, her schooling, and her on-the-job training. She tells about receiving special (favorable and unfavorable) treatment. She describes the investigation of lesbian activities, sexual harassment, and the effects of women's integration. She details her geographic moves, her housing, and women's different ways of coping. She airs many complaints, but also expresses satisfaction with a hard job well done, and acknowledges the opportunity which was presented by her enlistment. Because of her narrative's balance and perspective, any reader unfamiliar with the military should turn to it before reading further. The account is rich and it is authentic.

I am confident about its authenticity because I spent six weeks in the summer of 1982 interviewing hundreds of enlisted women and men of all ranks from the four military services. These individuals were stationed outside the continental United States—that is, in Germany, Italy, Hawaii, Okinawa, Korea, and "at sea." In the three previous years I visited a dozen stateside bases. My work did not involve scheduled interviews with a sample; it consisted of conversations with available enlisted women and men. My purpose was to observe and to hear about the life of enlisted women so that I could: (1) better understand the context and impact of policies concerning them, and (2) portray that life to civilians (especially women) who have rarely thought about enlisted women, much less had the opportunity to talk with them.

This chapter is culled from those interviews and from reflection on them. In developing the most often recurring themes, I have tried to go beyond reporting, to probe what was meant by what was said, sometimes by reformulating an idea or a set of ideas and then testing that reformulation with discussants to see whether it accurately reflects (or perhaps extends) their views. My goal has been to prepare an abstract and general essay that could have been written by (and that would be subscribed to by) the author of "I Am a Veteran . . ."

The themes come from conversations with enlisted personnel. They are not necessarily the topics that interest policymakers or women's commanders. They fall into three categories: experiences common to most enlisted personnel; the variety of experiences of enlisted women; and the experiences that enlisted women and enlisted men do not share.

### SHARED EXPERIENCES

The military is not only a uniformed, hierarchical institution; it is a class institution. That is, there are officers and there are enlisted people, and the two have quite separate hierarchies. (In contrast, U.S. police forces are only hierarchical: all professionals are "officers.") Some military personnel change their status from enlisted to officer, but most do not; and all enlisted people take orders from officers, even if the officer is twenty-two years old and devoid of experience and the enlisted person is forty years old with experience in eight countries and three wars. Most military women are enlisted, and most are in the lowest enlisted ranks. Most military men are, too. Nevertheless, senior enlisted people (who have substantial authority and act as spokesmen and role models) are virtually all men.

Moreover, today's military is sexually integrated. With the abolition of the separate or semiseparate women's corps, men can no longer be sure of having only male peers, superiors, and inferiors, and women in the services are submerged in a basically male institution. They no longer have organizations and commands of their own; they no longer have their own official network; often they both live and work apart from other women. Enlisted women are "unknowns"—even to each other.[1]

The military is also geographically, racially, and ethnically integrated, especially in the enlisted ranks. When there is a draft, the highly educated and economically advantaged may become enlisted personnel, too. Thus, both women and men must learn to cooperate with people different from themselves in order to achieve important military goals. But when women and men from distinct cultures interact in a personal way, and without learned or prescribed expectations, life can become complex. In addition to all the other things they need to learn, military men and women from a variety of cultures must also learn about others' understanding of the relationship between the sexes—their ways of flirting, their style of bargaining, the responsibilities each sex accepts and expects of the other. Both men and women undoubtedly make mistakes in receiving, interpreting, and sending sexual signals; for women such mistakes may be quite consequential.

Moreover, because of their relatively small number, military women absolutely cannot escape either signals or actual overtures. They cannot stand on the sidelines and observe until ready. They do not have the opportunity to learn slowly. Some who have never heard a vulgar word from a man in their lives may suddenly receive daily propositions, many of them indelicate. Junior enlisted personnel are at a sexually active stage of their lives. Many are away from familial and community restraints for the first time, and the culture seems to encourage (at least for the men) heterosexual experimentation. It is no wonder that many young women are overwhelmed.

The mobility of military life can be overwhelming, too. Enlisted personnel serve all over the world—in the Philippines, in Honduras, on Alaskan islands, and in Washington, D.C. They may move every twelve months, and they may interrupt longer tours for special training or for assignments across one or even several continents. Some of the geographic surprises are pleasant. Many women enjoy being in countries where, for instance, a woman can walk alone at night without concern. In fact, many claim to be unenthusiastic about returning to the dangers of their hometowns.

Even if one stays put, one's working conditions may be altered by the rotation of one's boss—or of one's boss's boss. Further, commanders exercise a great deal of discretion; thus, enlisted personnel with a large repertoire of responses are likely to advance over even the consistently compliant.

### VARIED EXPERIENCES

A woman's experience in the military depends in large part on which branch of the service she chooses. Air Force service is considered most like civilian life. Facilities are better, and the Air Force is interested in "people problems"—or at least Air Force women believe it is. Some Army women do, too, like the one who volunteered, "I love the Army, but I'd tell my sister: 'Go Air Force!'"

Marine women are few in number. They have all taken "women only" basic training at the same location, recognize limited assignments open to them, and often experience rather spartan facilities. Their working environment is likely to emphasize combat readiness and a capacity for immediate deployment. The "rough" quality about many Marine bases is accompanied by an *esprit* based on efforts to live up to the Marine image and mottoes.

The experience of Navy women is in transition as sea duty becomes a regular requirement and women move into blue- as well as white-collar jobs. Women officers have always been expected to be "ladies," just as their male counterparts have been expected to be "officers and gentlemen." When enlisted women were confined to traditional jobs and wore pumps, hosiery, and uniforms with skirts, they, too, were expected to be ladies. As they have moved into nontraditional fields, however, and began wearing men's work uniforms (blue shirts and dungarees) and began being identified by their supervisors not as "girls" or "women" but as "sailors," the earlier concept has begun to fade. Yet the new concept of respect for a woman who works with her hands and with machinery has not yet emerged. Moreover, any new concept will also have to incorporate the new attitudes of some women toward personal and sexual freedom, which would once have been thought most unladylike. Indeed, what proves baffling to some peers and supervisors of enlisted women is that while some women insist on such freedoms, others do not. Some with adventurous work lives lead conventional private lives, and vice versa. Further, some women insist on their right to behave differently at different times and to make their own choices, a right similarly claimed by civilian women.

Army women are in a difficult place. In the late 1970s the Army had a hard time meeting its recruitment goals. This meant that it had to enlist more women or no one. It enlisted more women, but with reluctance. Now it can more easily enlist men, and the Army seems to be constantly reevaluating its policies on women. The first formal reevaluation began with the 1980 election of Ronald Reagan. It resulted in a "pause" in the planned increase in women's numbers, the resegregation of basic training, and the closing to women of some specialties for which they had been trained and in which they were already (apparently successfully) employed. The continuing reevaluation and the Army's perceptible uncertainty about women's role have led to an unease among women interested in the Army as a career.

Many enlistees serve only in the United States; others have been sent to places they could never have expected to see as civilians. Those who serve abroad probably have a clearer sense of the military's essential activity (war). In Europe bombings and kidnappings of U.S. military personnel (often perpetrated by German and Italian "allies") have necessitated security precautions not required in the United States. Europe, Hawaii, and Okinawa preserve physical reminders of World War II and of the fact that yesterday's enemy may be today's best friend. Service in Korea, a country that operates on perpetual alert, brings the military's role home. Many personnel are assigned there only briefly, and they are not accompanied by family members. There, American women confront male–female relationships of a kind that many find loathsome. The fact that some American men find the relationships attractive—and in fact make a permanent commitment to them—is difficult for some American women to accept.

The work specialty or field that a woman chooses or is assigned to —her military occupational specialty (MOS), her rating, her Air Force Specialty Code (AFSC)—also has an important bearing on her military experience. Those who work as medical assistants and in clerical jobs may do these "traditional" jobs in an untraditional environment, but they can often count on some regularity and continuity in their work. Some have very responsible and even intellectually demanding jobs (e.g., as translators). The work, then, can be quite civilianlike. For women in "nontraditional" jobs, the entire setting may be both novel and doubtful. Indeed, women tend to try to leave these jobs for "traditional" ones— to "migrate" in service jargon.[2] This is seen as a problem by manpower planners, some of whom even conclude that women should, therefore, not be in nontraditional fields. Conversations with women suggest that there is more to migration than nontraditionality: after all, military women were unconventional enough to enlist in the first place.

Some women probably selected a particular specialty only in order to get into the military without going on a waiting list. Quite appropriately they later ask to switch—and the military could quite appropriately say no. But if it says yes, it should not blame the women, and if it led the women to believe that transfer is possible, it should expect women to be resentful if they are told no. Moreover, shift work, long hours, and/or alert status make some nontraditional jobs unattractive to both men and women—but, perhaps, more difficult for women with private responsibilities as wives and mothers.

Furthermore, women have been easier to recruit than men because they are enlisted in limited numbers. Thus, men who are harder to recruit, may more likely be offered inducements such as guaranteed locations or training or bonuses. This means women may disproportionately be getting less desirable assignments—the ones that people are likely to try to migrate from. On the other hand, the services, except for the Air Force, require higher entrance standards for women than for men. The average junior enlisted woman is both better educated and older than the average junior enlisted man (many women hold college degrees and enter service at twenty-five or even thirty). Thus, if more women are successful at migration, perhaps they are just better at working the system.

Finally, it seems likely that sexual harassment is more frequent in nontraditional occupations and contributes to migration. This topic will be addressed in the next section.

Enlisted women, then, have different experiences depending on service, location, and work assignment. They also have different experiences simply because of the different views held by commanders. These views can affect what women wear (skirts, pants, or camouflage uniforms), rules about dormitory visitation, standards for discharges requested (e.g., for pregnancy) or required (e.g., for homosexuality), the degree to which fraternization is tolerated, policies about assignments with or without spouses, whether or not a base has a women's coordinator, and requirements for physical training. Women report that commanders have widely varying practices. Some practices and local policies stem principally from a commander's personal conviction, some from a unit's mission, and some from physical arrangements. Whatever the cause, some enlisted women live in nearly open bays (as seen in films on basic training); others live in dormitories. Some of these resemble college dormitories of the 1950s, with well-guarded reception desks, or those of the 1970s, with men's and women's rooms separate but adjacent (for a while some women in Germany shared bathrooms with men). Some have motel-like accommodations with individual entrances or private off-base apartments. On some bases different commands share physical facilities. Thus, women in neighboring facilities might live by radically different rules.

With this amount of latitude, a commander can put together a set of policies women will find insupportable or do just the opposite. In civilian life employees can shop around until they find an employer who demonstrates the amount of paternalism, support, or neutrality that suits them. In the military, not only is there no shopping around, but life is ever-changing. Thus, one can go to a new assignment and find a new set of rules, or one can stay put and get a new commander with a new set of rules. This hierarchical institution requires adaptability for continued success.

Enlisted women can, in general, control their choice of service and specialty, but rarely the location of their work, and almost never the person for whom they must work. What they can be sure of is change.

## WOMEN'S EXPERIENCES

Wherever enlisted women meet, sexual harassment is discussed. Enlisted women's experience is clearly different from that of men (although men, too, can be sexually harassed) and from that of officers. New enlistees are young, and the low rank of most enlisted women makes them additionally vulnerable. Furthermore, commanders seem to be relatively unaware of the extent of the problem and are genuinely angry when a particular incident captures their attention. As one might expect, congressional hearings on sexual harassment held in 1980 did capture the military's attention and led to policy statements and educational programs. Nevertheless, sexual harassment is pervasive and often debilitating. Few women expect harassment to disappear, nor do they think that it does much good to resort to "channels." Few are even clear about what channels they could resort to. In fact, they can go to the Equal Opportunity Office, to the chaplain, to the legal office, to the enlisted women's adviser (where there is one), or to their supervisor (if he is not the guilty party). Still, it seems to many women that this is an area where everyone and no one is in charge, where one should not expect real relief or be surprised by retaliation.

Harassment involving a demand for sexual favors by a superior is rarely defended. Most women interviewed claimed to have heard of incidents in which enlistees in basic training, many away from home for the first time, were coerced or seduced by their trainers, non-commissioned officers (NCOs) who hold a great deal of formal and informal power over them. Most also claim to know of at least one woman who willingly exchanged sexual favors for work favors. Indeed, some argue that seduction and exploitation are sometimes the work of the young woman, and that the targeted NCO can hardly believe his good luck. Nevertheless, because of the rank differential and implied threat, the first type of interaction is clearly sexual harassment, whereas the second might be called temptation or exploitation. Some believe that the senior person should always be held responsible; others would consider who took the initiative and which party has the most to lose.

Views about how and whether to control mutually voluntary fraternization differ. In general, women are used to dating men older than themselves and with better jobs than theirs, and tend to resent having attractive men put "off limits." Indeed, they often complain that the males they must work with are "boys" who are still acting out—drinking and experimenting with reckless behavior—and whose childish bellicosity is condoned if not endorsed.

A second kind of harassment is workplace harassment by peers. Even new male members of a group have to put up with a certain amount of testing. Women who have not worked in a male milieu before may not expect this, but it is not surprising that "generic" harassment takes a sexual form when women enter a mostly male workplace. Nor is it surprising that women and men see such harassment differently. This day-to-day work environment may be the place in which women have the best opportunity to establish their point of view, to insist upon their definition of what is acceptable humor and horseplay, to win respect, and to bring the sexual harassment, if it is only "regular" harassment, to an end. Still, when a woman moves to a new assignment, she will almost certainly have to win respect again, and the form of her testing may again be sexual.

A third type of harassment, coming from anyone around, is a form of entertainment influenced by and done for a male audience. It can involve explicit invitations to a woman moving down the serving line in the mess hall, or it may take the form of pounding on the door of a woman's room or bold advances in an enlisted club. Even though most advances are verbal, physical intrusion, "copping a feel," is not uncommon. In discussing such harassment, men are more likely than women to state that things are not too bad "here," but "those guys" are really bad. "Those guys" sometimes means another unit, sometimes transients on temporary assignments, or infantry troops as opposed to technicians, or guys "just off the ship" or "just out of the field." Because this kind of harassment is more or less impersonal—that is, unrelated to any particular woman—it is impossible for individuals to establish themselves as persons deserving respect. Even Phyllis Schafly's "virtuous woman" could not avoid such incidents.

Still, avoidance is the solution attempted by many women. They simply stay away from public areas on base. The clubs, which are supposed to make leisure pleasant, are considered unusable by many women. Meals are seen as an ordeal, too—especially if one comes to the chowhall late and is, therefore, visible to gathered diners. Again and again women report skipping meals or eating soup heated on hot plates rather than run the dining hall gauntlet.

A second tactic is to ignore verbal assaults. All who have stayed in service have had to do this on at least some occasions. Some see this as making a woman "hard," and the persistence and pervasiveness of insult and the impossibility of developing full immunity (i.e., of forestalling rather than enduring insult) take a toll.

A third response, of course, is to give as good as one gets, to retort with vigor, scorn, or challenge. For some this is easier than for others, but one-liners can be learned, and counterattack can give satisfaction— both during the encounter and in telling a "war story" about it later.

Complaints about harassment diminish with rank. It is unclear whether this is because of higher rank itself (after a few years most enlisted men are one's juniors), or because the vulnerable give up, get out, or acquire a protector, or because women learn to avoid, to not hear, to deflect, or even, occasionally, to relish such incidents, or all of the above. A good-looking Marine NCO in her mid-twenties obviously enjoyed telling her story about the officer who would not leave her alone until she agreed to meet him at a motel. Once there, she arranged things so that he undressed and went into the bathroom—and she then departed by car with his trousers, which she gave to the bewildered (amused?) guard at the base gate. Sexual harassment training and policies thus far have been sober, reasoned, and legalistic. Instead of having equal-opportunity personnel reason with men, however, more might be accomplished if women were taught the variety of ways other women manage the problem—because some do learn to manage it. And perhaps retaliation, something women rarely think of and even more rarely do, is in order. After all, turning the other cheek seems a dubious tactic for success in a military organization.

Three other points concerning harassment should be made. Top leadership's views both filter down to the transgressors *and* give heart to the victims, who come to believe that some limit can be reached and that not all complaints will be futile. Second, the continual verbal aggression and insult in common areas, the catcalls from cars and dormitories, are often considered unimportant and uncontrollable by commanders; nevertheless, they are exhausting and corrosive for women. Perhaps women need to police such behavior themselves; and perhaps if women did take matters into their own hands, commanders would be as unwilling to sanction sexist epithets as racist slurs. (In part they do not tolerate the latter because they know private action will be taken if official action fails.) Third, young and junior women may need some protection even if women in general do not. When and how the transition from protection to self-assertion should occur, and how best to arm women so they can defend themselves, require careful thought. For men, basic training is supposed to be the military initiation, and once through that the civilian boy is considered a military man. For women, as noted above, testing continues in their first assignment, and base commanders who expect men to be "military" as soon as they leave boot camp may not be aware of the continuing trials women face and the need to give attention to the environment in which they work.

Many of enlisted women's experiences and concerns are related to their low absolute numbers or to their low numbers relative to men. Items and facilities that women want but men do not care about may be scarce or nonexistent (e.g., women's uniform items in the post exchange, or PX; a beauty parlor). Sometimes military and dependent women combined compose a critical mass, but enlisted women then may find that it is wives, not enlisted women, who are catered to. Thus, the PX may decide to stock women's civilian clothing, but principally with items styled to the taste and budget of "Mrs. Colonel," not those of Ms. Staff Sergeant. Day-care facilities, likewise, for a long time offered a volunteer-run, short-term convenience for wives. These facilities are converting to meet the needs of working women, but often they are still not appropriate for enlisted women in terms of availability and cost. One Air Force woman described her dilemma: the same Air Force that would not permit her child to remain at the day-care center for more than ten hours a day required her to work twelve consecutive hours.

Another facility geared to the needs of wives rather than enlisted women is the commissary. Hours of operation often assume an ability to shop during the day, which is when the dependents who constitute an important part of commissaries' staffs prefer to work. The needs of wives as shoppers and employees are met; enlisted women's need to shop after work is ignored.

Gynecological care is hard to obtain at small bases and at those with few dependents. Thus, having care at all often depends upon having dependents to share the facilities. A question of priority then arises: should military personnel always have first claim on services? Or should patients be seen on a first-come, first-seen basis? Or should a colonel's wife have priority over a young enlisted woman? Answers to such questions are both various and ambiguous. Rightly or wrongly, though, enlisted women perceive base facilities for women as more responsive to the needs of officers' wives than to those of enlisted women, whatever their relative numbers.

And the problem may extend beyond the base. On Okinawa, at least one beach has been reserved for families and senior enlisted personnel. The idea is that huge numbers of young enlisted men create a rowdy atmosphere unpleasant for older personnel and for families. This may not be unreasonable, but what should be done about the young enlisted women who may also desperately need a respite from throngs of young men? Should they be allowed to use the "family" beach or should they be required to use the "junior enlisted" beach? The disproportionate numbers of men and women often make it hard to establish a principle that is equitable and also yields a practice that is reasonable.

For if a certain number of persons are required to justify a facility or program, and if women are restricted in number, they can end up *never* getting any programs or facilities of special interest to them. Similarly, disproportionate ratios make it almost impossible for women to do things only with women. If the military does not authorize activities for women only, they must all day, every day exist in a male environment where guarded behavior may be considered necessary. In contrast, men can almost always choose between a sex-integrated or a male-only activity; they are sure to have times and places where they can "be themselves." This situation may have some bearing on the common view of enlisted women that women officers are not to be envied. Many enlisted women see women officers as having to be "too political." Enlisted women see the enlisted promotion system, which emphasizes tests, as fair. Female officers, they say, have, instead, to please everyone in every way—including appearance, style, and decorous behavior, with no distinction between on and off duty; their personal lives are not only followed, but have important bearing on their professional success.

Enlisted women endure a good deal of stereotyping. This is ironic, because out of uniform military women can "pass" more easily than men, if only because their haircuts do not distinguish them, and because "enlisted woman" is rarely a category in an encountering civilian's mind. Equally ironic is the tendency to describe the enlisted woman as antithetical to the "dependent" wife, because many enlisted women are in fact married to servicemen. Indeed, some join the military after marriage to a serviceman to ensure employment in the face of a good deal of moving. The stereotyping persists even though enlisted women have become increasingly heterogeneous. Once they were mostly single; now they may be single or married, and they may be mothers with or without husbands.

The combination of actual heterogeneity, continued stereotyping, and the integration that requires men to assume the command of women has led to some uncertainties in leadership. Some commanders who have no trouble at all dealing with husbands and fathers find it hard to require wives and mothers to act as they believe service people should act. This may in part be because commanders think that wives and mothers should *not* act the way enlisted people should act. For example, some units are on alert on a regular basis. Anyone with dependent children is supposed to have a plan providing for those children in an emergency situation. Many commanders are dubious about those plans, believing that they are "just paper," and that in an emergency deployment, servicewomen would not show up. There is also, I suspect, a belief that servicewomen who are mothers *should not* show up—that, as women, their first responsibility is to their children. Interestingly, many enlisted women who are mothers deny following such a script. Most say they have plans; most say they have a professional commitment; and several shared the opinion of the one who said, "My kid will have the best chance if I stay and fight while someone else gets him back to the States."

Again, some senior commanders see the children of military mothers as neglected. "Stairwell children" (the military form of latchkey children) may not be as well supervised as are (or were) the children of the commanders, and, assuredly, the children of some enlisted women lead hard lives, especially if there is no father present. An enlisted person's resources, both personal and financial, are easily stretched thin. Some commanders argue that single parents should be discharged to assume their family responsibilities. But at least some of those women are handling their responsibilities as well as they can, and are probably doing better in the military—which provides a number of services for dependents—than they could do outside it. The alternative, after all, is not being the commander's spouse; it might be welfare in the inner city. Further, and no words should be minced, these single mothers are being more responsible than are the single men who father and then desert children.

Few judgments are made and few questions are asked about the military value of men who are deserting fathers. Some of these men are the fathers of the children of single military women. (Others are the fathers of civilian women's children—children who go mostly unnoticed and un-counted—including the children of foreign women. Amerasian children have attracted some notice, perhaps because they are physically visible, often forced to live in conditions worse than those in our inner cities, and discriminated against in the culture in which they must live; sometimes they are the objects of organized private charity, offered by a military that assumes no legal responsibility for their well-being.) Yet it is single mothers who are seen as a management problem. Commanders doubt both their reliability as workers and their ability to be good mothers if they *are* committed to their work. Moreover, some commanders' un-spoken moral convictions cause them to believe that unmarried mothers reflect badly on the military, whereas unmarried fathers are not seen as a problem.

It is easy to understand why commanders would rather have male subordinates. They were once young men, and there is an agreed-upon code as to how young men should be treated. There is less certainty about how to treat young enlisted women. What is sure is that (1) young women are as heterogeneous as young men, and (2) questions and moral judgments are raised about women that are not raised about similarly situated men.

The tendency to stereotype probably means that commanders do not understand their female troops as well as they understand their male troops. Thus, their discomfort with women may be related to their own lack of confidence that they can lead women well. Indeed, when one talks with commanders about military women and then talks with military women themselves, the lack of common subject matter is striking. For example, one commander discussed pregnancy with me at great length before sending me out to talk with the women on his base. It was a matter of the gravest concern to him, and he estimated that the base had a 10 percent pregnancy rate. Later that morning I asked a group of seventeen women what trait in women gave their supervisors the most difficulty. Not one guessed pregnancy; and not one was pregnant. When I told them their commander's chief concern, their response was laughter. A discussion then ensued of the unease a woman's pregnancy causes the men who work with her. One told a hilarious story of having morning sickness, of hurrying to the coed bathroom, of bursting in and vomiting all over her NCO, who had forgotten to lock the door.

Women complain a lot about their uniforms and their living quarters, but one has the feeling that complaints about these items roll off commanders' backs. Living quarters for service personnel in general are often not ideal, and it may even be that more attention is given to women's facilities than to men's. Moreover, some changes are beyond a commander's control. Yet if these items are damaging women's morale, or if responding to them could have a positive effect, one wonders why they are not taken more seriously. Is it because women care more about such matters than men do? For example, women seem to desire a "room of their own"—that is, one with personal touches—and are likely to be less interested in an auto shop or transportation to a town catering to men's recreational preferences. One finds again and again, however, that efforts to achieve "uniformity" may give men things that they do not care much about, and, at the same time, take from women things that do affect morale. On one ship Navy women were allowed to have stuffed animals on their bunks. Men objected because they were not allowed to have them. The solution of permitting men also to have stuffed animals was rejected in favor of a policy that forbade women to have them.

Similarly, in one dormitory curtains, rugs, plants, and other "personal" materials had to be removed for every inspection, but could be put back (with much effort) as soon as the inspection was over. Women did this often; men, less often. Let me be clear. Some commanders permit attractive, personal dormitory furnishings; others require a uniform and identical austerity. The latter can be barren and depressing, and may be especially hard for women to accept, particularly when other individuals of the same rank are able to live off base and thereby avoid inspections altogether. Those living off base do so either because they can afford it or because they are married. Indeed, marriages of convenience, which make individuals eligible for off-base living, are not uncommon. In any event, the result is that people holding the same rank and doing the same job at the same base may have quite different retreats—different with regard to both privacy and aesthetics. Further, although such retreats may be differentially important to women and men, there are no differentials in treatment by gender.

A parallel move (at least in the Army) toward uniformity in clothing has not meant that men get skirts and tab collars, but rather that women are dressed more and more like men, sometimes in small-sized men's clothing. Clothing affects morale and performance. Even the young men enlisting in the Marines cite the dress uniform as a primary incentive, and men sailors created such a fuss over a uniform change that they got their bell bottoms and blouses back. In contrast, little has been done to give women uniforms with positive valence. In fact, one could almost suspect the Army of deliberately providing ugly clothing—for example, mint-green synthetic fiber summer dresses, bulky men's winter sweaters (not that the women's previous sweaters were any great shakes), and pants with a stripe down the leg, as on a band uniform. Compare the red-lined blue nurses' capes of World War II, and even the Marine green winter woolies, which provide a dash of red on the hat for women—gestures with positive results. Pride is a military goal, and appearance is crucial to pride. Military men wear ribbons and patches and berets. In fact, in the eighteenth century Mary Wollstonecraft likened military men to women because of their fondness for finery, gallantry, and appearance.[3] Why, then, are women so often put in inadequate, ill-fitting, unattractive clothes? Military women also like to look good. Too often they feel that they do not.

Conversations with men about women in the military tend to be laced with complaints. Surprisingly, some enlisted women believe that these complaints and the difficulties men make for them are rooted in jealousy. Men are seen as envious of women's options—that is, their ability to hold the same jobs men hold, or to be a mother and still hold a job, or to leave the service honorably and at their own volition to be a mother.

Women also think that men envy women's publicity, especially when women get credit for doing what men have always done, and women's "rapid" promotions, which actually occur at about the same rate as men's, even though women enter service (especially the Army and Marines) with higher qualifications.

One other envy goes largely untalked about, probably because women are too discreet to mention it and it would be too unmanly and unmilitary for men to admit to it. This is that men are envious of women's relative safety because of the legal and policy restrictions against the use of women in combat. After all, most men would probably prefer not to be in combat, and perhaps many men can be talked into the service only because they know that most men in uniform do not see combat either. (This is especially true of some services and some job specialties.) Everyone knows this on some level. Yet the myth remains that anyone might be required to do anything. This "myth of substitutability" suggests that the person who does die in war just happened to lose in a lottery that was fair and in which the odds were actually against losing. If numerous uniformed women are guaranteed safe jobs, however, men's chances to hold such jobs diminish.

Men must be assumed not to like the increased risk. But because the military ethic includes the protection of women and adherence to the policy that they should not be in combat, the envy of women's safe jobs cannot be expressed. One might fairly ask if there is a similar envy or resentment of men who do not see combat. The answer is probably yes. Verbal scorn and jokes are directed at such men; conversely high honor, awards, and pay go to those who do perform "combat" service.*

CONCLUSION

A few enlisted women fit the media stereotype of bold, independent pioneers challenging social taboos and relishing risks and trials, but most are personally conservative; many are politically conservative; few are feminists. Indeed, that last word is not part of the military vernacular. "Libber" is, but it is not something women call themselves. The Equal Rights Amendment failed to achieve ratification during the period of my interviews, and most military women did not mourn it. To many enlisted women the ERA was the project of women "sitting around their swimming pools wearing diamond rings."

Further, enlisted women seem only somewhat sensitive to the statement that "military women are whores or lesbians" (usually prefixed by "*people think* military women are whores or lesbians"). This World War II canard is thoroughly discussed in Mattie E. Treadwell's official history of the Women's Army Corps (WAC) in a section entitled "The Great Slander Campaign."[4] That account describes officialdom as so concerned about military women's bad reputation and its effect on recruiting that the Federal Bureau of Investigation was charged with seeing whether it was an Axis plot to harm the war effort. The FBI found that it was in fact just good old G.I. Joe grousing. Nevertheless, the impact on the women's branches was significant. After World War II great attention was paid to teaching women recruits ladylike behavior, including how to wear makeup, how to enter a car, and how to conduct a social conversation. In addition, a certain vigilance was maintained against "lesbian tendencies."

Although the old phrase was still being used in the 1980s, in my discussions with enlisted women its impact seemed muted. Women did not seem overly defensive, or fearful that one woman's behavior would reflect on all women. Some even attempted to explain why men thought (or perhaps, rather, said) such things. For example, it was noted that women are outnumbered ten to one. Thus, all of them have the opportunity to enjoy a very active social life, and, conversely, many men, even quite acceptable men, will not be given the time of day. Men's egos, they suggested, need an explanation for their lack of social life, preferably

---

*For many years combat pay has been higher for officers than for enlisted men. Some women stationed in dangerous locations have earned combat pay even though they may not have participated in exchanges of fire.

based not on their own deficiencies but on women's. Thus, if a woman will not go out, she must be a lesbian; if she goes out a lot, she must be a prostitute.

Many of the women found such slurs only temporarily daunting. However, being called lesbians—even when the charge is obviously rooted in the frustration of a rejected male—can be hard on women's cohesiveness. Some women worry that they must defuse the charge. One woman might feel this way because she is not a lesbian and is aghast that anyone would take her for one; another might feel that she must live the label down, even if it is true, and even if she is quite comfortable with the fact, because homosexuality is grounds for discharge. There is no possibility of coming out of the closet and staying in the military. For these reasons enlisted women can be loath to spend too much time together, or be too publicly affectionate in a way that male "buddies" find is actually encouraged. (The military has long sought to encourage "male bonding," although it prohibits homosexuality for men, too.) Now that the women's corps have been disbanded, military men can no longer leave women's bonding and lesbianism to women officers. Unfortunately, many commanders probably do not know what to think about relationships between women, either those the military wants to discourage or those it wishes to encourage. (No recent research studies have focused on women's morale and cohesiveness, or for that matter on how to teach women to lead men or men to follow women. Yet it is not at all clear that men consider enlisted women so "normal" that such studies are unnecessary.)

The young women with whom I talked are, as they assert, very normal. Frequently they see themselves as overqualified for their jobs but treated as though they were underqualified. They find their freedom curtailed by men's aggressiveness; they are, they feel, under constant surveillance. But they do not have world-shaping ambitions or generalize much. They have met many challenges, and they have adapted and endured. They have made their way in a variety of places, many of them a long way from home, but they do not consider themselves pioneers. Many have been aided by new laws, court decisions, and political pressures, but only rarely are they themselves consciously part of any change process. Most enlisted women have approached their military service in a matter-of-fact, individualistic way. Men's culture is no mystery to them. They have been close enough to realize that it is not always effective, and that some men are wimps, goof-offs, or hoodlums. The women respect themselves. Some believe that their military role is appropriately limited—because it is right, because that was the contract they signed, or because it is convenient and economical. Others believe that women should have a broad range of challenges and that they have met those presented and could meet more. While not inclined to stand on principle or to make claims for "all women," some do resent bars to "all women," especially if those bars prevent them from doing things they want to do and believe they can do. In short, enlisted women have found a variety of ways of surviving in a highly virile environment. Some like it, but some do not. Some think they put up with a lot, but they are also realistic about civilian alternatives. No one of the women could have written this chapter, but collectively and vicariously they have done so.

This is an overview. It is not comprehensive. It gives special emphasis to the parts of enlisted women's lives that they talk about among themselves. The remainder of the book is inevitably structured more as male officers would structure it. Still, it is important to remember as one proceeds that enlisted women are lively intelligences who should be queried directly and who may not see themselves precisely as those who report on or command them see them.

# 2

## The Generations of Enlisted Women

Recent policy changes have turned a single chronological generation of enlisted women into several attitudinal and behavioral generations, as interviews with enlisted women reveal. In this chapter the cohort method of analysis will be adapted to register important policy changes, with emphasis on how different changes have affected different women. In assessing these effects it is important to remember that all women who join the U.S. military do so voluntarily. They do not enlist expecting or wishing to change the Army, Air Force, Navy, or Marines. The services do change, though, and the changes can surprise service members—sometimes pleasantly, sometimes unpleasantly.

Rapid changes mean that women enter and continue their service under a variety of implicit contracts. Further, these contracts vary among services. For example, Navy women agree to meet higher enlistment standards than men; this is not required of Air Force women. Air Force women have long competed with men for promotion; Army women have not. On the other hand, Marine Corps enlisted women have always been segregated from men during basic training, whereas women in the other services have not.

Variations that have developed over time are even more dramatic: the introduction of weapons training, a shift from limited geographical assignments to involuntary remote and at-sea ones, and a shift from women supervisors and co-workers to otherwise all-male work groups. Each change reversed earlier assumptions. Perhaps the biggest change for military women, though, has been from an implicit agreement to remain childless to the acceptance of an agreement (at least by some women) to remain in service despite pregnancy and motherhood.

Most people learn the implicit terms of a work, marriage, or other contract through experience. Often one thinks of implicit terms as a natural part of what it "means" to hold a particular job, to be married, to be in the military. When the terms of a contract change, that contract no longer seems so natural, so inevitable, and individuals in the changing institution can more easily come to different conclusions about what is appropriate to and required by their role.

In a hierarchical organization with little lateral entry and a promotion system linked to time in service, the views of personnel are likely to vary considerably by rank. Moreover, in a sharply pyramidal organization, the views of those with senior rank (those with official power) may be the views of a small percentage of the membership. Thus, to understand American enlisted women today, it is helpful to remember that they entered the military with various assumptions, and that senior women (who are few in number) have enjoyed (or endured) several revisions of their implicit contracts.

Generational "differences" and "gaps" are a staple of public discussion. Generations (or, more precisely, cohorts) are also a tool for social analysis.[1] This method or approach is especially useful in the study of military personnel because people enter the military at approximately the same age, begin at the bottom of either the enlisted or officer ranks, and move through the system at about the same pace. Thus, date of entry is one of the most telling data one can have about a member of the military.

Since it does not permit lateral entry, the military must "grow its own" personnel. Even people recruited for newly valuable attitudes and skills must start at the bottom and proceed upward. Thus, if a new piece of equipment creates a need for forty mid-level technicians, that need cannot be met by hiring forty mid-level technicians. Either technicians already in service must be retrained, junior technicians must be induced to stay and rapidly promoted, or potential technicians must be recruited, trained, and rapidly promoted. Further, when people leave the military (and most do), they tend to be permanently lost to the services. This means a fluctuating policy that leads to the demoralization and exodus of different kinds of people at different times can severely thin the senior ranks.

Changes in military policy mean, then, that when policymakers solicit the views of senior military women, they get views colored by more than the usual generation gap. Discrepancies are further aggravated by the fact that the changed policies affect women differently at different points in their life cycle.

In the discussion that follows, it is assumed that today's military women are members of a number of distinct age cohorts. The policy and social changes cohort members experience at different points in their careers are discussed in detail. Traditional cohort analysis is used to assist exposition, but several facts prevent its full application. First, there are relatively few women in the military, and they represent a small percentage of those in their age group. Second, the principles of selection for entry into and exit from the cohorts are not clear and probably change as policy changes. Third, the cohorts shrink each year. Thus, the problem of causal attribution, which is difficult enough when one must consider both life cycle and impacting experience, is further complicated by emigration. Indeed, selective emigration may be a more important influence on measured attitudes and values than either age or events. Finally, women in the top ranks are so few that statistically significant comparisons by rank are all but impossible.

In spite of these limitations, the cohort model is a way to organize and make meaningful the changes that have affected military women since they became a continuing part of the military in 1948.*

### GENERATIONAL CHARTS

This analysis covers the period from 1948 to the end of 1986. Most men enter the enlisted ranks between the ages of nineteen and twenty. Because women tend to be slightly older and more varied in age, the age of their entrance will be assumed to be twenty. In the model, then, an individual's approximate age will always be her years of service plus twenty; thus, women with a full career would typically exit at age fifty with thirty years in uniform.

Women who enter service at the same time and at the same age experience particular events at approximately the same time in their life and career cycles. Groups who do this are called cohorts. The eight cohorts selected for detailed discussion here entered service in 1952, 1956, 1960, 1964, 1968, 1972, 1976, and 1980 (see figure 1). The four-year interval was selected because it is the length of a woman's typical enlistment. (After their initial commitment has been met, officers can usually resign at their discretion. Enlisted personnel, however, sign and are expected to honor enlistment and reenlistment contracts, which are often—not always—for four years.) The interval is important, then, because one cohort is considering enlistment at the same time another is considering reenlistment and still another is considering a career commitment. All these cohorts experience certain national and military events at the same time that they are assessing their desire for future or further military service.

Enlisted women put in from one to thirty years of service and range

*Military nurses obtained full military status in 1944; they had continuously existed in nursing corps since the beginning of the century.

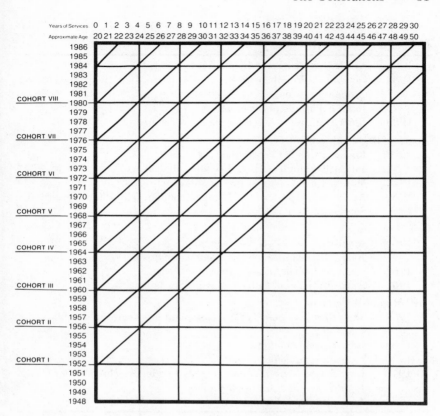

FIGURE 1.  Model Generational Chart for Military Women, 1948–1986

from about twenty to fifty years of age. All women now in service have had the opportunity to do "regular" (as opposed to auxiliary or temporary) service, and all have entered after World War II. Indeed, even in 1980 fewer than 700 servicewomen (0.5 percent) had enlisted before the start of the Vietnam War.[2] Public events that influenced these women's experiences are shown in tables 2.1 and 2.2. These experiences (and others) are also shown superimposed on the model generational chart in figure 2.

Since World War II, the number of active-duty personnel has depended on whether the country was at war. From under 1.5 million before the Korean War, it rose to more than 3.5 million, sank to under 2.5 million by 1960, increased to more than 3.5 million (again) during the Vietnam War, fell to 2.3 million at the beginning of the All-Volunteer Force, fell further to 2.0 million by 1980, and began a slow increase under the Reagan administration.

TABLE 2.1.   Events Affecting Military Personnel

| | |
|---|---|
| 1986 | April: U.S. Air Force bombs Libya. |
| 1983 | October: Marine base in Beirut is bombed; U.S. troops invade Grenada. |
| 1982 | June: ERA fails ratification. |
| 1980 | June: Draft registration for men is reinstated. |

Women's Rights Movement

| | |
|---|---|
| 1973 | January: Geneva Peace Treaty is signed. |
| | July: All-Volunteer Force becomes official. |
| 1972 | March: ERA is passed by Congress. |
| 1969 | April: At the peak of the Vietnam conflict, 543,400 troops are in Southeast Asia. |

Counter-Culture

| | |
|---|---|
| 1964 | August: Vietnam conflict begins. |
| | June: Mississippi Freedom Summer begins. |
| 1962 | October: Cuban missile crisis is resolved. |
| 1961 | April: Invasion of Cuba at Bay of Pigs fails. |

Civil Rights Movement

| | |
|---|---|
| 1954 | May: *Brown* v. *Board of Education* outlaws segregated public schools. |
| 1953 | July: Korean conflict ends. |
| 1950 | June: Korean conflict begins. |
| 1948 | July: Services are racially integrated under Executive Order 9981. |
| | June: Peacetime draft is instituted. |
| | April: Berlin airlift occurs. |

The recruitment of enlisted women did not follow the same pattern. During the Korean conflict women's numbers were increased fivefold, while men's increased by a multiple of less than three. On the other hand, the women's total during the Vietnam War was only 25 percent higher than it was in 1960, while the men's total increased 40 percent. By 1972 the men's total was below the 1960 total, but the women's was 50 percent higher; in fact, it was higher than the peak years of the Vietnam and Korean conflicts. The women's 1972 number tripled by 1976, almost quintupled by 1980, and continued to rise. Enlisted women today, then, are *not* replacing men going to the front, as women were said to do during World War II. If they are to be understood as replacements at all, they must be understood as replacements for men who prefer to remain civilians.

In addition, a higher and higher percentage of military women are now enlisted personnel rather than officers (most of whom used to be nurses). In 1948 enlisted women accounted for less than half of the 14,500 military women. In 1968 they accounted for 65 percent, and by

TABLE 2.2.    Events Affecting Military Women

| | |
|---|---|
| 1985 | Authorization bill mandates Air Force accessions of women. |
| 1983 | November: Pentagon Women's Corridor is dedicated. |
| 1982 | April: Resegregation of Army basic training is announced. |
| 1981 | June: *Goldberg* v. *Rostker* declares men-only draft registration constitutional. |
| | February: Army announces "Womanpause." |
| 1978 | July: *Owens* v. *Brown* permits Navy women to go to sea. |
| | April: Women's Army Corps is abolished. |
| 1977 | February: Army approves integrated basic training. |
| 1976 | June: Women enter military academies. |
| 1975 | May: Department of Defense ends involuntary discharge for pregnancy. |
| 1974 | May: Public Law 93-290 voids age differential for enlistment. |
| 1973 | May: *Frontiero* v. *Richardson* gives military women dependency benefits. |
| 1972 | Quigley and Zumwalt emphasize equality for Navy women. |
| 1970 | June: Two Army women become generals. |
| 1967 | Men enter Navy Nurse Corps. |
| | November: (Some) restrictions on careers of military women are removed under P.L. 90-130 |
| 1955 | October: Army Nurse and Medical Specialists Corps are opened to men. |
| 1951 | September: Defense Advisory Committee on Women in the Services is formed. |
| 1948 | June: Women's Armed Services Integration Act (P.L. 625) is passed. |

1980, 87 percent—just over the 86 percent figure for military enlisted personnel as a whole. Perhaps the most impressive statistic is the fact that in 1948 enlisted women were 0.4 percent of all military personnel, and by 1984 they were close to 10 percent.

Rank must also be incorporated into a discussion of the generations of military women. In general, promotions to ranks E-2 through E-4 occur rapidly and during the first enlistment. Promotions to E-5 through E-8 occur over the next four to twenty years and are related to the reenlistment cycle. Promotion to E-9 is likely to occur after twenty years. Women are concentrated in the lower ranks. In 1986, almost two-thirds of them were in ranks 1 to 4, and only 2 percent in ranks 7 to 9. (Among military personnel in general the numbers were 57 and 10 percent.) In large part this concentration is because women's numbers have expanded recently, and therefore as a group they have fewer years in service. (For more detailed demographic data, see Appendix C.)

Most women (and men), it should be noted, do *not* stay in service.

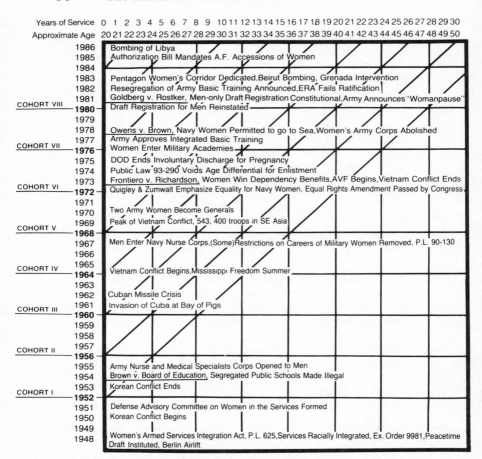

FIGURE 2.    National and Military Events Affecting Cohorts I–VIII

Most do not enlist for a second term. Because policies about women have been changing and because women's absolute numbers are so small after twelve years, it would be a serious mistake to generalize about women's behavior, especially that of senior women, on the basis of current data. The women who remain are a select few—but the criteria for their selection and self-selection are not clear. Stable and different policies might have led both to different numbers and to different women.

THE EIGHT COHORTS

The enlisted women of Cohort I entered service in 1952. Only four remained on active duty as late as 1980, but their rank gave them visibility and influence. These women responded to Korean War recruitment appeals; they elected to reenlist in a peacetime military supported by a male-only draft. In the military of their day, there was one woman officer for every two enlisted women. Most of the officers (77 percent) were nurses. Most others trained or supervised enlisted women. Over a third of the enlisted women served in the Army, where they had their own corps, the Women's Army Corps (WAC). During the day they may have worked for and with men, but their allegiance was to the WAC and their housing, command, and promotions came through it. Air Force, Navy, and Marine enlisted women also had segregated training, limited assignment possibilities, separate housing, and a sense of *esprit*. The women of Cohort I chose not only to stay in service but to be childless and in many cases single. (In the early 1950s marriage gave a woman grounds for requesting discharge, and 70 to 80 percent of these women's peers did not complete their first enlistment.)

The 1952 cohort of women accepted the terms of service as laid out in Public Law 625. This legislation provided a permanent place for women in a period of some uncertainty—just after the Russians cut off Berlin and just before Congress passed the peacetime draft for men. The women, however, were definitely *not* to serve on the same terms as men. Congress made it clear that women were not to serve in combat and responded to fears that women might be placed in command of men by leaving to the service secretaries the duty of defining "the military authority which female persons . . . may exercise and the kind of duty to which they may be assigned." P.L. 625 also imposed a 2 percent limit on active-duty women, reserving 98 percent of military slots for men. Women from eighteen to twenty-one could enlist only with parental consent (only seventeen-year-old males needed parental consent); and a woman of any age could claim a husband as dependent only if she could prove that she was in fact his "chief support." Finally, service secretaries were authorized to terminate the service of female members "under circumstances and in accordance with regulations prescribed by the President." This administrative authority for involuntary discharge was aimed at ridding the service of women who became pregnant or acquired children through adoption, marriage, or other circumstances.[3]

Because the Korean War was limited in scale, the male-only draft was able to fill U.S. manpower needs; some women were recruited, but they always composed less than one percent of the total even at the peak of the war. Thus, women of Cohort I entered during wartime to serve separately and under rules that limited their opportunity and required them to remain childless.

The women of Cohort II (1956) accepted the same rules. They, however, entered, in peacetime, a women's component reduced in size by one-fourth since 1952. Just over a dozen of these women remained in service in 1980, but like those of Cohort I, they had visibility and an average rank of almost E-8.

Cohort III, the women of 1960, accepted the same circumstances and rules. About forty of them remained in service in 1980, and their average rank was over E-7.

Today's senior enlisted women (those who enlisted before Vietnam) can be described as survivors. These volunteers met higher enlistment standards than male draftees and accepted both career limitations and childlessness. At the end of their careers they were equal in rank to men still in service, but they were submerged in a male cohort that made them almost invisible. (In 1980 there were 4 women in Cohort I to 1,400 men; 13 women in Cohort II to 4,500 men; and 42 women in Cohort III to 16,700 men.)

Women's programs were tenuous in the 1950s and 1960s, and even women military leaders feared that making waves might result in ending the programs. Indeed, one insider attributed the programs' survival "more to bureaucratic inertia and political expediency than to any conviction on the part of the military leaders that women were necessary to the national defense." During this period military women were concentrated in medical and clerical assignments. Only 7 percent held other jobs.[4]

With the women of Cohort IV (1964 entry), the experience of military women began to change. These women were volunteers during a war that was to prove unpopular with much of the public. By the time Cohort IV women had reenlisted (and Cohort V had enlisted), the Vietnam War was in full swing; women had reason to feel needed. Moreover, in 1967 Congress removed some of the restrictions on women's service, and the number of enlisted women slowly but steadily increased. Further, having large numbers of new recruits to train and command enhanced the promotion opportunities of women already in service.

P.L. 90-130 (1967) principally affected the promotion of women officers, removing the cap on their promotions and easing the restrictions at middle levels, where women were either being forced into early retirement or being given jobs slotted for persons of higher rank without getting that rank. The only part of the legislation directly affecting enlisted women removed the 2 percent limit on their numbers. Since that limit had not even been approached in the previous two decades, the immediate effect was primarily symbolic.

Cohort V entered service in 1968. The military continued to use a limited number of women in the medical and clerical fields, and these women accepted numerous limitations on assignments and personal advancement. However, they also enjoyed a special identity and a female support network. They were not urged into "men's jobs" or given remote or combat assignments. They had a niche. In 1968 no major changes in role or numbers were anticipated for military women. However, by 1970 two women would become generals, and the public would begin to realize that enlisted Marine and Army women were serving in Vietnam.*

The threshold year for military women was 1972. Those who remained from Cohorts I through IV were by then firmly established in their careers. In fact, Cohort I had already reached the twenty-year mark, Cohort II was entering its last enlistment before becoming eligible to retire, and Cohort III, after twelve years, had apparently made a commitment to a full career. The women in these cohorts (which included 100 to 130 women each) were then thirty-two years of age and over. The twenty-eight-year-old women of Cohort IV who reenlisted in 1972 were making both a life-cycle decision (probably never to have children) and a career decision. However, their careers would be in a military that would be very different from the one they had known up to that point.

The women of Cohort V (1968 entry), on the other hand, had just completed their first tour, had served during the urgency of war, had seen positive cues given to women, and now saw that more than 12,000 enlisted women would be recruited that year—almost half the total of all women then enlisted! Probably the first group of women to have "hopes," even Cohort V could not have foreseen what would occur in the next eight years. Some of those changes would be painful even if they were understood as necessary or as intended for women's benefit. In short, Cohort V was the group most exposed to, and also best positioned to benefit from, the coming changes. They were one step ahead of expansion, young enough to take advantage of change, and not too vested in the previous military women's culture. (In 1986 they would be about thirty-eight, have eighteen years of service, and be E-8s.)

In 1972 the ERA passed both houses of Congress with a two-thirds vote. During Congressional debate it was specifically decided *not* to give women constitutional protection from the draft. Indeed, Congress made it clear that women's services *could be* required. Some government officials also argued that women's services *would* be required if the ERA was ratified by the necessary three-fourths of the states. That possibility

---

*Most enlisted women in Vietnam had specifically volunteered for Southeast Asia and served in desk jobs. Most female officers were nurses, who worked where needed. Some were wounded and some died, but there was little debate about using them. In fact, the debate about "protecting" women focuses on women who take jobs usually held by men. Military women have made their first inroads as nurses, telephone operators, typists—jobs held by women in the civilian world—presumably because shortages could most quickly be met by already trained women. One suspects that in the future, women who are indispensable—for example, doctors—will again be used in war zones without debate.

began to affect the thought of military planners, as did the 1972 decision to end the draft. The United States had had a draft in war and in peace for over thirty years. Now it proposed to sustain a uniformed force of over 2 million without legal coercion. Even though the Gates Commission report on the All-Volunteer Force did not discuss women as a pool of underutilized volunteers, the Department of Defense (DOD) quickly recognized them as a resource. In 1972 the Army, Navy, and Air Force were instructed to plan to double the size of their women's programs by 1977. As it turned out, the absolute number of enlisted women tripled; their percentage more than tripled. In 1972 (the year of Cohort VI), one in thirty new recruits was a woman; by 1976, one in thirteen was.[5]

The women of Cohort VI (1972), then, entered the military in a period of rapid expansion of opportunities for women. Recruiters sought women out (men being hard to find), and large numbers enlisted. Of the 32,000 women in service in 1972, 20,000 were in their first or second year of active duty. Congress supported women, too. Congressional hearings held that year by Rep. Otis Pike (D–N.Y.) on the role of military women concluded: "We strongly urge the Secretary of Defense and the service Secretaries to develop a program which will permit women to take their rightful place in serving in our Armed Forces." The hearings also noted, "We are concerned that the Department of Defense and each of the military services are guilty of 'tokenism' in the recruitment and utilization of women."[6]

During this period the services opened more fields to women and spoke more and more positively about their integration. For instance, Capt. Robin L. Quigley, assistant chief of naval personnel for women, emphasized women's new and integrated role by announcing (by memo) that "there is no such thing as 'THE WAVES' (and) . . . I do not *direct* it or anything else." Chief of Naval Operations Elmo Zumwalt followed up with Z-Gram 116 announcing his intention to open *all* ratings to women, an "ultimate" goal of assigning women to ships at sea, and suspension of restrictions on women succeeding to command ashore.[7]

During Cohort VI's first four years, it must have seemed that each day held a new promise. Perhaps the most remarkable change occurred in 1975, when (in spite of the services' objections) DOD made discharge for pregnancy voluntary. Litigation on behalf of women who had become pregnant but who wished to remain in the military had been going on for several years. Seamen had won several victories, but the suits had no general effect, because the services sought to avoid adverse court rulings by mooting individual cases. (See Chapter 5.)

Pregnant servicewomen were anathema to many military women as well as men. Indeed, military maternity uniforms were probably beyond the imagination of most women in Cohorts I through IV. Those in Cohorts

I through III were over thirty-five when the policy was changed and were unlikely to be personally affected by it; women in Cohorts IV and V were over twenty-six, and not necessarily interested in taking advantage of it. In contrast, the women of Cohorts VI, VII, and VIII could simply assume that it was natural for young women to get pregnant and then decide whether or not to quit work.

By 1976 and the entry of Cohort VII, military women's role and status seemed to be better than ever. ROTC now accepted women; women were entering the military academies; and Air Force women had finally started pilots' training. (The Navy and Army had been giving them that training since 1973 and 1974 respectively.)

Between 1976 and 1980 there occurred the first changes, such as the abolition of the WAC, that could be perceived as negative. Some of the drawbacks associated with the new policies would affect senior women.

In their zeal to find women for the jobs most needed, military recruiters enlisted Cohort VI and VII women in a variety of "nontraditional" fields. Once in service, some women found their jobs too physically demanding, others discovered that they disliked a field after trying it out, and still others found that they were not well received in jobs that were not so extremely short-handed that a woman was considered better than no one.

During the 1960s, as noted above, "ladylike" appearance and behavior were prescribed for military women. Basic training included instruction on grooming and manners. Uniforms had skirts. Women had no fatigue uniforms and no boots. They did not learn how to use weapons. Men's and women's basic training programs were separate. In contrast, by the end of the 1970s women were expected to do many of their activities like and with men. Except in the Marines, women went through basic training and boot camp with men. Women's uniforms grew pants. Women were given defensive weapons training. Women began to wear fatigues and camouflage uniforms on a regular basis. Enlisted living quarters became integrated. Women began to command men and even served as drill instructors for integrated units. On the other hand, women's support systems were phased out—even the WAC was abolished in 1978. Finally, in June 1978 Judge John L. Sirica ruled (in *Owens* v. *Brown*, 455 F. Supp. 291 [D.D.C. 1978]) that Navy women could no longer be entirely excluded from sea duty. By November of that year, Navy women were at sea. The Navy decided that to be equitable it would not assign only women volunteers to sea duty and would not "grandmother" women who had enlisted when women *could not* go to sea. This meant that senior women were liable for tasks and tours they never could have foreseen. By the late 1970s, then, women had begun to understand that "equality" yields mixed, not just beneficent, results.

By 1980 seven cohorts of enlisted women wore military uniform. Cohorts I through IV had accepted a limited but defined sphere. They had accepted or chosen childlessness and found value and a comfortable way of life in the military. They had been in service for sixteen to twenty-eight years, were thirty-six to forty-eight years of age, and held ranks E-6 through E-9. Virtually all were in clerical and medical specialties. They totaled only 700 of the 150,000 enlisted women on active duty. Cohort V had completed its first enlistment in the "old days" but was in a position to ride the crest of every change. By 1980 members of that cohort were in their early thirties and were close to or had already earned the rank of E-6. Many were committed to a twenty-year career, and as senior enlisted personnel they were especially valuable to the services in helping to cope with a ballooning population of junior enlisted women. Generally, the growing number of women helped the forces of integration because, faced with shortages of senior women, the military was willing to try the supervision of women by men. (There was less enthusiasm for the reverse—the supervision of men by women—and since there was little "need" for it, it was not often attempted.)

Women of Cohorts VI, VII, and VIII (1980) were different. They were recruited and enlisted with high expectations. They had no experience and little knowledge of past restrictions. In addition, they knew only the peacetime All-Volunteer Force, which provided amenities unknown to a military geared to draftees fighting a war. (For example, in the late 1970s motel-like or dormitory accommodations became standard housing, replacing the open bays now mostly used in basic training.)

The year 1980 also marked a new development. Doubts about women's value to the military began to be openly expressed and were embodied in the Army's decision to "pause" in its recruitment of women. This was the first of several indications that the military intended to reassess its policies and might reduce the number of military women and the options available to them.

Thus, Cohort VIII began its career at the start of the backlash. (See Chapter 3.) Under the Reagan administration the period of rapid change was to end. Cohort VIII women experienced a period of relative stability; certain support programs for women began, but the atmosphere was uneasy. Service initiatives to roll back the changes of the 1970s were mostly thwarted. However, momentum, a sense of possibility, and official advocacy were lost. The trade-off, then, was consolidation (accessions secured) and honor (the Pentagon's Women's Corridor) for "benign neglect": a decline in the number of "firsts" and the attendant publicity that often says in effect, "Excellent—for a woman."

One would expect the women of different cohorts to respond to the "pause" and other setbacks in a variety of ways. Cohorts I through IV had made their commitment in and lived through far less supportive days.

Cohorts V through VII had experienced *only* advance and expansion. The women of Cohorts V and VI had twelve and eight years respectively invested in military service, whereas the women of Cohorts VII and VIII could more easily quit. Those who elected to stay would experience a new, somewhat uncertain atmosphere.

These younger women represented the bulk of military women. Not only were they numerous; they had other options and were also the women the military most needed, since many worked in nontraditional fields. These were also the women who simply expected to have military careers and spouses and children—just as men do.

The chill that became perceptible in 1980 will be detailed in the next chapter. First, however, we must consider the change commanders found the most radical—pregnant women and mothers in uniform.

## GENERATION AND THE GENERATIONS OF ENLISTED WOMEN

At one time enlisted personnel were mostly single. Then it became commonplace for enlisted men to marry and have families. Now enlisted women do, too. Dependents, of course, make the military costly. Still, their importance to morale and hence to performance and retention has caused the services to give a good deal of attention to families recently.

In 1980 about 50 percent of enlisted men, and over 90 percent of those with more than eight years of service, had dependents. In contrast, less than a quarter of enlisted women had dependents, and only a third of those with more than eight years of service (prior to Cohort VI) did. By 1985 women's and men's families were becoming more similar (table 2.3).[8]

Women who hold ranks E-1 through E-5 have family lives very similar to those of enlisted men. (Enlisted families will be discussed further in Chapter 9.) At senior ranks women are much more likely not to have

TABLE 2.3.  Family Status of Enlisted Men and Women, 1985

| Rank | Men | Women |
|---|---|---|
| Percentage Never Married | | |
| At entry | 86 | 83 |
| E1–E3 | 70 | 60 |
| E4–E5 | 37 | 33 |
| E6 and above | 5 | 21 |
| Percentage Households with Children | | |
| E1–E3 | 15 | 14 |
| E4–E5 | 43 | 41 |
| E6 and above | 81 | 51 |

children and never to have married. Some of this difference may reflect their decision that military service is incompatible with family life. Much, though, is residual—the result of the implicit contract the most senior women made when they entered service.

Previously, most young women left service soon after entering. Those who stayed were considered "serious"—the few who might grow up to be like the senior women, the "career" women. Some might describe the young women as modeling themselves after the older women. It is equally possible, of course, that they were chosen by the senior women for their similarity—as, in a sense, surrogate daughters. Role-modeling or successor-tapping cannot occur in the old way if most young military women are now wives and mothers while older women are single and childless. Today, senior women lack look-alike successors. They are less able to foster followers in their own image. For advisors and supporters, junior women now have boyfriends, husbands, and friends as well as senior women. And many senior military women agree with those military men who assert that mothers should not be soldiers.

Because policies have changed so dramatically and so recently, we do not have an adequate data base to describe the different views, performance, and behavior of women with different marital and familial ties. Let us consider the possibilities, however, for four categories of women (table 2.4).

For many years it was assumed that most enlisted women would be single and childless (category 1), and that they would serve for a short time before they married, just as other young women held low-paying, high-turnover civilian jobs before marriage. Only a select few were expected to find a vocation in the military. They would never have children, and many would never marry. Military women, then, were like Catholic religious and the Shakers: they drew upon others' children to serve as their successors.

Single, childless women formed a community in the military almost by virtue of wearing a uniform. They underwent the ordeal of entry training together and generally were housed together. The WACs might almost have been called a sisterhood. They had their own corps and managed and administered it separately. Its reason for being was biology, not

TABLE 2.4.    Marital and Familial Categories

|             | Single | Married |
|-------------|--------|---------|
| No Children | 1      | 2       |
| Children    | 4      | 3       |

function: women held a variety of jobs, but they were in the corps solely because they were women. In the other services the women were officially more integrated; they did not have the same control over their lives, but they did share housing and had a variety of both formal and informal networks for support.

There is very little literature on the communities of single, childless women, although some characteristics can be identified. Usually the dominant bond is work or an activity, not childlessness per se, even when childlessness is a prerequisite for group membership. Singleness, too, has often been required for women even when it has not been required for men (e.g., schoolteachers). Interestingly, even when women and their organizations are competent, effective, and powerful, they often remain under the formal control of men—for example, the WAC, Catholic religious orders, and in former times the faculties of women's colleges have had as their superiors the secretary of the Army, the pope, and a mostly male board of trustees.

It is hard to estimate the strength of women's bonding or identify its basis. One might, for example, assume a higher percentage of lesbians, whose sexual preference represents one kind of bonding, among single, childless, mature women than among women in general, but because lesbianism is specifically forbidden and is grounds for separation from the services, it is hard to know its incidence or influence. Since unit cohesion is of such concern to the military, it is surprising that so little attention has been given to the bonding created by women's corps. Those corps, with their multiple bonds, were dissolved in the 1970s. It was tacitly assumed that "integration" (even though it was actually submergence) was better. It was not assumed to be best; concern remains today that women's mere presence jeopardizes overall military effectiveness by diminishing unit cohesion.

Married but childless women (category 2) may hold the same jobs and have the same institutional locations as single women, but because they do not live with other women and because their social life is likely to revolve around their status as part of a couple, they are not as easily described as being part of a women's community. It is also not clear which is more institutionally advantageous to a woman—the ability to demonstrate undistracted commitment or access (through one's spouse) to the male communications network. (Two out of three military women with husbands are married to military men.) Some women in category 2 were, and are, in transition to civilian life, planning to stay in service only until they have children.

Married women with children (category 3) began to pressure the military for permission to remain in service in the 1970s. A few test cases were raised, a waiver policy for individuals was developed, and in 1975

DOD ended its policy of involuntary discharge for pregnancy or parent-hood.

When women of category 3 won the right to stay in service, so did the women of category 4—unmarried (including divorced) mothers, a group some considered not wholly reputable.

Some military women have felt a need to guard their own, and the group's, reputation. They expect others to do likewise and to be discreet if they choose to be unconventional. Unfortunately, the pregnancy of a working woman cannot be kept private, and when that woman is known to be single, she becomes visual evidence of the truth of traditional slurs about military women. Youth, low income, geographical transfers, and lack of family services combine to make it difficult for a junior enlisted woman to fulfill parental and military duties as a single parent. Thus many in this category leave service, and some who stay probably perform marginally. Both groups confirm doubts about single parents and make it harder for others—many of whom perform superbly—who elect to stay.

The relationships between women of categories 1, 2, 3, and 4 deserve probing. Category 3 (28 percent of military women in 1985) so dominates civilian and social science thinking that categories 4, 2, and 1 tend to be considered only when one is being conscientious. Yet category 1 (38 percent of military women) is still dominant, and category 2 accounts for 25 percent. (The newest group—category 4—comprises 8 percent.)[9] At present there is a balance among the categories, but it is not clear that members of the different groups effectively support each other. It may be that one category will eventually become so established that the others will have to hew to its line. In any event, the arrival of a younger genera-tion fundamentally different from the older one has to have been difficult for senior women, who, even though they hold rank, are overwhelmed by numbers. What is more, younger women cannot perceive the radical change they create just by having families—something civilian women and civilian and military men have always done.

CONCLUSION

There are two take-home messages. First, the military's policy of no lateral entry, its hierarchical structure, and the rapid policy changes of the 1970s created large differences in the experience of women of different ranks. Policy changes also mean that the kind of statistical projections normally used are not adequate for making decisions about women. For example, data showing women's low reenlistment for a third tour of duty might once have been attributable to a decision (at approxi-mately age twenty-eight) to start a family. The same statistics today may reflect a blocked career field or an inability (or unwillingness) to accept sea duty or a remote or unaccompanied assignment—neither of which was expected of women at the time of the individual's enlistment.

Second, only a small percentage and a relatively small number of women serve in the military, making the military experience different for women than for men. If promotion or uniform boards are selected without regard to sex, men can count on having a majority (and possibly a monopoly) on those bodies. Women cannot count on automatic representation. They must expect always to operate as a minority and sometimes to be wholly unrepresented. Women's small numbers also mean that senior military women are a select group. But for what are they selected? For professionalism? For a women's military as it was? For survivorship? For low expectations? Or for flexibility?

Maj. Gen. Jeanne Holm, USAF (Ret.), has noted that senior women again and again have resisted new jobs, new assignments, and new policies for women even when their apparent thrust was toward integration and equality.[10] On balance, those women may have been wrong, defensive, and protective. But their pessimism about the maleness of military culture, their suspicion about norms being suspended (because of pressures like the All-Volunteer Force and the ERA) rather than altered, their assessment of costs and the potential for backlash, all have some validity. Even if one does not come to the same conclusions, their views are comprehensible, as are the anti-ERA views voiced by younger women in base interviews. First, younger women have no experience or understanding of what it was like "before." Second, they have no knowledge of the benefits of the ERA—like their being there at all. They do know, though, that when they complain about the hardships of their job, they're told: "That's ERA!" or "You want equality, don't you?" For them the ERA is associated with negative results, not positive ones. It is used *on* them, not *by* them. In the interest of equality, they are required to participate in duties they might otherwise be able to avoid.

To an outsider and especially to a feminist, the antifeminism of both senior and junior women seems ironic and contrary to their own interests. But each group's positions are rooted in experience. The one has low expectations based on years at the periphery; the other is now experiencing the negative aspects of equality and the resistance to it that were suppressed or overlooked from 1972 through 1980.

Women who have known only the changed military—Cohorts VI, VII, and VIII—are the most likely to be (1) demanding on behalf of women but also (2) most disappointed by a backpedaling military and (3) best able to find rewarding civilian careers. If these women leave in excessive numbers, the military will have lost its pioneering generation. The women of Cohorts VI, VII, and VIII volunteered when not enough men would. They accepted the challenge of integrating an overwhelmingly male institution, undertook previously forbidden jobs, accepted the costs as well as the benefits of equality, and in some cases bore children while continuing their work. Its members are quite different from the survivors of Cohorts I through IV. The question is, will the difference be evident when some of these women become E-9s (around the year 2000)? Or will the military's screening (and women's emigration) cause the E-9s of the future to be very like those of today?

# 3

---

# Backlash
# and
# Freeze

As the previous chapter showed, military women experienced nearly constant progress toward equality from the late 1960s through the late 1970s. For a decade every change for women seemed to expand opportunity, to offer new (but not impossible) challenges, to reflect institutional respect and acceptance. Thus, a whole generation of women came to understand the military not as wholly fair, not as nonsexist, not as sweetly reasonable, but as a rapidly changing organization in which each change seemed to be for the better. In the late 1970s, and certainly by 1980, military women began to have a more mixed view of change. Some changes did not seem to be for the better. First, some changes in the direction of equality brought burdens—for example, women now had to stand watches and perform duties from which they had previously been excused. Second, some changes seemed to take away benefits, as when the military stopped routinely doing and paying for abortions. A mood of doubt, even apprehension, began to develop. What change would come next? What was really intended? Would women's numbers and opportunities be curtailed? Was a backlash, a counterattack, in progress? This chapter will review the events that led supporters of women in the military to conclude that a backlash had indeed begun in late 1980.

To the fisherman a backlash is an incapacitating snarl or, more generally, a sudden or violent backward whipping. In social relations, it has been defined as "an antagonistic reaction to some prior action construed as a threat" (*American Heritage Dictionary*).

A backlash is not always incapacitating, nor does it always involve a reversal. It may simply stop forward movement or it can actually have a positive effect if it causes proponents of a change to focus their energy and opponents to be embarrassed. Nor is a backlash necessarily either abrupt or violent. Frequently, in fact, it is erosive, composed of a number of small changes that unobtrusively shape a reversal. Still, there is usually one event or decision that comes to symbolize a general backsliding, and that event may, at first, appear to have come from the blue —to have had no precursor. In retrospect, though, one can usually tally a number of small events that preceded (and followed) the most visible setback. One then realizes that one should have seen it coming.

To many the Army's February 1981 announcement of its intention to "pause" in its planned increase in women's accessions was unexpected. It seemed a classic instance of backlash. However, a number of reversals in policies affecting women had occurred before then, and they were not restricted to the Army. At least in hindsight, antagonistic reactions to women's increased military role were not uncommon. What was uncommon before 1980, though, was any public expression of antagonism by high-ranking military or civilian authorities. Admission by antagonists that they felt threatened was to remain uncommon. Indeed, women were never described as threats to men, but rather as threats to military readiness and, therefore, to the nation.

A backlash, then, may cause a reversal in policy, it may arrest change, or it may only express antagonism and a desire to reverse or to arrest change. It can be composed of a single major event, a series of small, even insubstantial events, or both. It may involve no more than an expression of opinion, but when changes have been occurring in an atmosphere free of opposition, an expression of negative opinion can be chilling. After all, it is disturbing to find that principles assumed to be so sure that they could not be doubted, are in fact doubted. It is draining to have to spend energy defending what one believed was secure.

The identification of a backlash is left mostly to the complainant, who may take even minor and inadvertent words and deeds as evidence. An Anglo-American tradition of doing this dates back at least to John Locke's *Second Treatise of Government* and is preserved in the code of honor summarized in South Carolina's "Don't Tread on Me" flag and in the current, careful documentation of damage conducted by organizations like the Anti-Defamation League. Thus, in describing the backlash as perceived by supporters of military women, it is appropriate to list both major and minor events without seeking to balance or reconcile pros and cons. The proponent of change properly assumes a suspicious stance. In a dead calm, even a light breeze causes tattletales to flutter.

### EARLY SIGNS OF RETRENCHMENT

A first breeze appeared in the fall 1980 issue of the *Public Interest*, where Seth Cropsey of *Fortune* magazine charged in an article titled "The Military Manpower Crisis: Women in Combat": "What is going on today at the Pentagon is a social experiment of unprecedented magnitude and unimagined consequences."[1] A second hint was given on 17 November

1980, when Joseph C. Zengerle, Air Force assistant secretary for manpower, reserve affairs and installations, gave an address to the Defense Advisory Committee on Women in the Services (DACOWITS). After reviewing a number of achievements by and on behalf of military women, he said:

> But the circumstances leading to these kinds of achievements have changed today in at least two fundamental particulars. First, the honeymoon is over. Women have been in uniform long enough and in sufficient numbers for people to have developed some sense of the impact their presence will have on military institutions. That change would come about was inevitable. But the natural human tendency to protect the status quo now has a concrete set of targets to work on. Second, because of recently developed international tensions, the posture of our Defense establishment and public opinion about what that posture should be have changed. The Soviet invasion of Afghanistan, the taking of the hostages in Iran, and a growing sense of awareness of the disparity between Soviet and American military growth in the past ten years have combined to produce a heightened concern about national security in the sense of our war-fighting or war-deterring capability. . . .
>
> To me these developments have altered the relationship between national security and women's rights. Whereas before they were on parallel tracks, now there is a potential for conflict. Enthusiasm to enlist women to make the All-Volunteer Force work has been dampened by the inevitable struggle to make change a reality. Emphasis is shifting from the essentially domestic issue of equal opportunity to operational readiness, fundamentally a foreign issue.[2]

This speech was delivered shortly after Ronald Reagan was elected president on a platform that vigorously argued the need to enhance U.S. defenses. Questions about the appropriate use of U.S. power, the fairness of the draft, and the representativeness of the military had been abandoned in favor of advocacy of military pay increases, new weapon systems, and increased military preparedness. As is usually the case in politics, the old debates were not resolved; new issues simply took their place.

The opponents of women in the military were stymied as long as equal opportunity and citizens' rights held the limelight. When the debate was redirected so that readiness, effectiveness, and efficiency became the central issues, opponents of women did not have to address equality claims at all. They just insisted that other items had priority and that "rights" were a luxury—or even, in a popular phrase of the day, that women's presence in the military was a "social experiment." With the Reagan election, new items were given saliency. Supporters of women found not only that their items had been removed from the agenda, but also that the new issues were sometimes formulated in ways that reversed previously won gains.

The particular concerns about women cited by Zengerle emerged again and again in military managers' discussions and are therefore worth summarizing. The first concern was whether the nontraditional specialties women entered during the 1970s were really suitable for them. Specifically, questions were raised about women's strength, stamina, and agility; the special consequences for pregnant women of certain (especially chemical) environments; and women's apparent preference for administrative specialties as opposed to technical ones and their tendency to migrate from the latter. A second area of concern involved married military couples. These were considered hard to assign in terms of both location and career-enhancing assignments. How married military couples with dependent children and single parents would respond in the event of an emergency deployment also worried commanders. Perhaps the primary concern, though, centered on pregnancy: how was the safety of the woman (and fetus) to be ensured; how could military work be accomplished in small units where each individual was essential or in larger units with a high concentration of women? A related worry was the expense of new facilities made necessary by women, in particular facilities for day care. These, then, were the continuing themes. They are all legitimate management concerns, but they are also complaints about the "trouble" women create. Often the implicit message seemed to be: let's go back to the good old days and ways.

Even before Reagan's election, certain decisions or events could be seen as signs of an impending backlash. For example, the Air Force decided that women could not be security specialists after all. The Marines removed some women serving as embassy guards. The Navy tried to discharge a number of the first women at sea as lesbians. The Army failed to provide appropriate clothing for women (especially boots) and occupied itself with a proposal to issue unisex rather than men's and women's clothing.

Let us explore these items in some detail. The individuals who made these decisions probably did not see themselves as participating in a backlash. Plausible explanations for each decision are available, but when men make decisions about women as a category, there is always some suspicion about those decisions. The reverse experience (women making decisions about men as a category) is probably one that few adult men have had or can even imagine, but one suspects that men might be reluctant to accept such decisions.

The Air Force increased its proportion of women recruits and moved them into new specialties a bit earlier and perhaps more enthusiastically than the other services. In 1973 a goal was set of tripling the number of Air Force women over the next five years. In addition, 100 new fields were opened to them. This meant that only 7 of 230 job types and only 40,000 of 572,000 enlisted jobs were closed to women. These included air crew jobs as gunners and para-rescue/recovery specialists. Women were also ineligible to become tactical control and security specialists.

In 1976 the Air Force opened its academy to women and began training them as pilots and soon thereafter as navigators, thus acknowledging that not all its pilots and navigators had to fly in combat. In other words, rated officers did not have to be fully interchangeable. The Air Force described pilot training for women as a "test" and carefully monitored their performance. It was not, however, the kind of test where criteria for continuation or discontinuation of the program were established in advance. Those who saw it as a genuine test rejoiced, certain that women would do splendidly and that more and more women would soon join men in the air. Some, though, saw it not as a test of women's capability (which they also assumed), but as a test of public and/or congressional opinion. Would those publics insist on continuation, or would the opposition prevail? That opposition saw the test as establishing not capability or opinion, but only what special help and dispensations would be needed in order to keep enough women in the air to keep critics quiet.

With women officers in aircraft, it was inevitable that pressure would develop for enlisted women to serve in air crews. It did. However, the first of the few closed fields to be opened to women was not one of the air crew specialties but that of security specialist.

The Air Force described the opening of this field, too, as a "test." It is not an especially attractive field; it is difficult both to attract men and to keep them in it. In introducing women the Air Force "waived" its own combat policy, since the job involves guarding aircraft and weapons against sabotage and terrorist attack, controlling the terrain around a base, and protecting bases in hostile areas. This specialty and law enforcement are the two enlisted specialties that come under the general category of "security police." Women were already eligible for law enforcement, and women officers were already serving in the field (which was a single field at the officer level). The "test," then, covered the recruitment, training, and performance (at four bases in the United States and abroad, in hot and cold climates) of a hundred enlisted women security specialists over a period of one year.

Three years later the decision was made to "keep the field closed." The data had been collected in one year, but deciding what they meant took two more. The negative decision was said to be "principally due to combat relationship considerations." Three years later, then, (probably different) commanders decided that the combat "waiver" was to be un-waived. An official briefing given to DACOWITS in October 1979 by the Air Force general in charge of personnel planning, Maj. Gen. William Usher, focused on "test" data that implied that the female security specialists had failed.

In the Usher presentation the principal "test" turned out to be attrition. At the end of one year, 71 percent of the men, and only 47 percent of the women, remained at work in their units—a 24-point difference. Did that difference in fact represent failure? Fifteen of those 24 points were lost before basic training even began. Thus, when enlistees were screened for specialty assignments, 18 percent of the women, as contrasted with 3 percent of the men, were disqualified for medical problems, emotional instability, and enlistment contract misunderstandings. Clearly that difference represents not failure but (1) poor recruitment; (2) the Air Force's willingness to let women, but not men, change their minds; and possibly (3) women's superior ability to get their way (out). During training 18 percent of the men and 20 percent of the women dropped out. Where does the significant difference then lie? Presumably in the 8 percent loss of men and 15 percent loss of women during the first year on the job. Let us look at those losses more closely.

First, 16 men (of 199) left, but no breakdown is given for why they left or where they went. Twenty-four women (of 160) left, but 10 retrained for other fields and were not "lost" to the Air Force. Fourteen were discharged, 3 of them for pregnancy. In the group of 24, 14 had their jobs changed (or ended) because of "emotional problems" and 2 because of "fear of weapons." Although a number of men left service at all stages of their tour for "lack of adaptability," none were listed as discharged for "emotional reasons." These figures, like those for earlier losses, could be interpreted as showing that women who find themselves in an unpleasant job are better than men at getting out of it—and in this case most did not have to resort to pregnancy to do so. Yet the numbers were used to imply female incapacity and to justify banning *any* woman from the job. To some the explanation and decision looked like backlash.[3]

What about the Marines? In 1977 the commandant approved a "pilot program" to test "the feasibility and desirability" of assigning women to the Marine security guard. This coveted duty included embassy duty throughout the world. By 1979 the State Department had approved the program, and fifteen women were assigned to eight embassies. Shortly afterward three U.S. embassies were attacked in Teheran, Islamabad, and Tripoli (one male marine was killed). The State Department evacuated dependents and nonessential personnel from a number of embassies in Moslem countries, and the Marines removed female security guards assigned to Karachi, Amman, and Bamako (Mali). Women, it was decided, would not be assigned to "high risk" areas or jobs that "can reasonably be expected to routinely involve them in combat," defined as "a hostile encounter that involves the direct use of weapons against the enemy or exposure to the direct force of an enemy attack."[4] Again, Marine commanders must have seen women security guards as an experiment—one that they were willing to try but free to abandon. Women, on the other hand, could see the assignment as something they had gotten and lost—and they saw the loss as a victory for people who had been against the innovation from the beginning.*

In late 1978 the Navy assigned women to sea as a result of a federal court decision and a modification of the congressional prohibition against women on combat ships. Since 1979 was really women's "first year" at sea, the *Norton Sound* affair of early 1980 could not be overlooked. Indeed, it was front-page news in Los Angeles for a number of days.

A missile-tracking vessel, the *Norton Sound*, was one of the first Pacific-based ships to which enlisted women were assigned. In June 1980 nineteen of the sixty-one enlisted women on board were accused of homosexuality and received letters of discharge. Men and women are discharged for this reason with some regularity. What was not regular this time was that the women did not go quietly. Instead, they asked the Southern California chapter of the American Civil Liberties Union (ACLU) to represent them. It agreed. Ultimately charges against fifteen of the women were dropped. Of the four who were tried, two were convicted and two were not. The newswires sent the story across the country, and the picture painted of shipboard life—including sex, violence, drugs, and the loss of a sailor at sea—made it sound rough and unfair. In retrospect one might see the affair as simply "mishandled." However, some women saw it as a purposeful attempt to damage the Women at Sea Program and others saw it as intended to keep women from volunteering for the Navy at all.

And the Army. The Army would lead the 1981 movement to retrench, but before the presidential election its dissent was muted. One important

*In February 1988 DOD directed the Marines to assign women as embassy guards. A related question concerned U.S. willingness to honor the prejudices of foreign countries in assigning military personnel. The withdrawal of the women marines from embassies in Moslem countries represented a judgment about "combat," but the Marines also had a policy of honoring the views of "host" countries concerning the appropriate roles for women (interview with Gen. Anthony Lukeman, Arlington, Va., 15 November 1981). Some women saw this as permitting foreigners to decide what a U.S. citizen could do. However, few military women contested the policy, nor did DACOWITS find it an item of concern. Moreover, even under a system of free assignments, some individuals might prefer not to be assigned to an uncongenial location where they might find it difficult to accomplish their duties.

reason was that the Carter administration had a number of well-placed defense officials who considered it a part of their duty to monitor women's access to and participation in the services: Jill Wine-Banks, general counsel for the U.S. Army; Air Force Undersecretary Antonia Chayes; Deputy Undersecretary of the Navy Mitzi Wertheim; and Deputy Secretary of Defense for Equal Opportunity M. Kathleen Carpenter. Further, Secretary of the Army Clifford L. Alexander, Jr., heard no reservations and minced no words when it came to equal opportunity; in addition, the Army was under terrific pressure to recruit volunteers. The result was a lot of people in Army uniforms whom commanders would have preferred not to have there. Even with vigorous leadership at the top, many women experienced the Army as reluctant. Its attitude was exemplified by its apparent inability to provide the thousands of women recruits with properly fitting, sturdy boots. Often smaller-sized men's clothing was provided for work uniforms. Moreover, although women were allowed to be pregnant beginning in 1975 and were issued camouflage uniforms beginning in 1981, they could not get maternity "camis" until October 1984.

Retreats were being sounded in the civilian sector, too. Ratification of the ERA had begun to look doubtful. Congress did not include women in the newly instituted draft registration, nor did it remove the combat restriction on women, as the Carter administration had requested. Claims of "reverse discrimination" by white males became a subject of public concern, and the Supreme Court agreed to hear cases dealing with that issue. Finally, the Republican party, at Ronald Reagan's behest (and over his daughter Maureen's opposition), ended its forty years of support for the ERA. Clearly, many who had previously been silent now found it possible and appropriate to protest against women's changing role.

### AFTER THE ELECTION

Before Reagan was even sworn into office, the four military services sent a confidential memo to his transition team asking him to hold the line on women and refrain from implementing planned accessions (i.e., recruitment goals) and end strengths (the total number of personnel at a given time).[5] The end-strength goal in place for 1986 was 223,000 women; the women then in service numbered about 150,000. The joint-service position paper argued that women's attrition from nontraditional career fields, susceptibility to pregnancy, and need for dependent care, as well as the difficulty of reaching recruiting goals while maintaining standards, dictated a total reassessment. The services recommended that women recruits be held to "the minimum needed" to meet overall recruiting goals and that end-strength objectives be withdrawn until the services reestablished their "requirements." The Carter administration goals, they argued, were "arbitrary"; women impaired "preparedness"; and the services (not civilians) should determine the number of women they needed.

The Army did not stop with its part in the memo to the transition team. Representatives went before the Senate Armed Services Committee to make the same point again and to note that the Army was undertaking a "very extensive study" of women's impact on its "preparedness to fight." The Army referred to its new policy as a "pause" in recruitment, and those with a wry sense of humor called it the Army's "womanopause." The Army apparently informed DOD of its plan after informing the Senate.

The change in the wind was evident elsewhere too. As late as December 1980, *Army Magazine* had carried an article (written by a captain) that insisted: "Women are not a problem in Army." By February 1981 a research article in the same journal was arguing that women's deficiencies "in some soldierly skills that mean life or death in combat tend to lower the military—if not the functional—efficiency of support units with large numbers of women assigned." This piece (by a colonel) also noted that the "bothersome factor" of fraternization and the impact on men's families "should not be discounted or treated lightly." The same month the sergeant major of the Army held a press conference and said, "I think we need to re-evaluate women in the Army."[6]

By May the Reagan team was in place at the Pentagon, and the pause was an approved reality. At a news conference the new undersecretary for manpower and reserve affairs, Lawrence Korb, spelled out the situation.[7] Past goals, he said, had been based on "theoretical models"; moreover, it was appropriate to rethink all programs at the beginning of an administration. His own prediction was that after careful assessment women would be leveled out at 10 to 12 percent, "or lower." The shift in opinion he attributed to DOD's giving more attention to field commanders and their complaints. Indeed, one of those commanders, Maj. Gen. Robert Wetzel, was brought back to Washington to review Army policies on women and to prepare a report by the end of 1981.

One fact was unchanged: women's roles were directly linked to the volunteer force. The Reagan administration was firmly committed to that force. Some women took comfort in that, believing that recruitment pressures would keep women in service. Indeed, Korb himself enunciated what might be called the "policy of last resort": "No way [would we] ever leave a spot vacant rather than take a woman." More pessimistic women saw their opportunities as dependent upon a strong economy as well as the All-Volunteer Force itself.

The latter were right, for the economy ceased to boom, military salaries were raised, enlistments soared, retention increased, and women became more expendable. In June 1981 the Army stopped enlisting women (except for a small number in the Delayed Entry Program) for the rest of the year. It dropped its recruitment objective from 25,000 to 18,600 (to implement its pause at 65,000), and it tightened its female enlistment standards—that is, again raised them above men's.[8] All women would have to be high school graduates and be in mental category I, II, or III. Thus ended a brief experiment in equal standards, an experiment that had coincided with threatened litigation and with difficulty in recruiting the desired number of women.*

That same month one field commander, Lt. Gen. Julius Becton, whose policy of integrating barracks latrines had been rescinded after a photograph of integrated bathrooms appeared in *Stars and Stripes*, announced that first-term soldiers who get pregnant should "have an abortion or be discharged."[9]

In July the lash was felt from a new direction. The Air Force, with virtually no combat restrictions, abruptly announced a one-third reduction in its end-strength goals for women. The previous secretary of the Air Force, Hans Mark, had argued that there was no reason to register women for the draft, because there were so many volunteers—indeed, the Air Force was scheduled to be 18 to 20 percent female by 1985.[10] The new secretary, Verne Orr, authorized a dramatic cut in end-strength goals. The reasons will be explored in detail in Chapter 7, but the basic explanation was women's nonavailability or incompetence.

Reduced accessions and end strengths are the most thorough, raw, and unsubtle form of retrenchment. But women's alarms had been sounding for a year, some perhaps triggered by little more than misunderstandings, slights, or bad publicity. A suspected slowdown in women's promotions, or a decrease in their assignment to leadership positions, was hard to demonstrate. But when changes are made in numbers everyone knows, and when those changes occur suddenly and with little explanation the message is clear: retrenchment has begun.

The 1980 end-strength goals for women set by the Carter administration were the first set at the DOD level. That year active-duty enlisted women numbered almost 150,000, including 61,000 in the Army, 30,000 in the Navy, 6,000 in the Marines, and 51,000 in the Air Force. That same year Army goals for 1986 were set at 87,500; Navy goals at 47,000; Marine goals at 9,000; and Air Force goals at 90,000. In terms of percentages the 1980 end strengths represented 9.0 percent of the Army, 6.5 percent of the Navy, 3.7 percent of the Marines, and 11.3 percent

---

*The Navy and the Marines always held women to higher standards—because they could. The Air Force had high standards for women, but could and did require the same standards for men. The Army argued that women who had not completed high school had a much higher attrition rate than women who had, and also than men who had not. Data bear out this claim.

of Air Force personnel. Overall 8.5 percent of enlisted people were to be women. The projections for 1986 planned an increase to about 12.5 percent.[11]

As noted above, in January 1981 the Army indicated that it would maintain its current end strength of 65,000 but would not increase it.[12] The Navy indicated no change in its goals, which would not only substantially increase the number of enlisted women but would also increase their proportion to over 9 percent.[13] The Marines indicated no change in plans but announced that it was conducting three "major study and analysis projects for the purpose of improving present and future management and utilization of women Marine resources."[14] All this was reported to DACOWITS in April 1981. At that time the Air Force gave no hint as to any change in its recruitment plans, but it noted that it was having no problem in achieving the goals set for women.[15] However, in July the *Air Force Times* reported that the service intended to lower its end-strength goals from 90,000 in 1986 to 55,000 in 1987.[16] That represented only a small increase in absolute numbers over the existing end strength, and because there was to be an overall buildup, it represented a proportional decrease. In effect the Air Force was following the lead of the Army. It was "pausing." Yet there had been few indications of "problems" with Air Force personnel, in contrast to the Army situation. The recruits had been of high quality, there had been no difficulty recruiting them, and there were virtually no restrictions on the use of enlisted women. As recently as June the House Armed Services Committee had been told that no drastic change in plans was anticipated; apparently DOD itself was caught by surprise.

The Air Force presented this reversal smoothly. At the fall 1981 DACOWITS briefings, the other services sketched past, present, and future programs. The Air Force presented only past and present, without referring to its altered future. It appears that because the Air Force had more women than the other services, it was able to act like the Army —pause and reverse its commitments—without calling attention to its changed intentions. At the November 1982 DACOWITS briefing, the Air Force showed enlisted women increasing from 54,000 in 1982 to 61,000 in 1986. It looked as if the Air Force was moving forward. The fact that its goal for 1986 had dropped from 90,000 to 61,000 was deftly omitted.

In sum, during Reagan's first term the Army and Air Force retreated —the Air Force more quietly and further. The Marines considered and reconsidered. The Navy held a steady course. (Some might attribute the absence of backlash in the Navy's accessions to its successful resistance to earlier forces for change, but even the Navy had increased women enlisted personnel from about 6,000 in 1972 to almost 30,000 in 1980.) The discussion of retrenchment, then, came from the Army and its pause and study group. The activity of retrenchment, though, was equally the work of the Air Force.

August brought the news that the director of the Army's study, Maj. Gen. Wetzel, had been replaced by Brig. Gen. Ronald Zeltman. It was also acknowledged that the Army review group *was* considering discharge of first-term, pregnant women and that Lt. Gen. Becton, who had broached that policy, had left Germany and was now commander of all initial-entry training. In addition, the administration asked the services to reassess their position on the congressional ban on women in combat planes and on combat ships.[17] (Repeal had been requested by the Carter administration and was regularly recommended by DACOWITS on grounds of managerial flexibility—even after a majority of its members were Reagan appointees.)

In November the *U.S. Naval Institute Proceedings* published an article entitled "No Place for Women: The Fleet Marine Forces," by a Marine lieutenant colonel; and DOD issued *Women in the Military: Background Review*, which recommended increased management flexibility for the services, reduced emphasis on affirmative action plans, and increased emphasis on sexual harassment counseling and education, while endorsing the Army's pause "until such time as it completes its review of policies concerning women."

### YEAR TWO: REACTION TO RETRENCHMENT

The new year brought the Secretary of the Navy John F. Lehman, Jr., into the news when he told an audience of 250 women Navy officers that the Defense Officer Personnel Management Act (DOPMA) was "a non-issue." To the women it was very much an issue because it required Navy women who had been unable to go to sea to compete directly for promotion with Navy men who had. The secretary explained what he "meant" to a reporter the next day, but it was obvious that his audience had been disappointed. The 25 January *Navy Times* printed several revealing quotations: "I'm angry because of his total lack of understanding of the issues concerning women officers." "It appears to me that the Secretary was not well prepared to speak to this group, and that, in itself, suggested a careless approach towards his audience." Another said that Lehman had not treated women "as professionals" and was "cavalier" in his approach to them.

Lehman's speech was given almost exactly one year after the transition team received the services' memorandum. Retrenchment seemed to be in full swing, but a reaction had now begun, signaled by a well-publicized hearing held in November 1981. Conducted by Congresswoman Pat Schroeder, it featured Helen Rogan (author of *Mixed Com-*

*pany*) and officials who repeated the current policies of their services to a room full of uniformed and nonuniformed military and civilian women. It was a critical audience.

DOD began to respond in the second year. The sharp public comments made by women Navy officers about their boss had had an effect. Indeed, immediate action was taken to reassure the women. Secretary of Defense Casper Weinberger sent strongly worded memos to each service secretary: "This Administration desires to increase the role of women in the military and I expect the Service Secretaries actively to support that policy. I ask that you personally review your service policies to ensure that women are not subject to discrimination in recruiting or career opportunities." Further, Deputy Secretary of Defense Frank Carlucci asked each secretary for a report by 28 January 1982 on action being taken to remove institutional barriers for women and an analysis of how women's career paths are affected by limitations on their assignment to combat duties.[18]

Assistant Secretary of Defense Korb told the secretaries:

> I want to be sure that my office and the Services are together in understanding DOD policy relating to women in the military. . . . From my assessment of the recent POM [Program Objective Memorandum] and budget submissions and reactions to the preliminary Defense Guidance, I also sense a reluctance in the Services to expand the number of women in the military.[19]

A civilian response appeared in a series of articles beginning in the February 1982 issue of *Government Executive*. Evidently, after a year in office the Reagan administration's civilians were beginning to find themselves at odds with uniformed officials on the issue of women. The first article quoted Korb as saying that whereas once there were "targets," the services now had "planning numbers"; still, what they were saying was "first come, first serve" (*sic*). Dr. Sharon Lord, deputy assistant secretary of equal opportunity, described the "woman issue" as one of personnel management, noting that the military must decide how best to use its human power and not get bogged down in issues like "the draft" and "combat." Lord discussed the need for creative policy making (such as permitting interruptions in service) and advocated repeal of the combat exclusion. Although women may have perceived some support from civilians near the top of DOD, the article also quoted one staffer as saying, "During the Carter Administration, DOD officials at the sublevels were told to be silent on the issue of women in the military, but with the change in Administration, the new philosophy is to speak out even if it is negative."[20]

Korb personally undertook to control the Lehman damage by agreeing to address the same group of women officers at the end of February. (Three hundred, including a number of guests, attended.) Korb was direct. He acknowledged misunderstandings and the importance of perceptions and expressed his concern for "the morale of women"—a subject that had rarely surfaced before.

On 11 February 1982 there was a television panel discussion moderated by Phil Donahue and featuring Helen Rogan, Sarah McClendon (journalist and former member of the WAC), and (then Col., now Brig. Gen.) Evelyn Foot, a faculty member at the Army War College. Foot performed superbly, giving voice to women's aspirations, confidence, and frustrations: "If there's a group in the Army that has been studied to infinity, it's women. . . . You know, I just get tired of being studied. Leave me alone and let me do my job." Going beyond the party line, Foot stated her personal support for the conscription of women.

Finally, February brought the announcement that the report of the Women in the Army Study Group, due the previous fall, would not only be delayed once again but, further, would now be restricted in scope. All items that concerned both male and female soldiers—for example, joint domicile, single parenthood—would be removed from consideration. Only women-specific items would be addressed: pregnancy, the relationship between MOS assignment and combat, and physical-strength requirements (which one might think affected both women and men).[21]

The forthcoming report was kept under wraps. Nevertheless, one person who saw it predicted: "It will drive feminists crazy. It will reinforce most of the stereotypes we have always heard about the inherently weaker female who left to her own devices will probably get pregnant, is most concerned with parenting and can't be relied upon at certain times of the month." It focused, the reader said, on pregnancy, strength, female health problems, and female attrition.[22]

In fact, the wraps were so tight that Gen. Zeltman wrote a personal letter in March to Ann Banks, a member of the advisory task force of civilians, who had been taken on a field trip the previous September, saying, "I have deliberately chosen to solve the institutional issues within the institution—the Army. . . . Because of the readiness impacts the assessment (sometimes called the study) is classified and will not be made public."

Around this time the second of the *Government Executive* articles appeared, focusing on the January DOD memos, including one by Korb that specified that the services were not to change agreed-upon accession levels without coordination with his office. A substantial amount of attention was also given to the Air Force accession model, which was described by Gen. William Usher as "sex-blind." "We have no floor or ceiling with respect to recruiting women," he stated, "but we utilize a planning number." In fact, a "number" was specified for each and every one of the 200 skill areas. Ninety percent of Air Force jobs were identified as open to women—but Usher now described the Air Force as having low expectations for them: "Unfortunately, they [women] have more than their proportional share of problems associated with a very young group inexperienced in life in general and military life in particular." He expressed special concern about pregnant servicewomen, single parents, and married couples with dependent children.

The next setback occurred in April. The Army announced the end of integrated basic training, a program in existence for four years, ever since the abolition of the WAC.[23] Basic training would continue to be "the same" for women and men, the Army said, just separate, and women would be trained at only three of the six bases. The reason given for ending integration was that men were not being "physically challenged enough." At one time platoons (units of about 50) had been integrated. Then they were segregated, but companies (200 to 250 service people) were integrated. In the future companies would be single-sex as well, "to facilitate the Army's toughening goals and [to] enhance the soldierization process," although it was emphasized that all soldiers had been meeting standards, that women had not failed, and that both men and women would be used in training basics.

Although the Army's resegregation was officially said to be due to the need to test men's physical strength, the director of initial-entry training, Col. Charles B. Fountain, said to the *Army Times* (17 May 1982) that there was a "psychological impact on many of the young male soldiers" when they found that "their training environment included women." He seemed to be saying that men's lack of respect for women made them think less well of themselves and the Army, for, he went on to say, "tests" had found that all-male companies "improved esprit de corps," "fostered greater competition," and pushed individuals "beyond the minimum training standards."

Answering a letter of inquiry from the Women's Equity Action League (WEAL) in May 1982, an Army public affairs officer claimed that *both* men and women reached higher standards and had higher morale in single-sex companies, and that the decision was based on the "professional judgment of our training center commanders, their subordinate commanders and non-commissioned officers who are in direct, daily contact with soldiers." No "test" was mentioned.

What seemed to be wholly missing from policy making were women's judgment, women's morale, and consideration of what is best for long-term, integrated work. The decision was a surprise to most people, though internal memos had been circulating since March concerning "gender pure basic training." DACOWITS had no advance warning, and apparently no discussion was held with the Pentagon's Equal Opportunity Office. DOD did not announce or affirm the decision. The Army's offensive simply lumbered on.

The resegregation decision did, however, stir Maj. Gen. Mary Clarke (Ret.) to make a public statement. Clarke, director of the WAC until its demise, commander of Fort McClellan from 1978 to 1980, and director of human resources until her retirement in the fall of 1981, had always seen the best in and made the best of Army policy. She had earlier written a letter to Army women offering assurance about their future. The resegregation decision must have been a last straw. She told an interviewer that it was "the first step toward returning women to their old stereotypical roles in the military. . . . The next thing is they'll start closing military occupational specialties to women, and the third thing I see is that women will only be allowed to be typists, secretaries and medics," jobs that don't lead to a career that leads to the very top." Clarke concluded "that the women are being let down."[24]

Sharon Lord, director of equal opportunity and occupational safety, made no immediate and public comment, but by August she had criticized the Army's propensity to act first and study later: "No one provided any data that showed integrated training was not successful. I was alarmed that we would make a major change without data. The Army should have provided that. . . . The decision smacks of the old argument of 'separate but equal.' . . . It looks like a decision was made that implies the women aren't performing well."[25] Lord resigned her position shortly before the Army announced the withdrawal of more MOS at the end of August. A "top manpower official" said that Lord "often lacked data to back up her challenges to policies that she said would set women back."[26] The new question, then, seemed to be who had to furnish evidence—initiators or maintainers, integrationists or separatists.

In June Army Lt. Gen. Max Thurman noted that the Review Group was taking "a hard look" at a 1977 policy that permitted women to operate closer to the battle area than the rear of the brigade. Others predicted that the study would result in "lower recruitment quotas" and "greater restriction on the range of duties" for women. Moreover, it was argued, "the Army reassessment . . . is likely to affect the other services."[27]

That summer Congresswoman Schroeder expressed apprehension: "I think women have good reason to fear what this report will say." DACOWITS chair Maria Elena Torralva wrote to Weinberger that "the dragging out of the Army study is having a very definite effect on the morale of our military women. . . . [It] is going down, down, down." Although officials had tried to give her reassurance, she noted, "The Army has not been honest with us before."[28]

The third blow came at the end of August, when the Army announced that its massive eighteen-month study aimed at increasing the Army's combat readiness would result in (1) a reduction in the rate of increase in women's numbers, and (2) an effort to put them in "less demanding jobs." The Army had once planned to bring its female strength to 87,000. The new number was to be 70,000. Combat-related MOS closed to women would be increased from thirty-eight to sixty-one (principally in combat engineering), and physical-strength screening for all soldiers would begin, further limiting women's options. In all, about 1,400 women were then serving in fields that would be closed for reasons related to combat.

Army research showed that 64 percent of its jobs required lifting 100 pounds occasionally and 50 pounds frequently and that 42 percent of women soldiers were then in such "very heavy lifting" jobs even though fewer than 10 percent of women could lift 96 pounds. The Army argued that its new policies would "help women" by assigning them to jobs for which they were suited: "Men and women will be going into jobs with much more satisfaction."[29]

Responses to the September announcement were mixed. Schroeder asked: "What kind of career ladders are being dropped down on women? . . . Every time there is a new study [on women] it never helps morale. . . . The studies make it appear that the issues women face in the military are 'women problems.' . . . Why don't they include men?" Kathleen Carpenter charged that the recommended increases in the number of women were "a 'public relations' move," and that the final report indicated a "further stall, a non-decision." "The damage has already been done," she said, "the numbers have been held down and the future of women has been [made] uncertain." Sarah McClendon, however, was "upbeat" —"The report said women can do the job." Carolyn Becraft of WEAL called it "much better [on women] than I expected." And Torralva, who was given a three-hour Pentagon briefing, said, "The study is going to be a very positive thing."[30] All three would become less sanguine as fall progressed and no report was made public, although decisions were apparently being made. At length it began to appear that *faits accomplis* were part of the Army's strategy, even though Korb had promised that DOD would permit no changes in policies governing women soldiers until they had been thoroughly reviewed by the department.[31]

Lt. Gen. Max R. Thurman had said at a press conference in September that the report would be released on 30 September. In late October it was announced that "because of the complexity of data it contains, the review and final preparation of the report is taking longer than anticipated." Insiders said that the holdup was due to the pregnancy issue: a proposal was being reviewed to transfer pregnant women to inactive duty in the

Individual Ready Reserve for up to a year. The Army would pay medical expenses, but before returning to duty the servicewoman would have to accept stringent requirements concerning care for dependents in case of mobilization. Another proposal had called for discharging all pregnant first-termers.[32]

In an interview with *U.S. News and World Report,* Korb emphasized that there were *no* quotas on women. The numbers (such as an end strength of 70,000) were a "prediction," and if more women than that qualified, they would not be turned down. There were "plenty of jobs," there would be "no anti-female purge," and the Army was going to see whether pregnancy should be grounds to request discharge or whether women should fulfill their obligation. Korb's interview alone might have allayed fears, but it was an inset to a longer article titled "Women in the Army—End of a Honeymoon," whose subheading included the phrase "ambitious plans to expand the role of females in the service now are being put in reverse."

> The near-universal verdict here: a decade-long effort to put women into traditionally male jobs has not paid off in better combat readiness. Some even believe it has been harmful. . . . The Fort Bragg experience—high female attrition rates, troublesome strength differences between the sexes, pregnancy-related problems and the refusal of some males either to take orders from women or assign them to hazardous work—has been repeated throughout the Army.[33]

The Army Policy Review Group finally released its study at the DACO-WITS meeting at Fort Bragg on 18 November 1982 after a dramatic showdown that featured substantial press coverage, flights by generals from the Pentagon, and public statements by uniformed women stationed at Fort Bragg. Of the nineteen issues originally raised, only two emerged in the final report. The toughest—pregnancy—was passed on to DOD. "Other areas considered by the group are still under review and recommendations on them will be released as they are approved." In other words, consultation was not desired. No hands would be tipped.

The report's content was more or less as advertised. Women's numbers would be "increased" to 70,000 (instead of the planned 87,000). Jobs would be combat-coded P1 through P7 on the basis of job duties, mission of unit, battlefield location, and "Army doctrine." Women would be excluded from the 302,000 jobs coded P1. This would require closing twenty-three specialties to them while leaving 270,000 jobs open.[34]

The results of the "physical demands analysis" were not encouraging, either. No jobs were to be closed to women simply on grounds of strength. However, 368,000, or almost two-thirds, of the Army's jobs were classified as "very heavy"—work that only 3 percent of women could be expected to perform.[35] An additional 8 percent of women could be expected to accomplish the 71,000 jobs listed as "heavy." In short, the Army was saying that only 11 percent of women were able to do three-fourths of the Army's jobs.

By the end of 1982, then, the Army had developed policies on combat and physical strength that suggested that 1,400 Army women were "misplaced" in terms of "combat" and perhaps 30,000 more were misplaced in terms of physical strength. About half the women in the Army were being told that they could not, or would not be allowed to, do their jobs.

What is more, proposed policies involving pregnancy, single parents, and military couples would curtail women's participation even further. More subtle issues, like rotation base, career ladders, and facilities, had yet to be taken into account. Finally, it was clear that women's morale, opportunities to command, and uniform and housing complaints were not on anyone's agenda. (It should be noted, though, that much official attention was given to sexual harassment during this period.)

The events of the previous two years were summarized in two quite different documents: an article in *Human Rights* entitled "Reagan Modifying Carter's 'Co-Ed' Army Policy" (November 1982) and a June 1983 letter to Defense Secretary Weinberger from Dr. Mary Evelyn Bragg Huey, president of Texas Women's University and DACOWITS chair. The article, which applauded moves to end a "bizarre experiment in a fraudulent equality," spoke of the author's experience as a "buck" sergeant in Europe and charged that Carter's "fem-lib politicization" had breached the military's constitutional neutrality and pushed military women into combat positions "against the wishes of military women themselves." Impartiality is part of the camaraderie of being a soldier, the author concluded; you cannot have women soldiers for the same reason you cannot have homosexuals—they will "protect and promote their friends to the detriment of their military unit and their country."

Huey's letter objected to the premises, methodology, and implementation of the Army's study in light of the defense of the nation and the optimum utilization of women. Stressing DACOWITS's solemn obligation, Huey wrote:

> Our advice to you is to halt the current (and, we fear, precipitous) implementation of the MOS and unit closings. . . .
> We have serious questions regarding the merit of the continual studying of women's military participation. As a study reaffirms the

positive performance and contributions by those of our gender, a new one seems to be ordered. This finally raises the question of whether objectivity or the "right answers" is the purpose.

CONCLUSION

After the 1980 election, only the Navy and (reluctantly) the Marines maintained the 1986 end strengths for women projected under the Carter administration (table 3.1). The Army and the Air Force lowered theirs. The Army did so publicly and was criticized for its action and its attempt to justify it. Originally, its criticism of women had concentrated on their "lack of readiness" because of pregnancy, single parenthood, and marriage to another member of the military. Thus far there had been no changes of policy concerning those matters. However, women's opportunities to serve were now curtailed by a new method of combat coding and clouded by a new physical-strength testing program. The future for Army women had lost its luster.

The shocker, though, was the response of the Air Force. While admitting that over three-fourths of its jobs were open to women and that it had had no difficulty in recruiting them, the Air Force followed the Army's lead by abruptly and dramatically reducing its planned accessions of women. Queries produced only a verbal description of a new and "complicated" accession methodology based on propensity and ability.

Honeymoons must end and policy reviews and changes continue. From 1980 to 1982 military women experienced grave doubts about whether their gains of the last decade would be maintained. Most of the public's attention was focused on the Army's "pause," its resegregation of basic training, and its policy review. Far more disturbing in some ways were the Air Force's quiet cuts, which were larger than the Army's, left the Air Force with fewer women than the Army, and were not related to or justified by restraints on utilization. This last fact seems to confirm suspicions that concerns about women's utilization were not really the driving force behind the changes in their military opportunities. Perhaps the new Army and Air Force policies were justified. Perhaps suspicion and disquiet cannot always be avoided. Nevertheless, the period from 1980 to 1982 was unsettling for many military women. The Army's slow and secretive reassessment seems to have hurt the morale of career women, whose reenlistment rate fell precipitously.[36]

Honeymoons end, sometimes in happy marriage, sometimes in divorce, and sometimes in something resembling a war of attrition. Events from 1982 to the present suggest that the relationship between women and the military continues to be problematic. Thus, DOD opened a "Women's Corridor" in the Pentagon, the Army reopened thirteen MOS to

TABLE 3.1.    Women in the Military

| Service | 1980 End Strengths | 1986 End Strengths (Set 1980) | 1986 End Strengths (Planned 1982) | Estimated Potential End Strengths (1977)* |
|---------|--------------------|-------------------------------|-----------------------------------|-------------------------------------------|
| Army | 61,000 | 87,500 | 65,000 | 175,000 |
| Navy | 30,000 | 47,000 | 47,000 | 42,000 |
| Marines | 6,000 | 9,000 | 9,000 | 15,000 |
| Air Force | 51,000 | 90,000 | 61,000 | 363,000 |

*These figures are from Martin Binkin and Shirley J. Bach, *Women and the Military* (Washington, D.C.. The Brookings Institution, 1977), p. 108.

women and sent women to Grenada, but slacks became "nonauthorized" for women Marines except under specified circumstances.[37] In 1984 the secretary of defense announced the creation of a Task Force on Equity for Women, but the Navy announced that a civilian engineer would not be allowed to go on sea trials of her own work. (See Chapter 5.) In 1985 the Marines began weapons training for women, but the Air Force set recruitment goals for women so low that Congress mandated new goals in the defense authorization bill. In 1986 the Army opened some 10,000 slots in forward support battalions to women, but Secretary of the Navy John Lehman reneged on what some thought was a commitment to permit women on "mobile logistics support force vessels" by reclassifying those vessels as "other combatant." In 1987 the Navy froze women's accessions; the next day the secretary of defense rescinded the freeze.[38]

Such oscillations in policy have two negative effects. First, they make women feel unappreciated and unsure about their future. This hurts morale. Second, policies lose their legitimacy when they appear to be more responsive to officials' opinions than to evidence, logic, or agreed-upon assumptions. Institutions cannot thrive if some things are not settled.

A naval aviation electronics technician participates in a sunset colors ceremony as a member of a drill team.

An Army enlisted woman negotiates a three-rope bridge in a basic training confidence-building exercise.

An all-female platoon of basic trainees at Ft. Jackson, S.C. is attacked with tear gas during a road march as part of its graduation requirements. U.S. Army Training Center, Ft. Jackson, S.C. for Company C, 17th Battalion, 5th Brigade, C-17-5, 12 September 1975

An Air Force sergeant stocks aircraft tires.

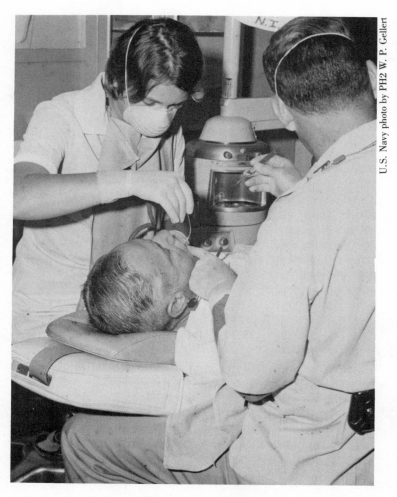

A dental technician assists in oral surgery.

U.S. Navy photo by PH3 Paul Mansfield

A male CPO instructs the first Navy woman to qualify as a heavy-equipment operator of a large crane.

A female drill sergeant teaches her troops the elementary defensive positions of hand-to-hand combat at Ft. Jackson, S.C.    U.S. Army Training Center, Ft. Jackson, S.C. for Company C, 17th Battalion, 5th Brigade, C-17-5, 12 September 1975

A (Marine) military policewoman practices firing an M1911-A1 automatic from a standing post position.

U.S. Navy photo by Warren Grass

The first female
Navy diver
prepares for a
dive in 1974.

Official U.S. Navy photo

A religious program specialist files books in the library of the USS
*Lexington.*

One of the women assigned to duty on the USS *Sanctuary* handles a line on deck.

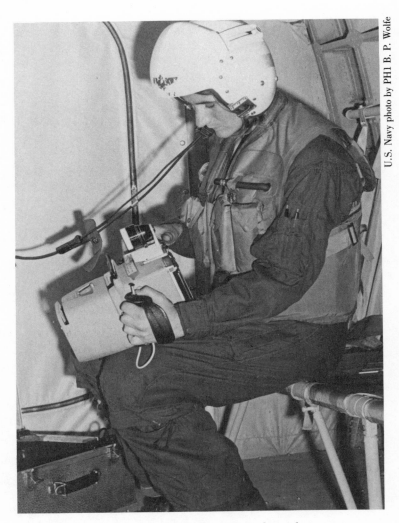

A photographer's mate adjusts her technical aerial camera during a mission on a Navy helicopter.

A drill sergeant coaches her trainees on shooting fundamentals in preparation for weapons qualification with the M16A1 rifle at Ft. Jackson, S.C. Authen- ticity training mandates live ammunition and pop-up targets. U.S. Army Training Center, Ft. Jackson, S.C. for Company C, 17th Battalion, 5th Brigade, C-17-5, 12 September 1975

Members of a women's softball team at Ft. Jackson pose long enough for a team picture.

An Army basic trainee "cools off" a grenade in a simulated bunker attack.

A parachute rigger relaxes before making her monthly "quality control" jump.

# PART II

Making
Policy for
Enlisted
Women

# 4

# Military Opinion

In the military, as in most institutions, policy is based more on opinion than on evidence. Thus, the opinions held about military women are important, and those of senior men are especially important.

Many studies of attitudes about and of military women were done during the 1970s. They reflect a variety of concerns and are therefore not completely comparable. Still, their findings are mostly compatible and also appear consistent with studies done during the 1980s. Constancy is not surprising, since two fundamental facts have not changed: women are proportionally few, and they are formally barred from the military's defining activity—combat. Study topics include the treatment and performance of women, their suitability for particular jobs, and their views of and degree of satisfaction with military life.

DOD, Navy, and Air Force studies will be summarized first. Army studies will be treated separately, since they are more extensive and interrelated. Further, the Army has the most women and appears to be the most uncomfortable with them, perhaps because it feels as required to protect women from combat as the other services, but lacks a congressional charge to do so and even a precise, well-bounded definition of combat itself.

We will see (1) that military women's views are quite different from those held by military men; (2) that "contact" does not appear to change attitudes or practices much; and (3) that individuals' summed (collective) views and their views of others' views are not necessarily consonant. Where it is possible, the views of different subgroups will be explored separately: women's views will be separated from men's, officers' from those of enlisted personnel, and the opinions of men who command women, are peers of women, or are subordinate to them from those of men who have had little or no contact with them.

## DOD, NAVY, AND AIR FORCE STUDIES

In 1979 DOD conducted a massive study of the opinions of active-duty personnel (table 4.1). Notable differences appeared in women's and

TABLE 4.1. Enlisted Personnel's Opinions About Women in Their Primary Work Unit by Sex

| Opinion and Respondents' Sex | Strongly Agree | Agree | Neutral | Disagree | Strongly Disagree | Total No. |
|---|---|---|---|---|---|---|
| 1. Women should be allowed to perform the skills in my primary MOS/rating/AFSC. | | | | | | |
| Male | 39.1% | 31.9% | 11.9% | 8.0% | 9.2% | 1,489,424 |
| Female | 73.1 | 19.2 | 5.8 | 0.8 | 1.1 | 106,762 |
| 2. Most women have the physical capacity to perform the skills in my primary MOS/rating/AFSC. | | | | | | |
| Male | 31.9 | 30.8 | 12.5 | 15.2 | 9.5 | 1,485,611 |
| Female | 65.0 | 23.2 | 6.9 | 3.7 | 1.1 | 106,747 |
| 3. Most women have the mental aptitude to perform the skills in my primary MOS/rating/AFSC. | | | | | | |
| Male | 39.2 | 41.8 | 11.1 | 4.7 | 3.1 | 1,479,700 |
| Female | 69.2 | 23.1 | 5.6 | 1.8 | 0.3 | 106,404 |
| 4. Women should learn to use weapons. | | | | | | |
| Male | 35.8 | 38.6 | 13.6 | 6.4 | 5.6 | 1,476,679 |
| Female | 43.6 | 34.2 | 14.5 | 3.6 | 4.1 | 106,274 |
| 5. Women should be allowed to engage in hand-to-hand combat. | | | | | | |
| Male | 22.2 | 23.3 | 21.5 | 17.0 | 15.9 | 1,479,772 |
| Female | 16.7 | 17.0 | 29.4 | 16.6 | 20.4 | 106,552 |
| 6. Women should be given training and used in combat situations. | | | | | | |
| Male | 23.5 | 27.4 | 18.6 | 14.3 | 16.3 | 1,485,137 |
| Female | 19.8 | 20.1 | 25.5 | 13.9 | 20.7 | 106,716 |

Source: Zahava D. Doering and William P. Hutzler, *Description of Officers and Enlisted Personnel in the United States Armed Forces: A Reference for Military Manpower Analysis* (Santa Monica, Calif.: Rand, 1982), table 475.

men's responses when asked whether women "should be allowed" to perform the same duties as the respondents and whether most women have the physical capacity and mental aptitude to do so. Other items dealt with training women to use weapons, the use of women in hand-to-hand combat, and women's training for and use in combat.[1]

To interpret the enormous difference between women's and men's responses to item 1, one must keep in mind the phrasing of the question. Men were responding from *all* jobs; women were responding only from the jobs women were already in. Thus, women might have agreed that they should not be in jobs that only men held; we cannot know. At the time of the survey, Air Force enlisted women were performing almost all enlisted jobs. Even so, almost a quarter of Air Force enlisted men did not agree that women should be allowed to do them; about the same percentage denied that most women had the "physical capacity" to do the work; and 6 percent denied that most women had the "mental aptitude" to do "their" work.

Responses to the first four items form a curve strongly skewed toward "agree." It would appear possible to find a widely acceptable policy on these issues. However, opinions on hand-to-hand combat are much more evenly distributed among the five possible responses, making it difficult to develop such a policy. Overall, 46 percent of enlisted men agree that "women should be allowed to engage in hand-to-hand combat," 22 percent were neutral, and 33 percent disagreed. This is not a consensus distribution, especially when one "strongly" category includes 22 percent and the other 16 percent of the respondents. Further, analysis shows that although majorities of both women and men disapproved of committing women to hand-to-hand combat, men (in all services) were more willing than women.

Whether or not they approve, many service people do work in sexually integrated settings. Their perceptions of how women are treated and how they respond and perform are important. Four items from the 1979 survey concern how women are treated; four other items concern women's behavior. Responses are available by sex and service and for officers and enlisted personnel. The data appear in table 4.2, which gives the percentages of respondents strongly agreeing and agreeing with the survey statements.

These data represent opinions based on experience and observation; in answering, respondents were asked to refer to their own "primary work unit." Male and female responses are consistently different. Among women officers the responses are quite similar from service to service, except that more female Marine officers believed that women get their complaints handled faster, that women expect special treatment, and also that women officers and NCOs receive less respect than male offi-

TABLE 4.2. Opinions About Women's Treatment and Performance

| | Percentage in Agreement | | | | | | | |
| | Enlisted Personnel | | | | Officers | | | |
| Opinion | AF | N | M | A | AF | N | M | A |
|---|---|---|---|---|---|---|---|---|
| 1. Get their complaints handled faster than men | | | | | | | | |
|     Male | 48 | 52 | 62 | 56 | 35 | 34 | 42 | 35 |
|     Female | 14 | 18 | 29 | 20 | 8 | 10 | 26 | 8 |
| 2. Have better opportunities for technical training | | | | | | | | |
|     Male | 9 | 14 | 25 | 27 | 7 | 7 | 13 | 12 |
|     Female | 2 | 4 | 9 | 9 | 4 | 4 | 4 | 4 |
| 3. Are promoted ahead of men even if the man is better qualified | | | | | | | | |
|     Male | 8 | 11 | 44 | 33 | 12 | 9 | 26 | 13 |
|     Female | 2 | 1 | 13 | 5 | 3 | 1 | 6 | 3 |
| 4. Receive less respect than men | | | | | | | | |
|     Male | 26 | 28 | 33 | 33 | 31 | 39 | 44 | 41 |
|     Female | 51 | 48 | 53 | 58 | 52 | 50 | 68 | 58 |
| 5. Cannot take criticism or discipline | | | | | | | | |
|     Male | 42 | 50 | 54 | 52 | 34 | 37 | 45 | 4 |
|     Female | 9 | 9 | 16 | 14 | 7 | 9 | 7 | 8 |
| 6. Will work extra hours when needed | | | | | | | | |
|     Male | 42 | 36 | 38 | 37 | 58 | 57 | 59 | 59 |
|     Female | 77 | 74 | 80 | 78 | 88 | 90 | 93 | 88 |
| 7. Expect special treatment | | | | | | | | |
|     Male | 40 | 47 | 55 | 53 | 25 | 28 | 33 | 33 |
|     Female | 6 | 11 | 17 | 14 | 3 | 4 | 13 | 8 |
| 8. Can supervise as well as men | | | | | | | | |
|     Male | 41 | 37 | 36 | 36 | 51 | 50 | 46 | 4 |
|     Female | 87 | 88 | 85 | 85 | 92 | 93 | 92 | 9 |

Note: Three of the first four items assume that women are given preference; two of the last four assume negative behavior, and another asks whether they can do "as well as men."
Source: Data extracted from Doering and Hutzler, Description of Officers and Enlisted Personnel, tables 485–494.

cers. Enlisted women generally agreed with women officers, although more enlisted women than officers thought that women's complaints are handled faster and that women are less willing to put in extra hours.

Problem areas would seem to be:

1. Men's widely held belief that women's complaints are handled faster than men's (a belief given some support by enlisted women in general and female Marine officers)

2. The belief of a majority of women that women officers and NCOs get less respect than men with the same formal rank
3. The belief of almost half of enlisted men and 30 to 38 percent of male officers that women expect special treatment and cannot take criticism or discipline
4. The fact that fewer than 40 percent of male officers believed women will work extra hours when needed and just half believed they can supervise as well as men.

The views held by enlisted men about women are even more daunting. In contrast, 90 percent of women officers believed women *will* work extra hours and can supervise. Three-fourths of enlisted women believed women will work extra hours, and 85 percent believed they can supervise.

Given these results, one might expect women to be dissatisfied with the military. However, when one compares the percentages of women and men in the two most "dissatisfied" and "satisfied" categories (dropping three middle scores) one finds that women, especially enlisted women, are more satisfied and less dissatisfied with military life than men (table 4.3). These findings are similar to those relating to Blacks.[2] Whatever their criticisms, neither women nor Blacks in the military seem to be seriously alienated by it. Perhaps their life expectations are low; perhaps the military is more equitable than civilian life; or perhaps they *are* being favored and appreciate it. In any event, whereas some 40 percent of enlisted women agreed that their family would be better off with "me" in a civilian job (38 percent in 1985), almost 60 percent of men (49 percent in 1985) said the same. (For officers the 1982 figures were under 30 percent of women and more than 50 percent of men.)[3]

The Navy also examined backgrounds and perceptions. One study found that men and women enter the service for the same reasons,

TABLE 4.3.   Satisfaction with Military Life (in percentages)

| | Officers | | | | | Enlisted Personnel | | | | |
|---|---|---|---|---|---|---|---|---|---|---|
| | AF | N | M | A | Total | AF | N | M | A | Total |
| Dissatisfied | | | | | | | | | | |
| Men | 19 | 36 | 31 | 27 | 28 | 14 | 15 | 10 | 13 | 14 |
| Women | 20 | 20 | 26 | 26 | 23 | 11 | 8 | 10 | 11 | 10 |
| Satisfied | | | | | | | | | | |
| Men | 22 | 12 | 18 | 18 | 17 | 25 | 27 | 39 | 33 | 29 |
| Women | 22 | 20 | 19 | 16 | 17 | 37 | 32 | 45 | 35 | 38 |

*Source:* Based on Doering and Hutzler, *Description of Officers and Enlisted Personnel*, tables 495–496. These tables include breakdowns by services and status (enlisted personnel and officers).

although their backgrounds and work histories are dissimilar.[4] On entry women are less likely to have had a regular job or to have lived away from home. They are likely to have participated in more activities, but not in athletics, and are less likely to have ever been detained by a police officer. Eighty-three percent of men, but only 33 percent of women, had first-hand information about the military from a member of their own sex. With regard to work, women are less anxious to win rewards, publicity, and opportunities to supervise. They do not like planning, repetition, or working with their hands, with machines, or outdoors. They do value a "cheerful," clean environment, working with people, and "personal" rewards.*

Another Navy study (1974–75) and its follow-up (1978) found that men's and women's perceptions of the Navy as an organization differ, and also that women of different pay grades have different perceptions.[5] In particular, the first study showed that the women who enter the Navy are selected from a pool four times as large as the number that can be accepted. They often have had to wait six months before being sworn in. They are better qualified than the men, and more positively disposed toward the Navy than men on every topic raised. However, by the time women reach E-6, they are *more negative* than men on 14 of 19 indices. Further, their scores are lower than those of entry-level women on 7 indices. Specifically, E-6 women do not find their leaders helpful in improving their performance. They also find peer leadership and work-group coordination less satisfying than when they entered. Finally, even though women's satisfaction and perception of equal opportunity rise with promotion, men's rise more. Apparently the rewards of rank are less for women than for men.

The 1978 follow-up found significant sex differences on 9 of 21 measures related to organizational climate, and 14 of 21 measures on sex-by-pay-grade variance. Women's scores are more negative than men's except among new enlistees without specialties. Both men's and women's positive responses tend to decrease following entrance and to bottom out at E-4. After that, men's positive responses increase more rapidly than women's. Again, women are especially dissatisfied with "command climate" and "supervisory leadership." It appears, then, that Navy women begin with high expectations that are disappointed. On the other hand, although they are more critical of the Navy than men, they are *not* less satisfied.

The Air Force conducted only a few personnel and opinion studies, and they were not always intended for public consumption. Some concerned the use of women in nontraditional fields, such as the study on security

---

*Such knowledge should be useful to recruiters, who match people to jobs, and commanders at all levels, who have "morale" as a responsibility.

specialists discussed in Chapter 3. A study of the use of women on (two-person) MX missile-launch teams involved a survey of men then assigned to these teams *and their wives*.[6] Military women were not asked their opinion; neither were their spouses. Spouses' views could be a legitimate consideration—there are more military wives than military women, and their views are believed to be important to the retention of men—but one would hope that they would not be a controlling factor in the development of personnel policy.*

Another Air Force study compared attitudes of people in the nontraditional (for women) career fields (NTCF) of (1) aircraft/missile maintenance, (2) civil engineering, and (3) security police with attitudes of people in the traditional career fields (TCF) of (1) administration, (2) personnel, and (3) supply. The subjects were enlisted women; their coworkers and their supervisors were queried, too.[7]

A majority of men were found to believe that women receive better treatment than men; about a quarter of women agreed. In the NTCF about 40 percent of men said that women are given less responsibility. About 70 percent of all respondents reported that women encounter "negative attitudes," and about one in five women found her supervisor resistant to her presence. In the NTCF a majority of supervisors viewed women as "not as capable," but a majority *also* said that they learn their jobs equally well, progress as well in training, and require less attention. One of four supervisors also reported his own leniency toward women; over one-half admitted that they would make allowances for women that they would not make for men.

Because there are so few Air Force studies concerning enlisted women, it is worth reporting the results from two studies that examined the attitudes toward women of Air Force Academy cadets.[8] In one study, female and male cadet scores on the Spence Attitude Toward Women Scale were found to differ by around 10 points. Further, that difference increased (slightly) from 1976 to 1980, a period when the number of women at the academy increased and so did interaction with them. On items concerning women's presence at the academy and women as military leaders, men and women cadets showed a 2- to 4-point difference on a 10-point scale.†

In general, the women believed in themselves. Although they real-

---

*The Navy assessed the views of wives in considering the management of its "Women in Ships" Program, but only in order to plan a smooth transition, not to determine what military women would be allowed or required to do.

†Interestingly, the gap between views on women's presence at the academy is substantially and persistently larger than the one between views on women's potential as military leaders. Women had no doubt about their belonging and little about their ability to lead; men had some doubt about women's ability to lead and more about their being at the academy.

ized that they were not fully accepted, they thought they were more accepted than the acceptors (the men) did. Similarly, the women rated their past and potential performance far higher than did the men. This study, then, showed a great difference between women's and men's views and also showed that "contact" had little effect. Both themes recur in other studies.

### ARMY STUDIES

Between 1975 and 1980 the Army produced numerous studies on women. One early study asked women taking Army basic training about their willingness to enlist if women's assignment policies changed to follow the (presumed) requirements of an Equal Rights Amendment.[9] The results showed women as having a strong desire to be able to volunteer for anything, but also a deep reluctance to be forced to do all that men are forced to do. The women approved of assignments to an active combat theater and training with defensive weapons, but were less interested in "direct combat duties." Indeed, 43 of 193 "strongly agreed" that they would not reenlist if women were subject to "involuntary assignment to any duty position for which they were fully qualified."

An Army Research Institute (ARI) study focusing on attitudes of personnel eligible for reenlistment with a rank of E-3 to E-4 found that men and women tend to agree on the combat issue, with about a third believing that "men and women can fight side by side in the battlefield."[10] Thirty percent of the enlisted women stated that they would like to go into combat in the case of war; 40 percent of the men gave a similar response. Views concerning the suitability of various jobs for men and women were especially interesting. First, jobs women had traditionally done were deemed suitable for both women and men. There was almost no support for any "women-only" specialties (e.g., dental assistant), but there was substantial support for "men-only" jobs. Second, the jobs that had recently been opened to women produced the strongest disagreement. Men disagreed with women and with other men over the assignment of women as, for example, military police.

The question of "quality" also separated the opinions of men from those of women. Thirty-four percent of the men gave women an average rating, and 28 percent rated them above average—approximately the same ratings that men gave men. Women, however, rated themselves much higher than they rated the men: 41 percent gave men average, and only 19 percent gave them above-average, ratings. In fact, 82 percent of the women and 59 percent of the men agreed that "in some ways, women in the Army are sharper and better soldiers than a lot of men."

Social science literature suggests that men (and often women) tend to rate men more highly than women when objective measures are equal, and are even more likely to do so when women are doing "men's" work.[11] The anomalous Army data may reflect the fact that enlisted women are significantly better on some measures than enlisted men, perhaps because of higher enlistment standards. As will be seen below, however, in studies done during field exercises, men rated women lower than they rated themselves, and women rated themselves about the same as they rated men.

The ARI study also showed that women who entered nontraditional fields were considered by men, by women in traditional fields, and *by themselves* (to a lesser degree) pushy, masculine, troublesome, unattractive, and hard. In fact, only 60 percent of women in nontraditional fields expressed "a lot of respect for women who go into nontraditional MOSs." The study also showed stronger support for women's equality from men than from women (75 to 62 percent). Since men also indicated that they believe women are given favored treatment, men committed to "equality" may actually be seeking equality for themselves! In fact, a majority of men *and* women believed that women successfully manipulate men through the use of their femininity; indeed, a majority of men believed that "a woman in the Army will use her femininity to get away with as much as she can."

Both men and women rejected women's full participation in combat but supported their training with weapons, although some believed that women would "panic and run under fire" (men: 31 percent; women: 18 percent). There was also disagreement over "allowing" women to participate in combat-related MOSs—61 percent of women approved, while 53 percent of men disapproved.

There is a coherency to these views. Men's roles and requirements seem to be taken as given. Women in general are seen as able to do some of men's roles. Some women are seen as able to do all of them, and some believe they should be allowed to do so. But women wish to serve as volunteers. As military personnel, they expect to be expected to do their jobs, but neither women nor men seem ready to coerce women to do all the things men are coerced to do.

Two other studies done about the same time also involved beliefs about job appropriateness and attitudes toward sex roles.[12] Although more and more women were being assigned to nontraditional fields, they still represented only a small percentage of total personnel even in the two new fields in which they were most numerous—maintenance and law enforcement. (It is noteworthy that even though women may not serve in combat, one of the first nontraditional fields to accept women in the military— military police—is the civilian analogue to the military, the organization charged with the use of legitimate violence. Thus, it appears to be more acceptable for women to shoot other Americans than foreigners!) Attitudes, then, were being examined at a time when real changes had been made in policy, but very little change had actually occurred in women's proportional representation.

In one study men and women agreed on the appropriateness of fifteen of twenty-four specific occupations. In fact, men were more accepting than women of women as statisticians, bartenders, and butchers. Women, though, were more accepting of women as commanders, military police, pilots, bomb-disposal specialists, and infantry foot soldiers. The largest discrepancy (20 percent) was between female and male support for women as jet pilots; the next largest concerned women as infantrymen and bomb-disposal specialists.

Officers and enlisted personnel agreed on only seven of the twenty-four items. In eleven of the other seventeen cases, a higher percentage of officers saw a job as appropriate for women. Officers were more able to see women in *both* civilian and military nontraditional jobs. There was no reversal (as there was between men and women) depending on whether the jobs had civilian analogues or were unique to the military.

When the data are broken down into four categories, however—officer men (OM), officer women (OW), enlisted men (EM), and enlisted women (EW)—it becomes apparent that the relationship between rank and sex is complex. Ninety-three percent or more of all groups agreed that cook, social worker, human relations officer, lawyer, and bandleader are appropriate jobs for women. Views were also positive and almost identical (though somewhat lower) for general's aide and truck driver: 91 percent and 82 percent respectively.

For the remaining seventeen jobs, OM, OW, EM, and EW gave quite different responses. The difference between the highest and lowest group response was statistically significant, but there were several different patterns in approval rates. The seventeen jobs are listed in table 4.4 in order of overall approval as suitable for women. The rate of approval of a particular job by each group is then ranked in comparison with the other three groups.

If the approval ratings of the four groups were distributed randomly, each of the twenty-four possible permutations would be equally likely to emerge. However, eighteen of the twenty-four patterns do not occur *at all*. Neither EM nor EW are *ever* the most liberal (twelve possibilities). When liberal, the views of OM are never polar to those of OW or EM (four possibilities), and when OW are the most liberal, they are never followed by EM (two possibilities).

OW gave the most liberal response for ten of the seventeen occupations. They were followed by OM on four (radar technician, navigator, plumber, diesel mechanic), and by EW on six (infantry, helicopter pilot,

TABLE 4.4.    Suitability of Nontraditional Jobs for Women:
Approval by Sex and Military Rank

| Job | OM | OW | EM | EW |
|---|---|---|---|---|
| Statistician | 1 | 2 | 3 | 4 |
| Radar technician | 2 | 1 | 3 | 4 |
| Bartender | 1 | 3 | 2 | 4 |
| Butcher | 1 | 3 | 2 | 4 |
| Navigator | 2 | 1 | 4 | 3 |
| Janitor | 1 | 2 | 3 | 4 |
| Parachute rigger | 1 | 2 | 3 | 4 |
| Plumber | 2 | 1 | 4 | 3 |
| Welder | 1 | 2 | 3 | 4 |
| Ammunition supply | 1 | 2 | 3 | 4 |
| Company commander | 4 | 1 | 3 | 2 |
| Diesel mechanic | 2 | 1 | 4 | 3 |
| MP–guard duty | 3 | 1 | 4 | 2 |
| Helicopter pilot | 3 | 1 | 4 | 2 |
| Jet pilot | 3 | 1 | 4 | 2 |
| Bomb disposal | 2/3 | 1 | 4 | 2/3 |
| Rifle-carrying infantry | 4 | 1 | 3 | 2 |

TABLE 4.5.    Patterns of Approval for
Women in Nontraditional Jobs

| Order | | | | No. Occupations |
|---|---|---|---|---|
| OM | OW | EM | EW | 5 |
| OM | EM | OW | EW | 2 |
| OW | OM | EW | EM | 4 |
| | | EM | EW | |
| OW | EW | OM | EM | 6 |
| | | EM | OM | |

MP, jet pilot, company commander, and—in a tie with OM—bomb dis-
posal. Thus, in almost 60 percent of the cases, OW were the most liberal.
In nontraditional jobs with civilian analogues, their allies were OM; in
nontraditional military occupations, their allies were EW.

For which jobs were OM the most liberal? For two civilian jobs,
butcher and bartender, they were the most liberal, followed by EM, with
EW last. In the other five—janitor, parachute rigger, welder, ammunition supply, and statistician—OM were followed by OW, EM, and EW
in that order. The patterns are compared in table 4.5.

Overall, reactions can be characterized as officers versus enlisted personnel 9 of 17 times and men versus women 8 of 17. As far as "fourth-place" rankings went, OW were never fourth, and OM were fourth only twice, but on the core jobs of company commander and infantry soldier. EM and EW were fourth 7 and 8 times, but EW were last when overall approval was high, and EM were last when overall approval was low. Thus, it appears to be women versus men when there is a controversy, and OM seem to be most resistant when a job assignment is most controversial.

The same sample was asked to approach the utilization of women somewhat differently through another set of questions.[13] Respondents were given two statements:

1. Under ordinary circumstances, women belong in the home, caring for children and carrying out domestic duties; whereas men should be responsible for financial support of the family. (Traditional)
2. Relationships between men and women are ideally equal and husbands and wives should share domestic, childrearing, and financial responsibilities. (Contemporary)

Respondents were asked not only to select the item with which *they* most agreed, but also to select the one they thought the following person or persons would most agree with:

Their mother
Their father
Their closest friend of the same sex
Their closest friend of the opposite sex
The majority of Army men
The majority of Army women

These responses give us information not only about men and women, officers and enlisted personnel, but also about their perceptions of others' attitudes.

Ninety percent of military women identified themselves as contemporary, and 85 percent overall identified the majority of Army women as contemporary. Officer women tended to identify their closest friend of the same sex as less contemporary than themselves; and enlisted women were substantially more likely to do so. Still, almost three-fourths of their closest same-sex friends were assigned a contemporary view. Seventy percent of Army men saw their closest friend of the opposite sex as contemporary. Presumably, many of these friends were Army women. Women's views and men's views of them were, then, quite coherent.

There is a remarkable difference, however, in the views held about men. First, 66 percent of military men identify *themselves* as contemporary; however, only 36 to 38 percent identify a majority of men in the Army as contemporary. (If perceptions of others matched others' self-perceptions, 100 percent would have so identified a majority of men.) Further, less than 25 percent of military women saw a majority of Army men as contemporary. In short, men's views of themselves did not match views of them held by either men or women. Either men are concealing their true attitudes, or they do not know how a "contemporary" man speaks and behaves.

After selecting a self-identity as contemporary or traditional, respondents were asked their opinions on drafting women, using women in combat, women's impact on military effectiveness, and the appropriateness for women of the role of infantry soldier. In every case the differences between those holding contemporary and traditional views were significant.

There were other important findings too. Women altogether were 15 or more points more opposed to drafting women than men. *But*, on items related to effectiveness and appropriateness, women scored higher than men. In fact, "traditional" women scored about the same as "contemporary" men! Further, more traditional women thought infantry was an appropriate role than thought women should be drafted! Apparently, to men being drafted was trivial (or a fact of life); to women it was similar to or worse than rifle-carrying infantry work.

The final report of the Women in the Army Study Group of 1976 drew on all available data in preparing a chapter on "Attitudinal Surveys." [14] Some of its summarized findings deserve note.

First, data from eight studies found that men were consistently dubious about women's participation as frontline combat soldiers. Women thought better of women than men did, but still only about half could see women in that role—and enlisted women were less enthusiastic than women officers. A majority of men believed that women's mere participation would make combat units less effective. Seventy percent of women disagreed.

An argument might be made that men speak from experience, but many of the men (even those in combat specialties) had not seen combat—and few of them had worked or trained with women. Thus, their "experience" consisted of single-sex combat *training*.

Another set of questions revolved around leadership and command. Again, there is a consistent pattern of men lacking confidence in women and believing that their use would decrease the effectiveness of the military. One study showed that half of the men questioned believed this versus about 15 percent of the women. Another showed 60 percent of men and 30 percent of women saying that they would not feel as secure in combat with a female commander as with one who was male. Yet another showed 31 percent believing that women are accepted by women but not men as leaders, and 13 percent saying they are accepted by no one. In still another men disagreed with the statement that women can command rifle companies, while a slight majority of women agreed.[15]

A third area of substantial disagreement between men and women is that of job performance. A 1975 survey showed men (around 50 percent) believing that the Army's mission is best carried out by men with "some women" in support roles. In contrast, around 60 percent of women believed that the mission is best accomplished "equally by men and women." About 40 percent of women agreed (and 40 percent denied) that women can perform jobs requiring "a lot of physical strength." Seventy percent of male officers and 54 percent of enlisted men disagreed. Overall, about 40 percent of men believed that women were performing "very well," but more than *70 percent* of women believed that they were performing very well. Men's low estimate of women is significant, because the military consists mostly of men, and they do most of the estimating.

In 1975 the Army was considering a change to integrated basic training.* Male officers and enlisted men then agreed that women should qualify with arms, that women's physical training should be "tougher," and that women should have exactly the same basic training as men. Enlisted women were more doubtful and did not agree that women should receive the same training. Overall, men believed that women are given preferential treatment during their separate training; enlisted women slightly agreed; women officers (who did most of the training) did not.

In the 1976 MAX WAC study of field performance, which will be discussed in Chapter 6, a number of subjective assessments of women's performance were collected.[16] They showed, first, that enlisted women gave slightly lower ratings to the unit as a whole than did men; but in assessing women's performance, 79 percent of E-5–E-9 women, 72 percent of E-1–E-4 women, 68 percent of (mostly male) officers, 56 percent of E-5–E-9 men, and 45 percent of E-1–E-4 men called it "outstanding." In contrast, the same groups rated men's performance "outstanding" in the following proportions: 76 percent, 70 percent, 79 percent, 76 percent, 73 percent. Thus, women rated men and women about the same. Ten percent more officers gave men a higher rating. But 20 to 28 percent more enlisted men rated men above women. Do peers know better, or are they more threatened? Do men have a same-sex bias that women do not have? How do these perceptions affect performance? Does competition spur men to higher achievement? Does relative disesteem inspire

*The change was made but then reversed in 1982.

women to try harder, or discourage them? Do women then lower their aspirations? Do they leave? *Are* women not performing well? If not, why do they think they are? Are supervisors providing women with negative as well as positive feedback? These vital questions remained unanswered.

During the early 1970s women not only increased in number and entered new career fields; they were also assigned to new locations. In particular, some were assigned to Korea—and to bases throughout the peninsula, not just to Seoul. A study of all women assigned to Korea was done, although analysis was confined to data collected from E-1s through E-5s doing their first tour in Korea. (The limited numbers of women with more than one tour [14], women NCOs [39], and women officers [54] meant that a statistical analysis of their responses would not be meaningful.) Data were reported for junior enlisted men and women in jobs traditionally and *not* traditionally held by women. Interestingly, women in nontraditional fields were least satisfied; women in fields traditional to women were as satisfied as men in fields traditional to men; but men in "women's" fields were the most satisfied group.[17] Perhaps women's jobs are satisfying ones, and it is only in the military that men can hold them without censure.

The Korean data are mostly self-descriptive and do not give us information about what others think of the respondent. Just over half the men and women in traditionally male fields reported that they did their job very well as far as their boss was concerned. In the fields of administration and medical work, 63 percent of women and 72 percent of men gave that report. How their bosses would actually rate them is unknown.

On the "attitudes toward women in the Army scale," more than 60 percent of men scored "low," regardless of MOS; for women, there was a significant difference in attitude between those in traditional and nontraditional jobs. Still, the difference between the traditional MOS women and men was twice as large as that between the two groups of women. When the question was exposing women to combat, though, the (negative) views of traditional women were very like those of men. Women in nontraditional jobs were far more willing to expose women to risk. Thus, any analysis needs to consider at least two kinds of women: traditional women who happen to be in the military, and nontraditional women who are *in* the military doing a variety of nontraditional specialties.

Leadership is always of concern to the military. Both men and women (in traditional and nontraditional MOSs) agreed that women make good leaders of women. However, men and women sharply disagreed over whether a woman can be a "good leader of men." More than 45 percent of men believed that they cannot. Answers relating to women's competence split along gender lines, as did views as to whether sex discrimination was being reduced in the Army.

"The Army's role is best carried out with women restricted to medical, nursing and purely administrative jobs" yielded different responses from men and women. Almost 40 percent of men, officers and enlisted, agreed; less than 20 percent of women did. Further, over half the men (and 30 percent of the women) disagreed with the statement: "Women would make just as good front-line soldiers as men if they were given the same training."

Forty to 50 percent of women, and 15 percent of men, agreed that "the Army would be more effective with more women in command positions."

The summary statement that "of all places in American society, the Army should be run by men" found support from 15 percent of military women and about 50 percent of military men.

A field study done in Germany also showed discrepant views for women and men.[18] REF WAC will be discussed in detail in Chapter 6. Only opinions about performance will be presented here.

Almost no one believed that women performed better than men, but 34 percent of officers and 42 percent of NCOs believed that men performed better. Further, NCOs who had worked with women rated them lower (as compared with men) than did NCOs who had not. Again, 93 percent of officers, 83 percent of NCOs, and 78 percent of enlisted men thought men did excellently or well in their MOS-related jobs. This was compared with 70 percent, 50 percent, and 35 percent (of officers, NCOs, and enlisted men respectively) who thought enlisted women did excellent or good jobs. Eighty-two percent of enlisted women thought women did excellent or good jobs. Only 69 percent of the women thought men did.[19]

Before the exercises enlisted peers were asked to state their expectations for men, women, and themselves. They were later asked how men, women, and they themselves had performed. Men predicted that they personally would do excellently, that men in general would do almost as well, and that women would do just about two-thirds as well. When the test was over, they reported being confirmed in their views about themselves and men; however, they thought women had done less than half as well! Women started out with expectations about as high as men's (and equally high for both men and women). A few women predicted that they personally would do less well than their women peers. When the exercise was over, they believed they and women as a group had done as predicted, but that men had not done quite as well as expected.

What should one conclude? If women were not doing well, they were not getting the message. If they were doing well, it was not being recognized by men. It is probably significant that the REF WAC researchers "observed considerable and widespread bias in units toward women." The most significant bias was attributed to first-line supervisors, who were, in many cases, described as highly vocal in their opposition to women.[20] But REF WAC researchers found not only low estimates of women's performance as a group, but also high performance ratings given to individual women by their supervisors. Perhaps, then, individual women were being fairly evaluated, and "other," unobserved women were simply assumed to be inferior.

As in other studies, almost half of enlisted men reported that NCOs treated women differently from—better than—men. A substantial number of women agreed that they were treated differently, but believed their treatment was negative. In particular, women believed they were denied ego- and career-enhancing opportunities. Since some of these "opportunities" may have been perceived as arduous by enlisted men, it is possible that a single NCO decision could simultaneously be seen as favoritism by men and as negative discrimination by women. Any particular assignment decision could involve the most rational allocation of skills within the unit, and thus be a "good" decision, but still damage the morale of men and women as long as it was perceived as discriminatory.

The combat question was probed in a new way in this study. The query was: "If enlisted women were allowed to go into combat, what do you think most EM / most EW / you, yourself would do about going into combat?"* The choices were as follows:

1. Would do anything to get to go
2. Would want to go but wouldn't do anything to get to go
3. Wouldn't care one way or another
4. Wouldn't want to go but wouldn't try to get out of going
5. Would do almost anything to keep from going

Responses were taken from officers and NCOs (both de facto male in this study) and from EM and EW separately (table 4.6).

These data are very interesting. Hardly anyone thought any enlisted person, man or woman, would "do anything to get to go," although 11 percent of EM, 20 percent of officers, and 27 percent of NCOs claimed *they* would.

The four groups of respondents agreed that the most likely response of EM would be: "Wouldn't want to go, but wouldn't try to get out of going." Officers believed that this would be the EW response as well. The other three groups, however, believed the most likely EW response would be to "do almost anything to keep from going." Further, 42 percent of EW gave this response for themselves.

*The question is ambiguous. Probably it was assumed that the conventional practice of drafting men and assigning them to combat would be practiced, and that undrafted women in uniform would be subject to compulsory assignment. However, respondents may have assumed that women would have to volunteer specifically for combat.

TABLE 4.6.    Responses to Women-in-Combat Query

| Rank | Yourself | Most EM | Most EW |
|------|----------|---------|---------|
| "Would do anything to get to go" | | | |
| O | 20% | 2% | 2% |
| NCO | 27 | 7 | 5 |
| EM | 11 | 4 | 5 |
| EW | 3 | 4 | 6 |
| "Would do almost anything to keep from going" | | | |
| O | 3% | 6% | 29% |
| NCO | 4 | 17 | 49 |
| EM | 16 | 24 | 58 |
| EW | 42 | 25 | 49 |

Source: Women Content in the Army—Reforger 77 (REF WAC), (Alexandria, Va.: Army Research Institute, 1978), tables B-45 through 48-Pretest.

Men consistently described themselves as more ready to go than men in general. Women did not.

Since being an enlisted man is something that happens to many young men, the views presented here may not be too different from those of young men in general. However, since so few young women enlist, and since the initiative is very much their own, with little or perhaps negative social pressure for enlistment, one is less confident that enlisted women's views are the same as those of women generally. Even so, their views are dramatically different from men's. Although many would submit to combat, women do not seek it, and more than 40 percent would, they say, strenuously avoid it.

Perceptions of bias were measured after the REF WAC field exercise called "Reforger" (Table 4.7).[21] Between 25 and 38 percent of the respondents in the different groups believed officers treated women differently; 39 to 47 percent believed NCOs did. There were a large number of "don't know" responses, especially from EM. EW and (male) officers were most likely to answer no (49 percent in referring to NCOs, and 63 percent in referring to officers). Less than 30 percent of EM answered no concerning either.

"Different treatment" can involve either preference or negative discrimination. The survey mentioned seven "difference" items, four involving discrimination in favor of women, for example, assignment of easier tasks to women, and three discrimination against men.* Thus, the only

*Supposed antimale discrimination took the form of using more obscene language against men and more discipline and harsher discipline for them. From 10 to 25 percent of officers, NCOs, and enlisted men perceived such discrimination.

TABLE 4.7.   Perceptions of Bias After Reforger Exercise

| Rank | Yes | No | Don't Know |
|------|-----|-----|-----------|
| "Did male officers treat men and women differently during Reforger?" | | | |
| O | 30% | 63% | 8% |
| NCO | 35 | 44 | 21 |
| EM | 38 | 28 | 34 |
| EW | 25 | 63 | 12 |
| "Did male NCOs treat men and women differently during Reforger?" | | | |
| O | 39% | 49% | 12% |
| NCOs | 40 | 43 | 17 |
| EM | 47 | 28 | 26 |
| EW | 43 | 49 | 8 |

Source: *Women Content in the Army—Reforger 77*, tables B-54–B-57.

way to register a perception of discrimination against women or favoritism toward men was to resort to the eighth category "other." Men did this rarely; women did it so often that "other" was the dominant category for them, showing a 32 to 42 percent response!

All of this is pertinent. It is important to remember that men often think it is *men* who are discriminated against. It is equally important to note that the Army did not even ask about discrimination against women, even though women widely and strongly perceive "other" kinds of "different" treatment.

A follow-up study of the Reforger data was done by the ARI in 1981 to assess the effect of contact on attitudes toward women in the Army.[22] Women's attitudes about women were found to be stable. Neither the proportion of women in a group nor the size of the work group had a bearing on their views. Women apparently knew what they thought. Men's views were also independent of the size of the group; however, they were significantly related to the percentage of women in it. Indeed, their attitudes were most positive in groups with no women; they were least positive in those containing 15 percent or more.

The authors speculated that in stressful conditions such as field exercises, when work is physical, and when favoritism is practiced (or perceived), women are not well accepted, and increased contact does not improve acceptance.* Whatever the reason, it seems clear that resist-

*The authors also noted that many of the women involved in these experimental exercises had never received training in skills they had to practice, but that junior women would in the future be trained in field skills.

ance to women by Army personnel remains substantial and widespread and that "contact" alone is no panacea.*

The ARI also ran a study using a Likert scale on half the sample and a choice item on the other half to evaluate attitudes toward women in the Army and correlate them not only with contact, but also with combat experience and with desire to stay in the Army.[23] Men and women, officers and enlisted personnel, were asked whether they agreed that "almost all" enlisted women and enlisted men have (1) the strength, (2) the stamina, and (3) the guts to be a combat soldier. A familiar pattern appeared. First, women officers thought at least as well of enlisted women as enlisted women did. Second, women rated women 20 points higher than men rated them. Close to 60 percent of women (versus 40 percent of men) thought women have the strength; 70 percent (versus 50 percent), the stamina; and 65 percent (versus 43 percent), the guts. Eighty-five to 93 percent of all respondents believed men have the guts, stamina, and strength. The most doubted quality was "guts." Women rated men lower than men did, but even so, 80 percent of women credited men with having the necessary guts. When men judge women, it is their strength that is most doubted.

In the past women have been pressed into service in time of need and, typically, a time of stress. Thus, individuals were asked whether they would prefer to be in a shorthanded unit (10, 30, or 50 percent under strength) or to have the shortage made up by women. In other words, would one prefer to have women or no one—and how many "no ones" would one accept before starting to utilize women? Interestingly enough, the 10, 30, and 50 percent alternatives seemed to have little effect on responses. The view seemed to be that one should fill the gap with women at once or not at all. Enlisted men were inclined to do without women, and officer women to fill without hesitation. But both male and female officers and enlisted personnel would fill light truck and military police assignments with women as soon as they became understrength. For infantry units, the numbers were quite different. Enlisted men were quicker than male officers to fill a gap with women, and two-thirds to three-fourths of women preferred women to no one.

---

*Some have suggested that women's acceptance is related to the "traditionality" of their particular jobs. Here there is a problem with definitions. After all, simply being in the military could be said to be nontraditional for a woman. Further, in one person's research traditionality may depend upon the proportion of women in the career field; in another's, it may depend upon the proportion of the whole population of working women in the field. That is, a field in which women make up 30 percent of the work force might still be called a "woman's" field if half of all women working were in it. Most military women in the past worked in medical and administrative jobs. These may be called traditional, but even there women are a minority of the workers.

Male respondents differed by rank. Generally, male officers are said to be more accepting of women than are enlisted men. However, this study and others show enlisted men as more favorable to women's use in the infantry. It may be that enlisted men's responses are more unidimensional—that is, they respond generally and negatively to "women"—whereas officers more carefully distinguish the particular role to which women would be assigned. Thus, officers may appear more open but may still be most opposed to women's use in combat, the infantry, and closely related areas. Indeed, "Women should not be assigned to combat jobs at all" was agreed to by 76 percent of male officers, 57 percent of enlisted men, 55 percent of enlisted women, and 53 percent of female officers.[24] This suggests that the general belief that male acceptance of women's equality correlates positively with education needs more careful analysis. It might be wise to compare acceptance in principle with acceptance in particular circumstances before judging that one group of men has "better" (or "worse") attitudes toward women.

A Military Personnel Center survey approached the question of willingness to accept combat service in terms of incentive (bonus pay) and context (peacetime versus a situation in which the United States was under attack).[25] In all situations women officers were much less willing than men to "attempt" a combat assignment. They were also (slightly) less willing than enlisted women, except "when the U.S. is under attack." Enlisted men were less willing than male officers, but more willing than women.* When asked whether they would have entered a combat specialty when they entered the service if that had been possible, 21 percent of enlisted women and 24 percent of women officers (not in health fields) said yes.

Using statements of willingness to move to combat units "now," the Army calculated that almost 40 percent of Army women would be willing to go into units then closed to them. Interestingly, close to 30 percent of women officers and 44 percent of enlisted women said that they would be concerned about the danger of sexual abuse by "our" (U.S.) troops. A majority (in the case of enlisted men and women a bare majority) thought it would be easy to achieve "battlefield privacy." In addition, particular combat hardships were listed and individuals were asked whether they believed they could endure them "at least as well as other soldiers." Enlisted men answered yes from 61 to 83 percent of the time on nine items. In both cases the lowest response was to the item that explored whether the subject could "endure consequences of enemy capture." Some women officers' self-expectations were lower even than those of enlisted women:

*In general, women responded less to economic incentives than men; everyone responded to "attack."

12 to 36 percent positive answers versus 34 to 59 percent. Women were least confident about their ability to engage in hand-to-hand combat. Enemy capture was at almost the same level. (It should be noted that 34 percent of the women officer sample were health personnel—mostly nurses, who have a long history of performing in an important noncombat role. Also, these women were older and were less likely to have had vigorous physical training.)

Three-fourths of the women in this survey believed women should join the combat arms. Sixty percent of enlisted men agreed. But only a third of male officers did. An important qualification is that both men and women believed women should have a choice about assignment to the combat arms. Again, men are not willing to coerce women as they coerce each other, nor do women wish to be coerced. However, there was support for coercion in the form of the draft. Drafting women was supported by 83 percent of female officers, 76 percent of male officers, 74 percent of enlisted men, and 65 percent of enlisted women.

Similarly, the deployment of women as combat replacements was supported by 45 percent of enlisted men, 43 percent of female officers, 40 percent of enlisted women, and 32 percent of male officers. Thus, male officers (the decision-makers) are ready to draft women, but not at all ready to use them for the military's central purpose.

Finally, let us consider a U.S. Army Administration Center's study of women's capacity to lead.[26] A sample of 7,600 (including only 200 women) were asked if they agreed that women "in general have the leadership skills, aggressiveness, and self-confidence to perform in any MOS or unit to which they might be assigned." The variable was wartime versus peacetime. As would be expected, women had more confidence in women than did men; women most doubted their own aggressiveness. Men showed rather high levels of disagreement with the four propositions —especially for "wartime." From one-third to almost one-half denied women's capacity to serve in wartime, levels from 13 to 18 percentage points higher than those offered for a peacetime context.

Men's lack of confidence in women in wartime could be serious because an emergency period is precisely the time when women are most likely to be used in new ways. Further, the abolition of the WAC means that if Army women are to receive *any* opportunities to command or lead, they will have to be placed over men. Women's "separate sphere" no longer exists, yet women are not welcomed into men's sphere. The notion that women are spectators and part-time help who will be withdrawn at the outbreak of hostilities is widespread. Grenada and Libya proved differently, but the perception almost certainly persists.

## SUMMARY AND CONCLUSION

Some would argue that even asking for opinions about women's capability and their appropriate role is to lend legitimacy to the views of those who seek to confine and limit them. Indeed, some of the surveys we have examined assumed women's deficiency as well as favoritism toward them and discrimination against men. Still, a number of interesting questions were asked, the findings were not always what might have been expected, and the same data were sometimes used in different ways. For example, although the Air Force used the opinions of spouses to bar military women from a job, the Navy used these data to develop a program to reassure spouses.

The major finding is a large and consistent difference between the views of women and men. Women believe that they do a good job and are discriminated against; nevertheless, they are at least as satisfied with the military as men. Men think that women in general do not do a good job, although particular women do, and that women are favored; still, men believe in equal treatment more than women do (e.g., with regard to combat assignments).

The issue of favoritism is tricky. First, as long as women are exempt from combat, women *are* being favored, no matter how well and honorably they behave, and no matter how responsibly a commander directs his unit. Moreover, a commander may find that the best use of individual talents and skills results in the allocation of particular kinds of slots predominantly to women. This may be fair at the individual level, and good for the unit, and still be seen as unfair to women and men as groups.

Many women seem to believe women are qualified for combat, and some would be willing to serve in it. However, women do not want to be coerced. That is, they are opposed both to being barred from and being forced into combat.

The combat issue is basic and it is divisive. Opinions range across a strongly agree–strongly disagree scale with a substantial percentage of opinion at each end. There is no modal view. More men favor combat for women than women, but women officers and Army personnel favor it the most. (Marines and male officers favor it the least.) Thus, opinions vary by gender, by rank, and even by service.

The substantial differences between the views of officers and enlisted personnel may reflect education, since officers are typically college graduates, and enlisted personnel are more likely to have only a high school diploma. However, they may also reflect differences in what the two groups do in the military. Male officers commit troops to battle and are sensitive to public opinion about their actions. Enlisted men may focus more on the assumed substitutability of enlisted personnel. Enlisted women's tentativeness about full equality probably reflects both a desire to maintain the terms of their implicit enlistment contracts and a realistic appraisal of the hard and heavy work avoided under current policy. Women officers, on the other hand, may be attuned to their lack of opportunity to exercise command and may feel a need to be available, at least theoretically, for all the managerial and leadership duties that go with rank. (Women line officers and nurses have such different roles that they should be distinguished from each other in any systematic study.) Finally, the apparently liberal global views of male officers probably reflect their understanding of the size and complexity of military institutions and their need for a variety of talents to function well; these men, however, are not liberal about women's fulfilling the core military functions of fighting and commanding.

These bi-modal and conflicting views about women predict little change in future policies. This is not a situation where disagreement exists but all views are taken into account. This is a situation where men and women disagree within an institution that is ten-to-one male and whose highest-ranked members (generals) are more than one-hundred-fifty-to-one male. Further, in this institution men (who are overwhelmingly dominant) see *themselves*, not women, as the objects of discrimination!

Army researchers asked good questions about job suitability, fitness to command, conditions in war and peace, and just when (if ever) "women" become better than "nothing." Women familiar with the findings are probably discouraged to learn that "contact" does not seem to enhance men's estimation of their competence. Changes in women's attitudes toward men as a result of contact have not been carefully explored, but the study of senior Navy enlisted women and the REF WAC study both suggest that contact may diminish women's regard for men—and, perhaps, their interest in participating in a male-dominated institution.

It is important to consider what these findings about opinions *mean*. Let us suppose that individuals are candid in reporting their views. Can the collective view be equated with the sum of the individual views? Are opinions about the collective view the same as the sum of individual views? Does knowledge of the summed views change beliefs about the collective views? Scholars have considered such questions under the label "pluralistic ignorance" or "false consciousness of kind." [27] In the contexts of the opinions of aged people and opinions about race relations, it was found that summed self-reports were often quite different from individuals' conceptions of their own group's views.* For instance, if

---

*This is different from the situation in which subgroups attribute different meanings to the same question, something that may occur more frequently than we realize. For

whites perceive others as prejudiced but individually deny that they are, they could be distorting their own view or misperceiving that of others. If the latter is true, there may be substantial room for social change. If the former is true, there may be some "slack," but only to the degree that people try to live up to their self-reporting.

Data on contemporary sex-role attitudes show that women's reports of their own views and their perceptions of the views of same-sex friends and of Army women generally fall within 9 percentage points of men's view of attitudes held by women in the Army. If, however, we compare men's own attitudes and their perceptions of the views of a same-sex friend and of men in the Army with women's views of attitudes held by men in the Army, we find a range of over 44 percentage points! Men collectively may be more disapproving of military women than they say individually—or less than they think men are in general.

In the same vein, predictions of whether most enlisted women "would do almost anything to keep from going" into combat varied widely from what enlisted women said about themselves. Officers underestimated their willingness by 13 percent, and enlisted men overestimated their reluctance by 16 percent. Enlisted women's self-reporting, though, was only 7 points away from their estimate for enlisted women as a whole. Enlisted men's self-reporting and others' estimates of their responses varied by less than 10 percent. Military opinion requires much more assessment. Since so many Army studies were conducted during a period of rapid but begrudging change, one might think them time-bound. The findings, though, are similar to those done by other services and by DOD, including some later ones. The effect of opinion on policy is related not only to the content and distribution of views, but also to their intensity, saliency, and stability. Nevertheless, after opinions have been fully analyzed, it must be remembered that the military has rich opportunities to require desired behavior and to coerce needed results. Thus, it is not enough to survey opinions on women's ability to lead and then to say, "Men will not follow, so women cannot lead." Men can be coerced to follow. The military does it all the time.

---

example, when new Navy recruits were asked how long they took to decide to enlist, 42 percent of women and 34 percent of men said they decided "quickly." However, only 39 percent of women decided in one month, and 34 percent took over six months, while 42 percent of men took one month and 26 percent over six months. Also, 45 percent of women (as opposed to 33 percent of men) inquired into all branches of the military (Patricia J. Thomas, *Why Women Enlist: The Navy as an Occupational Choice* [San Diego: Navy Personnel Research and Development Center, 1977], pp. 12–13).

# 5

---

# Litigation
# and
# Legislation

Policies about military women are affected by legislation and litigation as well as by military opinion. Legislation specifically related to military women is minimal, but it is mightily constraining. On the other hand, litigation—especially against the Navy—has proven surprisingly effective in increasing women's options.

The Navy seems especially prone to describing itself as bound by legal requirements. This would make change hard to accomplish if change were desired. On the other hand, it makes it possible to retreat with grace: for example, if a suit is brought and won, the Navy can portray itself as always happy to obey the law, and it can treat the litigant as a loyal service member because the challenge was to Congress and not the Navy itself. It is also true, though, that apart from Adm. Elmo Zumwalt, there have been few high-level advocates for women, and recent (civilian) secretaries of the Navy have projected especially macho images—*vide* John Warner, John Lehman, and James Webb.[1]

Courts usually do not let individuals sue the military. The Federal Tort Claims Act of 1946 forbids most suits based on a "discretionary function," which encompasses high-level policy decisions. Further, in *Feres* v. *United States* (1950), the Supreme Court specifically ruled that the government was not liable for damages to service people and veterans because legislation provides benefits and entitlements for them. In 1977 the Court extended the doctrine by holding that the government could not even be sued by suppliers for reimbursement of damages paid to service personnel because of malfunctioning products—even if the malfunction was primarily the fault of the government. In 1987 the Court reinforced its position by ruling that victims of radiation from atomic testing could not sue, that a Coast Guard pilot misdirected by a civilian air controller could not sue, and that a veteran who had unknowingly participated in an experiment with LSD could not sue.

Further, courts do not usually tell the military what to do. In 1983 the Supreme Court held that Black enlisted men could not sue their superiors in the Navy for violating their constitutional rights. Chief Justice Warren E. Burger summed it up: "The special status of the military has required, the Constitution has contemplated, Congress has created, and this Court has long recognized two systems of justice, to some extent parallel: one for civilians and one for military personnel" (*Chappell et al. v. Wallace et al.*, 462 U.S. 296, p. 1).

The military is hard to sue. Not only is it broadly exempted, but the rights of uniformed personnel are greatly restricted. Courts explicitly and the legislature implicitly defer to the military. Nevertheless, in the 1970s women won a number of significant victories over the military. The most important cases were *Frontiero, Crawford,* and *Owens* (*Frontiero* v. *Richardson*, 411 U.S. 677 [1973]; *Crawford* v. *Cusham*, 531 F.2d 114 [2nd Cir. 1976]; *Owens* v. *Brown*, 455 F.Supp. 291 [D.D.C. 1978]). Before detailing these cases, let us consider their background in legislation and military legal procedure as well as the impact of congressional passage of the ERA.

### BACKGROUND

The Women's Armed Services' Integration Act of 1948, P.L. 625, is the legal foundation for women's participation in the regular military. That law established the Women's Army Corps in the Regular Army and authorized the enlistment and appointment of women in the Air Force, Navy, and Marine Corps. It also limited women to 2 percent of total strength and refused enlistment to women under eighteen while requiring written parental permission for women under twenty-one. The act allowed enlisted women to achieve any rank, but did not permit women officers to hold any rank higher than that of colonel, and even that rank could not be held permanently. (The intent was to make the top woman officer in each service or corps a colonel or Naval captain for the period—and only for the period—during which she held the top position.) In addition, the service secretaries were authorized to prescribe regulations governing the discharge of women. This permitted the services to discharge pregnant women and even women who had minor children living in the home.[2] P.L. 625 also stipulated that the husbands and children of military women would not be considered dependents unless the women were their "chief support." Finally, it stipulated that Navy women were not to be assigned to duty on Navy vessels except hospital ships and naval transports, and Navy and Air Force women were not to be assigned to duty in aircraft "while such aircraft are engaged in combat missions." (The duties of women in the Army were not limited; they were simply to "perform such services as may be prescribed by the Secretary of the Army.")

In November 1967 P.L. 90-130 was passed. Its primary purpose was to remove restrictions on the careers of women officers, but it also removed a restriction of great importance to enlisted women: the 2 percent limit. Other skirmishes produced such changes as a requirement that DOD submit to Congress a definition of "combat," intended to prod the services into opening more positions to women. Other initiatives will be discussed below in conjunction with the issues they addressed, but some Carter administration proposals that failed in Congress should be noted here. One would have required women to register for the draft; another would have ended the combat exemption.

For most military personnel the relevant legal authority is the court-martial system, a system that has as its primary concern command control and combat readiness. (This purpose leads some to assert that the military justice system has the same relationship to justice that military music has to music.) Yet the Uniform Code of Military Justice (UCMJ), developed after World War II under the direction of James Forrestal, was specifically designed to civilianize and liberalize the military's criminal law and procedure. Further, the capstone of the system, the Court of Military Appeals (COMA), has, since its founding in 1950, rather consistently brought civilian procedural standards into the military system. COMA has not, however, held the military to civilian standards with regard to first amendment rights, especially those related to freedom of expression and privacy.[3]

As the military justice system has become more legalistic, there has been an increase in the use of administrative devices and nonjudicial punishments (Article 15s) as a way of maintaining discipline and order.[4] For instance, in 1966 the services created a new kind of discharge—"for the good of the service" (usually undesirable but not dishonorable). Some 300 of these discharges occurred in 1967; by 1972 there were 25,465. Even in 1975, when most personnel were volunteers, not draftees, there were 14,784 "good of the service" discharges. In the 1970s, two other categories for early discharge were created: "expeditious," which usually resulted in a "general" discharge, and "trainee," discharge. A third post–World War II change is that court-martial jurisdiction has been narrowed. In *Toth* v. *Quarles* (350 U.S. 11 [1955]), it was decided that the military could not call a civilian back to stand trial for a crime committed before discharge. Other cases have determined that although active-duty personnel are subject to court-martials, civilian dependents and overseas civilian employees are not. In the 1970s, moreover, judicial decisions began to treat enlistment contracts as contracts rather than as agreements subject to unilateral change at the discretion of the government.[5]

Between 1966 and 1973, there were from 400 to 2,000 federal court decisions involving military personnel each year. The numbers had never reached 400 before, nor would they after 1973. This was a period of heavy litigation on a limited range of issues. Most involved the limits of court-martial jurisdiction or the status of individuals who claimed to be conscientious objectors. In general, the courts deferred to the military. Strong statements on behalf of military authority by Justice William Rehnquist, including the decision in *Parker* v. *Levy* (417 U.S. 733 [1974]), argued the theme that the military is "a society apart." Still, changes did, rarely, occur. Some were almost certainly the result of the military's effort to anticipate judicially required changes; some changes were won. Both represent rare phenomena—successful litigation against the military or a response involved by fear of such litigation.

### THE IMPACT OF THE ERA

"Equality of rights under the law shall not be denied or abridged by the United States or by any State on account of sex," resolved 354 (to 23) members of the House of Representatives in October 1971. Eighty-four (to 8) senators agreed in March 1972. Almost immediately states began ratifying the ERA, and policymakers began to anticipate its consequences. Ratification, though, requires approval of three-fourths (38) of the states, and although 70 percent did ratify it, the amendment failed, even after the allotted seven-year approval period had been extended for three years (to 1982). Those who had predicted quick ratification had forgotten that our Constitution was originally designed to protect a "peculiar institution"—slavery—and that it provides an opportunity for the minority to veto both the will and rights of a majority. Although deeply embedded in the nation's history—slavery, the Civil War, "states' rights," and "civil rights"—the failure of the ERA was frequently attributed to uncertainty about what it would mean for women's participation in the military.[6]

Many politically active women took the position that a responsible citizen should accept all the duties as well as the benefits of citizenship. Others rejected the idea that equality implies responsibility to participate in an institution (e.g., the military) that one opposes. Few explicitly supported the current policy of permitting women to volunteer, but only for limited service. Many organizations that supported the ERA tried to sweep the military issue under the rug. However, when the Carter administration recommended to Congress draft registration for women and men, and when the *Rostker* challenge to male-only draft registration came before the Supreme Court, women's groups supporting the ERA finally had to face the issue. Many took the stance that equal rights would require equal responsibility.

Congress had faced the issue during its vote on the ERA, and had soundly defeated Sen. Sam Ervin's efforts to legislate that its passage would not prevent Congress from barring women from the draft or from combat units. Yet, although Congress was on record as prepared to accept full application of the amendment, some believed that it would have room to maneuver later by invoking the doctrine of military necessity, the need to maintain discipline and morale, and "national survival."[7]

Most authorities, though, thought that the ERA would require changes in a variety of existing military policies. The most obvious were the different enlistment standards used for men and women. Some of these involved age of eligibility to enlist and parental permission. Others required women to have higher test scores and higher educational attainment. Generally it was assumed that differential age and permission standards would be found illegal, and these were changed. There was more uncertainty about the education standards, which some believed could be justified by the (higher?) law of supply and demand. The argument was (and for the Navy and Marines always has been) that the services should take the best men and women they can get, even if the demand for each is such that the women must be better qualified than the men. (The Air Force has long required its men to match the standards for women.) Litigation was begun on this issue but did not proceed far.[8]

Organizational structure was another issue. By 1972 only the Army had a wholly separate corps for women. The services did, however, have a variety of special provisions for women—for example, some required higher standards for women's housing than for men's. All required that women be housed separately from men, and it seemed clear that the constitutional right to privacy would permit (if not require) separate bedrooms and bathrooms. Still, some observers thought that the Army's wholly separate basic training would have to come to an end.[9]

There were also questions about the justifications used for closing particular jobs to women, which went far beyond restrictions related to combat. They included the proscription for women of "strenuous physical labor," "hazardous duty," and "isolated areas." There were also strong feelings in the military about the "appropriateness" of certain jobs for women.[10]

Employment discrimination informed by such attitudes had become illegal in civilian life only with the passage of Title VII of the 1964 Civil Rights Act eight years before, and the full implications of that act were still being developed through judicial testing as late as 1971.* If the ERA was ratified, analysts expected that all military restrictions would require reevaluation. In the 1970s, then, the military voluntarily began to change a number of policies that it expected to be challenged. The fact that the decision to end the draft coincided with the passage of the

*See *Sail'er Inn* v. *Kirby* (5 Cal. 3d 1, 485 P.2d 529, 95 Cal. Rptr. 329) and *Phillips* v. *Martin Marietta Corp.* (400 U.S. 542), both 1971 decisions.

ERA, and that resulting recruitment pressures made women suddenly attractive to manpower planners, almost certainly made it easier for military managers to contemplate and accept changes in the use of women. Change is always easier when legal and practical imperatives converge. Nevertheless, the frequently successful challenges raised by women are equally deserving of analysis—an analysis that would not be necessary if the U.S. Supreme Court had not (previously and regularly) held that in the U.S. Constitution "persons" means men and legal corporations, but not women.

## WOMEN'S VICTORIES: *FRONTIERO, CRAWFORD, OWENS*

*Frontiero, Crawford,* and *Owens* were military women's major courtroom victories.

Sharron Frontiero, an Air Force lieutenant stationed at Maxwell Air Force Base, was married to a veteran who was attending college full time on the G.I. bill.* Because she was a woman, her spouse was not automatically considered her dependent, and she was treated as a single officer for entitlement purposes. Thus, the Frontieros were not eligible for on-base housing, nor was Joseph Frontiero eligible for the medical care routinely offered to female spouses. To become eligible, the Frontieros would have had to offer proof that he was, in fact, dependent on her for over half his support. Since the Frontieros were willing to stipulate that his monthly expenses approximated $354 per month and that he received veterans' benefits of $205 per month, the issue was posed as not just a procedural one (that women in the military had to bear a burden of proof not required of men), but also as a substantive one (that servicemen received benefits even when their spouses were not "in fact" dependent upon them, and that those benefits were denied to servicewomen). The challenge to federal statutes (37 U.S.C. §401, 403 and 10 U.S.C. §1072, 1076) was grounded on the due process clause of the fifth amendment. The contention of the defense was that the statutes existed solely and appropriately for the purpose of administrative convenience.

The Frontieros filed suit in December 1970. A three-judge federal district court denied their appeal two to one, surmising that Congress might reasonably have concluded that since husbands were generally "the breadwinners" and wives typically dependent, to presume that the spouses of the 1 percent of the military who were women were not dependent would result in "considerable saving of administrative expense and manpower."

By the time the Frontieros' appeal reached the Supreme Court (*Fron-*

---

*Today she writes Harlequin romances. See Martha Brannigan, "Women Who Fought Sex Bias on Job Prove to Be a Varied Group," *Wall Street Journal,* 8 June 1987.

*tiero* v. *Richardson*, 411 U.S. 677 [1973]), Congress had passed the ERA and the Supreme Court had ruled (in a case involving an Idaho law giving preference to males in the appointment of estate administrators) that "dissimilar treatment for men and women who are . . . similarly situated" is "the very kind of arbitrary legislative choice forbidden" by the fourteenth amendment's equal protection clause (*Reed* v. *Reed*, 404 U.S. 71, 92 S.Ct. 251, 30 L.Ed.2d 225 [1971]). This decision, the first in which the Supreme Court invalidated legislation using sex as a classification for legal distinction, had been unanimous. A new standard for measuring sex discrimination, sometimes called "strict rationality," was established.

Justice William Rehnquist agreed with the lower court about *Frontiero*. The other eight justices did not. However, the eight did not fully agree with each other, and their reasoning is important. Justice William Brennan, writing for himself and Justices Douglas, White, and Marshall, asserted that

> there can be no doubt that our Nation has had a long and unfortunate history of sex discrimination. . . . Our statute books gradually became laden with gross, stereotyped distinctions between the sexes and, indeed, throughout much of the 19th century the position of women in our society was, in many respects, comparable to that of blacks under the pre-Civil War slave codes. . . . We can only conclude that classification based upon sex, like classifications based upon race, alienage, or national origin, are inherently suspect, and must therefore be subjected to strict judicial scrutiny.

Brennan noted that Congress itself had suggested that classifications based upon sex are "inherently invidious" by passing the ERA by overwhelming margins.

Justice Potter Stewart concurred that the legislation was unconstitutional, citing *Reed* v. *Reed*, but made no reference to the higher standard of "strict scrutiny." Three other justices (Powell, Blackmun, and Burger) agreed that the statute was unconstitutional but specifically refused to apply the "strict scrutiny" standard used in "civil rights" cases. *Reed* v. *Reed*, they noted, did not use that standard, and the recent approval of the ERA was a reason for not invoking the "strictest test of judicial scrutiny." That is, the adoption of the ERA would resolve the substance of the question, and the Court should not act "prematurely and unnecessarily" at the very time when state legislatures are debating the proposed amendment:

> Reaching out to pre-empt by judicial action a major political decision which is currently in process of resolution does not reflect

appropriate respect for duly prescribed legislative processes. . . . Democratic institutions are weakened . . . when we appear unnecessarily to decide sensitive issues of broad social and political importance at the very time they are under consideration within the prescribed constitutional processes.

*Frontiero* came close to granting equal rights for women: only one more vote was needed. The three justices who felt that it was "unnecessary" to concur with the Brennan decision evidently expected the ERA to pass; probably they did not consider the position they might have to take later if it did not. *Frontiero* thus looked like a good "win," but it was only a "due process," not an "equal protection," decision, and it only overruled Congress and convenience, *not* the military or "necessity." It is ironic indeed that women may have lost a stronger Supreme Court decision only because congressional passage of the ERA had created expectations that later proved to be false.

Women also took on the military over their right to become mothers. The definitive case was *Crawford* v. *Cushman* (531 F.2d 114 [2d Cir. 1976]), but the issue developed over a number of years.

The traditional view was that service was something young women did for a few years before getting married, that they made good clerks or medical assistants, and that they could effectively supervise other women. In 1972 there were only 32,400 enlisted women in uniform; 29,400 of them had been in service less than five years.[11] Further, some may have doubted that a servicewoman could also be a married woman, and many thought there was no doubt at all about whether a servicewoman could be a mother. She could not.

During the 1960s the military's desire to reduce attrition, especially of trained and senior women, and the wishes of a few women to stay in service but to alter their family status, converged enough to modify the policy that required discharge of any woman with personal custody of a child under eighteen who resided in her home more than thirty days a year. Waivers were given to a limited number of women whom the military wished to retain. Thus, motherhood became a possibility for women in uniform. Pregnancy and giving birth, though, remained taboo.

In spite of these attitudes, military women won the right to give birth in the 1970s. They won that right through the courts, following the example of civilian women. (Interestingly, some of the crucial decisions involved women in that most traditional of occupations—schoolteacher: *Green* v. *Waterford Board of Education*, 473 F.2d 629 [2d Cir. 1973], and *Cleveland Board of Education* v. *La Fleur*, 414 U.S. 649, 94 S.Ct. 791 [1974].) They won even though the director of the WAC and the Navy's assistant chief of personnel (the de facto director of the WAVEs) did not support a change in family policy. The WAF director at that time, Jeanne Holm, did support a change in the policy on minor children, but even though the judge advocate general's office gave her an opinion that "the signs of the times and the demands of justice require that discriminatory rules which are essentially based in sex must be discarded," the Air Force did not change its regulations until after Capt. Tommie Sue Smith, a judge advocate (i.e., lawyer) herself, filed suit in federal district court charging a violation of her equal protection rights, since no restrictions were placed on men with minor children—and, as she noted, a general on her own base had eight children and no wife living with him![12]

Because she had given up legal custody, Smith was allowed to join the Air Force in 1966, even though she had a four-year-old child. Once in service, she learned that she could not have him in her home more than thirty days a year. She resolved this problem by placing him in a nearby boarding school. In 1969 she was assigned to the Philippines and was told that her son could not accompany her because of the thirty-day rule. Refusing the waiver that the Air Force offered her, she went to court. The day after her suit was filed, it was mooted because the Air Force had changed its policy. The Air Force claims to have made the decision to do so a month earlier; but whether this is true or not, the threat of litigation clearly exercised an important influence on the policymakers.

It was Seaman Anna Flores who took on the U.S. Navy over the question of pregnancy. Essentially she lost her case but won the war. In 1970 Flores, who was single, became pregnant. She later miscarried, but the Navy insisted on discharging her because it could not "condone" an unwed pregnancy or a "dilution of the moral standards set for women in the Navy."[13] With the assistance of the American Civil Liberties Union (ACLU), Flores brought a class-action suit charging that the Navy maintained one standard of behavior for women and another for men. The Navy then changed its mind, allowing her to stay and even making her eligible for promotion (which she later received) and for reenlistment (which she did not elect). In this case, however, Flores' retention did not moot the case. Her suit proceeded and she "lost"—but only because the Navy had meanwhile changed its policy.

In the *Flores* decision the Court found that a review of case histories from January 1971 to January 1972 showed that an unwed pregnancy was indeed a factor in a woman's retention, but unwed paternity was never a factor in a man's retention. Moreover, the deputy chief of Naval personnel, Rear Adm. Douglas C. Plate, had stated that he "did not accept the rationale that men and women should be held to a single standard of morality." He also worried that discharging men for causing a pregnancy would make it too easy for a man to get out of the military. The Court also found, though, that records from January 1972 through August 1972 showed *no* evidence of a double standard and that the new deputy chief of Naval personnel, Adm. Robert B. Baldwin, had stated that there was no longer a policy of applying one. The Court's conclusion was that the Navy's policy at the time of its decision was acceptable, and that it was that a woman on active duty who acquired dependency or pregnancy status and who wished to remain in the Navy must request a waiver, which would be considered on a case-by-case basis.

Meanwhile, the Air Force and the Army continued to play the mootness game, issuing individual waivers to avoid legal challenges. For example, Capt. Susan Struck, a pregnant Air Force nurse, took her case to court and lost (*Struck* v. *Secretary of Defense*, 460 F.2d 1372 [9th Cir. 1971]). Struck then appealed and was granted *certiorari*. At this point the solicitor general, who believed that the case could not be won by the Air Force, and the three service judge advocates general (JAG), agreed to give Struck a waiver rather than risk an adverse decision.[14] Air Force Lt. Mary S. Gutierrez lost in the district court (v. Secretary of Defense Melvin Laird), filed an appeal (unpublished order, D.C. Cir., 6 February 1973, amended 8 May 1973), and then received her waiver, as did Airman Gloria D. Robinson, who won in district court (*Robinson* v. *Rand*, 340 F.Supp. 37 [D. Colo. 1972]).

The Marine Corps was unwilling to call retreat, however. It defeated a challenge by Stephanie Crawford. Crawford had been discharged in 1970 when she became pregnant out of wedlock; she applied for reenlistment and was refused because she had a child. Marine regulations then denied enlistment to a woman even if she had surrendered all rights to custody or control of the child, and even if the child had been formally adopted by someone else. The Marines also had a policy of notifying parents of a pregnant woman's discharge and the reason for it. The lower court held that the requirement of *Reed*, a "fair and substantial relation to the object of the legislation," had been met, in view of the Marines' special requirement for ready and mobile personnel. The decision came in 1974. The Marines had won; when Crawford appealed, the Corps took no action to moot the case.

Then, DOD, wishing to reduce attrition and seeing that many more waivers were being granted than refused, told the services on 1 June 1974 that they should develop new policies making separations for pregnancy voluntary by May 1975. The Air Force and Navy (whose policy covered the Marines) complied. The Army resisted until November. The *Crawford* decision, finally given in February 1976, confirmed the opinion of JAG— the time had come. The appeals court ruled that it had the right to review the Marines' regulation, that the regulation was unconstitutional on both equal protection and due process grounds, and that allowing the plaintiff to serve out the remaining twenty months of her original reenlistment was an appropriate remedy. Pregnancy was the only temporary disability that resulted in a discharge. This was irrational (hence wrong), since no evidence was offered to show that it was different from other disabilities in terms of mobility, readiness, or even convenience. "Pregnancy," the court concluded, "is no longer . . . a dirty word." The previously applicable regulation penalized the decision to bear a child, a decision protected by the Constitution.*

Women in the services now regularly bear children. This does not mean that the services are happy about it. Any number of new policies have been discussed internally to limit this right; often they are aimed at enlisted women in their first enlistments. It also seems clear that feelings about the immorality of unwed motherhood remain. What is new is the feeling that women with responsible jobs and expensive training should be required to honor their commitments. Indeed, policies have now evolved to the point where a woman may ask to be released when she becomes pregnant, but the service does not have to let her go.[15]

Meanwhile, the Army and the Air Force have won the right to deny enlistment to single parents who have custody of children, first through a 1981 decision in the Tenth Circuit Court of Appeals and, finally, through a 1985 U.S. District Court (Western New York) decision, *Mack* v. *Rumsfield*. The latter decision was "upheld" by the U.S. Supreme Court when it refused to review it.[16]† Because the enlistment policy is applied to men as well as women, and because an Army affidavit cited inordinate management problems, morale problems, and assignment inflexibility, the Court held against the plaintiff, Irene Lendenau, even though it acknowledged that more women than men might be affected. Thus, it would appear that because the military believes it requires so many more men than women, it cannot afford a policy that turns away men and women equally (such as a ban on parenthood), but it can and does apply restrictions that affect women more (such as a ban on pregnancy or single, custodial parenthood).‡

Some military policymakers probably believe that mothers and fathers have different roles and that motherhood, but not fatherhood, is incom-

---

*Interestingly, the 1975 policy change had little effect on women's attrition. Forty percent of the women who entered service in 1973 left before completing their third year of service. Thirty-seven percent of those entering in 1977 dropped out before completing three years. Apparently the previous waiver policy had combined with the continuing policy of voluntary discharges to prevent an abrupt transition.

†Congress is considering legislation that would permit active-duty single mothers to enlist in the National Guard or in the reserves (because they are already trained), but that would not permit civilians to do so (Rick Maze, "House Eases Single Parents' Reserve Signups," *Air Force Times*, 15 September 1986).

‡Since 90 percent of U.S. women bear a child at some time, the military would grievously reduce the pool of women eligible for a service career if it were to return to the old policy.

patible with military service. However, it should be remembered that accommodations are regularly made for fathers that are not compatible with the myth that every service person is always available for world-wide assignment. For example, when marines were sent to Lebanon, men whose wives were scheduled to deliver a child within the next twelve weeks were not required to take the assignment.[17]

The third major 1970s case involved a congressional restriction. Known as the *Owens* case (*Owens* v. *Brown*, 455 F.Supp. 291 [D.D.C. 1978]), it challenged the code that prohibited Navy women from serving on Navy ships—except hospital and transport ships, neither of which were in use in November 1976, when the complaint was filed. At that time, civilian women could serve on board ship, but Navy enlisted women and female line officers could not. The original complainants were four enlisted women; three officers (including then–Lt. Comdr. Kathleen Byerly, who had been featured on the cover of *Time* magazine as an out-standing young woman) joined the suit in early 1977. In spite of Adm. Elmo Zumwalt's (in)famous Z-Gram of 16 August 1972, which opened all ratings to women, assigned women to the U.S.S. *Sanctuary*, and even announced as "the ultimate goal" the assignment of women to ships at sea, there had been no change in Navy policy or in congressional legislation in years. Women who entered Annapolis in 1976 were faced with the probability that they would not be allowed to participate in summer train-ing cruises; women in uniform faced constricted careers and promotions —all because they could not do what the Navy is about—go to sea.

Yona Owens, an electrician, had applied for a billet on the U.S.S. *Michaelson*, a Naval Survey ship. This civilian-operated ship frequently had civilian women aboard as well as male Navy personnel. The Navy JAG recommended disapproval of her application but said that women could be assigned to non-ocean-going ships—tugs and other harbor craft. Owens was ready to do battle. She and other plaintiffs pointed out that since the last transport ship was decommissioned in 1973 and the last hospital ship in 1975, Navy women had no opportunity to serve at sea at all. They argued that 10 U.S.C. §6015 was overly restrictive— that it was "not substantially related to the achievement of an important governmental objective," and, therefore, violated the due process clause of the fifth amendment.

*Craig* v. *Boren* (429 U.S. 190, 197 [1976]) and *Califano* v. *Goldfarb* (430 U.S. 199 [1977]) were decided between the time Owens filed and the time the case was decided in July 1978. These were the cases that finally established that any sex-based legal distinction had to be "sub-stantially related" to an "important objective." Men were the plaintiffs in both. The first involved a statute under which women were allowed to buy beer at age eighteen but men were not, presumably because of men's higher rate of alcohol-related auto accidents. The second was brought by a widower who was denied Social Security benefits granted to widows. The latter regulation was disallowed (over Rehnquist's opposition), even though the correlation between "widow" and "surviving dependent spouse" was 90 percent.

The *Owens* plaintiffs showed that the relevant section of the U.S. Code had not been requested by the Navy or DOD but was inserted (without explanation) at the direction of Congressman Carl Vinson of Georgia, chair of the House Armed Services Committee at the time of the legislation— 1948. The plaintiffs argued that they sought only a ruling that the Navy could not base assignments on "unproved and overbroad assumptions about proper sex roles and the capabilities or proclivities of women."[18] The Navy responded that to find for the plaintiffs would lead to day-to-day interference with Naval affairs—or, possibly, to immediate and total integration.

In May 1977 Sen. William Proxmire of Wisconsin introduced a bill that would have repealed the Navy and Air Force combat restrictions and made the task of determining women's assignments an administrative responsibility (as it was and is for the Army). This meant that the Navy was being challenged simultaneously by its women in federal court and by legislators on Capitol Hill.*

The two previous Navy secretaries, J. William Middendorf and John Warner, had both opposed any change in the combat legislation, although some of their senior officers had recommended it. Nor did the Navy JAG offer generous advice. Thus, ROTC women who had taken the traditional orientation cruise in the summer of 1976 had dressed in civilian clothes and been designated as "guests."[19]

With the election of Annapolis graduate Jimmy Carter, the roles were reversed. The new secretary of the Navy, W. Graham Claytor (who was married to a lieutenant commander), was committed to change, but now his senior officers were not. The new DOD officials were not just seeking modification, however: they wanted §6015 repealed.[20] DOD's position was that the Air Force and especially the Navy should "have the same direction with regard to the assignment of personnel as the Army." Claytor's compromise recommendation was to change the wording of the statute to say: "Women may not be assigned to duty in vessels or aircraft that are engaged in combat missions nor may they be assigned to other than temporary duty on vessels of the Navy except hospital ships, trans-

*By 1986 Proxmire had (with the support of Sen. William Cohen of Maine) abandoned his efforts to remove the combat exemption and introduced legislation to open all combat-support positions to women. The Navy was reported as opposed to, the Air Force and Army as supportive of, the proposal (Rick Maze, "Bill Would Let Women Work Closer to Combat Zone," *Air Force Times*, 13 October 1986).

ports and vessels of a similar classification not expected to be assigned combat missions." Claytor described himself as a "great believer in the step-by-step approach" and noted that this policy would open more billets for women than the Navy could expect to fill.[21] In his view, the limitation was not billets but the small number of women in nontraditional fields and the small number of experienced women petty officers. DOD supported Claytor's suggestion as an interim position, but continued to believe that repeal was the only satisfactory long-term solution.

During House Armed Services Subcommittee hearings, however, doubts about women at sea resurfaced. Language even more restrictive than that proposed by Claytor was discussed; soon thereafter, the secretary of the Navy proposed a new policy under which women's temporary duty would not involve the filling of a billet or last more than six months, and, further, if a ship on which women were serving was assigned to combat, every reasonable effort would be made to disembark the women. Such a policy, in DOD's view, would make women second-class citizens and was far more restrictive than current policies governing other military women. Some argued that DOD should go for complete repeal. Then came the Sirica decision.

The decision authored by Judge John Sirica in the *Owens* case was rendered in July 1978. This summary judgment for the plaintiffs found existing legislation overbroad and restored discretion of assignment to DOD. A "moral element" was identified as well as the practical ones. The court found that women were excluded from sea billets, from job opportunities, and from training that would benefit them in the private sector; that a ceiling on assignments resulted in limited veterans' benefits and privileges; and, in addition, that individuals were denied the right to take part in an "essential national enterprise to the limits of their abilities." The code was just "too broad to pass muster." The court required executive authorities to "move forward in measured steps to approach these issues free from the absolute bar erected by section 6015."[22]*

---

*The case of Pamela Doviak Celli suggests that the Navy has not yet made its peace with women. Celli, a civilian technician, went on a sea trial on the U.S.S. *Benjamin Franklin* in 1981. In 1982 the Navy refused to let her go on a similar trial on the grounds that her presence lessened crew privacy and thus could impair crew "readiness." (The alleged violation of privacy occurred when Celli walked through the crew's lounge.) In May 1986 Celli received a "final" ruling in her favor from the Equal Employment Opportunity Commission (EEOC). The Navy declined to honor it. A federal suit was brought in March 1987 seeking implementation. In June 1987 the new secretary of the Navy, James Webb, announced that civilian technicians could participate in nonoperational, short-term sea trials. However, individual decisions would be left to "the appropriate commander in the operational chain of command," and restrictions for the sake of "readiness, safety, the nature of the work to be performed, or other appropriate considerations" would be permitted. Celli and others see this as an effort to moot the case with no change

In October the original Claytor ("incremental") proposal passed as § 808 of P.L. 95-485, the Department of Defense Authorization Act, 1979. The Navy's "Women in Ships" Program began the next month (see Appendix B).

## MEN'S CHALLENGES TO SEX DISCRIMINATION IN THE MILITARY

Two of the most important civilian cases concerning sex discrimination (*Craig* v. *Boren*, 1976, and *Califano* v. *Goldfarb*, 1977) were, as we have seen, successfully raised by men. When men raised the same issue in a military context, though, they tended to lose. Two important cases involving military men were *Schlesinger* v. *Ballard* (419 U.S. 498 [1975]) and *Rostker* v. *Goldberg* (101 S.Ct. 2646 [1981]).

Robert C. Ballard was a Naval officer who had not been promoted within the required time period and was discharged after seventeen years of service. Women Naval officers were given more time to attain promotion, and Ballard charged that this policy discriminated against men. Congress allowed women Naval officers (only Naval women and only officers) the extension because their assignments were so restricted by the prohibition against their going to sea. The intent was to provide women with an equal opportunity for promotion. The Supreme Court (5–4) found that the different treatment was "rationally related" to an "important" purpose. The Navy's reasoning, which was apparently adopted by the Court, was that organization policy affected military action in a way that benefits (Frontiero) did not, and also that a standard less stringent than one assuming sex to be a "suspect category" was appropriate in this case. Three of the dissenters—Brennan, Douglas, and Marshall—said that "suspect category" *was* the appropriate standard, and White agreed "for the most part" with their dissent.

The decision that most strongly suggested that judicial standards concerning sex discrimination in the military and civilian worlds are different was *Rostker* v. *Goldberg*, brought during the Vietnam War. Rostker argued that the exclusion of women from the draft increased men's chances of being drafted (and perhaps injured or killed). The case became moot when the draft was abolished, but was revived when President

in policy ("Navy to Allow Female Technicians Aboard Submarines for Sea Trials," *Los Angeles Times*, 6 June 1987. See also Don Edwards, "Navy Duty Nearly Impossible for Women," *Los Angeles Times*, 15 April 1987; Rosemary Purcell, "Secretary of the Navy Clears Way for Woman to Go on Sub Trials," *Navy Times*, 29 June 1987, plaintiffs brief in Civil Action No. 87-0072 p, U.S. District Court of Maine, *Pamela M. Doviak Celli* v. *James H. Webb*, 29 June 1987, EEOC. Decision in Appeal No. 01860381 in *Doviak* v. *Department of the Navy*, signed 21 May 1986).

Carter requested that Congress appropriate funds to renew the registration of men and begin the registration of women following the Russian invasion of Afghanistan. By appropriating funds only to register men, Congress defied both the president and the service secretaries. The Court upheld Congress by deciding 6–3 on 25 June 1981 that Congress need not require women to register for the draft just because it required men to do so. The decision did not state, but seemed to assume, two very important points: that Congress could register and draft women, and that combat-exclusion legislation and policies were constitutional.

By the time of the decision, the *Craig* v. *Boren* standard that any sex discrimination must be (1) "substantially related" to (2) an "important governmental objective" had been fairly well established. Justice Rehnquist's decision in *Rostker*, however, overruled the district court that had decided *Boren*. Rehnquist declared that the Constitution's equal protection clause could be superseded by the deference due to Congress, a deference that should reach its "apogee" in the area of military affairs, but he in fact used "administrative convenience" as the basis for his decision, even though "convenience" had been found insufficient to justify gender discrimination in *Frontiero* and other cases both military and nonmilitary. Rehnquist did not specify what standard had to be met in order to overrule equal protection rights; he did state, though, that the draft was necessary for raising *combat* troops, and that women (who could not participate in combat) and men were therefore differently situated. Justice White, on the other hand, specifically stated that the record did not show that sufficient volunteers would be available for all noncombat positions.

*Rostker* is usually discussed as though the rights involved were women's, or as though the question was whether or not it was necessary to draft women, but the suit was raised by a man on behalf of men as a class, and (as Justice Marshall pointed out in his dissent) the question answered should have been whether there were grounds for *excluding* women, not whether there were grounds for including them. An *amicus* brief, prepared by the National Organization for Women (NOW) and citing more than seventy relevant studies, argued that it was women's equal rights that were being damaged. (A second brief was filed on behalf of WEAL and eleven other women's organizations represented by an attorney from the Women's Legal Defense Fund.) NOW's brief focused on the damage done women by reinforcing sex-role stereotyping and on the damage done to the standing as citizen or leader of a person who is excluded from playing a part in the protection of the community and thus consigned to second-class citizenship. (The 1857 decision *Dred Scott* v. *Sandford*, 60 U.S. [19 How.] 698, 1857, is one of many in which military service and citizenship are explicitly linked.) NOW pointed out that the draft pool would be doubled and the quality of recruits improved if women were included, even though the average woman is smaller than the average man. Utilizing current sociological and psychological literature, the brief also argued that the results of taking only women who were volunteers were (1) small numbers, (2) a deviant label, (3) inadequate provision for housing and uniforms, and (4) relative deprivation of the many benefits provided veterans. The Court was unpersuaded.

OTHER CASES

As late as 1979, a number of issues related to discrimination against military women remained unresolved. These included Air Force policies against letting women participate in contact sports and limitations on their assignments (especially overseas) because of inadequate housing and inadequate facilities for the care of dependents. Unsettled even today is the Marine and Army practice of requiring higher enlistment standards for women. Also not put to judicial test is the practice of limiting women's assignments because of discriminatory policies or views of foreign countries.

Two other areas with potential for litigation concern women's sexuality. One involves heterosexual activity, the other homosexual. The latter is simply forbidden and is grounds for discharge. The former involves tensions among (1) the military's concern for the reputation of those who wear its uniform; (2) its expectation that its women should be chaste if single, faithful if married, and discreet if not (coexisting with the expectation that many of its men will be adventurous and proud of it); and (3) a legal, if not general, presumption that the same standards of conduct should apply to women and to men.

The military environment includes large numbers of young men temporarily gathered in places without effective, local, social controls and without a lot to do. Men greatly outnumber available women, and most of the available women are civilian. "Realism" has dictated that military officials know about, condone, and to some extent regulate prostitution. This can be justified on health and even on readiness grounds. The "businesswomen" involved are not the direct responsibility of the military, however, and the military has not given sustained thought to the roles and the rights of the women with whom its men are sexually involved.[23]

When large numbers of women came into the services in the 1970s, they found themselves greatly outnumbered and energetically pursued. The opportunities and temptations, as well as the pressures, were enormous. Promises and invitations of all kinds, welcome and unwelcome, with every kind of intention, never ceased. These women, however, were not "businesswomen" but *military* women, and the men to whom they were relating were also in the military. The problem was no longer just "medical." Further, military commanders who had been accustomed to having women officers manage the sexuality of young enlisted women found themselves having to make decisions about women. Moreover, the sexual revolution had arrived. Many young women simply did not hold the view of morality that had guided previous policies. To many of them, abortion, birth control, and single parenting were reasonable choices. Some may even have been "businesswomen" in the sense that they saw the rewards available for sexual favors and were willing to make the exchange. The male–female imbalance, disparate views of propriety (which probably derived from subcultural as well as generational heterogeneity), and the need to make decisions about women in service and in uniform disconcerted commanders. They did not want to have to manage such concerns, they did not want the military embarrassed, and still problems occurred and recurred; often they were very time-consuming. In fact, Assistant Secretary of Defense for Manpower Affairs Lawrence Korb once said, "No issue has taken more of my time than women in the military."[24]

One trivial yet embarrassing and time-consuming incident was sparked by the April 1980 issue of *Playboy*. A popular feature of this mass-circulation magazine consists of photographs of nearly nude women purportedly representing some collectivity—for example, women at Ivy League schools. In 1980 (at the suggestion of one of the models), it found seven young "Women of the Armed Forces"—three from the Navy, an airman, and one member each from the Coast Guard, the Army, and the Marines—willing to pose in uniform, in parts of their uniforms, and in very little. In the background were pictures of Air Force jets, Navy ships, and Marine tanks. One of the women was photographed while parachuting. The group included an electrician and a machinist. One of the Navy women was assigned to sea duty. One might say that these women combined a very traditional female role (pinup) with a very untraditional (military) one.

The Marines responded quickly. Sgt. Bambi Finney was discharged (honorably) "for the convenience of the Marine Corps," which "does not tolerate posing in the nude." A spokesman said:

> We have a philosophy in the Marine Corps, a longstanding one, that a Marine is on duty 24 hours a day and while there may be time for outside employment and outside activities, whatever activity is undertaken by the Marine is to bring credit upon the corps and not discredit. It's without a doubt that every action a Marine takes—both good and bad—reflects not only on herself, but on every Marine wearing a Marine uniform now, in the past and in the future.[25]

It was reported that one of the other women got a letter of reprimand, a second had her duties changed, and several others were called before their commanding officers.

Immediately, it was asked: "What if it had been a man?" Sure enough, two instances turned up. One involved an active-duty Marine major who in 1974 had posed naked with fellow members of the San Diego State rugby team (he was studying there at the time) for *Playgirl* magazine. He was recalled to Camp Pendleton and received a letter of reprimand. The incident would, in his view, have resulted in failure to win promotion and ultimate discharge if he had not been decorated with the Silver Star for service in Vietnam. It was also reported at the same time that a male (Navy) petty officer would be discharged for appearing as a stripper in a night spot catering to women in Fremont, California.[26]

The lesson was apparently not wholly absorbed. Only a year later another Navy enlisted woman was honorably discharged after seven years of service—again for posing for *Playboy*. Yeoman Second Class Darlene Aubrey was held past her original discharge date so that she could be court-martialed for "showing disrespect to a superior commissioned officer and . . . violating the good standards of the Navy." Her lawyer was prepared to argue that her superiors at the Pentagon had actually provided her with the kimono and fan with which she posed, and that her immediate superior had stated that her posing "would bring no discredit to the Navy." In addition, her lawyer said, he intended to subpoena two admirals to testify that they had sanctioned the yeoman's posing. Because of "delay" and "costs," the Navy decided to discharge rather than court-martial Aubrey. Her attorney claimed that a classified message was sent from one high-ranking official to another saying, "Stop the embarrassment to the Navy and get rid of the thing."[27]

When an institution is unsure of a policy or procedure, bringing it to public notice can be an effective way of fighting it. For the most part, though, young enlisted women do not challenge the military. In the infamous *Norton Sound* case of 1980, a group of young Navy women did make such a challenge.

Homosexuality has long disqualified an individual from military service and has long been grounds for discharge. Homophobia often seems to characterize military thought—a striking example is the Marines' refusal to pick up toys from a Los Angeles homosexual bar as a part of its 1983 Christmas Toys for Tots campaign. A Marine spokesman said: "I wouldn't send a U.S. Marine into any gay bar for any reason. . . . You have to understand that this is the U.S. Marine Corps. We're a very proud Corps. We've got a proud tradition and we're very very proud of our uniform. We're not only concerned about how we wear our uniform, but where we wear it."[28] The same month a Navy commander, a decorated nineteen-year veteran, was convicted of engaging in homo-sexual relations with a member of his own crew. He was dismissed and forfeited all pension and veteran's benefits. The Navy prosecutor empha-sized fraternization (not homosexuality per se) as the issue. Yet that year the Navy alone dismissed 1,167 individuals for homosexuality.[29] In all, 1,796 service members were discharged for homosexuality in 1983, a 64 percent increase over the year before. Of these, 670 received other-than-honorable discharges—twice the 314 of the year before.[30] These numbers suggest differential enforcement over time and, probably, by service.

The danger of blackmail (and hence the threat to national security) is often invoked to proscribe homosexuality. Because this danger is most potent when homosexuality is illegal or denied, some public agencies no longer require the immediate dismissal of admitted homosexuals. The military, though, has not eased its policy. Its arguments involve the close living conditions of service personnel, conditions that are perhaps at their extreme for enlisted personnel at sea. Nevertheless, one suspects that the all-male ethos of the institution has something to do with the taboo. The sexual repression required of servicemen much of the time might become intolerable if other men were finding gratification within the community. Moreover, since homosexuality is apparently practiced in other all-male communities (such as prisons) by men who would not do so if women were available, it may be that the rule actually works to protect weaker men from (usually) heterosexual aggressors. That is, the bar may limit a kind of exploitation that would not develop in a sexually integrated population.

The Army's JAG, Maj. Gen. Hugh J. Clausen, defended the Army's position on homosexuality in a 1982 letter threatening six universities (Columbia, New York University, Yale, Harvard, University of Califor-nia at Los Angeles, and Wayne State) with the loss of ROTC units and defense contracts because their law schools prohibited recruiting by dis-criminatory employers, including those who discriminated against homo-sexuals.[31] "The uniqueness of military service," Clausen argued, means that the service cannot adhere to prohibitions against discrimination on the basis of age, physical handicap, or sexual preference:

> Soldiers are required to live and work under entirely different con-ditions than civilians. . . . [They] must often sleep, eat, and perform personal hygiene under conditions affording minimal privacy. The presence of homosexuals in such an environment tends to impair unit morale and cohesion as well as infringing upon the right of privacy of those service members who have more traditional sexual preferences.

Furthermore, homosexual conduct is a crime in the military. Exclusion of homosexuals from the armed forces is a practical means of precluding from military service a group of individuals who have a natural proclivity to violate the Uniform Code of Military Justice.

The case of Sgt. Perry Watkins reveals the discrepancy between policy and practice. Watkins was drafted in 1967, even though he told the military he was a homosexual. In 1968 he told an investigator about relations he had with two other servicemen, but the criminal probe was dropped for lack of evidence. He was discharged in 1970. He reenlisted in 1971 and began performing as a female impersonator—with the permission of his commanding officer. In 1975 his commanding officer initiated proceedings to dismiss Watkins, but he was found "suitable for retention" by a board of inquiry. Then, in 1982, fifteen years after Watkins was drafted, the Army adopted a regulation requiring, mandating, forcing the discharge of avowed homosexuals instead of making it a "motive for disqualification." Watkins was discharged, and the discharge was upheld by a federal appeals court (the government had lost at the district court level), which ruled that it had no power to intercede and "no function of questioning Army regulations or of forcing Watkins' superiors to disobey them." [32]

The military prefers to have all men available for service. In time of war it drafts men. The military does not want to let the estimated 10 percent of men who are homosexuals out of serving, nor does it want men to be able to evade service by declaring themselves homosexual. The homosexual male, then, is often coerced both into serving and into concealing his sexual preference. A homosexual woman is *not* coerced into service. She voluntarily joins an institution that defines her as unacceptable. Further, it is only since 1977 that an honorable discharge for homosexuality has been routinely obtainable. In the past, the price of being caught was high. Why, then, do homosexual women enlist in an apparently hostile institution?

The only book-length study of homosexuality in the military estimates that three-fourths of the homosexuals who serve do so with no problem, although enforcement policies seem to fluctuate (the Navy is the most vigilant). [33] Those "discovered" are the inexperienced, the defiant or indifferent, and the high-frequency homosexuals. [34] A majority of discoveries occurred because of a third-party report—often the result of a "tiff." Over a third of the homosexuals studied were self-acknowledged; under 10 percent were exposed through indiscretion. At the time (1971), the accused almost never fought to stay in service.

It is estimated that 25 percent of military personnel dismissed for homosexuality are women. [35] Another source gives the 1979 rate of dismissal on these grounds for Navy men as 0.158 percent (778 men out of

493,000) and for Navy women, 0.230 percent (76 women out of 33,000). For the Marines, the overall rate was 0.020 percent; for the Army and the Air Force, 0.040 percent. For these three branches, the dismissal rate for women was two to seven times the rate for men.[36] Service-supplied figures say that in 1979 the Air Force discharged 172 men out of 499,000 and 78 women out of 59,000, and the Army discharged 190 men out of 698,000, and 104 women out of 64,000. This suggests a strong attraction to a punitive institution by lesbians, discrepant enforcement between men and women, and/or mistaken enforcement. Several observers believe that enforcement is primarily directed toward enlisted women, and that homosexuality is treated as an individual activity in the case of men but as a group activity among women. One result is what has become known as a witchhunt.[37]

The Navy's Women at Sea Program has been small and carefully managed. Nevertheless, the number of dismissals for homosexuality caused concern that women who take nontraditional jobs are under particular suspicion. Several women were discharged from the U.S.S. *Vulcan* (one of the first two ships to take women) in August 1982. That same month the Pacific Coast U.S.S. *Dixon* had twelve of its women and seventeen of its men under investigation. Six were charged; of these, one's tour expired, and three were discharged. Shortly afterward, some seventeen women were charged with homosexuality at Millington Naval Air Station in Tennessee. Nine were discharged.[38]

The case of the U.S.S. *Norton Sound*, then, appears to be an example, not an aberration,* unusual only because of the publicity and support given the accused women. This support developed when one woman (against whom charges were ultimately dropped) sought help from NOW, which put her in contact with a newly hired ACLU lawyer assigned specifically to handle cases involving the rights of homosexuals. The attorney, Susan McGreivy, was the daughter of a naval commander father and was, perhaps, less intimidated by and less naive about military culture than other new women lawyers would have been.

The story began in May 1982. Twenty-four young women were told by officials that they were under investigation for being lesbians. They were questioned, and then they were given ten-minute screenings for "mental disease" at the Long Beach Naval Hospital. On 4 June nineteen of the women (almost one-third of the women crew members) were charged

---

*"Witchhunts" are not confined to the Navy. A group of eight Army women were investigated for homosexuality at Fort Carson in 1984, and eight military policewomen stationed at West Point were discharged as lesbians in 1986 (Sue McMillin, "Female GI Wins Fight; Army Mum," *Colorado Springs Gazette Telegraph*, 10 April 1984; James Feron, "Army Dismisses Eight Women on Sex Charges," *New York Times*, 4 October 1986).

before a captain's mast, so that the charges were made known to any member of the crew who had missed out on the ship's hottest item of gossip. The women also received "letters of discharge" as being "unsuitable" for service because of "homosexual tendencies."

On 13 June ACLU attorneys held a news conference and indicated that the women would insist on a full hearing on the charges. On 20 June charges were dropped against eleven; the charges against the remaining eight were upgraded to "misconduct" (homosexual acts). The upgrading entitled them to a formal hearing; if the charges were found true, discharge would be mandatory. Originally all the Black women on board had been charged. Three of the four who came to trial were Black, and both of the women who were ultimately convicted were Black.

The charges originally came from other women rather than from male crew members. The Naval Intelligence Service (NIS) was alerted by the Executive Officer—a male commander who had said women did not belong at sea—working in conjunction with a woman lieutenant commander and a petty officer who had opposed the Women at Sea Program on national television. The investigation was conducted by twelve civilian NIS employees, who could not be compelled to testify at the hearings, although defense attorneys wished to try to show that statements to them had been both coerced and falsified.

Each defendant had a Navy attorney; in addition, two ACLU lawyers, a man and a woman, defended the group collectively. The women were tried singly, although the original plan had been to try them in groups of three, three, and two. The board was composed of three members of the Navy.

In the proceedings, character and work references were important, but so was testimony concerning an individual's sexual activity and motherhood. In fact, it was the kind of situation where a defendant's case was helped by a man's description of a one-night stand on the beach with her!

During the course of the hearings, the Navy had to prove that each defendant had solicited, attempted, or engaged in homosexual acts. Thus, testimony to the effect that "everyone knew what was going on down there" or a statement that a defendant had patronized a gay bar or gone to "Gay Night" at Magic Mountain (amusement park) would not be sufficient. Witnesses had to be (and sometimes were) quite specific as to what had been said and seen. Some of the women denied all charges, but at least one woman refused to make a statement about her sexual preference, insisting that what should matter was her record as a sailor. Some referred to sexual play, such as giving someone a hickie to get that person in trouble with a mate, and noted that this was done, in fun, by both women and men.

The first two defendants (Gaskins and Underwood) used "boyfriend" testimony as a part of their defense. Gaskins, the mother of an eight-year-old, denied being a homosexual and was acquitted 3–0. Underwood emphasized her excellent seamanship, refused to make a flat denial, and was also acquitted, 2–1. She "seemed stunned" by the acquittal. Defense lawyers had argued that although there may have been "normal expressions of affection," both women were good sailors whose sexual preference should be of no concern; nor should misinterpretations of their behavior by others be a basis for punishment. As Gaskins said, "It's all right for a male to grab ass, but the Navy didn't know that females did the same thing." In Gaskins' trial, the Navy offered only three witnesses. One had, she said, lied to NIS agents because she had been threatened; one admitted having had four fights with one of the defendants; and the third testified to giggles, whispers, and the sound of zippers. The defense had a list of twenty-five witnesses, including fiancées, ex-boyfriends, and a hypnotist.

The third and fourth sailors to be tried were two Black women, Alicia Harris and Wendi Williams, both firemen. Harris, just eighteen, denied being a lesbian to the end, but there were witnesses to a kiss in the boiler room. Harris, her attorney said, "made the mistake of being very good friends with Wendi Williams." Williams said, "They must think that I am the dumbest nigger in the Navy to do it in the room [the berthing area] with 60 people." Both were convicted and ordered discharged. Many believed Harris' testimony.

After the first four hearings, charges against the remaining four defendants were dropped. The Navy had been through an embarrassing ordeal —an ordeal apparently begun because regulations against homosexuality provided a way for individuals to hurt each other; an ordeal in which Navy officials were manipulated; an ordeal for the innocent as well as the guilty; an ordeal that did not stand the test of daylight well. Relatively powerless young women had been badgered into statements by investigators who could not be called as witnesses. One of the witnesses testified that she "hated" one of the defendants; a second testified that she wanted a transfer—*and* that her boyfriend had had sex with one of the women charged.

It is hard to estimate the effect of such incidents on the morale of Navy women, but their morale did not seem to be a consideration. Nor was there much sense that justice, however unpleasant, had been done. Even if one accepted a "no homosexuals" policy as reasonable, the services' incapacity to enforce it and the damage done to the unconvicted and even uncharged would seem to cast doubt on current practice. Nevertheless, the services are not seeking repeal of this policy, dubious, destructive, and embarrassing as its enforcement seems to be. Indeed, the services seem almost to take advantage of most defendants' desire to avoid publicity, and perhaps prosecution would be less assiduous if it were less unpublic.

The regulation that called for the discharge of individuals for lesbian "tendencies" is now under attack because, as attorney McGreivy says, it calls for punishment for thoughts and the expression of those thoughts, no acts being necessary.[39] McGreivy has pursued this line as the attorney for an Army Reserve officer, Carolyn Pruitt, who acknowledged in a newspaper interview that she was a lesbian and also the pastor of a church that serves a largely homosexual congregation. Pruitt's position is that her activities as a civilian minister are "beyond the military's reach."

Some homosexuals, then, are both admitting their preference and insisting that they be allowed to stay. During World War II, homosexuality was apparently tolerated if concealed, even though it was then against the law in every jurisdiction. Today it is not tolerated, although homosexual behavior *is* legal in more than half the states.[40]

In sum, homosexuality is not permitted in the military. Even though there is more homosexuality among men than women in the civilian population, a much higher percentage of enlisted women are discharged for homosexuality than enlisted men or male and female officers. Does society permit concrete expressions of affection (such as kissing, hugging, and even sleeping in the same bed) between women in civilian life that are interpreted as homosexual in military life? Are enlisted women more closely supervised? Are lesbians attracted to an institution that bans them? Is the military willing to lose women in situations where it would be unwilling to lose men? Does the military environment create homosexuality? Are women homosexuals more vindictive and, therefore, more likely to report each other? Is the military's willingness to investigate and to charge the same for women as for men? These questions remain unanswered and, for the most part, unasked.

CONCLUSION

Military women won several dramatic court victories affecting military policies in the aftermath of the civil rights movement and the Vietnam War. These were won while the nation was at peace, but also in an environment where most assumed that women would not be used in combat even if a war broke out. The legality of constraints against the use of women in combat now seems established. It also seems clear, however, that particular restrictions derive from particular interpretations of policies and will therefore vary with election results and executive appointments. In the near future, military women are unlikely to successfully challenge policies in the courts. Judges seem to have returned to a "hands off the military" line of reasoning—a position energetically argued by the new Chief Justice, William Rehnquist. Thus, military women's day in court may be over. Frontiero, Crawford, and Owens won fine decisions, but their latter-day sisters should not expect to repeat their success.

# 6

## Research

In the fall of 1983, most of the community doing research on military women, as well as representatives of military policymakers from both Congress and the Pentagon, gathered in Chicago at a special meeting of the Inter-University Seminar on Armed Forces and Society.[1] This may have been the largest and most professional gathering of its kind; nevertheless, the climax of the meeting was the impassioned plea by a woman Marine officer: "No more research!"

The warm reception given this apparently perverse appeal was due partly to the irrelevance felt by many in the audience, who had learned only hours before that some 265 marines had been killed when their barracks were blown up in Beirut. (Although no one in the room knew it then, at the moment the officer spoke other marines were already on their way to invade the island of Grenada.) The audience's approval probably also reflected the feeling that research had too often been directed toward limiting the participation of and opportunities for women and emphasizing the ways in which women were different from and inferior to men. By 1983 many military women wanted to get on with their work and let that work speak for itself.

During the Carter administration (1976–1980), executive branch policymakers were committed to women's increased participation. Thus, "getting on with it" may have been a good strategy. In a less benign environment, however, research and knowledge about research techniques can be most useful to women and their supporters. In-house studies can be evaluated (and if necessary countered) by insisting that queries be placed in context. For example, at one time a great deal of attention was given to collecting information about time lost from work because of pregnancy. Military women familiar with research methodologies asked the question basic to all research: "Of what is this an instance?" When it was seen that the general issue was "lost time," it was recognized that all reasons for lost time—including being absent without leave—should be considered. When this was done, the Navy's data actually showed men losing more time than women—even with women's higher losses for medical reasons generally and pregnancy in particular. Later studies also came to the conclusion that women and men lost similar amounts of time, even though pregnancy-related lost time is substantial and exclusively female.[2]

Research on women can also help analysts construct more adequate studies of such continuing problems as attrition and failure to reenlist. Over the years the military has developed certain beliefs about attrition. One is that high school graduates are more likely to complete their enlistments than nongraduates. This has justified the use of educational requirements as well as minimum test scores and has led to the assumption that the "quitters" are the less able. One study of Black men showed, however, that nongraduates have lower rates of discharge than high school graduates for personality disorders and expediency and fewer in-lieu-of-court-martial discharges.[3] Another study found that marriage and children affected men's and women's reenlistment in opposite ways.[4] Such findings suggest that more suitable predictors should be sought or that different predictors are better for different groups.

Research can also raise issues that would not otherwise be raised because of lack of sensitivity, or because of an excess of sensitivity—for example, women's morale under different commanders.[5]

Two things must be remembered in assessing research findings on military women. The first is women's heterogeneity. The second is that the questions about women have characteristically been *should* and *can* they serve. For men service is assumed, and research on them is directed toward "how best?"

Let us turn now to an examination of military research on women, its content, and its link to military policies.

## STUDIES BY THE AIR FORCE AND THE NAVY

The Air Force Human Resources Laboratory (AFHRL) at Brooks Air Force Base (Texas) publishes an annual annotated bibliography of technical reports it has produced or sponsored. Other studies are conducted by students at the Air Universities (Maxwell and the Institute of Technology at Wright-Patterson). In addition the Air Force Academy has sponsored a set of conferences on "Psychology in Department of Defense" and published the proceedings.

The Air Force also conducts numerous studies at its Manpower and Personnel Center (AFMPC) at Randolph Air Force Base. Typically these studies (such as "Integrating Women into Non-Traditional Jobs: Air Force Rated Women," prepared in 1979) are for internal use. Even though no classified material is presented, access is sometimes difficult, and often replication "without the expressed consent of HQ USAF" is forbidden.

In addition, the Air Force personnel office in the Pentagon (DCS/MP) maintains a *Fact Book* that provides ready answers to the questions most often posed by media representatives, elected officials, and other members of the military (including the Air Force). The mimeographed 137-page *Fact Book* for 1980 covers fifteen topics (including civilians, discipline, enlisted personnel, medical care, reserves, strength, and women). The last item under "Miscellaneous" is a list of Air Force Personnel Surveys. In 1980, ten were listed as having been completed that year, three as in the field, and four as projected. Sample sizes ranged from 657 (Reserve Readership Survey) to 28,000 (Commissary Patrons Survey). Two were specifically on women: Women's Uniform Items, and Women in Missile Operations.

In briefings to selected audiences—for example, DACOWITS—these quite different studies are sometimes treated as though they were equally reliable, valid, and appropriate bases for the making of policy. But even if one somehow learns of the existence of a particular study (often through a reference to it in the *Air Force Times*), it can be difficult to obtain for independent assessment. Even a senior Air Force officer seconded to a research institute for the purpose of writing a book on women in the military found that she had to threaten to sue under the Freedom of Information Act (FOIA) to get copies of studies necessary to her research.[6] Sometimes copies of studies will be promised but not mailed. Ironically, the Air Force, which appears to have the fewest problems with public relations, with personnel in general, and with the integration of women in particular, often appears less willing to share information than the Army, whose efforts and motives concerning women have more often aroused suspicion.

Studies conducted at the Naval Personnel Research and Development Center (NPRDC) in San Diego are available through the Defense Technical Information Center at Cameron Station, Alexandria, Virginia, and through the National Technical Information Service in Springfield, Virginia. Continuity in the professional staff as well as a willingness to share research findings with the scholarly community allow researchers to get a good handle on the issues and data through direct contact. Although Navy research addresses issues that concern policymakers, the studies seem to be insulated from policy pressures; they adhere to research conventions and appear to be free to offer results different from the ones one might guess were wanted. For instance, in assessing women's propensity to enlist, one study used queries based on different policy conditions: (1) the present (combat-restricted) policy; (2) increased use of women in nontraditional fields; (3) use of women in close support and aboard support ships and aircraft; and (4) equivalent use of men and women. The results showed men and women with similar low inclinations to enlist at all. Both were least likely to enlist under condition 1 (present circumstances), more likely under conditions 3 and 4, but most likely under condition 2.[7] The answers are relevant to an assessment of women's willingness to take nontraditional jobs. Although a substantial portion of potential recruits might not be interested in nontraditional jobs, another group of applicants *may* be interested. Therefore, a different policy might change the kind of women who enlist without changing the number enlisting.

Navy studies on pregnancy found that women missed two weeks of work during the prenatal period and six weeks after giving birth, for a total of eight weeks. The Army has claimed an average of fifteen weeks off the job and considerable damage to morale and productivity. The Navy found negligible effects on each.[8] This suggests the importance of having the different services conduct their affairs and research in relative independence. If each service were not studying women separately, the only controls would be civilian women, and differences might be attributed to differences between military and civilian life, when in fact other causes, such as service, leadership, location, and policy differences, may be more relevant.

ARMY RESEARCH

It is impossible to review every study done on women by the various services and DOD in the 1970s and 1980s, but it is worth following the research program of one service to note the questions asked, the answers discovered, and the policies resulting. The Army research program will serve as an illustration of the process. It must not be assumed that the other services asked the same questions, found the same answers, or arrived at the same policies. In each case mission, leadership, and precedent had a good deal to do with decision making.

The nine major studies conducted by the Army were:

Women in the Army Study (WITA), December 1976, by ODCSPER*
Utilization of Women in the Army, July 1977, by MILPERCEN
Women Content in Units (MAX WAC), October 1977, by ARI
Evaluation of Women in the Army (EWITA), March 1978, by ODCSPER
Women Content in the Army (REF WAC), May 1978, by ARI
Comprehensive Evaluation of Total Integration of Women in the Army, March 1980, by ODCSPER
Enlisted Women in the Army, April 1982, by the Army Audit Agency

*Office of the Deputy Chief of Staff for Personnel.

Lost Time and Utilization, October 1982, by ARI
Women in the Army Policy Review (WITAPR), November 1982,
ODCSPER

These studies came after the first rapid buildup of women and before the stabilization of both their number and policies about them that
occurred in the mid-1980s. During the period of the studies women's
numbers doubled, they were integrated into existing corps, some 90 percent of MOSs were opened to them, mandatory weapons qualification
training for women was begun, and a shared core curriculum for men's
and women's basic training was developed.*

The Women in the Army Study (WITA, 1976), then, was charged with
examining an institution that had already undergone change and faced
even more change. The WITA study sought to integrate the judgments of
field commanders and evidence drawn from social science research.

Concerns expressed by commanders at that time included the perceptions that:

1.  Women's relative lack of physical strength impaired their
    performance.
2.  Pregnancies resulted in understrength units and/or lack of
    deployability.
3.  Women needed more physical, weapons, tactical, and field
    training.[9]

The WITA study recommended, first, that attrition studies dealing with
actual specialty training be used to determine the rate of failure due to
physical incapacity, and that physical standards then be developed to reduce attrition to an acceptable level.[10] Second, it recommended that "the
retention option" for pregnant women be returned to the Army and that
data justifying this position and data on single parents be systematically
developed. (Data then available showed that at any one time approximately 3.8 percent of women on active duty were pregnant or on postnatal
leave, and therefore nondeployable. Another study showed pregnancy as
the cause in only one in ten instances of nondeployability.)[11]

Third, WITA noted that a core Basic Initial Entry Training (BIET) Program would soon be tested at Fort Jackson on 880 male and 880 female

*These changes were not a subject the Army enjoyed acknowledging. Even a lieu-
tenant colonel conducting a research project as an Army War College student was not
allowed to see a copy of the Army's report on the potential impact of the passage of the
ERA (Charles J. Garvey, *Analysis of the Changing Role of Women in the United States
Army* [Carlisle Barracks, Pa.: U.S. Army War College, 1974], p. 116).

trainees, and that provisions were being made for military and physical training for women who had already completed their basic training.[12]

WITA also observed that much of the research relating to women concerned attitudes and demonstrated (1) that men were more conservative than women; (2) that men's attitudes and perceptions were so varied that further study was necessary; but (3) that "the belief that men do a better job is so widespread that it could affect unit capabilities."[13]

While noting the critical nature of psychological and sociological responses to stress and combat, WITA concluded that "only limited information is available with regard to psychological and sociological factors impacting on the utilization of women." Commanders had not reported psychological and sociological factors as a significant problem. Nevertheless, the report concluded that women should not serve in combat, that "questions must be answered before any significant changes are made to current policies and programs," and that the Army's central concern should be the number of women it can absorb "without degrading mission capability."[14] In short, women were assumed to be handicapping, and the burden of proof was placed squarely on the advocates of change.

How did WITA propose to compute the magic, "nondegrading" number of women the Army could absorb?[15] First, it reviewed the Woman's Enlisted Expansion Model (WEEM) and the list of MOSs open and closed to enlisted women; next, it sketched a design for a "quantitative program" for determining accession requirements. Again, the Army's primary fear was that it would enlist too many women and degrade effectiveness.

The WEEM model was designed to establish the maximum number of women the Army could use in each MOS at each rank, taking into consideration women's combat exclusion, rotation equity, and "career progression," i.e., ensuring noncombatant males opportunities for the variety of jobs they needed for career development. Also, women's enlistments were limited so that they could have a "normal" career progression, that is, avoid being capped at a particular rank. This is discussed more fully in the next chapter.

The Army's WEEM analysis was based on particular job slots, but WITA also analyzed accessions on the basis of MOS. Some whole MOSs were (and are) closed to women because of the combat exclusion, while some slots in other MOSs were closed or restricted for the reasons listed above. Ultimately the 1976 report concluded that only 31 MOSs should be closed for "combat" and 13 for management (mostly rotation) reasons —a great change from the 297 closed in 1972. The 53,000 jobs classified as "available" to women likewise represented a great increase over the 19,000 positions defined as open in 1972, but "available " jobs remained a small proportion of the Army's 677,000 slots.[16]

WITA also recommended that the distribution of women "be equitable among units."[17] The effect of such a policy, of course, would be to distribute women broadly and isolate them from each other. WITA also proposed that units closer to the front have lower proportions of women because those units might be drawn into combat, the work was likely to be heavier, and mobility demands would be high.[18] These recommendations, then, were the foundation for the Army's new policies on women.

The next year (1977) the Army staff was charged by DOD with the further task of considering just how women could be utilized, and what the effect would be of expanding their number to 100,000 (85,000 enlisted) by 1983. (The goal then in place for 1983 was only 51,000.) The Army's response was unenthusiastic, and new concerns came to the surface. These included women's purported reluctance to enter nontraditional fields and the "bow-wave" that would develop, and perhaps lead to "disproportionate" promotions for women, if large numbers of them were rapidly recruited and nearly all at the entry level. Concern continued about the lack of readiness of the unknown number of pregnant women, single parents, and military couples. The Army did agree, though, to begin letting women reserve training seats and to cease letting men reserve women's seats—that is, women would be able to reserve a time and a specialty for enlistment, as men had long been able to do, while men would no longer be allowed to reserve desirable slots planned for women. (The old policy had had the effect of giving women only "leftover" assignments.)

Yet the Army resisted DOD's instruction to plan on doubling its women, instead urging that women be held at the current level at least "until data becomes [sic] available from current research initiatives."[19] The Army argued that more data were needed before it could establish MOS physical-strength requirements or estimate the likelihood of its being able to recruit and retain women in nontraditional MOSs. Thus, the Army's response to pressure to increase the number of women wearing its uniform was to call for and to wait upon "research."

That same year saw the publication of the Army Research Institute's first major social science study on women. Titled *Women Content in Units Force Development Test*, the ARI study was usually referred to as "MAX WAC." This field experiment was designed to test the effect of different percentages (up to 35 percent) of women on the "operational capability" of company-sized support units, including signal, maintenance, military police, transportation, and medical companies.[20] This was a direct response to Army concerns and assumptions about the need for an "equitable" distribution of women, and about the appropriate proportion of women in different units.

Forty companies, eight of each of the five types, were given performance tests during a three-day field exercise. These were conducted by a team of officer–observers; judgments about performance were also collected from company NCOs and company members. The results showed that the proportion of women in the company was *not* related, positively or negatively, to performance. In addition, officers were asked to indicate what factors they believed contributed to overall performance. The officers gave leadership, training, and morale ratings of 32, 30, and 19 percent respectively. Personnel turbulence was given a 10 percent rating; the proportion of women, a 7 percent rating.[21] Thus, the study showed no degradation, and the officers involved did not see women as a primary influence on overall performance. The study did say, though, that women were better utilized when they were numerous and when a unit was short of men, that protectiveness could lead to additional work for men, that acceptance was a function of command attitude, and that women were not receiving adequate field training during basic training.[22]

A critique of the ARI study by the Army's Operational Test and Evaluation Agency (signed by Gen. Julius Becton) concluded that it did not offer "an empirical basis to objectively support establishment of an upper bound on potential female content of military units." The Becton recommendations were as follows:

1. The proportion of women should be determined by MOS, not by company.
2. Women's performance in extended field exercises should be studied.
3. Basic training should be integrated.
4. Women's uniforms should be improved.
5. Field commanders should be given guidance on pregnancy, fraternization, and billeting.

The report also noted important uncontrolled variables in the study, which included a lack of women NCOs, a lack of command support for the study, and the high quality of the women. It queried what the long-term effect would be of having women NCOs in command of men, and how problems would differ if the Army recruited women of the same quality as its men instead of women of higher quality. In the long run, Becton's report noted, male NCOs would acquire experience working with women, which should reduce gallantry, shyness, and low expectations, and women would come to the units better trained—for example, with weapons training.[23]

Because the effect of long-term stress remained a question for many, a team of observers visited a free-play exercise ("Braveshield") conducted at Twenty Nine Palms, California, in July 1977.[24] Their findings suggested that sharing the training ordeal encouraged the acceptance of women by peers and supervisors. It appears that women were more "shocked" by field circumstances than men, but they adjusted—and maintained hygiene and grooming while men eased up on both. (The women did complain about unnecessarily unpleasant sanitary facilities.) Again, neither the "test" nor the "observation" produced any evidence that the percentage of women affected performance. Thus, the Army's own research failed to prove what had been assumed. Yet these data were not used to shape new policy, and the unease of commanders was not dispelled.

The next year the ARI tested the effect of longer field experience. *Women Content in the Army—Reforger 77* (or REF WAC) issued in May 1978, concluded, "The presence of female soldiers on REFORGER 77 did not impair the performance of combat support and combat-support units." But, it noted, eighteen of ninety MOSs, in the participating units, were designated as physically too demanding for women by 50 percent or more of the supervisors, and a number of "leadership and management problems" were evident.

Besides reinforcing the previous year's finding that "women content" did not affect performance, REF WAC produced a variety of supplemental findings. First, 15 percent of enlisted men and 29 percent of enlisted women were not deployable from CONUS (Continental United States)—2 percent of men and 11 percent of women for personal reasons. Second, "considerable and widespread bias against women was observed in units, most significantly among first-line supervisors. . . . As often occurs with targets of bias, women as a group were rated poorly (questionnaire responses), whereas they were rated as highly as their male counterparts when rated individually." Third, "most NCO's just do not want them around." [25]

These unit evaluations were part of a research program that also included individual performance tests, an assessment of physical requirements, and an investigation of ways to modify equipment or procedures to reduce required time and physical effort. A substantial future research program was outlined in the report. In fact, however, after the ARI had produced two major studies showing that it could not be shown that women decrease performance, its five-year research plan dematerialized. The studies on women that would appear in the future would tend to be based on field judgments rather than social science measurement. The conclusions would be different, too.

The inches-thick *Evaluation of Women in the Army* (EWITA) was also prepared in early 1978. In this report, prepared at the Army Administration Center (Fort Benjamin Harrison), the Army acknowledged the difficulty of defining "combat." Previously, definitions were based on organizational units and their relationship to the "forward edge of battle." It had been assumed, though, that women working in, for example, communications, repair, or supply would be required to move into and out of zones to which they could not be assigned. EWITA added yet another dimension to the Army's latest definition by arguing that women should be eligible to operate weaponry fired in a non-line-of-sight (mechanically aimed), indirect mode.[26]

The EWITA data were based largely on interviews and questionnaires about perceptions of women (discussed in Chapter 4). The report specifically recommended that the Army:

1. Open three MOSs now closed to enlisted women
2. Close twenty MOSs to them, primarily because of the combat ban
3. Close seventeen now open for reasons of career progression
4. Close fourteen now open for reasons of physical incapacity[27]

EWITA estimated the theoretical maximum number of enlisted women as 159,700 (27 percent of service personnel), although it predicted significant management problems if the Army attempted to reach that number quickly.[28] In fact, given women's interest and current enlistment standards for them, the Army could recruit only about 20,000 a year, a number that would raise the total to 75,000 in 1983. (DOD was proposing a total of 100,000.) To recruit the maximum possible number of women (an end strength of 159,700), the Army said, it would have to lower admission standards, which would result in higher attrition, or some MOSs would have to be closed to men and others controlled (i.e., slots appropriate for women would have to be saved for them). Thus, the problem was not just setting limits on women, but also properly distributing them.[29]

EWITA identified four "critically significant" issues in the integration of women. First, as "location" is primary to real estate, so "pregnancy" seemed to be to integration: "In general, unit leaders do not cope well with the entire pregnancy issue. In many cases the women do not pull their share of extra duty, are exempted from field duty, draw full pay and allowances without earning them, and are not required to maintain minimum dress standards."[30] The report estimated that full-term pregnancies actually resulted in twenty-one weeks of lost time rather than the "normal" ten, and urged as a solution discharge or absence without pay until deployable—even to locations where dependents are not authorized.

To cope with the second issue, physical strength, a gender-free test system was recommended. The third issue involved substandard overseas housing, especially in isolated duty sites, and improvement was recommended. Inadequate field uniforms and equipment for women were next. The report not only urged improvement, but recommended that "clothing/ equipment be designed/engineered for the average soldier without regard to sex when possible." One result of this suggestion was an amazing and elaborate Army program directed toward "unisex" uniform sizing. Almost unheard of, interestingly enough, were engineering efforts to make equipment more manageable by women (and, presumably, by allies of small stature).

EWITA emphatically called attention to the existence of other problems that were not "just women's": (1) leadership and supervision of women by men trained to lead only men; (2) lack of field and military training for women; (3) nondeployability of sole parents; (4) fraternization; and (5) intraservice marriage. Questionnaire data showed continued concern about men's reaction to women's responses to stress, and women's self-image, emotionality, and (lack of) aggressiveness.

This report, then, portrayed difficult problems, including many perceptual and attitude problems. Of the twenty-nine people assigned to develop the report, close to half (thirteen) were women, and the director was a female lieutenant colonel. Perhaps this accounts for the spirit of the study, which seems to focus on solving integration problems rather than the grudging admission of outsiders into a previously homogeneous group.

By 1980 the (always reluctant) Army was committed to 96,000 women by 1985, and the office of the deputy chief of staff for personnel was again undertaking an in-depth review of policies and programs affecting the "career opportunities and quality of life of Army women." (One begins to understand the plea for "no more studies"!) The "Comprehensive Evaluation of Total Integration of Women in the Army" reviewed thirteen items and asked sixteen commanders of major units to comment.

By this time the Army was coding 75 percent of officer spots and 58 percent of enlisted spots (454,000 of 783,000) as "interchangeable." The Army was committed to continuation of the combat-exclusion policy, but its commanders recognized that if hostilities were to break out, some women would be exposed to combat and become casualties in spite of that policy. It was important, they felt, that the public understand this. The 1980 decision to equalize recruiting standards for women and men had resulted in a surge of enlistees, but the women continued to enter traditional fields. The Army noted that the 1974 experience with nongraduates suggested that as many as 60 percent of the women might not complete three years of service. Thus, attrition remained a grave concern. Men's rates were bimodal: high school graduates left at a rate of about 25 percent, and nongraduates at a rate of over 40 percent. Women high school graduates attrited at about the same rate as male nongraduates, but women nongraduates left at a rate of over 55 percent. No satisfactory explanation was offered.[31]

The study noted that a training package on issues such as rape, sex education, and leadership was being prepared for Common Military Education and Training (continuing education). Sexual harassment, it said, was not tolerated, although the Army had no plans to address the subject beyond an already issued policy statement that enjoined commanders to educate, to inform, and to enforce policies related to harassment.

Pregnancy rates were reported as high; however, they were calculated to include women who left the Army, those who stayed in, and even those who terminated their pregnancies. (Beginning in 1979 abortions became difficult to obtain under military auspices, and many women may have gone private. This would account for a substantial drop in reported pregnancies.) In spite of their general discomfort with pregnancy, however, commanders did not report that pregnancy affected the deployability of their units.

A number of commanders expressed a need for child-care facilities and frustration over women's uniforms. There was not much enthusiasm for single-sizing or for offering women small men's clothing—especially boots. One commander recommended adding a stripe to women's pants and the "recision of the policy to allow females to carry umbrellas."

Women's need for privacy and personal security was given special emphasis. At least one commander insisted upon the need to address and solve the problem of harassment. Others reemphasized the lack of gynecologists and the failure to counsel women about reenlisting as men are counseled. Several emphasized the need to teach women assertiveness and the kind of responses to verbal harassment that would swiftly and successfully put an end to it. One candid response noted that because women who plunged into nontraditional jobs were labeled lesbian or "bull-dyke," many women shied away from those jobs.

A number of commanders urged the provision of maternity uniforms. One declared, "The simplest uniform purchase becomes a long-term Herculean undertaking." Another asserted, "The Army causes its low female retention rate. Fewer studies and more action should be the order of the day."

Army studies followed a pattern of looking at women and only occasionally looking at women and men. Moreover, they appeared to look at women as a problem, and to imply that the solution was to limit their use. Data *from* women rather than *about* them were not collected as often as they might have been, nor were such data analyzed as carefully as commanders' complaints. A notable exception was the briefing presented at the World Wide Symposium on Women in the Army in July 1977. In addition to the standard "women questions," it presented thirteen pages of strong comments offered by women who had filled out questionnaires about their service experience. Many complained of being underutilized and underchallenged—a perspective dramatically different from that of their commanders and supervisors. Yet these data were not analyzed or made the basis for policy recommendations.

The next major studies did not appear until 1982. The two-year hiatus was not filled by the quiet implementation of policies harmonious with previous studies and plans. In fact, recruitment goals were greatly altered (by being held steady), and the integrated basic training program put into place in the fall of 1977 was ended. Instead of having platoons of women and men and integration at the company level (a unit of about 200 persons), companies were resegregated. No research studies were made public to justify either major policy change.

The Women in the Army Policy Review (WITAPR) went through several transformations and was kept under wraps until it was finally released in November 1982. It found women to be of only limited use and was energetically criticized. Established in May 1981, the review group was originally scheduled to have ready for the Commander's Conference that October a report assessing women's retention and the impact of women on the Army's mission and readiness, quality of military life, *and* cost effectiveness.[32] Of the nineteen issues on its original agenda, it developed only two: physical-strength requirements and the combat coding of MOSs. Little reference was made to such earlier studies as WITA, EWITA, MAX WAC, and REF WAC. The issue of pregnancy was sent to DOD for resolution, apparently because the Army's wishes could not be squared with what was thought to be legally required. Lost time, single parents, clothing, child care, harassment, and similar items were defined as "institutional" problems, to be dealt with in a routine way by the responsible Army unit, and were left out of the final report. Cost effectiveness was not systematically studied, although the extra uniform and medical costs associated with women would almost certainly have been balanced by women's fewer dependents and ease of recruitment.

Work began on WITAPR under the direction of Maj. Gen. Robert T. Wetzel, assisted by five officers from ODCSPER, an enlisted woman, and a civilian employee, Cecile Landrum. An advisory group of several dozen women and men—including distinguished scholars, civic leaders, and businesswomen was taken on a field trip to two bases in Georgia in late August. By the time of this trip, Wetzel had been replaced by Brig. Gen. Ronald Zeltman, who found the civilian women on the tour "radical" and eased them (and Landrum) out of the picture after a December meeting to which not all of the women on the panel were invited. (Among those omitted was Sarah McClendon, journalist and former WAC known for her cross-examination of public figures.) Zeltman, who planned to classify the study, said it was designed, "to develop corrective action." He did not expect child care to receive a high priority, but he did predict that a plan to assist civilian spouses in finding employment would be put in place!

At a dramatic meeting of DACOWITS in the fall of 1982, members insisted on learning the contents of the report and of the Army plans. Women in uniform spoke from the floor about women's issues, a DACO-WITS social scientist called the report "nothing but a snow job," an Air Force officer charged that "the Army developed its conclusions and then began looking for rationale to support them," and a retired Air Force general said that the study had created "major morale problems among female troops."[33]

The Army was clearly uncomfortable about its women. It would espe-cially have liked to discharge pregnant women, but felt that the law would not permit this. Since it could not change what was really bother-ing it, and since the issues that the Army itself deemed most essential to its mission—leadership and morale—were poorly defined and under scrutiny elsewhere, the directors of WITAPR focused on tangible and less controversial matters: physical strength and the government's wish to shield women from combat. The way in which strength and participation in combat were assessed appeared technical, objective, and irrefutable. The assessments were in fact based on judgments made by individuals who were not necessarily impartial and their result was to limit the use of women. The assumptions and line of reasoning suggest that this was what was intended.

The study of MOS assumed that each individual must be able to fulfill every MOS requirement under combat conditions. This ignored the fact that women were not to be in combat, that most work is teamwork, that the military has always found it possible to work with small men, and that new techniques and modified equipment could make it possible for women to do tasks that are now difficult or impossible. The finding that only 26 percent of women but 100 percent of men could meet the Army's heavy, very heavy, and medium heavy work standards seems to demon-strate that standards and equipment were designed to accommodate all men but set without regard to women.[34] The study did not demonstrate that particular standards were tied to military requirements. Nor did it follow the WITA recommendation that standards be set by the schools —that is, be tied to training for the specialty. The study argued that 92 percent of the women in the Army were physically unfit for the very jobs held by over half the women in it—! even though field studies had not shown that women's presence affected performance.

The fact that Army women's exclusion from combat is based on Army regulation made an Army definition of combat necessary. One was offered in December 1977, a second was recommended by EWITA after Congress required both a definition of combat and recommendations for expanding job classifications for women. The exclusion provision used for Army policy purposes said: "Women are authorized to serve in any officer or enlisted specialty except those specified, at any organizational level, and in any unit of the Army except Infantry, Armor, Cannon Field Artillery Units of battalion/squadron size or smaller. Women may not serve on Scout or Attack helicopters."[35]

This definition focuses on what a unit or MOS does. The WITAPR study used a definition involving direct exposure to fire, high probability of direct physical contact, and substantial risk of capture. Thus, geography became central, with MOS diminished in relevance, for example, because noncombat MOS could be assigned to positions not only in the combat zone but forward of that zone. Individuals and fighting could both be mobile, and supply units, for instance, would have to bring matériel to the front. For these reasons WITAPR argued that the definition of direct combat (from which women should be excluded) should take into account not only unit mission and assigned duties, but also location (potential enemy presence) and tactical requirements (the committing of reserves to combat).

The WITAPR approach was to examine each position in the Army and assign it a "probability of direct combat" code number ranging from 1 to 7. The intent was to remove from direct combat the women whose noncombat jobs placed them in geographical jeopardy. In essence, a geographical exclusion was added to the mission exclusion. Further, the coding incorporated the Women Enlisted Expansion Model, which excluded women from other assignments on the grounds of promotion and rotation equity, saving some good and safe jobs for men as well as some difficult and dangerous ones.

The WITAPR coded 302,000 of the Army's 572,000 jobs, well over half, "P1," and therefore men-only. One result of the coding was a recommendation to close twenty-three more MOSs to women. Again, analysis was limited to slots, but closure recommendations involved MOSs— whole categories.[36]

Army policy was being driven by managers' studies, not by research. Often those studies were summations of opinion; sometimes they were based on reports that were not generally accessible. Those reports were in turn based on assumptions that were not necessarily widely shared or supported by evidence.

It is clear that the rapid expansion in the number of women and their integration represented a challenge to the Army. Its arguments about location, rotation, and promotion were not improper. Its emphasis on the ability to do its job was appropriate. What casts doubt on the enterprise is that available data that might support an expanded role for women seemed to be ignored, and deficiencies in women's performance seemed to be attributed to their being women rather than to any other element of the situation.

A case in point: it had long been assumed that women detract from readiness. The Army had even directed the ARI to collect data to prove this assumption in the form of a study of lost time. When those data became available in preliminary form in the fall of 1981, they were not made a part of the WITAPR report to the public. Why not? Perhaps, because once again, the research did not support the perceptions of commanders.

The new study showed, first, that two-thirds of all soldiers were away from their jobs during a five-day observation period. Second, women did not lose more time than men for health-related reasons. Third, they did not lose more time for home and family reasons. Fourth, they lost less time for disciplinary reasons. Overall, women did not lose significantly more time over five days of record keeping than men. However, data *recollected* (as opposed to recorded) over a four-week period *did* show women as losing more time.[37] The findings of this carefully managed empirical study were withheld from the public for at least a year (the technical report is dated October 1982) and were not used to dispel doubts and reservations about women soldiers. By the time the data were released, the Army had already shifted its grounds for limiting women's accessions to physical testing and combat-probability coding. It was as if "studies" and research were means to an end of minimizing women's participation in the Army—tools not for the shaping of policy, but for the defense of policy.

In the same way there seemed to be a general belief that although women were most needed in nontraditional (for women) jobs, they did not want those jobs and left them (attrited) at high rates. Yet an ARI study of attrition (on 1976 cohort data) showed women's attrition from such jobs at 41 to men's 35 percent. (Black women's attrition was 28 percent.) While the data showed less attrition in traditional MOSs, there were substantial variations within the two categories. Moreover, men left women's nontraditional jobs at a high rate too. Clearly traditionality and gender were not sufficient explanations.[38]

A study with a profound bearing on women's utilization is set forth in a series of spring 1982 base reports conducted by the Army Audit Agency. The report from Fort McClellan, where women were trained as military police and in chemical specialties (two nontraditional fields), emphasized a need for physical standards, but also noted widespread perceptions of sexual mistreatment. It did not find that pregnancy affected unit readiness or that women were improperly assigned more frequently than men were.[39]

The report from Fort Hood also raised the issue of physical standards, reported a substantial amount of sexual mistreatment, and found that pregnancy did not affect readiness (although it saw a need for better implementation of dependent-care plans). Women soldiers were not being required to meet the physical standards necessary to their assignment, it noted, but men did not always meet them either, and *both* men and women were being certified as proficient in weapons firing when in fact they were not.[40] To a civilian, an over 50 percent variation between reported and observed hits in weapons training is hard to understand. A reported thirty hits with an observed three (as happened in one instance) is incomprehensible. Again, when it is found that women are not measuring up to standards, it is important to put the finding into context—the context of what men are doing, what is necessary, and how one "knows" that they are not measuring up.

Because sexual discrimination and harassment were reported as widespread, let us consider this finding further.[41] "Preferential" discrimination was more often described by men (65 percent) than was negative discrimination by women (45 percent). Neither women nor men reported harassment to a superior, but 71 percent of women said they had experienced or observed it. Indeed, 44 percent of the women believed that complaints about harassment would be treated as a joke. They felt threatened by harassment at service clubs (66 percent), at dining halls (46 percent), at theaters (35 percent), and at post exchanges (30 percent). A probably related report by one commander was that 50 percent of male soldiers, but only 15 percent of female ones used the dining facility.

The intensity of the Army's feelings about the "mismanagement" of women's assignments is demonstrated by the audit's overall recommendation that assignment policies be revised on an "interim basis" should an extended delay in developing new policies occur. Again, the apparent message ("Do it—do not wait for studies!") fitted a continuing pattern of acting on conviction and getting the studies later. It was awkward for the Army, however, if the later studies did not show what was expected. By 1982 the 65,000 Army women were in many specialties and holding 25 percent of the jobs open to them; moreover, the Army was actually constraining their use in traditionally female jobs because it wished to reserve many of those jobs for men. The deployment question still bothered commanders, but its form had shifted from assertions that women were unwilling to doubts about dependent-care plans. A new element in the discussion of pregnancy was the acknowledged variability of its incidence. Auditors had found great variation both between units and between specialties, which suggested that factors such as "leadership" might be playing an important role. (Auditors also found that half the pregnant women were single.) While recommending no change in policy until a more thorough analysis had been completed, the audit noted the need for a proper response to "pregnancy incidents."

The one new area covered in the 1982 audit was sexual mistreatment. The audit found policy clear and adequate but implementation emphatically inadequate: "Local commanders, officers, and senior noncommissioned officers generally seemed to be unaware of the significance of the problem." Data on *reported* incidents, which suggested that 9 percent of women had experienced mistreatment of some kind, may not seem overwhelming; however, a survey of 500 enlisted women suggests serious underreporting.[42] Two-thirds of the 500 women reported being victims of or observing sexual harassment; one-half said they had been victims of or had witnessed sexual discrimination; one-third of a group separating from the Army said they were doing so because of improper treatment.*

Related to underreporting is the fact that the very people to whom women would properly complain were often the villains. Forty percent of both men and women said privileges were offered to women soldiers in exchange for sexual favors, even in basic training. Moreover, many women not only did not trust the chain of command to act positively, but actually feared reprisal if they were to complain. The auditors also reported that women received little training in this area, that the training was usually voluntary, that classes on rape prevention "were not prescribed in the context of seriousness that it [the crime] deserved," and that "some instructors could not refrain from vulgar, insulting sexual connotations during their presentations." The report called on local leaders to encourage complaints, observe trouble areas such as barracks and service clubs, and deliver immediate and stern admonishments as the most effective means of creating a proper environment for women in the Army."

Finally, a study of enlisted women in Korea offered a new way of looking at these issues. One finding (consistent with other data) was that men in traditionally female jobs were the group most satisfied with their military experience. Thus, women may prefer to stay in "traditional" jobs because they are the best ones, not because the women themselves are "sexist." The second finding was that military women held strongly nega-

---

*In an Army "exit survey," about one-third of the women called sexual harassment a "very" or "extremely" important reason for leaving service. However, nine other reasons were (on average) more important, including a desire to return to school or find a civilian job, lack of respect, and poor NCOs (Glenda Y. Nogami, "Army Exit Survey," briefing for DACOWITS, 24 April 1985).

tive attitudes toward Korean-American relations and especially toward Korean women,[43] particularly those encountered in military clubs, whom they considered prostitutes. The study made no effort to interpret this finding, which may have related to the treatment servicewomen experienced when off duty in Korea or when working with Korean military personnel in an official capacity; or they may have been jealous of the attention Korean women attracted. But it seems likely that the extremely asymmetrical relationship between U.S. servicemen and Korean women, a relationship perhaps summed up in the role of *yobo*, or "temporary wife," was deeply troubling to the U.S. women.* Perhaps their feelings about Korean women represented displaced anger toward U.S. men ("So that's what men really want!") or empathy ("There but for the grace of God go I"). The strength of the findings, and intensity of the feelings reported in informal observations and conversations, suggests a need for further research and reflection.

CONCLUSION

Beginning in 1972 the Army (and the other services) recruited ever larger numbers of enlisted women. Because the women remained a small percentage both of the whole and of any unit to which they were assigned, were dispersed through a variety of noncombat jobs, and were integrated into many previously all-male units, their presence disturbed without altering. At the workplace they were perceived as novelties, not as necessities. Understanding this makes the nature of the research done about them more comprehensible. In general it assumed them to be liabilities, took for granted the legitimacy of any man's presence but tested that of every woman, and attempted to see women as men saw them, but rarely to see women *and* men as *women* saw them.

The women had a hard time. In "After-Action Report on Seminars Held for the Army Chaplains," a social scientist offered several examples: a woman going through a food service line was asked by the counterman, who had grabbed his penis, "Would you rather have this or mashed potatoes?" A second woman, who asked if there was room at a dining table, was told, "As long as I have a face, you have a place to sit." The response of commanding officers and NCOs, the report continued, was that "there was no way to prevent this kind of behavior since it's only natural for men to behave like animals."[44]

Officials' apparently cavalier attitude may be derived from the belief that if things were really bad, women would do something about it—

---

*Many Korean women are legal wives. It is estimated that more than a quarter of Air Force men stationed in the Pacific are married to Asian women.

that, like men, women could and would retaliate informally. However, women are not socialized to be their own enforcers, nor does the Army give them that training. In fact, the Army may be positively averse to it: witness the conviction of a woman soldier for sexual harassment, a conviction that included a sentence to "hard labor" for "grabbing" a man.[45] Since any number of Army women have endured frontal snatches with no recourse, one reads the news stories about this incident with a sense that the Army must be wholly out of touch, intent on running women out, and/or unwilling to let them settle their own accounts.

Thus, Army research appears to anticipate "bad news" *about* women and ignore "bad news" *for* them. "Good news" about women—for example, MAX WAC and REF WAC—evidently did not affect Army policy, except, perhaps, to encourage a deemphasis on ARI research on women.

In fact, Army policy was not shaped by research but by the judgment of commanders, a tendency exemplified by its decision to resegregate basic training in 1982. This was done without warning (and in particular without notifying DACOWITS), without evidence as to the negative effect of integration on men, and without consideration of resegregation's effect on women.

Precisely because experience is rooted in the usual, the familiar, it may not be adequate to guide decision making in changing circumstances. Research can be helpful, but it must be well designed and ask pertinent questions, and it must be conducted in a spirit of inquiry. It is important that it ask general questions about both women and men. It must ask crucial questions, and it must be subjected to public scrutiny.

Often the military deplores the risk involved in "social experimentation," but the hard fact is that if it does not experiment during the relative security of peacetime, it will almost surely be forced to do so in the exigency of war. So, if policy is as rational as pretended, shouldn't experiments be conducted?* Shouldn't research continue? Shouldn't policy be guided by it? If "opinion" is more important than "objectivity," how can one be sure that one knows the content, shape, intensity, saliency, and stability of opinion? Surely one can be surest if one conducts research.

In the recent past, research that might have reached negative conclusions about Blacks was unpopular because it was feared that such results might lead to discriminatory policies. In particular, questions that might lead to exclusion just were not asked: no one would have done a study like MAX WAC or REF WAC with race as a variable. The nation's need for cohesiveness simply requires the assumption of Black adequacy and

---

*One reason for the deep resistance to research that involves treating military personnel differently is the military's commitment to uniformity, to the identical treatment of personnel.

participation. At present the nation does not find debate and research about women's competence and participation intolerable. Indeed, some have argued that the "woman debate" has been functional for the military because it enhances the unity of Black and white men, whose own integration is relatively recent. Thus, when questions about women arise, it is important to remember that in the long run, men, women, and the nation may be best served by the pursuit of fairness as well as efficiency. In any event, good research is an essential. It is neither a luxury (because it is expensive) nor a liability (because it yields undesired answers).

# 7

# The
# Bottom
# Line:
# Accessions

Qualified women volunteers cannot count on being admitted to the military. Enlistments are guided by detailed accession plans that prescribe or predict the number of women to be inducted. That number is the bottom line. It represents the resolution of forces for increasing and for decreasing women's military participation.

In general, forces in favor of increase include war, the All-Volunteer Force, low military pay, and low civilian unemployment. Countervailing forces include limited assignments (because of the combat exclusion), and concerns about women's attrition rate, their preparedness, their preference for "traditional" jobs, and their cost.

Since women's accessions fall far below the proportion of young people who are women, this chapter will emphasize the reasons offered for keeping their numbers relatively low. These reasons can be summed up in three assertions: (1) that women have limited "use"; (2) that women are less available; and (3) that women are less valuable.

It is important to understand that accession goals are but one element of the Pentagon's very large-scale personnel planning. Each year the services induct, train, assign and reassign, evaluate, promote, reenlist, and/or discharge more than two million people. Most of these are enlisted; indeed, most are junior enlisted. Numerical goals are set for every step of the process: for geographical districts, for prior- and non-prior-service accessions, for trainees in the many and various specialties, for promotions to each rank, and for retention by rank and specialty. Thus, the setting of goals for women's accessions is wholly conventional; it long preceded the concept of "affirmative action" and has had as its principal purpose restricting (not increasing) the number of women. Let us begin by examining the military's conclusions about the "use" of women.

## THE "USE" OF WOMEN

The most important limit on the military's ability to "use" women derives from those laws which prohibit their (even voluntary) participation in combat. If recruitment were open, too many women might enlist, and the result would be an insufficient number of combat-eligible men in service. Establishing goals for accessions may not sound like a conceptually difficult problem, but setting specific goals by sex is not simple. One does not just say, "These are combat jobs. They are reserved for men. All other jobs will be filled by the best-qualified individual." Even when a definition of "combat" can be agreed upon, other problems remain. First, there is the problem of rotation. Because the Navy considers it unfair and impossible to assign anyone to permanent sea duty, a substantial number of shore jobs must be reserved as a rotation base for the (mostly male) sailors coming off ships. Thus women must be excluded from numerous jobs ashore as well as from those at sea. The other services have similar, though perhaps less obvious, needs to reserve rotation slots for men.

Slots are routinely withheld from women for reasons of "career development." Because a variety of assignments and also particular assignments enhance an individual's chance for promotion, it is thought that it would be unfair to men if women held too many desirable jobs—for example, as Pentagon aides. Hence, additional jobs are "reserved" for men (as opposed to "restricted" to them). An attempt is also made to ensure the possibility of a full career progression for women, although the combat restriction clearly impairs their promotability. Some argue that because one needs certain assignments to win promotion to top jobs, and because women may be ineligible for certain intermediate assignments, their careers will be "capped," they will become frustrated, and, thus, they should not be in those careers at all. Finally, some jobs are restricted for diplomatic reasons and others because of inadequate housing. An estimate of the number of jobs open to enlisted women was made in 1977 (table 7.1).[1]

Data of this kind call for analysis rather than acceptance. For example, the Army has no statutory restriction on its use of women, and the strictly Army-made policies and definitions that control service women's role are subject to different interpretation at different times by different administrators. At least one contemporary (1977) expert estimated that a slight modification in policy would allow the Army to absorb 175,000 women rather than 55,000.[2] The Army did not make that modification, but in 1982 it adopted a new method for combat-coding its assignments and closed a number of fields in which women were already serving. In 1983 it reopened some fields. By 1986 it had more than 69,000 women among its 667,000 soldiers. (One should note that while over 400,000

TABLE 7.1.  Jobs Open to Women, 1977 (in thousands)

|  | Total Jobs | Restricted to Men | Reserved for Men | Open to Women | Goals for Women |
|---|---|---|---|---|---|
| Army | 676 | 415 | 206 | 55 | 50 |
| Navy | 464 | 287 | 153 | 24 | 21 |
| Marines | 171 | 128 | 35 | 9 | 7 |
| Air Force | 477 | 31 | 83 | 363 | 48 |
| DOD | 1,788 | 861 | 477 | 451 | 126 |

*Note:* Rows do not add up precisely because of rounding.
*Source:* Martin Binkin and Shirley J. Bach, *Women and the Military* (Washington, D.C.: Brookings Institution, 1977), p. 106.

Army jobs were "restricted" to men, half as many more were "reserved" for them.)

When the estimates presented in table 7.1 were made, Navy women could not go to sea. Now some can, and the Navy's estimate as to the number of enlisted women it can use has doubled. The number of "usable" women is now set at under 10 percent.

The Marines combines the Army's and the Navy's problems. Women marines can neither serve in combat nor travel on Navy combat ships, even to work "in the rear with the gear." Moreover, Navy personnel fill many support functions for the Marines, which further reduces the ways Marine women can be used. For women, then, the Corps is the most restrictive service, both proportionally and in absolute numbers. Current plans are for some 10,000 women marines in a force of about 179,000.

Compare the last two columns in table 7.1. The 1977 Army, Navy, and Marine goals for women can be seen to approximate the number of positions open to them. Thus, these services appear willing to recruit all the women that (they say) they can use. Their concern is overrecruitment —the supply's exceeding the demand.

An independent assessment of the services' ability to use women is difficult to make. Personnel data are massive, detailed, and hard to obtain. Moreover, rotation, career progression, and other factors involve judgment calls. One wonders, though, about the legitimacy of restrictions designed to enhance men's career opportunities. When women are barred from 830,000 of 1,311,000 jobs in three of the services, is it really necessary to reserve additional jobs for men? That is, is it necessary in order to be fair? Or is it thought necessary for reasons of men's morale, whether it is fair or not?

One wonders about housing restrictions, too. Many "unsuitable" facilities are small. If the problem is one of separate bathrooms, why not make some units all female? Why is it assumed that when only single-sex facilities are available, they must be male? And, finally, why do the numbers of women who can be used change with the political situation? Why did the Army reduce its planned accessions after Reagan was elected? Why did the Air Force, which inducted almost 14,000 enlisted women in 1980, reduce the number to 9,000 in 1982?[3] And why are Air Force goals for women so low when compared with the number of slots open to them?

### AVAILABILITY

The answer given by the Air Force is, essentially, that qualified women are unavailable. Because the Air Force is quite successful in its recruiting, its enlistments and its goals have been more or less congruent; neither standards nor numbers have been stretched. The Air Force is also the service with the highest percentage of women, and its women have been the most integrated for some time. Even in 1977, and by the Air Force's own estimate, three-fourths of all enlisted jobs were open to women, and women were barred from less than 7 percent of the jobs. But the Air Force did not follow its sister services and set a recruitment goal that would fill all slots open to women with women—or even half of them. (The latter endeavor would have resulted in an Air Force that was about 38 percent female.) In 1977 its goal was to fill less than one in seven of the slots open to women with women. In absolute numbers it sought *fewer* women than the Army.

Accession goals are set each year. The process begins when personnel requirements are developed by the separate services and negotiated within DOD. DOD then submits to Congress a Program Objective Memorandum (POM) that states (and justifies) its manpower requirements for the next five years. One might think that the name of the game would be to maximize personnel. Without the draft, however, recruitment was difficult before 1981, and military planners were ambivalent about recruiting large numbers of enlisted personnel if it meant more women or poorly educated or poorly disciplined men. Moreover, if the services requested a total they were unable to recruit, they were setting themselves up for public failure—or for arguing a return to the draft.

Congress sets both military end strengths and minimum criteria for enlistees: for example, limits on the number of recruits who have scored low on intelligence tests.* Until recently, Congress has not stipulated the number of women any service should recruit, although it once legislated

---

*Recently there has been criticism that the services' standards are too high. A highly technological military needs skilled enlisted personnel, but not everyone needs to be skilled.

an upper limit of 2 percent, and goals for women have appeared in the POM.

In developing personnel requirements, military planners assume a permanent need for a strong military. They know that the pool of seventeen- to twenty-one-year-olds will continue to decrease until the mid-1990s. This means that if U.S. strength is to be maintained, a higher percentage of young people will have to enter military service, or they will have to stay in service longer.

In the short run, the military's ability to recruit men in the absence of a draft is probably most influenced by the civilian unemployment rate and the military compensation rate. In 1979, when unemployment was moderate and compensation was low, all services failed to make their recruiting goals. (The success rate varied from the Air Force's 98 percent to the Army's 89 percent.) All the services except the Army met their goals for women, although these were only a fraction of the goals for men. Because the military's policy of equal pay for equal rank is attractive to women, who make only 60 to 88 cents on the male dollar in the civilian world, the fears of the Army, Navy, and Marines—that women might enlist in numbers larger than could be used—had some credibility. (Young Blacks, whose unemployment rate is double that of young whites, enlist in large numbers; in recent years 42 percent of eligible young Blacks have enlisted.)[4]*

After Reagan came into office the economy slumped, and the military received more praise and also more pay. Suddenly the services discovered that they could (1) meet their recruiting goals, (2) raise enlistment standards, and (3) reduce the number of planned female accessions —and all at once! As noted above, the Army and the Air Force, though scheduled to continue increasing their women's end strengths through 1985, called a near halt to that increase. The Army argued that this was necessary because it could not use more women. The Air Force, in contrast, argued that this was necessary because it could not get more women! Thus, similarly restrictive decisions were justified by opposing assumptions. The Army sought to avoid being swamped by women volunteers. The Air Force (which polls show to be the most attractive service to women recruits) claimed that it could attract only two-thirds as many women recruits in 1982 as it had attracted in 1980.[5]

The Air Force focused on the importance of guaranteeing interested, qualified men an opportunity to enlist equal to that of women. If too high a goal was set for women, men who wished to enlist would be

---

*Blacks reenlist at a higher rate too, so that among enlisted personnel, the concentration of Blacks increases with rank. While there is no great disproportion between the percentage of Blacks in the population as a whole and in the Navy and Air Force, some analysts are concerned about the "blackness" of the enlisted Army. (See note 4.)

discriminated against, it argued. The Air Force's solution was to use "a highly sophisticated formula" to estimate the number of qualified women and men interested not just in joining the Air Force, but in filling each job specialty within it. It then sought to recruit women and men in proportion to its estimates.

It is true that the Air Force was not always able to meet its goal for women. In 1951 (during the Korean War), President Harry Truman launched a drive to enlist 72,000 women (40,000 were already serving). The Women's Air Force (WAF) ambitiously planned to grow from 8,200 to 50,000 in ten months by increasing monthly recruiting goals from 400 to 1,200. In fact, the Air Force was able to enlist only 500 women a month, and end strength peaked at 13,000. Maj. Gen. Jeanne Holm, USAF (Ret.), attributes the "failure" to (1) women's having to meet higher standards than men; (2) the special processing of women, including an individual psychiatric exam; (3) an unpopular and winding-down war; (4) "poverty-level" pay, and (5) no draft for women.[6] After Korea none of the services was interested in even approaching the congressionally imposed limit of 2 percent.

During the 1960s women's interest in the military increased. The services' response was not to increase their number, but to improve their "quality"—even though women were already meeting higher standards than men. Moreover, quality was understood to include personal appearance: Marine recruiters were told to look for "attractive" women, and Air Force recruiters sought "better-looking WAF."[7] (WAF officer recruits had to submit photographs and were required to wear girdles.) By 1966 women volunteers were being regularly turned down by military recruiters even though men were being drafted. Finally, a decision was made to recruit to the 2 percent limit; in 1967 the limit was removed. Significant change, though, occurred only when the All-Volunteer Force came into existence. It was then that the services committed themselves to a 170 percent increase in the number of women over the next five years, and the Air Force committed itself to *tripling* its women.[8]

The Carter administration continued the Nixon policies of an All-Volunteer Force and an increased percentage and number of women. Indeed, Harold Brown, Carter's secretary of defense, ordered that the number of women be doubled (again) by 1983.[9] At no time did the Air Force fail, or even find it hard, to meet its recruitment goals for women.

Then came the Reagan administration. The Air Force, which had been committed to an end strength of 90,000 enlisted women by 1986, suddenly set a new goal of only 61,000. But the new administration was philosophically opposed to the concept of goals (even though the whole military system is managed in this way), and so the new doctrine on the management of women was that the services would create "program development methodologies designed to accommodate their own mission and management"—in sum a "method" for deriving a number would be substituted for a number.[10]

And just what was the Air Force methodology? Two interviews in the Pentagon and three written inquiries produced a written formula but not its supporting references. Still, the principles involved and the justification offered for those principles can (and will) be outlined (below). The "answers" obtained by application of the formula were two: what proportion of the individuals recruited should be women, and what proportion of the recruits assigned to each particular specialty should be women. The reason for seeking these answers was criticism of an Air Force decision of the mid-1970s to enlist 15 percent women and to endeavor to assign them so that they would make up 15 percent of every specialty.[11] This decision posed two difficulties. First, women were kept out of some fields that they desired and for which they were well qualified in order to avoid "overrepresentation." Second, some women enlisted in fields that they were not interested in, with the expectation that they could later transfer to a field of their choice. When they were not allowed to transfer from shorthanded specialties to well-supplied ones, they were unhappy.

The goal of the Air Force formula was to achieve a distribution of women and men based upon their "propensities" and "capacities"—thus, the goal was to "afford qualified and interested persons of both sexes an opportunity to enlist which is at least equivalent to their proportion of the civilian population."[12] Again, "interest" was described as a driving principle in Air Force recruitment—*not* Air Force needs, or the market, but young people's registered "propensity" and measured ability.

After applying its formula, the Air Force concluded that there should continue to be fewer women in the Air Force than in the Army, and that they should compose about 12 percent of the force.* Its reasoning was as follows:

1. The populations of men and women between eighteen and twenty-four years were assumed to be equal.
2. It was assumed that 6 percent of men and 2 percent of women were interested in joining the Air Force.
3. It was assumed that 56 percent of males and 46 percent of females met minimum enlistment standards.
4. The percentages of women and men interested in particular AFSCs were estimated.

*In the 1985 Military Authorization Act, Congress directed the Air Force to make women 19 percent of its recruits in 1987. The Air Force then did another study using similar principles but deemphasizing "interest." In the latest model, intended to be in place by 1988, the Air Force estimated that women would make up 12.5 to 17.5 of 1985 accessions, and 18.5 percent of 1986 accessions. They did.

5. The percentages of the remaining men and women who qualified for particular AFSCs were then estimated.
6. The numbers of men and women were reduced by the number of each expected to fail on the basis of "X-factor" strength testing. (See Chapter 9.)
7. Allowance was made for positions "restricted" for any reason.
8. Finally, a ratio for the number of recruits who "can reasonably be expected to be women" was set for each specialty. This number was multiplied by the total needed in each specialty, and the results were summed. The result was an overall percentage of female accessions and also a series of percentages by specialty.

This system, first fully applied in 1982, was occasionally described as a "free flow" system. It was not. It simulated a free-flow system, but the goals actually functioned as limits, at least during the first part of the recruiting year. Since recruitment was generally successful, so that goals were met early in the year, little deviation from the model occurred, although the Air Force was prepared to permit "cross-overs" if there were shortages near the end of the recruiting year.*

How would a critic respond to this formulation? First, by noting that the second assumption—that 6 percent of men and 2 percent of women are "interested" in joining the Air Force—is used to determine that women will not be more than a third of the Air Force no matter what. Great power is given this datum even though it does not consider the intensity of interest, the level of information, the ability of those interested, or the number of competing interests and opportunities men and women have. Further, in the DOD report on *Women in the Military* (1981), it was stated that women are (almost) *half* (not one-third) as interested in the Air Force as men.[13] Further, marketing data of this kind are normally used in planning how to create interest, rather than in setting a limit on results. Interest in the military *always* has to be created. DOD now enlists about 14 percent of available eighteen-year-old males (many more than the number who indicate interest), but only 2 percent of available eighteen-year-old females (not necessarily the same ones who are said to be "interested"). Are women's minds so hard to change, and shouldn't one try to change them if one tries to change men's minds?

If one considers military service per se, the pool of men willing to enlist have about 300,000 positions open to them each year. The pool of women have about 50,000. That six-to-one ratio means that recruiters have to interest many more uninterested men than uninterested women

---

*The Air Force has maintained that no women were or are turned away. However, women are said to have been given DOEs (dates of entry) more distant than those given to men.

in order to achieve their goals; further, DOD itself has suggested that "negative propensity" females may be easier to recruit than "negative propensity" males.[14] The Air Force, then, uses existing "propensities" to set its final goal for women, but does not do so in other situations—for example, propensity varies by state, but recruitment goals are set to reflect demography, *not* already existing propensity. By using "propensity" instead of a market or supply and demand model, then, the Air Force severely restricts its planned accession of women.

Let us examine other details of the Air Force formula. The Air Force estimates that there are an equal number of women and men between eighteen and twenty-four, but also that 56 percent of men and only 46 percent of women are qualified to enlist. The primary enlistment standards are physical health, nonuse of drugs, lack of criminal record, level of education, and Armed Forces Qualification Test (AFQT) scores. It is not clear that young men and women have markedly different health statuses; one would expect more men than women to be disqualified for drug use and criminal records; and women are more likely to complete high school than men. Do AFQT scores account for the discrepancy? An Air Force Pentagon personnel manager told me that they do. Let us look at these tests in some detail.

Each potential enlistee takes an Armed Services Vocational Aptitude Battery (ASVAB). This includes ten subsets:

1. Arithmetic reasoning
2. Numerical operations
3. Paragraph comprehension
4. Word knowledge
5. Coding speed
6. General science
7. Mathematics knowledge
8. Electronics knowledge
9. Mechanical comprehension
10. Automotive shop information

Scores from the first four tests are combined to produce the AFQT score.[15]

Scores on the AFQT are grouped into five categories. Those in category V (8 percent of men, 6 percent of women) are ineligible for service. Those in categories III and IV are required by the Air Force to hold a high school diploma. Data from 1980 showed 52 percent of male youths and 59 percent of female youths in categories III and IV. On the other hand, only 20 percent of all women in this age group lacked a high school degree or its equivalent, while 24 percent of men did.[16] The reason for the male–female discrepancy in eligibility is not yet clear.

In 1980 the Air Force also required (1) a composite aptitude score of 170 or higher, (2) a general aptitude score of 45 or higher, and (3) a qualifying score in the particular area of enlistment before a recruit was considered eligible to enlist. The four composite scores, supposed to reflect mechanical, administrative, general, and electronics aptitude, were based on performance in various ASVAB subtests (table 7.2).[17]

TABLE 7.2.    ASVAB Subtests and Composites

| Composite | Subtests |
|---|---|
| AFQT | 1, 2, 3, 4 |
| Mechanical | 9, 10, 6 |
| Administrative | 5, 2, 3, 4 |
| General | 1, 3, 4 |
| Electronics | 1, 8, 6, 7 |

Note that subtests 8 and 10 specifically test "information" (electronics and automotive). Mechanical comprehension (9) may also test information. This means that scores on two of the composites are probably affected by previous course work of a kind that was often restricted to and required of males. Today shop courses are usually open to all students, but enrollments continue to be mostly male. Tests being used for enlistment eligibility, then, may be giving weight to previous course study rather than capacity for training. This is an important issue, not just because it may restrict opportunity for individuals, but because it may inhibit identification of talent.

For the youth population (of 1980), the male mean percentile score on the AFQT was 50.8; the female score was 49.5. On the general composite (identical to the AFQT with the omission of "numerical operations"), the male mean was 52 and the female 48. In the administrative composite the women's score was 51 and the men's 44. (This composite substituted "coding speed" for arithmetic reasoning in the AFQT.) For the electronics and mechanical composites, the only ones clearly using "information" tests, men scored 53 and 51 to women's 41 and 26. These are significant differences, and differences that make men more eligible to join the Air Force than women *regardless of the job* they will have there. Should anyone's eligibility to join the Air Force be tied to electronic and mechanical information and comprehension, areas that may be of low relevance for many Air Force jobs? Is it appropriate to tie enlistment to acquired information at all? If so, should this not be made clear? Is there any information women may be more likely to have than men that is or should be tested for in general eligibility screening?

The weight given to tests of acquired knowledge seems to account for much of the 56 to 46 eligibility difference between men and women. Surely the possibility that the difference is rooted in secondary school training should be acknowledged and explored; probably qualifying tests should be tied only to those specialties where the particular knowledge is relevant; and perhaps the "trainability" of persons without specific knowledge should be taken into account.

The women's pool is reduced further by the application of an Air Force formula designed to reflect the interest recruits express in particular job specialties. This formula is derived from tests of recruits in basic training. According to Air Force planners, there are male recruits interested in 100 percent of Air Force jobs—therefore, the male pool is not reduced at all. Women, though, are described as interested in only 78 percent of available jobs, and their pool is reduced accordingly. Let us assume that these preference data are accurate. Is a 22 percent reduction in the number of women to be enlisted the only possible outcome? Should the Air Force recruit for interest? Should it try to create interest? Individuals can become interested in assignments they have not previously considered. Moreover, if women's interests are less broad than men's and they are better qualified, shouldn't they be permitted to have *all* of the jobs they are interested in? What would happen if all qualified recruits were simply placed in a pool and assigned by interest and by competence? Would a quarter of the women end up unplaceable? Or would their greater interest and higher scores in, for instance, administration mean that they would get more than their "share" of those jobs—and that men who were interested in them would just have to make another choice? Does the Air Force give men's "interest" such weight that interested men are recruited over more qualified women who lack interest but who could become interested? Does the Air Force give the "interest" of all recruits too much weight? Does it give the "interest" of all recruits equal weight? Don't some have the opportunity to select specialties before enlistment, while others have to wait for leftover slots after basic training? It would seem that the questions of specialty assignment and recruit interest need more consideration before women's more focused interest becomes the basis for reducing their pool by 22 percent.

The Air Force next matches interest and qualifications. Here the men's and women's pools are reduced by almost exactly the same amount—one-third. Since women's scores are so different from men's on two of the composites, the fact that they qualify for the jobs they choose at the same rate as men suggests that the women may be self-selecting according to their estimate of their qualifications and expressing their self-appraisal in terms of interest or lack of interest. Since the areas of women's low interest tend to be areas of Air Force need, it might be worth considering whether interest could be developed by offering information and, possibly, training. After all, once women enter a pool from which they have been excluded (or which they have chosen to ignore), that pool is doubled in size.

Physical testing by the Air Force involves strength and endurance. According to the Air Force, men qualify physically for 99 percent of Air Force jobs; women qualify for 77 percent. Although the Air Force has been using physical testing for years and has even revised its tests (upward) once, no data have been made public that validate the tests either in general or for particular AFSCs. Standards have been set and equipment designed so that virtually all physically fit men can pass. It is clear that the tests are really asking to what degree women are like men, especially since the test that most often disqualifies women involves lifting a weight overhead. If the goal were to enable women to do Air Force work, equipment or work redesign, not physical testing, would be the chief concern of the Air Force. After all, if manufacturers of cars did not care whether or not they sold to women, it would be very easy for them to design equipment that would be attractive to all men but only some women. Since the manufacturers' desire is to enable everyone to use their product, they do so.

The present policy of losing one-eighth of the pool of eighteen- to twenty-four-year-old potential recruits because of limited equipment design (or "lack of strength") seems profligate. If redesign must come slowly, and if physical requirements are, at least temporarily, essential, then it would seem wise to maximize the number of individuals able to serve by reserving jobs not requiring strength for the less strong.

Women's accessions are reduced another one-fifth on the grounds that Air Force policy restricts them from serving in that proportion of available jobs. Again, men are the norm, eligible to serve in 100 percent of jobs. Because women's access to particular jobs is restricted, their total numbers are restricted.

In sum, the Air Force accession formula is constructed in terms of proportions, and each female "deficiency" is built into it in turn. Thus, the formula says that with the men's pool used as a norm, the women's pool must be reduced by two-thirds (interest in Air Force), one-fifth (qualification to join), one-fifth (interest in AFSC), one-quarter (strength), and one-fifth (job restricted). According to the Air Force, these calculations would have women constituting 11.5 percent of accessions. The fact that it had without difficulty recruited enough women to make up almost 20 percent of accessions the year the formula was constructed apparently did not shake Air Force confidence in its formula—the formula "too sophisticated" to be shared with outsiders. The extraordinary weight given "interest" and the lack of weight given to market factors and men's other options is notable. The use of men and of knowledge they are more likely to have as norms is also notable.

The bottom line is that the Army, which fears enlisting too many women, and the Air Force, which believes it cannot find enough (interested and qualified) women, have come to very similar conclusions about the number and percentage of women they can use. It is almost as though there were a magic percentage of women who can be absorbed—not for whatever reasons are cited, but for the maintenance of a properly male military identity.

The Air Force grew out of the Army forty years ago. It has acquired generals trained in its own academy only in the last decade. Its attitudes and values are very close to those of the Army even though many of its activities are similar to those of civilians. Is "Army" thinking relevant to Air Force performance, or would that service do better with a new ethos —one that acknowledges that in the Air Force it is air crews that "fight" while the remainder (and bulk) of that force is really, like Marine women, "in the rear"?

## THE VALUE OF WOMEN

Some argue that even if women are usable and available, they are just not as valuable to the military as men. Emphasis is often given to attrition data. These require discussion, but so do other elements of the personnel system, such as retention and promotions.

Just as the services do not wish to enlist all or even half the nation's eighteen- to twenty-four-year-olds, they do not wish to reenlist all first- or second-termers, or even to retain all enlistees for a full first term. Attrition and retention goals fluctuate each year and differ by service and by specialty. In some periods deficiencies are overlooked that would not be tolerated in another. For example, in 1983 and 1984 the services energetically enforced drug regulations, partly because new screening devices made stronger enforcement possible, but partly because the services could afford to hold their personnel to a high standard at a time when civilians were eager to enlist and enlisted personnel to reenlist.

In general, Air Force expectations about retention follow the pattern outlined below:

100 individuals enlist.
27 attrite during their first enlistment.
11 are not eligible to reenlist.
39 choose not to reenlist (23 do).
7 choose not to reenlist at end of next term.
4 do not reach retirement.
12 complete a twenty-year career.[18]

Thus, the Air Force expects fewer than one in eight enlistees to complete a career—and its expectations are higher than those of the other services.*

*These expectations are detailed in its Total Objective Plan for Career Personnel (TOCAP), which is intended to manage both the overall structure of the force and the

For those who stay in service for the maximum allowable time (there are "up or out" constraints), the goal has been to provide the following promotion opportunities. For E-1 through E-4, promotion is supposed to go to all who are "fully qualified"; there is no limit on overall promotions, although they can be delayed until vacancies occur. Promotions to E-5, E-6, and E-7, all of which would normally occur after at least one reenlistment, are competitive—that is, they go to the "best-qualified." Selection is based on a Weighted Airman Program System (WAPS). This system is still evolving, but in the recent past scores were based on a specialty knowledge test (100 point maximum), a promotion fitness test involving general military knowledge (100 point maximum), time in service (40 point maximum), time in grade (25 point maximum), airman performance reports (APR, 135 point maximum), and decorations. There is a 90 percent promotion opportunity goal for grades E-5 and E-6, and an 84 percent goal for E-7. This does not mean that 90 percent of E-4s seeking promotion each year are promoted, but that 90 percent of those who enlist in a given year *and* stay in for the maximum number of years (8 for E-5, 20 for E-6, and 23 for E-7) will eventually be promoted. Note that tests and seniority dominate the promotion criteria for ranks E-5 through E-7.

Promotion to E-8 and E-9 depends on a differently weighted formula.[19] In addition, a three-person evaluation board reviews and grades the record of each candidate by AFSC. Candidates are then ranked, and a quota based on available vacancies is devised. The quota is stated as a percentage of eligible service people, and the same quota is applied to each AFSC. Thus, each eligible individual should have the same chance of being promoted. In fact, however, the Air Force has not been able to keep opportunity equal just by controlling enlistment and reenlistment. In recent years it has had to use a two-tier promotion system for senior airmen in the approximately 30 percent of its skills described as "chronic critical" or "sortie-generating." Airmen in these fields have been given a 5 percent promotion advantage over airmen in others.[20] The Air Force plans a 75 percent opportunity rate for promotion to E-8 and a 60 percent rate for E-9. Overall, 2 percent of enlisted personnel are authorized to hold the rank of E-8, and 1 percent may hold the rank of E-9.

Again, it is important to remember that the Air Force does not want to retain all of its people. Most are expected to leave and do so; still, Air Force personnel are older and more career-oriented than those of the other services.

Since one's opportunity to be promoted and retained varies by spe-

career development of individuals (Edward A. Richter and David A. Thorp, *A Comparative Analysis of Enlisted Career Progression Systems* [Wright-Patterson Air Force Base, Ohio: Air Force Institute of Technology, 1980], pp. 28–45).

cialty, and enlisted personnel do not routinely change or add specialties (one can retrain into shortage AFSCs), one's original choice of field is consequential. Yet it is often made in some ignorance and before enlisting. An attractive job can be used as an inducement to enlist, or immediate enlistment in a less attractive field can be offered with the suggestion that one can change fields later. If women receive fewer preenlistment guarantees than men because they are easier to recruit (and apparently they do), or if they make less informed choices, or if they are in less desirable specialties, one should expect them to leave the Air Force at a higher rate than men. Further, if women recruits are considered a means of averting shortages, and if they are given a disproportionate number of hard-to-fill assignments, or if they do not receive their share of most-desired assignments, and if, in addition, they are sometimes not welcomed to or trusted in their jobs, a higher attrition rate might be attributed not to gender, but to recruitment and assignment procedures.* Finally, if women receive more delayed DOEs than men, it would seem that the Air Force considers interested and qualified women to be in good supply, even though its accession goal suggests the opposite.

Civilians often perceive the military as the kind of coercive system that permits no dropouts, no attrition. In fact, however, 22 to 42 percent of 1982 military enlistees left service within three years.[21] (Because attrition is concentrated in the first years and because some services use a three-year enlistment, DOD uses departure within three years of enlistment as its conventional measure of attrition.) In the All-Volunteer Force, personnel typically enlist for a four-year period. This term is seen as providing a good balance between the costs of training and the costs of attrition. The highest attrition rates are for Marine Corps and Army women (over 40 percent). The lowest rates are for Air Force men, but even these are more than 20 percent. The rates for Navy women and men and those for Air Force women and men are within about 5 percentage points of each other.† Thus, even though women have an "easy" exit from service (being honorably discharged when they become pregnant), for two of the four services this policy does not make them significantly less enduring personnel than men.‡

---

*A study of male attrition showed attrition is "heavily influenced" by occupational specialty and location of first assignment ("Recruit Dropout Rate Tied to Experiences," *Air Force Times*, 25 January 1982).

†Women's and men's attrition differs in two ways. First, women's occurs early—during basic. This could mean that the recruitment process selects poorly, or that women are allowed to quit more easily. The second difference, of course, stems from pregnancy, which accounts for about one-third of women's attrition.

‡Before the All-Volunteer Force, and before pregnant women were permitted to remain in service, this was not the case. In 1972 the (DOD) three-year attrition rate was about 20 percent higher for women than for men.

In general, enlistees without high school diplomas have a higher attrition rate than those with them. This is true for both women and men. However, since few women are accepted for service without diplomas, the military's highest attrition rate is not that of women but that of male nongraduates. Overall, then, one would expect women with diplomas to be a better bet than men without them. Still, the Marine Corps has always taken *only* women with diplomas, and it loses more than 40 percent of them; thus, even "high-quality" women leave the Marines. A significant reason for this appears to be their lack of acceptance.[22]

Let us look at Air Force attrition in more detail. Male attrition rose with the All-Volunteer Force. It rose with cohorts entering in 1971, 1972, 1973, and 1974. It then leveled off at a rate between 25 and 30 percent.* In contrast, (Air Force) women's attrition dropped after the All-Volunteer Force was created to match the men's attrition rate exactly; it then leveled off at about five points above that of men.

Even though women's attrition has been similar to that of men, in two of the services a perception exists that women get out of service much more frequently. This may be because they do it more visibly but also more smoothly than men by becoming pregnant instead of becoming delinquent.

Of the men who entered service in 1975, 20 percent were given involuntary or disciplinary discharges; 4 percent received "voluntary or interest of the Air Force" discharges; and another 5 percent were given medical or hardship discharges or died (such discharges are considered "uncontrollable"). One out of four of the Air Force's "high-quality" male recruits does not last.[23]

Moreover, some personnel losses can be beneficial to the services; for example, individuals with large families are costly; so is retirement pay. Women who leave in mid-career increase the opportunities of their male peers for promotion and may do so without damaging the services, since the rank pyramid is steep. Thus, higher attrition by women or a lower reenlistment rate for women does not necessarily harm either the military or the men in it. Because retention is of only relative importance to service needs, the raw numbers that show women reenlisting at a higher rate than men and men signing up for a third term at a higher rate than women do not really tell about either fairness to women and men or the best interests of the military.

Among the several devices used to manage retention is the selective reenlistment bonus (SRB), intended to retain enlisted personnel in shortage specialties. Such bonuses can be as much as $30,000; thus, such a bonus (even when spread out over a four-year enlistment) can signifi-

---

*Just about one-third of college entrants finish four years of college on schedule.

cantly modify what is conceived of as a system of equal pay for equal rank. In the spring of 1987 there were 120 skills on the Air Force SRB list, with bonuses ranging from one-half to three times base pay for the period of reenlistment. The list is revised every six months. The SRB is used to manage force structure: even if the draft were reinstituted, some device would be needed to retain skilled personnel. The SRB is just one of numerous means used to adjust the military's equal pay scale to market realities. Others include flight pay, hazardous duty pay, and family separation allowances.

Do promotion rates suggest that women are less valuable? No. Enlisted women who stay in service are promoted earlier than men at every rank and in every service.[24] Yet caveats should be made. First, Air Force promotions are slow; it can easily take thirteen years to reach E-6. Second, the buildup in women's numbers did not really begin until 1972. Thus, the women in ranks E-8 and E-9 are drawn from a very small pool. In fact, in 1986 their numbers were 459 and 64, whereas men's absolute numbers in those ranks were 38,514 and 15,390. Third, Air Force data on enlisted women's promotions show a bottleneck at the E-6 level, where the average Air Force promotion rate for the period 1980 through 1985 was 19.7 percent, while the women's rate was only 11.9.[25] One explanation is that because junior women receive a high proportion of the early promotions, they are penalized when time in service and time in grade begin to be significant promotion factors.* The pattern may also reflect the fact that women are concentrated in the most competitive specialties, where being "fully qualified" is not enough. That is, for E-5 and above, promotion requires one not just to meet specified criteria, but to be better than other qualified individuals. Senior Air Force promotions are very competitive. At present candidates have to have nearly perfect APRs. This means that even a little discrimination, negative or positive, can have important consequences.

Another way of looking at promotions would take into account the fact that most people leave service. If one looks at the percentage of a cohort still in service and at a particular rank at a particular time—for example, the cohorts entering in 1973 through 1978—it appears that a higher percentage of men achieve high rank than do women of their cohort.[26] Alternatively, one can look at rank by years in service. Roughly 45 percent of men who hold the rank of E-4 have been in service three years or less; another 46 percent of E-4 men have been in service from four to six years. Only 39 percent of E-4 women have three years of

*Air Force enlisted women meet the same entrance standards as men. Nevertheless, their APRs were consistently higher than men's through E-6 for the period 1980 through 1984. From E-7 through E-9, men's and women's APRs are both very similar and very high.

service or less; 54 percent have four to six years. For ranks E-5, E-6, and E-7, men's and women's patterns are dissimilar. At each rank women's years of service are more compressed than men's; that is, there are fewer long-term holders of any particular rank among women. This is partly because the proportion of women with many years in service is small. It may also be that women who are not promoted early or on time are more likely than men to leave the military. At E-8 and E-9, the patterns are different again. About half the E-8 men have been in service for fifteen to twenty years, and half for over twenty. Ninety percent of male E-9s have been in service over twenty years. For women the pattern is about two-thirds below and one-third above twenty years at E-8, but only one-half have over twenty years in service at E-9, and almost a quarter of the women E-9s have been in service less than fourteen years. Again, this reflects military women's age distribution and possibly their unwillingness to linger.[27]

## OTHER PERSONNEL CONSIDERATIONS

The Air Force Personnel Center at Randolph Air Force Base in San Antonio has the jobs of maintaining a force with the proper distribution of skills at the proper rank and also of placing almost 600,000 individuals in particular assignments throughout the globe. This includes assignments to some 135 major installations, 30 of which are in foreign countries, and some 2,700 other installations, more than 600 of which are in other countries. Between a fifth and a quarter of Air Force personnel are stationed abroad: some 80,000 in Europe, some 34,000 in East Asia and the Pacific—Japan, Okinawa, the Philippines, and South Korea. Air Force bases need space (to land and take off) but do not require a high concentration of troops. Base populations are often low (as compared with the other services), and bases are often remote.

In making geographical assignments, the Air Force must meet its needs and also deal equitably with its people. Economy suggests minimizing permanent changes of station (PCSs). Finally, retention can be influenced by individual preferences related to geography, rapid or slow rotation, and desire to be stationed with a military spouse.

For the Air Force, getting personnel into overseas assignments is the chief problem. Women's availability for such assignments may be less than men's if the Air Force grants exemptions from overseas duty for pregnancy and if certain countries reject the assignment of women, but under current policies 40 percent of Air Force personnel, the vast majority of whom are men, are "unavailable" for overseas assignment at any given time. On the other hand, cooks, avionic specialists, and linguists are likely to have extended overseas assignments, and there are others, such as enlisted personnel with foreign spouses, who prefer overseas tours.* Again, assignments, especially for senior personnel, rarely come as bolts from the blue: one's next assignment is relatively predictable. Moreover, Air Force jobs are actually advertised; they can be applied for, bargained for, and even "exchanged." Some personnel successfully "nest" in a particular area for years. Just as it is inappropriate to study women's lost time in isolation, it is inappropriate to study their supposed lack of readiness except in the more general context of "assignment availability." Further, as will be discussed later, "spouse" programs affect men as well as women; and civilian spouses, like military ones, have an effect on availability and retention.

Doubt about women's value to the military also stems from their supposed reluctance to select "nontraditional" as opposed to "traditional" AFSCs. (These are awkward categories because many military jobs have no civilian analogue, and because, as noted above, for a woman just being in the military is nontraditional, even if what she does is type.)

What do airmen do all day? Like enlisted personnel in the other services, most "support." Few airmen fly, and there is no principal specialty. The two largest fields are Support and Administration and Electrical and Mechanical Repairs; each includes about a fifth of Air Force enlisted personnel. Forty-three percent of women are in Support and Administration and 10.2 percent in Medical and Dental specialties. However, even in these fields, "traditional" ones for women, most enlisted personnel are men. Men outnumber women three or four to one in Support and Administration and more than two to one in Medical and Dental occupations. *No* enlisted specialty is dominated by women.[28]

Further, in spite of widespread beliefs that women leave or perform less well in "nontraditional" fields, the evidence does not show this to be unambiguously true.[29] Again:

1. Every military woman is in a nontraditional job.
2. Military women *and* men like clerical and medical jobs.
3. Women migrate from different "nontraditional" jobs at different rates.
4. Women may be encouraged to leave certain jobs.
5. Regular hours may be a high priority for women, regardless of "traditionality."

Other issues related to personnel management will be discussed in Chapter 9. The concern here has been large-scale personnel manage-

---

*As late as 1978 the Air Force did not assign single, junior enlisted women abroad. Most such restrictions have now been removed.

ment done by the numbers. Like the big items in a budget, big issues in personnel often go unprobed even though their effect is controlling. Accessions are the heart of the women-in-the-military matter. If women are not accessed, all other considerations become moot. Questions about technical training, opportunities for professional military education, discrimination in APRs, and availability of medical care will not arise if women are not in uniform. Thus, a constant check on and analysis of women's accessions by service is important. It is also important that the judgments behind accession goals be explicitly critiqued. When the most popular service attracts as many women as the least popular, the need for inquiry is obvious. The need may be just as great where it is not obvious.

## MAKING JUDGMENTS ABOUT ACCESSIONS

Even under existing policies, U.S. Air Force enlisted personnel could be mostly women. The modest recruitment goals now set for women are attributed to their lack of interest and qualifications. One might conclude that if large numbers of interested and qualified women suddenly sought to join the Air Force, the number of female airmen would increase and debate cease. This might not be the case. Even though Air Force women's attrition, retention, and promotion statistics are similar to those for men, many commanders continue to perceive women as a problem.

Pregnancy is described as a problem; so are single military members with dependent children or parents and married military couples. Other questions are raised about women's stamina (in addition to their strength), their ability to lead, their availability for assignment, and the effect they have on male cohesion and morale. Other questions are cast in economic terms—for example, increased costs for medical care. Yet men cost more to recruit and have more dependents and higher retirement costs. Moreover, the nation's defense involves other and more fundamental concerns than economy, including certainty of success and public support for the military.

It is worth repeating that no enlisted jobs are allocated to women formally or informally. No effort is made to maximize the use of women. It is almost as though military leaders think of the services as belonging to men, who "use" some women when convenient. The military does not belong to men. It belongs to the citizens of the country, over half of whom are women. The military is a national institution intended to protect all citizens. It is under, and not apart from, government; it is not a vehicle for the aggrandizement of individuals. It is a burden to the country, and those who participate in it serve their fellow citizens and take direction from an elected commander in chief.

Men who command should not think of women's participation in the military as just a matter of emergency "use." Instead, the whole population of young people should be considered potentially available to serve the nation—and not just in a particular service, but in the services as a whole. If service is thought of in this way, the assignment of "less-usable" individuals to reserved slots because they are the only slots those individuals can fill might make sense.

For example, if the Air Force needs 300 speakers of French, it assigns French-speaking enlistees to slots requiring French even if those individuals prefer other slots. English-speaking-only positions are, in essence, reserved for the English-speaking-only. Similarly, if certain jobs require men for combat, physical strength, and mechanical knowledge, men are assigned to them even if they would prefer office jobs. And shouldn't the only jobs women *can* qualify for be reserved for them in order to use them? Why shouldn't women predominate in the jobs that are available to them and for which they qualify, even if men can also do them and want them—especially if the men are needed elsewhere?

The 88 percent male Air Force is concerned that it is discriminating against men. But even if women were to get more than half the jobs for which both men and women are eligible, and even if women were to get them when there were eligible men who wanted them, men would not necessarily be discriminated against. As long as only men can be used in certain crucial jobs, a "pull" to an area of need, rather than a barrier to an area of preference, cannot be considered discrimination. Some other "discrimination" occurs now because equipment is designed so that more men can use it than women. This means that men are siphoned off to tasks that they might not prefer, leaving a reduced number of men to compete with all women.

The Air Force's stated reverence for the existing propensities of young people and its lack of interest in affecting existing predispositions are hard to take seriously. The best utilization of the country's human resources may be quite different from its past utilization when the services' needs and citizens' needs for participation are fully considered. Congressman Les Aspin (D.-Wisc.), who became chair of the House Armed Services Committee in 1985, was chair of the Subcommittee on Military Personnel and Compensation in 1984. From his readings of documents similar to those discussed above, he concluded that "the service that at first blush appeared to have the best record of utilizing women suddenly turns out to have the worst record." Even if one accepts the combat exclusion as a given, Aspin noted, the Army was filling 22 percent of jobs open to women with women, the Navy 23 percent, the Marines 30 percent, and the Air Force only 12 percent. Aspin's committee therefore recommended that the Air Force be directed to recruit more women (up to 25 percent of recruits by 1987), thus increasing its use of women and decreasing its use of men, who might then become available to the other services.[30]

Tydal McCoy, assistant secretary of the Air Force for manpower, reserve affairs and installation, found Aspin's arguments "superficial" and asserted that the level of female Air Force recruits under the Carter administration (20 percent) was "artificially high" and "actually lowered women's status in the service." Moreover, he argued, mandated female quotas would "discriminate against males who might consider military careers" but would be forced aside. Air Force concern about discrimination against men extended even to "gender oriented recruitment," which it forbade. McCoy concluded that increasing female accessions from 15 to 22 percent would lower Air Force productivity, increase its accession and training costs, exacerbate attrition, and "hurt" enlisted women.[31] Meanwhile, the Air Force opened some of the few remaining fields then closed to women, including the long-debated position of security specialist. (This change opened 26,000 of the 60,000 previously closed jobs.)[32]

Aspin prevailed. The Fiscal Year 1985 Defense Authorization Bill required the Air Force to make women 19 percent of recruits by the end of Fiscal Year 1987 and 22 percent by 1988. It also directed the Air Force to (1) determine its actual ability to utilize women, and (2) replace its accession methodology with one based on "capacity" or "demand." McCoy continued to resist, describing the mandated change as "micro management" and warning that it would force "certain inefficiencies" not in the best interest of the United States. "We're doing our own study of women," he said; ". . . we'll be looking into what kinds of jobs could be suitable and proper for women. Once we're finished, Congress may want to reconsider."[33]

That Air Force study, "An Analysis of the Effects of Varying Male and Female Force Levels," was conducted by Maj. Gen. Robert C. Oaks and reported in May 1985.[34] Its two foci were the "youth market" (i.e., the nation's supply, as opposed to the requested focus on the Air Force's demand) and the "effects" of women on the Air Force, a topic in which Congress had expressed no interest.

The study showed that an increased percentage of women would lead to an increase in the percentage of military spouses, military spouses with children, and single parents, but after considering retention, availability, and performance, the Air Force concluded that expanding the representation of women, even to 22.4 percent, would not be constraining.

"Interest" (or "propensity") was deemphasized, although it was noted that women's interest would have to double to equal that of men. Moreover, by 1985 more was known about "propensity." First, it was shown to be inversely related to age, level of education, aptitude, social class, and employment. This meant that the *least* desired were the *most* interested. Second, those who are actually enlisted are of a higher quality than those who express a propensity to enlist.[35] Recruitment, then, involves (1) screening out undesirables who would like to enlist, and (2) attracting those without a propensity. Further, two-thirds of women who *did* enlist had previously had a "negative propensity" to do so, as did a substantial percentage of men who enlisted. Thus, propensity or interest predictors work better for men than women, and many who "lack propensity" do in fact enlist. Moreover, interested women who do not join tend to cite familial reasons, whereas interested men tend not to join because of low pay. This fact suggests that different and perhaps relatively cheap inducements could increase women's propensity.

It is also of interest that women's propensity is very like that of "older" males (twenty-two- to twenty-nine-year-olds), and that "young" men's positive propensity data are greatly inflated by the responses of sixteen- and seventeen-year-olds.[36]

Finally, in view of the Air Force's ban, it is worth noting that "gender-oriented" recruitment apparently occurs anyway—but oriented away from women. One study reported that 46 percent of men received recruitment literature while 28 percent of women did, and that 40 percent of men, but only 27 percent of women, had contact with a recruiter.[37]

The Oaks study disputes two assumptions made by Aspin and most military planners. The first is that there will be a decline in the number of youths available for recruitment as the pool of eighteen- to twenty-four-year-olds diminishes. The Air Force now argues that women and immigrants seeking civilian jobs will pressure men to turn to the military. Second, the Air Force claims that the other services will not gain access to a larger pool of men just because more women enter the Air Force. It asserts a displacement of 6,000 men would produce only 70 to 520 more Army enlistees.[38]

Overall the Air Force concluded that "gender-free" recruitment would make annual accessions about 18 percent female, and that to "deviate" from this mix would be to (1) risk increased costs and attrition, (2) risk the creation of unequal opportunities for qualified men and women (i.e., favor women), and (3) jeopardize the comparable quality of men and women (i.e., men would have to be more highly qualified).

When the Air Force, which is attractive to women and which can use larger numbers of them, argues that it should access only a fraction of the number of women accessed by the Army, which is less popular and substantially constrains its use of women, one wonders if the Air Force really wants women. If the Air Force does not want to enlist women, should one believe that the Army, Navy, and Marines really want to do so? If the

Army, Navy, and Marines profess both willingness and deep regret over their constraints, should their description of those constraints and their accession goals be accepted uncritically? Probably not, but such criticism will be difficult, because the savvy, the data, the interest, and the energy for analysis are in short supply. Air Force women are not actively complaining. If they do not complain, who will or should? Watchdog women? Crotchety academics? If Air Force women *did* complain, who would listen? What would happen to them?

Apparently women are still considered "filler"; the size of women's accessions is influenced primarily by external forces such as acts of Congress, declarations of war, and the end (or beginning) of a draft. The military describes itself as bound by Congress, and Congress describes itself as the embodiment of public opinion. Since the work of political institutions is an imperfect reflection of public opinion, it is worth turning now to an examination of what is known about public opinion regarding women in the military.

# PART III

Meta-
Influences
on
Policies

# 8

## Public
## Opinion

President Jimmy Carter proposed draft registration for women and men following the December 1979 invasion of Afghanistan by Russia. But even before Carter had formally submitted his proposal, Speaker of the House Thomas P. O'Neill announced that the registration of women "wouldn't go," that it would be "anathema around here."[1] He was right; it did not go, probably not because Congress was so opposed to women's registration, but because it was opposed to debating the issue. The problem was not that there was a consensus, but that there was not. Thus, the result was less the product of a majority decision than of a desire to avoid creating a majority that was likely to be slim, composed of disparate views, and confronted with intense opposition.

The Supreme Court also evaded the issue. In *Rostker* v. *Goldberg* it overturned a district court decision that had held that a men-only draft registration was unconstitutional sex discrimination. Instead, the Supreme Court honored "the customary deference" accorded the judgment of Congress, especially in the area of national defense and military affairs.

And what did the American people, the public, think about the draft, registration for the draft, and women? In March 1980 (according to the Gallup Poll), 59 percent thought we should return to the draft, and 51 percent thought young women should participate in it. Moreover, 83 percent believed men should register for the draft, and 56 percent believed women should (5 percent or less had no opinion on these items).[2] Thus, by requiring only registration and only that of men, Congress ensured a policy that was overwhelmingly supported. (Congress may have perceived that many who ostensibly supported women's registration would be secretly happy to lose, while those who were opposed to it were more passionate in their views and might even resist registration.)

This chapter will bring together existing information on opinions about women in the military. It will include data going back to World War II and data from samples representing both the public as a whole and young men and women. It will cover a variety of issues: registration, the draft, combat, appropriate jobs, and national service. Because different studies are not strictly comparable, I will not attempt meta-analysis.[3] Still, patterns can be shown, and a discussion of concepts such as chivalry and patriarchy may help to shed light on some of the findings. Because no military can be effective without civilian support, it is essential that the views of the public be known.

## CURRENT OPINION AND ITS CONTEXT

It is primarily men—the commander in chief, the members of Congress, the federal judiciary, the civilian military secretaries, and military commanders—who make military policy. It is they who determine what men and women may and must do. Women have a say about their role in the military only indirectly: they vote in elections and on referenda; they support interest groups and participate in demonstrations. Women need no one's permission to participate in these ways, and they do so. In general, they are more opposed to war and preparations for it than are men. Still, it should be noted that (1) recorded views are *not* polarized by sex; (2) questions intended to elicit opinion are often ambiguous; (3) opinions are solicited in a particular context (for more than a decade all opinions have been expressed during peacetime); and (4) law and past practice have placed numerous restrictions on military women, so that the slate is not clean. Finally, and most important, U.S. citizens are almost uniquely able to think of war as an out-of-country venture, as something one goes to—probably by airplane. This makes it possible for Americans to believe that chivalry is possible and that a law can actually prevent as well as simply prohibit women's participation in combat.

The best recent data on this topic (collected by the University of Chicago's National Opinion Research Center)[4] showed 44 percent of the population favoring a return to the draft in 1982, but only 24 percent in 1984; these numbers shifted to 88 and 84 percent "if there were a national emergency."[5]* Fifty-five and 50 percent of those favoring a return to the draft favored drafting women. Further, 84 percent supported national service for women if they supported a national service at all, and 35 percent of the general population thought women should be assigned to hand-to-hand combat if they were trained to do it![6] There was a statistical difference (at the 0.05 level) between the sexes on attitudes toward women's participation in the military; the more significant difference, though, was between men and working women, on the one hand, and

---

*Fifty-eight percent had favored restoration of the draft in 1980. Increased pay and higher civilian unemployment eased recruitment for the All-Volunteer Force during the Reagan years and reduced pressure for a return to the draft.

housewives, on the other. Support for women in the military was also associated with more education, youth, and low religiosity.[7] (Those who most strongly supported women in the military were also the least supportive of the military itself.)

Overall, the NORC data showed "strong national support for extensive feminine involvement in the military, including the 'military military.'" "To anyone brought up to hold the door open for females," the authors noted, "the finding that a third of the contemporary U.S. adult population endorses assignment of females to hand-to-hand combat is astounding!"[8]

These findings may have surprised the finders, but Gallup Poll data going back to the 1940s—*before* U.S. entrance into World War II—show that the U.S. public has long expected women to share in the nation's defense, even if not exactly on the same terms as men. Although the questions asked over the last forty years are not perfectly comparable, a summary of Gallup results is, nevertheless, instructive.

POLL DATA

Society has always been ready to ask more of its young men, particularly when it comes to the military, than of its young women. Nevertheless, almost one year *before* Pearl Harbor 48 percent of the population was ready, "starting now," to draft women between twenty-one and thirty-five and "to train them for jobs in wartime." After Pearl Harbor almost 70 percent approved of such a policy.[9]*

In mid-war (late 1943), only 45 percent of the population favored drafting single women in that age range to serve in women's branches of the armed services. However, when the choice was between drafting 300,000 women for "non-fighting" jobs in the WACS or drafting "married men with families for the same work," over three out of four Americans favored the drafting of single women. Similarly, three out of four favored the drafting of nurses (gender and marital status unspecified).† Apparently women were seen as an emergency force, for in peacetime there was much less interest in service for them. Thus, in February 1945, 69 percent of Americans supported one year of compulsory military training for men, while only 22 percent supported it for women, "after this war is over." Fifty-three percent, though, did think there should be units in which women "could enlist" in peacetime.[10]

---

*After Pearl Harbor the question was altered to: "single women between the ages of 21 and 35."

†During the Korean War (1951) a plurality of 48 percent (to 44 percent) favored drafting women into the armed forces specifically to do "typing and clerical jobs."

National military service is clearly more compelling to the public than other kinds of national service. Thus, 55 percent said women should be drafted "for non-combat duties" if a third World War broke out, but even during the Vietnam War 58 percent *disapproved* of drafting women to fill nonmilitary medical service needs "on the same general basis that young men are drafted for war service." In addition, although 79 percent of the population felt that men should give one year of service (military or nonmilitary) to their country, a 49 percent plurality opposed such service for women. By 1977, 62 percent continued to favor some kind of compulsory national service for men, while 51 percent opposed it for women.[11]

When the issue is national defense as opposed to national service, women *are* expected to participate. Thus, in 1979 only 40 percent favored one year of required national service for women, but 43 percent believed women should be drafted for military service if men were drafted, and 50 percent said that if men were required to register for the draft, women should register too. Indeed, one of five surveyed said that women "should be eligible" for combat roles! These figures were slightly elevated in March and July 1980, when draft and registration issues were debated by Congress. A majority of 51 percent (March) and then a plurality of 49 percent (July) believed that women should participate in any draft.[12]

Gallup data from 1940 through 1969 were usually developed during wartime, and sex was usually reported as a variable. In nearly every poll before 1970, women were substantially more in favor of women's participation in the military than were men.* On eight items measured between 1940 and 1969, women's support was an average of 7.6 percentage points higher than men's, with a range of 6 to 12 points higher.

Men's and women's views were within two percentage points of each other only twice: on an item concerning the drafting of women for nonmilitary service in hospitals and nursing homes, and on the issue of making volunteer, peacetime service available to women. When women between twenty-one and thirty-five (the women most likely to be affected) were analyzed separately, they were even more supportive of women's participation than were women in general. But on the one occasion when single women were measured separately, they fell below the mark for women generally, apparently because married women, whose husbands might

---

*Public opinion and public opinion polls are not always clear and consistent. In an August 1981 poll, people were asked, "Do you approve or disapprove of the Supreme Court ruling that women cannot be drafted?" Fifty-nine percent approved of a decision that (1) had not in fact been made and (2) contradicted most recorded opinion! What the Court had actually said in *Rostker* v. *Goldberg* was that Congress did not *have* to draft women just because it drafted men; that is, if Congress saw no need, it did not have to draft women just to be "fair" to men.

get to stay home, were even more enthusiastic about single women's participation than were single women themselves![13]

The data for the 1970s are quite different. Again and again, men are more supportive of women's participation than are women. On eight items measured between 1970 and 1973, men scored an average of 8.3 percentage points higher than women with a range of 2 to 13 points. There are several possible interpretations. One is that the ERA debate caused men to think that women should assume a full share of life's responsibilities as long as they were asking for a full share of its rights and privileges; a second is that women are more opposed to military (and compulsory nonmilitary) service than are men, and this applies to service for themselves as well as for men; a third is that women would prefer to reap the benefits of citizenship and avoid obligation, if possible.

The difference between men's and women's views was typically about eight points both before and after 1969, but the reversal of their views produces a relative change of sixteen points. Such a large change may reflect the fact that the three proposed interpretations are all operative. The first (men's response to women's demand for equality) cannot be proven or disproven by the data, but the average male score for the items considered during the period from 1940 to 1969 was 53.5; for the period 1970 through 1980, it was 51.8. The average item score for women was 61.0 in the first period and 43.6 in the second. Thus, the change seems to lie with the women. It must be reiterated, however, that the items are not comparable. In the first period items clearly referred to a limited role for women; in the second period, even the possibility of hand-to-hand combat for them is considered. Thus, women's views may have been stable even though their scores changed, and men may have moved from a chivalrous view toward a more egalitarian one, even though their scores appear unchanged.

As for the second possibility women are indeed more opposed to military and other forms of compulsory service than are men. But is the third possibility also true? Are women even *more* opposed to service for themselves than to service for men? That is, given women's opposition, is the difference between men's and women's views *larger* when the issue is women? The answer seems to be no. First, only in 1970 and after did polls systematically ask both men and women about both men and women. Male–female differences on such items is consistently small (1 to 5 percent), and those differences do not always vary in the same direction. Thus, the data do not appear to demonstrate that women are trying to shirk their responsibilities while seeking their rights.

In the 1970s no distinction was made between single and married women in the phrasing of questions. This is interesting in itself. It seems to represent a final break with the patriarchal assumption, derived from

TABLE 8.1.    Support for Compulsory Service

| Item | Race | | Sex | | Age | |
|---|---|---|---|---|---|---|
| | W | NW | M | F | 30–49 | 18–24 |
| Data from 2 March 1980 | | | | | | |
| Return to the draft | 60 | 49 | 66 | 53 | 67 | 41 |
| Draft for women too | 53 | 42 | 58 | 45 | 53 | 49 |
| Registration for men | – | – | 85 | 81 | 85 | 77 |
| Registration for women | – | – | 59 | 52 | 57 | 58 |
| Data from 20 July 1980 | | | | | | |
| Return to the draft | 61 | 36 | 62 | 54 | 64 | 37 |
| Draft for women too | 52 | 31 | 55 | 44 | 51 | 45 |
| Registration for men | 82 | 67 | 81 | 80 | 82 | 66 |
| Registration for women | 53 | 28 | 50 | 48 | 52 | 44 |

English common law, that upon marriage a woman loses her separate legal identity—or that marriage is so different for women and men as to require a blanket exemption for all women who are wedded.*

Another interesting finding appears when respondents' views are examined by age group. The young and the old have quite different views about what should be required of the young. Patriarchy is so often discussed as an institution in which men oppress women that the control of children given to fathers, the power held by the old over the young, frequently goes unremarked. War is the most explicit instance in our society of old men's coercive exploitation of young men. Unfortunately, Gallup did not report peacetime opinion about items relating to war and the draft until the 1970s. Perhaps during wartime (or at least during World War II and the Korean War), the young accept (or accepted) the "inevitable." During the post-Vietnam or "peaceful" 1970s, the young do not seem resigned. A consistent pattern appears in the age differences Gallup has recorded. The young are the most opposed to coercive military or nonmilitary service; those between thirty and forty-nine—"householders" in the Hindu age-cycle, those with special responsibility for the affairs of this world—are the most exacting and coercive; and those fifty and over sometimes support the householders and sometimes have more temperate views. In table 8.1 support for coerced participation, as stated in all the Gallup polls, is broken down by age, race, and sex.

*The United States has at times exempted husbands and fathers from the draft. In Israel any married woman can claim exemption; married men cannot. To some degree "single and married" have stood, for women, as surrogates for "working woman" and "housewife." Differences in the attitudes of these two groups are significant enough that a woman's possession or lack of an independent income should become a routine variable in any social science analysis.

When the issue is "generic" or specifically involves young men only, the pattern is clear. The older are more willing to coerce than the younger to be coerced. When the question involves women the curve is flatter, but there is no increase in the desire to shield women with age. Older people are demanding of young women. No age group is as prepared to coerce women as it is to coerce men, but society *is* prepared to require involuntary social and military service of women.

Region, party, and income have some effect on the items considered here, but sex, age, and race have more. Women, the young, and nonwhites, those with least authority and "stake," seem least willing to coerce participation. The "householder," older, white, and male, the kind of person who makes society's decisions, is more prepared to coerce. He has the larger stake and is willing to use others to act for him. The nonwhite and the young are overrepresented not among the "deciders" but among the prospective "servers." Note that nonwhites are the group *least* disposed to support coercive recruitment into coercive institutions, but, ironically, they are *in them*—voluntarily or through economic coercion.

When attention shifts from "should" to "expect," 59 percent of women and 54 percent of men believe that it is likely or fairly likely that by the year 2000, "women will be drafted into combat units just as men are," if there is a draft. Some 69 and 68 percent believe women will be electable as vice-president by that time, but only 46 and 45 percent believe women will be ordained as priests, ministers, and rabbis. Apparently coercive authority seems more attainable for women than moral authority![14]

These findings are reinforced by a 1978 Louis Harris survey in which two-thirds of the public supported draft registration and a majority favored a return to the draft. But women split 47 percent (for) to 49 percent (against), and among adults between eighteen and twenty-nine, two-thirds rejected the draft and half opposed registration. Perhaps more important, 70 percent of the public indicated its belief that the Vietnam draft had been "unfair," and three-fourths believed that "all young people of military age" should be eligible for a draft.[15]

THE VIEWS OF YOUNG PEOPLE

Young people had several other opportunities to register their views. A Gallup Poll of 30 April 1979 showed 80 percent of men and 74 percent of women favoring an opportunity for *voluntary* military or nonmilitary national service, but only 20 and 12 percent had a definite interest in it for themselves, and only about one in three would select military as opposed to nonmilitary service. Gallup data from 1978, representing the views of thirteen- to eighteen-year-olds, showed a majority of both boys and girls supporting women's service in Army or Marine combat units and more than two-thirds supporting their use as combat pilots. Girls and young people from white-collar families tended to be more supportive, but not to a statistically significant degree.[16] *

Data analyzed by Faye Dowdell on the attitudes of high school seniors toward the military found that young men were more occupationally oriented toward the military and that women were more service (in the sense of "help") oriented. Women (Black and white) expressed unwillingness to volunteer for a "necessary" war† at a rate of 5 to 2; Black men were unwilling 5 to 3; white men were evenly split. Conversely, Blacks and white women were *more* likely to see the military as an opportunity. This was especially true for Black women; white women and Black men had rather similar views. Moreover, Blacks and women perceived discrimination as well as opportunity, and Black women, who saw the most opportunity, also saw the most discrimination. One of three Black women saw discrimination against both Blacks and women; one of four Black men saw discrimination against both Blacks and women; one of five white women saw discrimination against women, but only one of ten saw it against Blacks. Finally, about one of ten white men saw discrimination against Blacks, while a slightly higher percentage saw it against women. Nevertheless, Blacks saw themselves as generally receiving fairer treatment in the military than in civilian life by a rate of 2 to 1; white women split evenly; white men saw civilian life as fairer by better than 2 to 1.

White women (7 percent) were least likely to want to serve, and half of those felt that they were likely to. Three times as many Black women (21 percent) wanted to, but, again, only half expected to. White men fell in the middle in terms of wanting to serve (14 percent), but as many who wanted to serve saw service as likely. A quarter of all Black males "wanted" to serve, but almost 40 percent thought it likely that they would![17]

An April 1982 *Glamour* magazine survey found that its readers supported the registration of women 44 to 28 percent, and the draft of unmarried women rather than fathers 62 to 38 percent. Thirty-three percent believed women should be trained for combat, but 23 percent thought women were not strong enough, and 27 percent thought they were not emotionally equipped to handle combat. Almost 40 percent felt that using women in combat "would create more problems than it would solve."[18] While not systematic, these results fit what is known from other polls.

A spring 1980 poll of Berkeley students showed 40 percent supporting registration, one-third supporting registration for women, 40 percent

*The 1978 question referred to women's being "allowed," not "required," to serve.
†About one-quarter of the women and 15 percent of the men said that "there was no such thing."

saying women in the service should be available for combat roles, but only 12 percent supporting a peacetime draft, and 40 percent (a majority of women) saying they would not serve if a draft was instituted.[19]

A University of Southern California student survey taken about the same time showed that even among respondents with a high "Attitudes Toward Women" (AWS) score—that is, generally egalitarian—only a quarter thought women should serve in the military and in combat, and most of them thought the Army was not as appropriate as the Air Force or Navy. The USC study's attempt to show correspondence between general views about women and views about women in the military was highly successful. On one item the correlation was nearly perfect. When asked to agree or disagree that "on the battlefield, most women would probably panic and run under fire," all those with low AWS scores agreed; those with middle-range scores split 53 to 47 percent; and all those with high AWS scores disagreed![20]

SO WHAT?

Public opinion is important, first, because it affects the decisions of elected officials and, second, because it affects public support for the military. The views of the young are especially important, since they are most likely to be asked to volunteer for or compelled to enlist in the armed forces.

With some justice, elected officials complain that analysis of public opinion rarely yields a clear message. Indeed, public opinion might have more control over events if its contents were clearer. But it is not just a matter of content. There is the question of shape—is there a modal view shading to extremes, or are there two or more strongly held views with no middle ground? There is also the question of intensity—do "disagreers" care enough to resist? And are views informed and consistent—is the size of the draft-eligible pool known, and is that pool large enough to meet requirements if all publicly supported exemptions are offered? Is opinion stable—do new information and changed circumstances alter opinion? Is the issue salient—is it *the* issue on which voters vote?

Further, officials can go a long way toward shaping opinion, especially on defense issues. Nationalism is an intense and widely shared value; agreement can almost always be forged to support the United States as opposed to an "enemy." In addition, knowledge can be controlled; keeping information from the enemy is usually an acceptable justification for keeping information from the public as well (or instead). But defense and especially war call for sacrifice and even self-sacrifice, and people are not always enthusiastic about such sacrifice. Further, the means for resistance lie in the hands of the people. Citizens can refuse service, and even if they suffer for that decision, entering service and encountering combat could be worse. Or citizens can submit to service and then resist —passively by "dogging it" or more actively by "fragging." (There is little public discussion of mutiny or internal resistance, but the military's intense discipline and its emphasis on "leadership" should alert the public to the fact that the commanded do not always obey.)[21]

Women play an important part in the effort to shape public opinion. Accounts of atrocities featuring the rape of virtuous women (such as nuns and virgins) are a part of the justifying story of every war. Similarly, women's preparations for war—for example, arms training for Iraqi, Nicaraguan, and Guinean women—are a sign of a nation's unity and commitment. After the war many atrocity stories are neither verified nor remembered; similarly, the women trained to use weapons are rarely committed to battle, and it is not clear whether their mobilization has primarily affected the enemy (Look how serious we are!) or the nation's men (Women will do it if you don't)!

Poll data make it appear that the U.S. public expects women to contribute to the nation's defense and is prepared to coerce them if necessary. It is equally clear that society does *not* expect women to kill, and that it hopes to protect them from being killed. Thus, there is no dispute over women's serving as nurses and typists, some dispute over their service in less traditional fields; and a good deal of resistance (which is by no means unanimous) to their service in combat arms and/or on the battlefield. These attitudes could be called chivalrous.

A patriarchal perspective is reflected (1) in the support of older persons for young people's participation in the military, (2) in distinctions made between single and married women, and (3) in apparent support for an exemption for "married men with families" as opposed even to single women.

About 1970 an arresting shift occurred. Before that date more women than men supported military participation for women; afterward, more men than women supported it. Is this a case of men's seeing war as an ever-present possibility and believing that if women want equality elsewhere, they must accept it in the military as well? Or is this a case of women's believing that war is avoidable and that refusing to prepare for and participate in it is an effective way of preventing it? If the Vietnam War had been more widely approved of, would women have been more eager to participate? Would men, seeking the opportunity to become heroes, have sought to keep women out? Or does the difference between Black and white attitudes toward service suggest another explanation?

Blacks consistently give less support to coerced military participation than whites. Perhaps because of their very high *actual* participation, this point has been overlooked. It suggests that support for the military and the draft comes from those with a stake, whereas participation comes

TABLE 8.2.   Policies on Military Service for Women

|          | Restricted | Unrestricted |
|----------|------------|--------------|
| Volunteer | A | B |
| Coerced | C | D |

from those searching for an opportunity. Women's lower support may reflect consciousness of their relative stake in existing institutions; since their military participation is currently so restricted, it is not clear to what degree they see the military as an opportunity.

Two important considerations are not covered in the various polls. One is capacity: many Americans do not see women as capable of service. It would be helpful to assess views about the appropriate roles of "able and trained" women as opposed to "just" women.

The second is the relationship between voluntary and coerced participation on the one hand and restrictions on combat on the other. Even though feminists protest against and ask for public solutions to the private violence women experience (e.g., rape), they are less energetic in protesting against the public violence done to young men. Women in the United States have never been drafted or ordered into combat; war is, simply, not as salient to them as it is to men. Further, questions about women's military participation are often not clear as to whether voluntary or coerced participation is intended. When the words used are "allow" or "assign," it is hard to know just what the respondent believes.

In a survey of undergraduates at Northwestern University in the fall of 1982, students were asked to indicate whether or not women should be assigned to particular military jobs. They were then asked if they had assumed the women were volunteers. Two-thirds answered yes. Next, the students were asked to respond to the first question again, this time assuming that women had been drafted, and also that they had been trained and were physically and psychologically qualified for the various jobs. The responses were very similar. Finally, the respondents were asked the same question but told to assume that the women were trained and qualified volunteers. This time responses assigning women to nontraditional and arduous jobs were consistently and significantly higher! Responses treated women most like men when it was explicitly stated that the women were volunteers. In that instance 55 percent of the respondents supported women as soldiers in hand-to-hand combat, 71 supported them as commanders of large military bases, and 78 supported their service as crew members on a combat ship.[22] Thus, if two sets of variables (coerced versus volunteer, restricted versus unrestricted) are taken into account, there are four possible policy positions (table 8.2). ·

A represents current policy. B would be coherent with the classically liberal position of letting each individual be "all he/she can be"—that is, not imposing restrictive legislation or policies. *C* is a position that the U.S. public would almost certainly support in an emergency; even *D* might have substantial, but not majority, support. Unfortunately, no survey to date has worded its questions clearly enough to permit a confident allocation of public views among the four categories.*

Some military commanders believe that the American people "won't stand for women coming home in body bags." They fear that the nation's nerve will fail, or that the public will insist that women be withdrawn from dangerous situations. Therefore, they argue, women should not even be allowed to volunteer for dangerous assignments. Obviously, it would be foolish to make oneself (or one's country) dependent on persons whose capacities one is unwilling to use, but the "body bag" question is not simple. It may be that the public *will* be distressed by dead women soldiers, and *will* ask itself, "Is this goal worth the death of our young people?" And it may answer no. One can well understand a commander's desire to keep such questions unasked in the midst of a campaign. Nevertheless, the root question is, indeed, "Is it worth it?" and if women's participation forces the issue, if it makes defense policy salient sooner, does society not benefit? Conversely, women's deaths might stiffen the U.S. backbone (or upper lip). During World War II the bombing of English civilians did not lead to English surrender. The bombing of Japanese civilians did, presumably not because women died, but because it seemed possible that the whole population would perish.

Clearly there is more to learn about the public's opinion concerning military women. At present public opinion is invoked to justify restricted opportunities for women who volunteer during peacetime. Yet it is clear that women will be called, and probably coerced, to assume more responsibilities if war should come.

---

*Congress could complicate the issue further by allowing the coercion into any position of volunteer women, while guaranteeing that drafted women would serve only in restricted roles. Or, as has essentially been done to men, the opposite.

# 9

## Biology, Sex, and the Family

When civilians with unformed opinions about women in the military first begin to think about the subject, they often begin with biology. They question women's capacity, their fitness and strength; they ponder the meaning of sex between soldiers; and they reflect upon military families —particularly those in which mothers and wives wear uniforms.

Fitness is a concern both at the time of enlistment and during service. Establishing physical standards for enlistment has proven relatively easy and noncontroversial; establishing and, especially, enforcing standards for continuing service have been more problematic. Physical strength has become an issue only recently as women have (1) moved into jobs that require heavy work and into previously all-male units, and (2) become a significant proportion of the personnel in particular units and specialties.

Sex, on the other hand, has always permeated the atmosphere of enlisted life. This is partly because so many enlistees are young single men away from home, surrounded by peers, and with little access to marriageable women. Thus, talk about sex and the pursuit of it are rampant, both at home and abroad.[1] The military endeavors to some extent to make sex safe: at Camp Casey in Korea, for example, a billboard at the exit gate lists the ten houses of prostitution with the highest venereal disease rate for the last reporting period. But no official and ongoing responsibility is assumed for the local women with whom enlisted men consort.

The sex life of the enlisted women is quite a different matter. Traditionally the women's corps insisted upon a ladylike or an asexual image in order to counter the rumors and stories associated with women who associated with military men. Further, any woman who became pregnant was discharged. When the services were integrated in the 1970s, and when pregnancy was no longer grounds for the involuntary discharge of even unmarried women, it became harder for the military to maintain what was, in fact, a double standard. Further, maternal responsibilities,

which the military could ignore when mothers were only civilians associated with military men, could no longer be ignored when the mothers
themselves wore a uniform.

"Family" is also a prominent theme in military conversation. The context is different from that of "sex," though; indeed, it invokes near reverence, for the protection of the family justifies the military's existence.
In addition, the services' guarantee that families will be taken care of is
essential to getting soldiers to take risks; they have to be confident that
by offering protection to the nation they are not endangering their own
families.

The importance of families to the military is demonstrated by DOD ex-
penditures of $10 billion a year on family programs. It was symbolized by
placing a day-care center in the Pentagon and by the introductions made
at an Army War College Seminar, where officer participants introduced
themselves to guests not by rank, specialty, or even academic training,
but by name, wife's name, and childrens' names and ages.[2]

### FITNESS

Lack of fitness has not been described as a major barrier to women's
enlistment as compared with men's, nor has it been a major reason for
women's discharge from the service. Still, military service *is* selective.
Some 22 percent of youths are automatically excluded on the basis of
their AFQT scores or for failure to meet educational standards; if another
15 percent are excluded for failure to meet physical standards (usually
for being overweight),* and if still others fail to meet moral standards,
the pool for enlistments may be composed of as little as 60 percent of
young people. (Both physical and mental standards can be reduced in
time of emergency. It has been U.S. policy, however, to have a single
enlistment standard at any particular time, the myth being that every
member of the military is available for "worldwide assignment.")

Today, women's entrance physicals routinely include gender-specific

---

*A 1985 DOD study found that the rigorous fitness standards developed by the sepa-
rate services in the 1980s had resulted in height/weight standards that made 96 percent
of men between sixteen and twenty-four eligible to enlist, but only 74 percent of women.
It recommended that men's standards be tightened and women's loosened so that only
7.3 percent of women (and 5.8 percent of men) would be defined as overweight. The Air
Force modified its standards in 1987; the Army already had the more equitable standards
in place for its active-duty personnel. Under the new Air Force standards, the maxi-
mum allowable weight for a woman five feet, four inches tall was raised from 139 to 146
pounds. The desired weight was raised from 125 to 131 pounds (P. J. Budahn, "DOD
Wants Weight Rules for Women Recruits Eased," *Air Force Times*, 8 December 1986; Pat
Dalton, "Weight Limits Raised for Women," ibid., 6 July 1987; and John W. Overbey II,
Phillip E. Winter, and Michael T. Lawrence, *The Medical Fitness of American Youth for
Military Service* [Alexandria, Va.: Defense Manpower Data Center, 1986]).

items such as pelvic examinations, and standards for non-gender-specific items (such as vision) are the same for women and men. This was not always the case. When women were first recruited for the Women's Army Auxiliary Corps (WAAC, which became the Women's Army Corps, WAC, in 1943), men's standards were used and therefore no pelvics were given. Later a consultant for women's health and welfare was appointed to establish appropriate health standards for women. The director of the WAC wished to hold women to generally higher standards than men and also to screen them more thoroughly. Her goal was to reduce disability discharges (principally for gynecological and psychoneurotic reasons) and build a corps above criticism. She also sought careful monitoring of women once in service. For instance, she requested that all women scheduled to go overseas take a complete physical, including a test for pregnancy. The Army refused, on the grounds that such a procedure would be too time-consuming and expensive, and that men were not screened at embarkation.[3] As it turned out, the medical evacuation rates for women in the European, Indian, and Chinese theaters were approximately the same as those of noncombatant men in the same theaters; the rate was substantially higher, however, for the Southwest Pacific, a difference apparently due less to women's physical health than to command attitudes and policies.[4]

Another World War II inclusion-of-women problem involved the Army's practice of checking every soldier every month for healthy feet, mouth, and teeth and for the absence of vermin and venereal disease. For women, an adequate venereal examination would have included a monthly pelvic, and some commanders insisted on this. Eventually a regulation was issued stating that pelvic examinations would be done (1) only as needed, (2) rectally "where indicated," and (3) with a woman officer present. If women's "higher degree of modesty" and the consequent need to provide women officers as witnesses were experienced as a bother, the source of the problem was the mostly male nature of the military medical setting. Whether women would have been "near rebellion" if their physicians had been women, or whether men would have become suddenly modest in a setting dominated by women physicians and aides, is unknowable.[5]

Maintaining fitness for active-duty personnel is a chronic problem. In July 1981 DOD directed the services to develop new fitness programs that would (1) base measurements on percentage of body fat, (2) include those over forty in fitness programs (thus ensuring participation by those holding the most rank), (3) add strength and flexibility training to aerobics training, and (4) put teeth into the enforcement of standards.[6] All services now conduct annual testing, and the results are reported to DOD. Penalties for failure to meet standards range from a reprimand to demotion, denial of reenlistment, and discharge. Most fitness failures are due to overweight, and the usual remedy is to place the individual in a weight-management, or, as the Air Force calls it, a "fat boy," program.* Physical training practices vary by service and within the services by unit; however, all members of a particular unit usually participate in the same programs.

Physical training is a major component of basic training. Although fitness is one goal, in that setting physical training is also used as a tool for the development of unit cohesion and discipline. Programs are not designed solely to build bodies; they are also intended to build commitment and to develop the habit of compliance.

The Marine Corps has always conducted separate and different basic training for enlisted women and men. So has the Army, except for the period from 1978 to 1982.† Basic training is supposed to be just that—basic, the shared introductory experience of enlisted personnel. (In the Air Force all basic training actually occurs at the same location.) Basic is not the same as combat training; even the infantryman goes on to Advanced Individual Training (AIT). Thus, "basic" is the common denominator—except that it is not common for Marine and Army women and men.

Basic is highly structured. Trainees sleep in open-bay dormitories. They are together and their activity is directed around the clock. Organization is both hierarchical and residential. Because dormitories are segregated by sex, the smallest and lowest unit of organization is, by definition, sex-segregated. Integration, then, occurs at a particular level. Any activity at the lowest organizational level, the squad, is conducted according to dormitory residence and is de facto sex-segregated. This means that rugged physical conditioning could be conducted in sex-segregated groups simply by controlling the level at which it is offered. Platoons (which are composed of squads) of women could be combined with other platoons of women to maintain sex segregation at the next level of organization, the company (some 150 people), or they could be combined with men's platoons to integrate the company level of training. In fact, the Army's "resegregation" did not institute a return to the com-

---

*In 1985 the Air Force discharged 258 individuals for being overweight; in 1986 it discharged 1,061. This was a dramatic jump, but the trend had been upward since 1981 (Pat Dalton, "Separations of Overweight Members Up Fourfold," *Air Force Times*, 16 March 1987).

†Before that, women's basic was conducted by the WAC. When the WAC was disbanded, women were integrated into the Army, and basic training was also integrated. Resegregation occurred four years later. The Army explained that women's presence harmed men's performance, because integrated basic training was not sufficiently challenging for men (see Chapter 3).

plete separation and difference of the past. Basic for women and men remained similar; what was new was the fact that it stayed separate up through the company level. Female and male instructors were retained to train both women and men.

The Air Force and the Navy describe themselves as conducting integrated training. However, because of residential segregation, they can and do conduct some elements of training in sex-segregated units.*

After basic is completed, Marine and Army work units are more likely to conduct regular and strenuous physical exercise than are Navy and Air Force units. Physical training that is conducted by work (in contrast to residence) group is sex-integrated and may involve daily, hour-long workouts. Running is a favored activity, but calisthenics are also a normal part of the routine. Thus, women may be spared physical training with men in basic only to have to participate with them in their first work assignment!

Training or conditioning sessions typically begin or end a day. Their arduousness depends very much on the commander and the work of the unit. At one Army base in Korea in 1982, early morning runs (in combat boots) were the norm; at a base in West Germany, a late afternoon run (in jogging shoes) was a regular but not a daily event. At the first base alternative forms of exercise were permitted, but the effect of this policy was blunted by the offering of a unit prize based only on competition in running. This meant that women who were permitted and might have preferred aerobics, dance, or another form of exercise felt pressured to run instead. Unless women had been athletes before coming into service, most would not previously have experienced such a strenuous regime. If they were in poor shape, it would not be fun. Still, one suspects that the social climate surrounding exercise (including whether it rewards effort and offers positive reinforcement) is as important to women's attitude and performance as its specific content.

The Army's fitness program includes testing on pushups, situps, and a two-mile run for both active-duty and reserve personnel.† The minimum required and maximum scores for seventeen-year-old Army men and women in 1986 are given in table 9.1. These figures were substantially more rigorous than those in place as recently as 1983.[7]

The Navy program emphasizes "fitness for life" and includes education

---

*If the problem were one of providing equally taxing workouts to a heterogeneous population, one would think ability grouping would be the best answer. This, in fact, was the solution chosen by West Point in the assignment of its cadets to running groups; however, it is at odds with the principle of uniformity—a principle believed to be crucial to the development of cohesive units.

†The "Fit to Win" program also included a change in the Army's master menu to reduce both salt and calories.

TABLE 9.1.   Army Fitness Scores, 1986

|  | Minimum | | Maximum | |
|---|---|---|---|---|
|  | M | F | M | F |
| Pushups (no.) | 42 | 18 | 82 | 52 |
| Situps (no.) | 52 | 50 | 92 | 90 |
| Two-mile run (min.:sec.) | 15:54 | 18:45 | 11:45 | 14:45 |

about nutrition, exercise, smoking, accidents, substance abuse, high blood pressure, and stress management.

The Air Force has required an annual 1.5-mile run for some time. In 1983 personnel under twenty-nine years of age were expected to complete that run in 14:30 minutes if male and in 15:36 if female. Personnel over fifty could use up to 17:00 minutes if male and 18:15 if female. At that time the Air Force was planning to shorten the running time for men (whose standards had been set in the 1960s) and to add a situp test for both men and women.[8] A new height/weight standard without age differences was being phased in, and those who did not meet the minimum standards were directed to join a rehabilitation program that required women to lose three pounds a month and men five.

The Marine Corps does not just give tests; it gives mandatory training. All Marine personnel regardless of age, sex, or rank do a minimum of three hours of physical training a week during duty hours. In addition, a test consisting of a flexed arm hang, situps, and a 1.5-mile run is required. A woman who is five feet, four inches tall can weigh 102 to 138 pounds *or* can have under 26 percent body fat. "Food abusers" enter a six-month program to "take care of the problem."

Clearly there is pressure to maintain fitness. It is strongest in the Marine Corps, which details its expectations in its public-affairs pamphlets. Fitness standards seem reasonable and do not affect women more adversely than men. The increased attention given fitness may in part be a response to the fitness habits of the 1980s and in part a response to a "more military" presidency. Attention to fitness may also derive from questions about women's capacity to do their share of heavy work. Such questions have given rise to a new personnel issue—physical-strength testing for job specialties.

PHYSICAL-STRENGTH TESTING

Being strong and being fit are not necessarily the same. Weight-lifters and football linemen serve as an illustration. Indeed, an Air Force

Academy football coach was once incensed to learn that a star player was not eligible for an officer's commission because he was overweight.[9] Similarly, the Navy has noted that bulky enlisted personnel can be extremely useful aboard ship even though they are not very "fit."[10]

Strength testing became an agenda item when a 1976 report by the U.S. comptroller general noted that military women in new job specialties were not always doing the tasks associated with those specialties. The report suggested that the attitudes of supervisors and women themselves and women's lack of physical strength might all play a part. It specifically recommended that attention be given to developing physical tests for job specialties.[11]

The Air Force had actually already developed such tests, and the Marine Corps had plans to do so. The Air Force called its "Physical Work Capacity" score the "X-factor," and new Air Force enlistees were being assigned physical-strength profiles at the Armed Forces Examining Entrance Station (AFEES) by January 1976. Subsequent testing showed that the AFEES' subjective testing was underestimating men's and overestimating women's scores. A machine was therefore ordered for this testing in 1978. Lifting seventy pounds to six feet (the X-1 standard) was held to represent a capacity for "heavy work over a prolonged period" and was required for placement in 85 skills with 123,000 slots, or 28 percent of all Air Force enlisted jobs. (Air Force officers are not tested for strength.) These jobs were principally in mechanical or electronic specialties. A score of 2 qualified an individual for "sustained moderate work over prolonged periods." The test was to lift forty pounds to elbow height. This score applied to 227 specialties with 190,000 slots, or an additional 43 percent of enlisted jobs. Thus, 71 percent of Air Force jobs were deemed to require more than mere fitness.[12]

Virtually all men, but only 29.4 percent of women, were able to meet X-1 standards. This meant that Air Force strength testing eliminated 70 percent of women from 28 percent of Air Force jobs—jobs open to all men—presumably because equipment had been designed so that men in general can use it. (The X-3 factor, the minimum score, involved lifting twenty pounds to elbow height. Virtually every enlistee could meet that requirement.)

At the end of 1981, the Air Force raised its standards for X-factor scores. The new X-1 standard became lifting 100 pounds to six feet; X-2 became lifting 70 pounds to six feet; X-3 became lifting forty pounds to elbow height; and X-4 became lifting 20 pounds to waist height. Although 82 percent of men can meet the new X-1 standard, only 4 percent of women can do so. Four percent of Air Force jobs fall into this category. Ninety-five percent of men and 31 percent of women meet X-2 standards. Twenty-nine percent of jobs fall into this category.[13]

Air Force physical-strength standards were put into place with little notice or justification to the public. Still, the lack of test validation caused no outcry, perhaps because the test ostensibly made sense. Meanwhile the Air Force, describing the current system as an interim measure, contracted with the Texas Institute of Technology to develop validated scores for assignment to AFSCs that would include stamina as well as strength as a factor, and that would also provide physical tests appropriate for those to be assigned flying duties.

The Navy approached strength testing more conservatively. Although women accounted for 8 percent of Navy personnel by 1983, they made up only 2 percent of the personnel in the twenty-six occupations the Navy had identified as requiring special physical strength. After a study of the strength requirements of these jobs, the Navy concluded that it would not be worth the time and money to set standards and implement a physical-screening system. The Navy noted as part of its assessment that there were common shipboard demands (such as fire fighting) that might be made of all persons aboard ship regardless of their work assignment; there were other tasks required of everyone on a particular work team; and still other tasks to which only the strongest crew members need be assigned. Its conclusion was that most work was done in a group, a fact that must be taken into account in any study of the implementation of individual strength testing.[14]

Acknowledging the wide separation of score distributions between men and women, the Navy suggested that its effect could be minimized by (1) applying standards only to the limited number of jobs demanding substantial physical strength, (2) using only tasks required of everyone as criteria, (3) reviewing tasks to identify ways of redesigning equipment and procedures, and (4) allowing for gains in function through better technique. (For instance, it was found that virtually all women could open a water-tight steel hatch with one arm if they kept their arm straight and lifted with their legs by climbing up the ladder, instead of climbing the ladder, grasping the handle, and then trying to lift the handle by straightening the arm.)

The Army has long considered the problem of physical strength in estimating just how many women it can "utilize." A 1958 study concluded that 25 percent of the Army could be female, using the same criteria that are used today—physical strength and relation to combat.[15] To arrive at this number, the 1958 study estimated that fewer than 25 percent of its MOSs required lifting and carrying fifty pounds as part of the serviceperson's regular duties; it prescribed no strength testing for either women or men. By the late 1970s, however, discussion inside the Army about the utility and utilization of women was vigorous. Questions about the effect of women's participation on Soviet perceptions of U.S. strength, on unit morale, and on civilian support for the military excited strong feel-ings. At least one memo said, "The Army should take no more women." Strong as these views were, they did not prevail—at least not immedi-ately and directly. What would make it possible for the Army to "take no more women"—to hold the number of women in the Army constant in 1980—was the development of a new rationale for restrictions. This was based on the old (1958) criteria of physical strength and proximity to combat, but the Army's conclusions were quite different. The 1978 EWITA study proposed restrictions based on the percentage of women estimated to be able to do the work of some 133 MOSs. In EWITA each MOS was given a difficulty rating based on a description of its most strenuous aspect and stated in terms of weights (50, 75, 100, and 125 pounds). Forty-three were held to require the ability to lift 100 pounds; 48, 75 pounds; and 18, 50 pounds; and 22 were declared to have no lift-ing requirement. After twenty years of advancing technology, the Army now found that 70 percent of its MOSs required the serviceperson to lift more than 50 pounds! The 1958 figure had been only 25 percent.

Having assigned requirements to particular MOSs, EWITA estimated what percentages of women and men would be able to meet them. Take, for example, the 43 jobs said to require the ability to lift 100 pounds. Not all men were expected to be able to do all 43. In fact, 100 percent of men were estimated to be able to do only 36 of them, and there were 2 jobs that only 50 percent of men were expected to be able to do. Estimates of the percentages of women capable of doing the 43 jobs were both lower and more varied: 100 percent were believed capable of doing one; no women were believed capable of doing 6. Other estimates were 9 jobs, 5 percent; 5 jobs, 10 percent; another 5, 25 percent; still another 5, 50 percent; 4 jobs, 35 percent; 3 jobs, 15 percent; 2 jobs, 75 percent; and one job, 40 percent; another, 80 percent; and another, 90 percent. Overall it was estimated that 95 percent of men could do 121 of the 133 jobs studied; and that 95 percent of women could do only 32 of them— and 22 of these were MOSs with no strength requirement at all.

Physical strength had not been a primary concern of commanders. Nevertheless, as job analyses emerged based on each person's being able to do every element of a job, and with equipment and job definitions designed for a male population, physical strength requirements emerged as a sure and "objective" way of dramatically reducing opportunities for women by restricting both the number and the range of jobs available to them.

Work on work continued. A new method involved rating by job incum-bents of the physical demands, criticality, and teamwork requirements of particular MOSs. The ratings proved reliable (i.e., repeatable). In gen-eral, the overall rating of a MOS was similar to that of its most demanding task. Estimates of criticality (learning difficulty, tolerance of delay, and consequences of inadequate performance) were also reliable. However, efforts to assess which tasks were, in fact, performed as a team were not at all reliable. Moreover, the 1980 work did not establish the validity of the ratings.[16] The data, then, were not adequate.

The Office of the Deputy Chief of Staff for Personnel continued the extensive effort to establish valid physical-strength standards. When physical standards were finally ready to be put into place late in 1983, however, they were used for recruit counseling but *not* for assignment. Adherence to the standards was described as voluntary on the part of the recruit. One interpretation holds that this policy was generous, leaving the choice of MOS to the individual woman. A different interpretation is that the policy was rooted in the knowledge that the standards would not withstand scrutiny.

In developing its ultimate set of standards, the Army did not begin by making a list of tasks for each MOS and then identifying the physical demands of those tasks. Instead, it created job clusters of MOSs based on the amount of upper-body strength required *under combat conditions* even though women, being barred from combat, would presumably have served in such MOSs in noncombat assignments only. The method used, then, held women to the standard of the most vigorous, not the most likely, duty.[17]

The Army made much of its use of long-established Department of Labor (DOL) standards for physical testing. However, it was Army Training and Doctrine personnel who assigned individual MOSs to particular categories. Moreover, the Army did *not*, in the end, use the categories—sedentary, light, medium, heavy, and very heavy—established by DOL.

According to DOL, "medium" work consists of lifting weights up to 50 pounds and frequently lifting 25 pounds. "Heavy" work consists of lifting weights up to 100 pounds and frequently lifting 50 pounds. "Very heavy" work involves lifting over 100 pounds. The Army found 100 percent of men and 74 percent of women qualified for "medium" work, 82 percent of men and 8 percent of women qualified for "heavy" work, and 80 percent of men and 3 percent of women qualified for "very heavy" work.

The Army separately determined that the 100-pound lift disqualified some individuals (18 percent of men and 92 percent of women) from 64 MOSs that required more than a 50-pound lift but less than the next cut-off, 100 pounds. It then argued that "the heavy category neither conforms to the distribution of jobs nor does it optimize the physical capacity of women." Based on this observation, a new category—"moderately heavy" —was created, requiring a lift of 80 pounds and frequent lifting of 40 pounds.[18]

What was the effect of the new category? It was to create for 64 MOSs (44,000 jobs) a separate category with standards that 26 percent of women could meet. But it *also* created a standard that 100 percent of men could meet. Thus, the cut moved the 18 percent of men who had previously been in the 74 percent female "medium" category into a new category that was only 26 percent female. The male–female "overlap" was minimized, and, perhaps most important, no group of men was left as a minority in a group of women. The new category included the top 26 percent of women, but *all* men. One hundred percent of men were now in and dominated the top categories. Small men were not left behind.*

The net effect of the Army's standards was that only 8 percent of women (compared with 82 percent of men) were expected to be able to do heavy or very heavy work. These categories included 440,000 of the Army's 572,000 slots, or 76 percent of all jobs. Again, 92 percent of women were expected to be ineligible for more than three-fourths of the Army's jobs on physical-strength grounds alone, yet in 1982 over half the Army's women were serving in those very jobs! Their lack of strength had not previously been a primary complaint, nor was there any evidence that it affected unit performance. Still, a vigorous application of the system as developed in 1982 could have sharply reduced recruitment possibilities for women.

Physical-strength testing was begun in 1984. In effect, the Army had two clusters—"light" and "heavy." Over 99 percent of men and 21 percent of women were able to lift 80 pounds, thus qualifying for "heavy" work. Most of the new male recruits took heavy jobs, but 17 percent of those eligible for heavy jobs took light ones. Women eligible for heavy jobs divided about equally between heavy and light; however, almost a third of the women eligible for only light work actually took heavy jobs. In absolute numbers, more than 40,000 men and 3,000 women took heavy jobs. Some 8,700 men and 5,300 women took light jobs.[19]

Cutoff scores for mental qualification are regularly varied; the military wishes to get "enough" draftees or enlistees and does so. The same thing will surely occur with physical standards, but when the categories are large and the tests skip from 50- to 80- to 100-pound lifts, adjustments will be both more difficult and more visible than they are for changes in mental standards, and may be perceived as more compromising. At the same time, questions about scaling equipment and tasks to women's size have gone almost unaddressed. U.S. forces regularly share equipment with men of other nations whose size and strength are significantly less than that of U.S. personnel. This leads one to wonder how serious the problem really is, since no literature has appeared to suggest that small allies (as contrasted with women) create any difficulty.

---

*And such men were eligible for infantry assignments. Apparently commanders could not see declaring one out of five men unfit for combat duty, especially when the same man might be able to enlist in either the Marines or the Navy on the same day that the Army turned him down.

Moreover, the U.S. population is becoming more ethnically diverse, and different groups have different average heights and weights. Does the Army really want, for instance, to have men of Asian or Latin descent concentrated in particular types of jobs because of size and strength measures? Or do the Army and the country want all male citizens available for any assignment? During World War II, Japanese Americans were used as fighting men; Sen. Daniel Inouye has described himself at five feet, six inches as a big man in his unit and noted that some of his men wore size-four shoes![20] In the past and even now, the military seems to have been able to accommodate men of many sizes. Physical strength has not been an issue. Individuals were simply used as needed. The real issue, then, seems to be extending the range of size (and strength) to include *women*, not extending the range per se.

Strength has never been a criterion for men's participation except in certain elite units. It is not clear that the Army really wants to use it as a criterion for men, because a crucial element of military service is fairness, and "fairness" is usually taken to mean inclusiveness—equal risk. Further, no one seems to have analyzed how less physical strength might be balanced by the other desirable qualities (e.g., education) an enlistee might offer. It is almost as though physical-strength testing is being used to reduce opportunities for women in an "objective," "gender-free" way because women are a problem, not because strength is a problem.

Finally, if the Army wishes to utilize fully the available pool of personnel, should it not reserve the "light," "medium," and "moderately heavy" jobs for people who cannot meet higher standards? This would mean that about a quarter of the Army's jobs would be reserved for the 74 percent of women and 0 percent of men ineligible for heavier jobs. Competition for jobs would then be more balanced, although over a third of the youth pool would still be competing for a quarter of the jobs. Certain MOSs might become all or mostly female if this were done but all-female units have not been an obvious disservice to the Army—consider, for example, the Army Nurse Corps.

One study the Army did *not* undertake was to see how women who could not pass the proposed physical-strength test were doing in their jobs. Were the estimated requirements valid? Or have women found ways to do the work? The Army analysts found five jobs rated "heavy" or "very heavy" that had substantial numbers of women working in them. In these cases the Army actually redefined ("separated") the MOS to remove the onerous duties from the job description.[21] Thus, the Army made women more likely to qualify for the jobs they were already in: wire systems installer/operator, ammunition specialist, motor transport operator, medical specialist, and military police.

The Marine Corps has taken an entirely different approach to the question of strength. It considers basic training its physical-standards test: if one can get through basic, one is fit to be a Marine. The Marine Corps claims to wonder exactly what other services' "basic" is all about if large numbers of women and men can pass it and still not be able to do the services' jobs.

## SEX

Three topics coexist under the rubric of military women and sex. One is harassment; a second, its antithesis, is fraternization; the third is pregnancy. Although some forms of harassment have been discussed previously, it is so pervasive and so fundamental to women's military experience that it must be considered here as well. "Fraternization" is the name given to behavior, perfectly ordinary in civilian life, that may (or may not) be punished in the military. Pregnancy will be discussed again because the military discusses it again and again.

There is nothing uniquely military about the harassment described by enlisted women. Harassment by superiors demanding sexual favors, analogous to rape, and harassment by peers making lewd remarks, analogous to racial intimidation, are well known to young enlisted women.[22] Even older and senior women admit incidents, although they do not share the resignation that accompanies the narratives of younger and junior women.

Five conditions promote the harassment of young military women in the All-Volunteer Force: (1) the lack of both older women supervisors and a separate women's corps, where shelter and good advice could be sought; (2) the isolation experienced by women who have moved into new job fields, integrated living quarters, and remote locations; (3) the degree to which many women are outnumbered, constantly exposed to men who do not know them, cannot reasonably expect to get to know them, and therefore feel entitled to test and tease them; (4) the fact that many young women (and men) are away from home for the first time and find themselves immersed in a culture where people play the game of courtship according to rules very different from those followed in their high school or home town; (5) military living quarters and dining arrangements that ensure that even during off-duty hours women are exposed to comments, pressure, and intrusions. They have no "space," no place for a "time out."

Commanders frequently claimed to see no harassment and to hear (of) no harassment, and they spoke not of harassment. Then in 1980 the iceberg's tip emerged. The Subcommittee on Investigations of the House Committee on Post Office and Civil Service issued a report entitled *Sexual Harassment in the Federal Government*, giving legitimacy and visibility to a subject of longstanding concern to working women.[23] Around the same time the Army issued a report suggesting widespread harassment and very publicly court-martialed two soldiers for using indecent language to a woman soldier.[24]

It was a series of *Baltimore Sun* articles about Fort Meade, though, that forced action in the form of an on-base investigation and investigations by I.G. (Inspector General) officers from the Pentagon and by the House Armed Services Committee. The latter not only held a hearing but provided television coverage.[25] (Fort Meade is in Maryland, whose voters have sent several women to the House of Representatives. One of them, Marjorie Holt, is a member of the House Armed Services Committee. Only a year before the investigation, Holt had questioned whether harassment was a serious problem for military women. When it became evident that it was, she may have felt a special need to respond conscientiously. These factors may have helped to bring the issue into the spotlight.)

The February 1980 hearing included testimony from soldiers stationed at Fort Meade, the top-ranking woman officer from each service, and ten "randomly selected" female enlistees.[26] The bulk of the testimony suggested that it was particularly young enlisted women who experienced harassment, that it was practiced especially by senior enlisted men, and that women believed that they had no recourse. Even if one considers that it is part of the ethos of an institution like the military to harass newcomers and low-ranking personnel, and even if one assumes that some harassment of women is sexual only incidentally (the chief aim being to harass), it remains clear that many military women were plagued by constant verbal assault, bullying, and restraints on their freedom: for example, many avoided going to service clubs alone and felt that other dining and recreation facilities were not worth trying to use. Many sought protection in marriage.

Finally, in 1980, the military took heed. Policies were developed. Commanders who had rarely had harassment brought to their attention were told that ending it was part of their duty. But getting men to assume responsibility for ending harassment was difficult. Commanders do not want to forbid activity that they cannot police, and peers do not want to side with victims. To the degree that harassment decreased, it was probably the result of publicity, which made the threat of punishment at least somewhat credible and persuaded women that harassment was not condoned and that their own efforts to control it would not be punished.*

What the Army did not do was look for and try to eliminate the structural causes of harassment, such as the isolation of women and the threat

---

*News stories concerning punishment for sexual harassment, or protection for its victims, began to appear with some regularity. For example, in 1982 a court of military review overturned the conviction of a woman sailor who had gone AWOL rather than face an "initiation" threatened by her male co-worker. "Men Will Be Boys," *Air Force Times*, 6 December 1982.

they posed to their immediately senior but often less well educated male superiors. Further, the Army did not address the problem of "bonding" its women and men soldiers, even though it was greatly concerned about the problem of bonding men to men.

Systematic training in this area was slow to begin, although the services launched a variety of educational programs. "Sexual Harassment: What Is It and What To Do" appeared in the February–March 1981 *Commanders Call*, and training for advanced Army NCOs, initial-entry personnel, and troop units began in 1982. The Navy introduced training for its civilian employees before it began compulsory training for its commanders. But none of this occurred until a decade after the buildup in the numbers of military women.

In August 1981 DOD issued a directive from Secretary Casper Weinberger declaring sexual harassment "unacceptable conduct" that would not be condoned or tolerated. Complaints were to be given "high priority."[27] A report, *Countering Sexual Harassment*, was prepared by Nina Beth Gilder for the deputy assistant secretary of defense, which summed up most of what was known and believed.[28] Several points should be emphasized: first, harassment is closely tied to attrition in women's minds, second, spending twenty-four hours a day on a military base makes harassment far more debilitating than it would be in a civilian job, third, more harassment seems to occur overseas and in the field (where U.S. women are in short supply).*

When the Army began its enforcement campaign in 1980, one of the first widely reported convictions was that of a woman private who was reduced in rank, sentenced to thirty days hard labor, and fined $298 for placing her hand in a man's groin area and "squeezing." This sentence attracted a good deal of attention and some derision because at about the same time, an Army colonel charged with attempted rape, indecent assault, and sodomy against three women pleaded guilty to lesser charges and was permitted to retire with full benefits after paying a fine of $15,000.[29] Some may have thought justice had been done, since the Army had proved that it would prosecute both men and women; others considered the action against the woman out of proportion. Still, military men who are asked about being harassed report it with regularity. The exact nature of the men's harassment and its impact on them, however, are not at all clear.

One aspect of sexual harassment that has not been discussed or studied involves the influence of race and class. One wonders whether Black women receive different treatment from white men than from Black

*In the fall of 1987 DACOWITS reported "overt and blatant sexual harassment" especially in the U.S. Navy and Marine Corps in the Pacific. This sparked a new round of investigations and admonitions. Molly Moore, "Pentagon Unit Finds Sexual Harassment," *Washington Post*, 18 September 1987.

men, and if white women do, and if harassment is different and more degrading or threatening for a woman when it comes from a person of another race or background. It seems clear that even though Black and white enlisted men have learned to work together, they do not usually socialize together.[30] Nor do Black and white women often date interracially. (Women who do often experience social pressure if not ostracism.) Given these facts, it would not be surprising if codes for work and social relationships that cross sex and race (and even class) lines have not yet been worked out.

Finally, it is possible that women do not fully appreciate the depth of disdain some men have for some women. One account of male enlisted life describes three kinds of women: "nice girls," "whores," and "sweathogs."[31] The first two categories are familiar; the third comprises women who can be "viciously" abused verbally and physically and shared among friends, and who submit to this treatment voluntarily and without payment. Many individual men seem to be comfortable relating to any of these categories while seeing individual women as confined to one of them.

The military may wish its women were all "nice girls." It may frown upon whoredom. But has it considered the possibility that some military women are being treated as "sweathogs"? What does the military teach about women who wear uniforms? One might hope that the training and group membership the uniform signifies would bring respect and protection to women; or that the large number of them married to other service personnel would convey the message that military women, like civilian women, like military and civilian men, are enormously varied. Unfortunately, these goals have not been fully realized, and it is apparent that no military woman can afford to be "sensitive," nor will she have much opportunity to experiment while developing her sexual identity. The numbers game is such that each woman is besieged, and each is likely to be treated simultaneously (but by different persons) as a nice girl, a whore, and perhaps a sweathog. Each woman will be talked about all the time. Young women fresh from home and high school, used to a 50–50 environment and to being treated as individuals, will find themselves in an overwhelmingly male environment where they are always perceived as members of an opposite category. Increasing the number of women (the solution followed by private colleges and universities that "went co-ed") is not presently possible. The method followed for nurses —to make them officers and give them their own corps (still modestly integrated)—has been discarded.* Military women today find their niche within a male culture.

---

*The Navy does cluster women's assignments, especially at sea. It also has the lowest pregnancy and attrition rates.

The military has long frowned on personal relationships between a senior and his or her subordinate. Although "fraternization" has never been precisely defined, as far as male–female relationships are concerned it seems clear that one should not date a person whom one commands or who commands one, and that junior enlisted personnel should probably not date NCOs or officers. (Some believe that the reason nurses were made officers was to avoid the awkwardness of trying to keep nurses and doctors from dating.) [32]

The Army left fraternization issues to custom and local commanders until 1978, when it finally prepared a regulation (600-20) dealing with the "relationship of superiors toward subordinates." This was revised in November 1984 and provided examples of improper relationships that would lead to the perception of "favoritism" or "undermine" morale, discipline, or authority. [33] The particular goal at that time was to prevent dating between trainers and trainees, especially during basic training. Having outlined the problem, the regulation concluded, "No canned solutions are available."

The Air Force revised its one-sentence regulation (AFR 30-1) prohibiting friendships between officers and enlisted personnel that interfered with "judgment or duty performance" only after the service lost a conviction of an officer who openly picked up enlisted women and had sex with them. Even the revision did not forbid dating between enlisted personnel and officers, and the Air Force routinely assigns military living quarters to married officer–enlisted couples. The Air Force now requires only that "the circumstances" not prejudice "the good order and discipline of the unit."

The Navy had no service-wide policy on fraternization. Since August 1984, however, Article 134 of the "Manual for Courts-Martial" has forbidden it. "Frat," then, remains an issue, but it is punished locally and because of its effect in particular circumstances rather than because of the act itself.

The marriage of the Olympic diver and Air Force officer Miki King and the newly graduated Air Force Academy cadet she coached demonstrates the leniency of some practice. The other end of the enforcement spectrum is represented by the discharge of a Marine officer who requested that his enlisted fiancée be given an early discharge so they could be married, and the dismissal of a woman Army officer but not that of the two men (an officer and an enlisted man) with whom she committed adultery. [34]

Mattie E. Treadwell has told the story of U.S. military women and pregnancy through World War II. Then the issue was primarily the reputation of the corps. In general, the services sought to protect their reputation by guarding their women. In at least one camp, the women's barracks were surrounded by barbed wire and floodlights—to protect the residents from their fellow troops! [35] Nevertheless, rumors about the immorality of military women persisted, even though the 1943 pregnancy rate among unmarried Army women was approximately one-fifth that of civilian women. In the North African theater, the pregnancy rate among enlisted women was lower than that of civilian women at home and about the same as that of nurses in the theater. Some 1944 data suggested a rate less than half that of civilians.[36] While the data are inexact, it is clear that pregnancy was not endemic and that the "morality" of military women—as measured by out-of-wedlock pregnancy—was probably better than that of civilian women.

The fastidiousness that impelled the use of the word "cyesis" rather than "pregnancy" in official data and the "less than honorable" discharge of unmarried pregnant Army nurses was modified during the course of the war; and pregnancy was less punitively managed in the other services.[37] Needless to say, though, men who fathered children rarely received punishment; and all men, married and single, were regularly provided with prophylactics "to prevent disease." Women were not, and in the European theater sex education that was "very frank" rather than "moralizing" was "obliged to desist"—the WAC did not want "chemical or mechanical" information.[38]

During the war just getting married was grounds for requesting discharge, and discharge was required for pregnancy. By the 1960s marriage alone was no longer grounds for requesting discharge, and married women could even join the military. Concern had shifted to the presence of minor children in a woman's home; even if the children were teenagers and the husband's from a previous marriage, military women had to obtain waivers on a case-by-case basis in order to remain on active duty. By 1973 some 60 to 80 percent of waivers were being approved; still, 6 percent of military women were leaving service each year because they were pregnant.[39]

In June 1974 DOD directed all the services to make discharge for pregnancy voluntary by May 1975. The Army adopted this policy for officers but requested postponement for enlisted women. That request was denied. However, the Army has, ever since, periodically requested a return to the old policy of involuntary discharge. The other services seem content to let the Army take the lead; they have not engaged in the same public debate.

Discussion today focuses not on "morality," but on "readiness," "the mission" and "deployability." A second line of discussion focuses on disrupted or exempted training, the need for special medical facilities, and dangers to women and their fetuses. Sometimes it is also argued that pregnant women damage unit morale.*

*A Navy study of pregnancy and its costs in time, productivity, and morale suggests that the facts are quite different from these assumptions (Marsha S. Olson and Susan S.

If morale is impaired, one reason may be that military policies do not permit the temporary replacement of a pregnant woman, so that other personnel must make up any work she cannot do. In addition, men feel that they get extra and more onerous assignments when pregnant women are present but protected, as when medical staff women are taken off X-ray work or wards for contagious illnesses. This resentment is interesting, for it suggests that convergence creates problems and hostility that do not occur when the sexes are kept quite separate. That is, the same people who resent women's doing almost but not quite the same work as men may be quite content to have women doing no work at all or working as civilians. It should be remembered, though, that pregnant women are just one of several varieties of "work-arounds," people who do not carry their own weight. Indeed, an Air Force study on the effect of women in the Air Force found three major reasons for "working around": poor motivation, ineptness, and inexperience. None of these is gender-related.[40] Moreover, similar special consideration in the form of arranging work schedules is often given to enlisted personnel so that they can "moonlight" in civilian jobs or go to school. Thus, while accommodations for pregnancy do occur, other accommodations occur as well.*

The data on pregnancy suggest that pregnancy rates vary significantly among the services, within different units, and, possibly, at different points in time. In its 1976 Women in the Army Study, the Army reported 3.8 percent of its women as pregnant. It also gave the average number of work days lost by a pregnant woman as 105. Only two years later, its 1978 *Evaluation of Women in the Army* said that "pregnancy is perceived by the Army in the field as the greatest impediment to the full integration of women." It declared that 15 percent of enlisted women became pregnant in 1977 and that 39 percent of them carried to term.

The basic post-1975 policy on pregnancy for military women has been that (1) pregnant women could be honorably discharged on request; (2) pregnant women would be discharged if they were participating in training that they could not continue because of their condition; and (3) pregnant women would be discharged if they were pregnant prior to entry.

---

Stumpf, *Pregnancy in the Navy: Impact on Absenteeism, Attrition and Work Group Morale*, NPRDC # TR 78-35 [San Diego, Calif.: Navy Personnel Research and Development Center, 1978]). A more recent study captured headlines when it reported that during a ten-month period 41 percent of pregnant sailors in San Diego were unwed. Nationally the rate is 30 percent (Robert Dietrich, "Sailors Pregnant to Avoid Rough Duty?" *San Diego Tribune*, 25 February 1988).

*If the policy of not replacing pregnant women creates morale problems or work overload, it would seem reasonable to change that policy, especially since replacement needs for pregnancy and maternity are very predictable. Yet the policy seems to be taken as immutable. One must conclude either that sharing the work is practicable or that some hope that by maintaining an irritating policy they can obtain a different change— the discharge of pregnant women.

Pregnant women are not sent overseas. They work as long as "feasible," go on "sick-in-quarters status" before delivery if necessary, and receive four weeks maternity leave after birth. New developments include military facilities for infant care. (Typically these do not accept children under six weeks of age, although mothers are expected to return to work after four weeks.) Women were once allowed to wear civilian maternity clothes, but, in the interest of uniformity, the services have one by one created regulation maternity uniforms. Further, one by one the services have begun to *refuse* discharge to some pregnant women who request it.[41]

Complaints about letting women be discharged "just because" they are pregnant arose first over women who had received expensive specialized training or enlistment bonuses. Thus, the military often finds itself moving in two directions at once when it reviews its policies. Both directions involve a reduction in women's choices: if it had its wish, the military might simply retain those women it wished to retain, and discharge those it wished to discharge. That is, the decision would be transferred wholly from women to the services.

By 1981 each of the services had done its own studies putting pregnancy in the context of "lost time." Each had data to show that although women lost more time than men for medical reasons, overall lost time was not very different.*

The 1982 Army study on women was considerably delayed by DOD's failure to settle on a new pregnancy policy. A proposed policy that met with some favor was that first-term soldiers who became pregnant would be discharged if discharge was determined to be in the Army's best interest; another proposal was that pregnant women be sent to the Inactive Ready Reserve until fully deployable. The Air Force proposed involuntary discharge during the first three years of service. In all cases the crucial constraint seems to have been legal: that is, changes desired by the military were limited principally by what the services estimated the courts would permit.

In one memo gathered for the 1982 Army study it was noted both that pregnant soldiers would be evacuated with other noncombatants and also that it was "not indicated that pregnancy has a significant effect on the deployability of their [the women's] units." This is not "evidence," of course, but it does suggest the possibility that deployability data are like "lost time" data. That is, they are not readily available, and if they were, they might show that men and women are not so different in deployability, although their reasons for nondeployability may differ. More than one commander has noted that non-English-speaking wives who cannot drive are in some ways as dependent as the child of a single mother.

---

*Moreover, pregnancy rates should decrease slightly with time because military women will be less concentrated in the prime child-bearing years.

Some deployability problems are the result of too few rather than too many women. For instance, when women became widely diffused following the abolition of the WAC, facilities like beauty parlors, which were heavily used where women were concentrated, became an economic burden to small units. Similarly, women may now have to fly hundreds of miles for a Pap smear or drive all day to see a gynecologist. However, the visibility of these costs does not make them unnecessary, nor does it prove that women are more expensive than men; it is simply that men's costs have long ago faded into budgets as overhead.

The concern about pregnancy (a condition that affects only women) has focused on women's availability for work and on attrition, both of which are indeed affected by it. One conclusion has been that restrictions should, therefore, be placed on women's enlistment. Fortunately, it now appears to be understood that policies about women must not be made in isolation from policies (and facts) about men. It is equally important that policymakers be fully aware of the variation among women. For instance, available data show marked variability with regard to completion of enlistment. In particular, Black women's attrition is significantly lower than white women's.[42] To restrict women's enlistment generally because of white women's high attrition, then, would be to penalize Black women for white women's behavior. Finally, wouldn't it be ironic if fully analyzed data were to show that single mothers are more likely to stay in service and serve well than married ones? Wouldn't it be ironic if the data were to show that policies that seek to discharge single mothers and that prohibit their enlistment actually impair readiness and effectiveness by barring an inordinate number of ready and devoted enlisted personnel?

## FAMILY

The "military family" includes all who wear the uniform and their nuclear families. A familiar formula describes these relationships:

1. Husbands and wives are deeply bonded.
2. He is in uniform and his primary responsibility is to fulfill his military duties.
3. Her primary responsibility is to the members of her nuclear family.
4. The military has a responsibility to support all in the military family, even if the member of the military is absent or dies.

The military's commitment to support family members (previously called dependents) is unique among U.S. institutions. It is almost tribal. It meets needs instead of rewarding individual performance. It is almost un-American.

Nuclear military families need support because they experience exceptional stress. They move a lot; husbands and wives are separated a lot (two-thirds for more than a month, and one-third for more than four months, in 1985); they live in isolated parts and abroad (one-fourth overseas); their income is modest; and death and danger, as well as arbitrary and abrupt change, are a part of daily life.[43]

Although military leaders may think of officers as mostly married and enlisted personnel as single, the fact is that 51 percent of enlisted people are married, 13 percent divorced, and 3 percent unmarried with children. (See Appendix C for more data on families.) Thus, the military must deal with a variety of families. To exclude those who do not fit the norm would be to exclude too many.

In dealing with families, the military faces several problems. The first is the enormously expensive and logistically complex problem of caring for them. Currently there are more than a million spouses and as many children as there are personnel. Since 1942 support has included numerous benefits and services, including housing, education, medical care, even shopping facilities. Indeed, the military "safety net" is so extensive and so complex that family service programs have been developed by all the military branches to help families use the programs that exist.*

The second need is to keep families happy in order to attract volunteers and retain trained personnel. This need has spawned a series of conferences on, programs for, and studies of military families.

The Army's first Family Symposium was held in Washington, D.C., in 1980 and was sponsored jointly by the Association of the United States Army and the Army Officers' Wives Club of the Greater Washington Area under a slogan offered by Gen. Edward C. Meyer: "We recruit soldiers, but we retain families!" Recommendations made there and later implemented included replacing the word "dependent" with "spouse" or "family member," and establishing an Army Family Liaison Office. The right to employment of family members and their need for assistance in acquiring appropriate jobs were central issues—it had become clear that military families now have working wives.† It also became clear that

---

*Air Force, Army, and Navy *Times* newspapers and handbooks for service personnel devote large amounts of space to current information on housing allowances, housing eligibility, moving expenses, commissary and exchange privileges, travel, educational benefits, and more. These constantly change and often vary by rank. No individual is likely to be fully informed on benefits even if she or he endeavors mightily.

†Forty-four percent of the spouses of enlisted people are employed and 12 percent are unemployed. Since 1986 preference for federal civil service jobs and non-appropriated-fund jobs has been given to military family members. Even so, over half of the employed spouses of enlisted people made less than $5,000 in 1984 (Janet D. Griffith, Zahava D. Doering, and Bette S. Mahoney, *Description of Spouses of Officers and Enlisted Personnel in the U.S. Armed Forces: 1985* [Arlington, Va.: Defense Manpower Data Center, 1986],

the military's established volunteer activities did not meet the needs of working wives and that volunteer programs were becoming difficult to staff. Further, there were fewer individuals available for such "wifely" chores as relocating a family to a foreign country.[44]

"The Navy Family: It Matters," proclaimed the Navy's guide for planning and operating Family Service Centers.[45] These centers are supposed to ensure that necessary services and information about resources reach Navy families. These services are considerable and wide-ranging: they have to be to meet the needs of itinerant, young, low-income families. * Included are personal, marriage, and family counseling, child care, health benefits assistance, deployment assistance, resource management, legal assistance, and assistance to families with special needs, such as handicapped children or non-English-speaking spouses. This, of course, is the intention. Any particular family on any particular base may not find the resources it needs, but the Navy has found that the officer retention rate went from 40 to 57 percent and the enlisted rate (for a second tour) went from 37 to 45 percent after family support programs began functioning.[46]

The Air Force, too, held a family conference, which highlighted research findings from a study commissioned by the Office of the Chief of Chaplains. The study found far more dependents than military personnel, many families living off base, and airmen and their families often holding several civilian jobs.[47] (Among junior enlisted personnel, one of three held a second job, and two out of three civilian wives held a full-time job.)[48]

The third problem concerns those families in which the wife or mother is in the military. Even though an effort is made to think about, and to make policy for, spouses and parents of both sexes, it is clear that questions about the compatibility of certain martial and marital statuses arise most often when it is the woman who wears the uniform. Let us examine the effects of particular marital statuses on one's martial status.

The relevant variables are being a man or woman, being married or single, having a civilian or a military spouse, and having or not having children. The permutations number twelve, as shown in table 9.2.

In 1985 DOD reported the following distribution of personnel across these statuses: single with no dependents (3, 6): 36 percent; married to

---

pp. vii, 107 ; see also P. J. Budahn, "DOD Defends Record on Employing Spouses," *Air Force Times*, 7 September 1987; Rick Maze, "Study: Spouses Have Trouble Finding Work Overseas," *Air Force Times*, 2 September 1987).

*Officers' wives have an additional difficulty—pressure from their husbands' superiors to participate in military volunteer programs. An extended series of articles appeared in the *Air Force Times* in 1987 on this subject. In 1988 DOD formally announced such pressure was inappropriate.

TABLE 9.2.    Possible Marital Statuses

|       |           | Spouse   | No Children | Children |
|-------|-----------|----------|-------------|----------|
| Men   | Married   | Civilian | 1           | 7        |
|       |           | Military | 2           | 8        |
|       | Unmarried |          | 3           | 9        |
| Women | Married   | Civilian | 4           | 10       |
|       |           | Military | 5           | 11       |
|       | Unmarried |          | 6           | 12       |

a civilian wife (1, 7): 56 percent of men; married to a civilian husband (4, 10): 19 percent of women; married to a military spouse (2, 8, 5, 11): 6 percent (4 percent of men, 34 percent of women); single parents (9, 12): 4 percent.[49]

The single, childless enlisted person (3, 6) is viewed as the most deployable, but young singles are also the most unreliable group in terms of discipline, drugs, and other problems. Older singles are considered very desirable, but feel discriminated against and resent, for instance, having to live on base in quarters with limited amenities and having to stand quarters inspection. They also feel that they get extra "Hey, you" duties and other undesirable assignments.*

The value of a male soldier married to a civilian (1, 7) is also rarely questioned—even though the costs of supporting military families are enormous. Childless men married to military women (2) and unwed fathers (9) are not seen as requiring special policies; if problems have arisen, the services seem to have managed to respond to the particular circumstances.† Thus, men's marital status has generally had little effect on their martial status.

Married women without children (4, 5) are now seen as presenting

*For example, in a 1986 economy measure "career bachelors" (singles past their first enlistment) had their overseas tours involuntarily extended by twelve months.

†There are more male sole parents than female ones, although the incidence among women is much higher. Few commanders want a policy requiring the discharge of all unwed, divorced, or widowed fathers—many are senior, many are officers, some may be academy graduates with sensitive or essential positions. In addition, the status "wifeless father" is likely to be temporary. Commanders are less enthusiastic about single parents who are junior enlisted women, but because sole-parent policies must be general, the women are presently protected by the services' desire to retain similarly situated male NCOs and officers. The current ban on the enlistment of sole parents affects more women than men, since they are more likely to be caring for children and to be legally identified as a parent.

only a limited problem—that of making geographical assignments that permit spouses to stay (and to prosper) together. The greatest stress for the services has come from the women who elect to stay in service after giving birth (10, 11, 12). The handful of women who are married to civilians (10) have not been singled out as a problem: presumably their husbands are expected to function as "wives" in an emergency. However, mothers married to military men (11) and unmarried mothers (12) have become the subject of much discussion. These are the military parents who entirely lack "wives," who lack the support of an adult not under military discipline to provide competent, on-demand child care. Likewise, the one group of men whose value is questioned are military fathers married to military mothers (8). In a sense they, too, are wifeless. Thus, it may be that the primary problem military women present is that they lack wives! The services worry that if called, some parents might not go, and those that do go may leave the services with uncared-for children on their hands. Even if the services were to provide institutional care for the children, public opinion might not support such stringency.*

The military has not been unresponsive to the changes in the American family. One response has been to provide preferential employment opportunities for civilian spouses. A second has been to provide day-care facilities. A third has been to become more attentive to the needs of "service couples."

Although the Reagan administration has not generally been perceived as enthusiastic about military women, the development of child-care facilities began in the 1980s. The stimulus was a 1982 General Accounting Office report particularly critical of the Navy's and Army's lack of facilities. The Air Force, which began providing child care in 1974, has a goal of a center for every base by the mid-1980s. The Army built twelve centers between 1980 and 1985 and scheduled nineteen for 1986. All told there are 554 centers and 400 installations with an average daily

*Data are now available on (self-reported) responsiveness to no-notice recall and no-notice deployment. Only 65 percent of enlisted personnel (and 76 percent of officers) say they can respond "very quickly" in the first case; 54 percent (and 66 percent) can respond very quickly in the second. Dependent care was cited as the chief obstacle by 7 percent in the first instance and 15 percent in the second. Lack of phone, lack of transportation, distance, and school attendance were also reported as "significant obstacles."

Self-reported "workable dependent arrangements" for a short-term and a long-term emergency do vary among personnel with civilian spouses and children, those with military spouses and children, and those who are single parents. Personnel with civilian spouses and children lack short- and long-term arrangements in 6 and 14 percent of cases respectively. The figures for those with military spouses are 9 and 19 percent; for single parents, 14 and 20 percent (*Description of Officers and Enlisted Personnel, 1985: Supplementary Tabulations* [Arlington, Va.: Defense Manpower Data Center, 1986], vol. 1, chap. 7, esp. pp. 7-20, 7-23, 7-29, 7-32, 7-128, 7-133).

attendance of 95,000 at a monthly cost of $160 per child. Two-thirds of the annual cost is covered by parent fees.[50]

The scale of the "service couple" problem differs from service to service, but involves about 6 percent of enlisted personnel. About 4 percent of Army and Marine, 5 percent of Navy, and 9 percent of Air Force enlisted personnel have military spouses. The crucial problem here is geographical assignment.

In 1985, 86 percent of married couples were at the same base, 5 percent "would be," 6 percent were not because they could not be, and 4 percent were not for reasons unrelated to the assignment system.[51] Failure to assign spouses together will increase women's attrition, if servicepeople mean what they say, for in 1985 men and women gave different answers when asked what action they would take if geographically separated from their spouses in their next assignment. Thirty-six percent of men and 41 percent of women said they would accept the assignment; 28 percent of men and 53 percent of women said they would leave the service; and 36 percent of men but only 7 percent of women said their spouse would leave.[52]

The Air Force has had a "join spouse" assignment program since the 1950s. As late as 1982, it had an approval rate of 95 percent for such assignments. In 1983 regulations were tightened, and the approval rate dropped to 89 percent in 1985. Obviously, making assignments to the same base becomes harder as more and more couples are involved (the number of Air Force couples rose from 3 to 9 percent of service personnel in a single decade), as individuals rise in rank and need particular assignments, and as the size of military bases diminishes.[53] One element of the new Air Force policy provoked special criticism. Reversing a ten-year-old policy, it forbade the independent assignment of both members of a service couple to the same "unaccompanied" location. There would be no military housing at such locations, and conditions might be primitive, but the couple could be together, and both would complete a mandatory remote or hardship tour. Particularly galling to some was one reason offered for the change: the "perceived inequity" of military spouses' being together while other service personnel and their civilian spouses were separated. As service couples pointed out, each member is required to fulfill remote and hardship assignments. If they could not do them simultaneously, they would have to endure twice as many separations. At present military personnel can expect to be separated from their families from 15 to 20 percent of the time. Thus, service *couples* could be separated over a third of the time.*

---

*Separations require a skillful alteration of roles. Stay-at-home wives describe having to be effective, single parents one month and nurturing, grateful dependents the next.

Remote tours are not unlike the Navy's sea rotations, which are also required of each spouse and which may involve a one–one rotation. The Navy has decided that married couples (who are few in this service) may not serve on the same ship. Because of the way benefits are managed, it has also found it necessary to discourage couples from accepting simultaneous sea-duty assignments. Thus, those couples with average bad luck can expect to be living together only rarely. The Army, which did not begin its "Married Couples Program" until the fall of 1985, has a higher proportion of married couples than the Navy but an 82 percent success rate in assignment matching, the lowest of the services.[54]

Current benefit policies provide each individual with his or her own benefits at the "without dependents" rate if there are no children. This system provides service couples with a windfall for travel allowances, variable housing adjustments, and money to apply to housing.* It wreaks havoc with couple's affairs, though, when one family member goes to sea or on remote assignment and loses his or her housing allowance. A sensible resolution might be to offer the couple the benefits of the person of higher rank at the "with dependents" rate. This would result in a similar living standard for individuals at the same rank, and it would take care of the at-sea and remote-assignment problem, since those allowances are continued in the absence of a sponsor. However, the Army vetoed this general solution, it is said because the genderless formula would have designated some of its men—even battle-hardened leaders—as "dependents."

CONCLUSION

Achieving physical fitness is not a special problem for women. Particular training programs and the spirit in which they are conducted can have different consequences for morale, but separate standards are set for women and men, and most are able to meet those standards.

Physical strength is another matter. The debate is not (or should not be) over how strong women are, but over how strong they need to be. Strength testing and other physical requirements have a potential for unnecessarily excluding and limiting women and doing so with an aura of objectivity and certainty that is hard to counter.

The reliability or validity of any test is important. But there are more fundamental questions to be asked. What is the appropriate unit of analy-

---

An enlisted woman often has to add a third role—that of adventuring returnee. It is the reentry, the reunion, that seems to be the most stressful phase of deployment.

*It has also led to marriages of convenience to secure additional benefits and the opportunity to live off base.

sis? Is it the individual? Or is it some group of individuals? Is the measure work accomplished, or is it equal capacity to do work? That is, is the issue really the mission, or is it substitutability of personnel?* Further, if tasks are now designed so that almost all men can do them, couldn't those tasks be redesigned so that all citizens can do them?

The Air Force is now studying how much strength is needed to be a pilot. One can confidently predict that if the study is ever released, it will show that a substantial number of women are not strong enough to be pilots. One can also predict that if women were the purchasers and intended operators of military planes, manufacturers would design them so that 100 percent of women would have the strength to fly. It is merely a matter of design and market. Unfortunately, there is almost no evidence that any of the services are serious about redesigning physically demanding equipment for women's use. †

The sexual pressures experienced by the greatly outnumbered enlisted women are frustrating for commanders, who see little prospect of reducing them, and for the women who experience them. But the pressures are not just negative and harassing. Enlisted women are also energetically courted. This sometimes leads to fraternization and often to marriage. Indeed, some women describe a "need" to be married, believing that it offers them protection. This, plus the great mobility of junior enlisted personnel and the need to be married to have even a hope of being stationed together, can lead to quick marriages, which then experience the special stresses of military life.

Overall, more than half of enlisted women are married and more than a third are mothers. Thus, these women have family as well as military roles to fulfill, and their roles as mother and wife are widely perceived as (at least) less compatible with their military role than are the roles of father and husband.

Some enlisted women complain that when the military talks about "families," it means those of male officers and their civilian wives, and that when it talks about the families of enlisted women, it means "a problem." They cite the attention devoted to finding jobs for civilian wives

*The Army's 1982 revision of the scale it uses to define work categories suggests that the issue is really the substitutability of male soldiers.

†The most recent physical-standards struggle involved standards the Navy and Marine Corps wished to apply to future pilots. The length of torso, arms, and legs was the issue. Standards in use up to 1 January 1984 excluded 39 percent of college-age women and 7 percent of men. Standards set in January and in place until May excluded 73 percent of women and 13 percent of men. These were rescinded by the secretary of the Navy as "unintentional" discrimination. Nothing was said about safety (the original justification for the change), the remaining discrimination, or existing Air Force standards that are close to the suspended ones (Jack Dorsey, "Navy Rescinds Size Rules for Pilots That Made Most Women Ineligible," *Norfolk Virginia Pilot*, 30 May 1984).

(to assist in retention of their husbands). The feeling is that enlisted women's retention is not seen as essential, and good strategies to retain them are not being employed. For enlisted women, those might fall principally in the realm of social services or guaranteed assignments with spouses. The military regularly asserts that it is not a testing ground for social experiments or a social service agency. However, military life is racially integrated, there are numerous bicultural families, and the Army, in particular, has served as a vehicle of upward mobility for Black Americans, especially with the All-Volunteer ("economically drafted") Force. Moreover, the military not only offers employment; it provides for dependents. This makes it even more attractive to low-income families who lack access to high-quality civilian services.

Since the military clearly supports low-income married couples, and not just with income, but with professional services as well, why shouldn't it support sole parents and their dependents too? Would the nation be better off if single mothers were on Aid to Dependent Children instead of serving military enlistments? Would their children be better off? Would society in the next generation be better off?

The fact is that the All-Volunteer Force is composed of the most competent needy, and the largest pool of competent needy in the country today may consist of single mothers. Thus, their needs and the military's almost unique provision for dependents may have created a perfectly symbiotic relationship.

The military's anxiety about sole parents highlights its traditional dependence on the unpaid labor of wives. This dependence, like its role as a dispenser of social services, is something the military might prefer not to recognize, but it must, since civilian wives, too, are redefining their relationship to the military—institutional wives are just becoming scarcer and scarcer.

The "morale" factor (the supposed hostility of those who are not parents and who take up the slack when a mother requires a particular schedule or when a pregnant woman must use half a day for a prenatal checkup) is hard to estimate. All units have "get-overs," and they are all resented. Still, military schedules are adjusted for people who hold second jobs, for people who have especially dependent dependents (such as a wife who cannot speak English or drive), and for others. Thus, it is not clear that adjustments made for parents are especially hard on morale.

In the military there is an expectation of readiness for unaccompanied tours, temporary duty assignments, deployments, field exercises, alerts, extended hours, shift work, and changes of station. Not everyone is always ready, however. Some personnel are on leave; some are given a "humanitarian" exemption from moving or have a disciplinary status that prevents reassignment. Perhaps sole parents and new mothers do have an adverse affect on mobility but it is not at all clear that they are the principal cause of reduced mobility: perhaps they are an easy rather than a critical target. It may well be that the lack of preparedness of "emergency essential civilians" employed by DOD or by civilian contractors, inadequate communications, lack of troop carrier capacity, and faulty equipment are far more critical to readiness than the marital status of personnel. It may also be that military parents and sole parents are made a target not because of the costs of pregnancy and child care, not because of commitments to dependents, not because of presumed higher loyalties, and not because of their lack of value or their unreliability, but because of their lack of substitutability and because they are a definable and manageable "problem." Again, few military personnel are actually asked to be ready to leave the country and abandon all familial and community responsibilities within hours. But some are asked, and the myth is that *any* could be. Thus, the presence of individuals who might refuse, or whom the military might not wish to use, is unsettling and disturbing, not because particular persons are exempt, but because their exemption draws attention to the fact that *many* are exempt, that all service members are *not* alike—and that more will be asked of some than of others.

# 10

## Myths Necessary to the Pursuit of War

How is one to understand the competing and sometimes contradictory views, data, and analyses presented above? What sense can be made of the explanations given for policies enacted and rejected? Should one simply ignore the abrupt changes in accessions? Should one disregard the tenuous relationship between research and policy? Should one overlook dubious legal distinctions and contradictory yet sincerely held opinions? Must one simply accept incongruity, disparity, the apparently surreal, or is there a discernible pattern in what has been set forth?

One thing seems certain. To the professional military, the enlisted woman is a raw nerve. To discuss her too thoroughly is to open Pandora's box. To make her, her role, and her status the object of careful scrutiny is to display what the military (and probably civilians, too) would prefer to leave decently draped.

But just what *is* revealed? It appears to be the fact that certain ideas that are essential to the military as we know it are not literally true. That is, the mere existence of enlisted women seems to make it difficult to believe certain myths that are thought to be necessary to the pursuit of war.

A myth is a widely shared, deeply rooted belief that gives meaning to action. Whether true or not, myths are functional. They can encompass contradiction. They are also not very susceptible to either logical or empirical disproof. This means that demythologizing is an often futile exercise—myths are hydra-headed; they possess many lives. Indeed, wide acceptance and "irrefutability" are identifiers. Empirical evidence of the width and depth of belief in a particular myth can be obtained; functional or psychological explanations can be developed; however, the red flag, the sure cue, is the acceptance of the logically and empirically dubious.

In *The Disappearance*, Philip Wylie neatly displayed the separate worlds in which men and women, even those who sleep together, may live.[1] Today, the thoughts and acts of women seem scarcely to impinge upon the managers of legitimate violence in the United States. Women may or may not understand how irrelevant they and sometimes logic and evidence are to those who direct that large, expensive, awesome institution we call the U.S. military. But to at least this outsider, women do not seem irrelevant at all. In fact, they seem to be absolutely essential to the military. Their essentialness, though, lies in their absence. It is this which explains why enlisted women, who are by definition present, are unsettling. Their mere existence contradicts three ideas fundamental to the military enterprise:

1. War is manly.
2. Warriors protect.
3. Soldiers are substitutable.*

## MYTH NUMBER ONE: WAR IS MANLY

Today's U.S. military violates national tradition, first by being a "standing army" (more than 2 million in uniform with a million civilian employees), and second by being committed to fighting anywhere, anytime (an ideal embodied in the Rapid Deployment Force). It also violates a broader norm that holds that peacetime militaries—legitimate, trained, bureaucratic, honored, professional institutions prepared to wield violence—are the exclusive domain of men.

Women have always fought and died in war. However, they have usually been called to difficult and dangerous tasks only to replace men who have assumed even more difficult and dangerous tasks—or to replace those whose tasks have led to death. Cynthia Enloe has referred to women as a "reserve Army," and it seems clear that women will be used should the going get rough.[2] Ordinarily, though, women are not allowed to serve in peacetime when it is safe and when one can acquire enough rank to have real responsibility and authority in wartime. Again, what is unusual about U.S. military women today is their number (10 percent of the total), the number of traditionally male jobs they hold, and, most

---

*All the services are committed to these myths, but each comes to different "therefores" in developing its policies. This makes the myths more accessible than they would be if the services had developed uniform policies. Also, the myths' patent inapplicability to the Air Force (in spite of that service's devotion to them) makes it easier to see that they are not necessarily true for the other services either.

important, the fact that they serve as "replacements" for men who have chosen to stay at home rather than for men who have gone to fight.

In every war, in every mobilization for war, and even in countries where women are ordinarily kept in seclusion, pictures of young women in uniform and carrying rifles are widely displayed. Such pictures in part reflect the reality of a war fought close to home. Interestingly, though, few historical accounts mention women's military service. This is consistent with the need to think of (or to remember) war as manly. In fact, however, few armed women are actually committed to combat, and the pictures may not really be "about" women, or directed toward the mobilization of women, at all. Instead, they may be intended to shame reluctant *men* into the war. The message, then, would be that "*even* women . . . ."*

Again, Russia is a country of statues. Most are of identifiable men. Statues of women tend not to be identifiable; they tend to stand for "woman" or women in general or some abstraction. One particular genre is that of the woman warrior—a colossus (note the masculine ending) that stands guard on a hilltop or in a central square with a sword. This message, too, I believe, is, at least in part, "If you men fail, women can and will save the homeland."

One response to such messages might be that women should not let themselves be used by some men to manipulate (mobilize) other men. Women should, therefore, refuse to serve even as a reserve force. A second response might be that if the military does depend on women's absence, it can be subverted or radically altered by joining it, especially by joining it in large numbers and as full partners. One must be clear, though: the women in today's military have not altered it. In fact, their limited numbers may have made them more conventionally loyal and uncritical than military men. (When I asked a young officer whom she considered her role model, she responded in a sweet drawl, "General Douglas MacArthur.") And men may have become more "military" in order to distance themselves from the women.

Not only are U.S. women not allowed to join the military in large numbers; they are not allowed to join as full partners. They may serve, but they may not serve in combat. The manly role of warrior thus remains as intact as a virgin's hymen. The belief that war is for men, then, is fundamental. Is it essential?

In discussions of the combat restriction, men make it abundantly clear that they do not want *their* women hurt or jeopardized, that they do not

---

*In the 12 March 1984 issue, *Time* magazine ran a photograph of Iranian women in chadors carrying guns and ammunition belts. Other photographs showed the bodies of boy soldiers who had marched through Iraqi mine fields to clear the way for older Iranian troops. These pictures of real and symbolic sacrifices made by women and children must have made it very hard for an Iranian man to resist military service.

want women fighting *with* them, that they do not trust women's competence, that they are concerned about women's reliability, and that they mistrust women's effect on men's cohesion. Further, men are concerned that the use of women in combat conveys desperation to others. But there is another argument against women serving in combat. That is that society will lose its specialists in nurturing and healing—that military women will lose their "femininity."

When men deplore women's loss of femininity, they are usually objecting to women's acting as men act. In general women find this view puzzling. They do not perceive themselves as "losing" something when they learn new skills and information. Instead, when they adopt a new role, women see themselves as adding to their repertoire, as growing, not as diminishing or losing.

When women do what men do, men sometimes describe themselves as losing something—their masculinity. They describe themselves as castrated. Imitation is frequently thought of as a form of flattery. Why, then, do men feel that their very identity is threatened when they are imitated? Perhaps because their gender identity is fragile, and Simone de Beauvoir had it backwards: that is, the root problem may be that it is men, not women, who are "the second sex," and men know it. Surely this is the message of Chodorow, Dinnerstein, and others.[3]

Women know that they are women. They do not require the reservation of a social role as a guarantee of their nature. Women may reject a destiny defined exclusively by biology, but their biology apparently gives them enough definition that they are not uncertain about their identity. Thus, women, unlike men, have not been trapped into defining themselves through opposition and through the claim to an exclusive social role. This means that women are not as easily manipulated by the assertion that they are "not women" if they do *x* or do not do *y*.

Young men are vulnerable to the charge of being "not men" (or "boys" or "girls" or "women"). It would seem no accident, then, that it is young men who do most of the military service. Appeals to manhood are an integral theme of all enlistment campaigns. They are also important to the discipline of basic training. But are such appeals necessary? The best, but not a sure, answer is that no military has yet been willing to try doing without such appeals. Some argue that a volunteer military is actually based on economic coercion. It would seem, though, that *all* militaries have additionally and regularly been rooted in the psychological coercion of young men through appeals to their (uncertain) manliness.

This leads us to the conclusion that a central aspect of patriarchy that feminists have neglected is the oppression of young men by old men and the price young men are required to pay to acquire old men's privilege.

The patriarch, the father, dominates young men as well as women, and demands enormous sacrifices, sometimes including life, from the former. Patriarchs brutalize young men. In Freud's *Totem and Taboo*, young men are depicted as finally uniting and overthrowing (actually killing and eating) the patriarch. Women and young men, then, should have a shared interest in abolishing patriarchy. Indeed, arguments feminists are developing about maternal thinking may be related to this shared interest; the difficulty is that young men secure their adult and gender identity precisely by separating themselves from their mothers.

Patriarchy promises power and benefits to the young men who ultimately prove themselves. But is that proof one of talent, of merit, or of morality? No. It is, in fact, proof of submission. It is evidence of obedience. It is a demonstration of compliance and of willingness to risk and sometimes sacrifice. Military training is the most naked form of surrender old men require of young men, but hierarchy, coercion, and discipline are well understood in the culture of U.S. men. The kind of violence and discipline to which young men are exposed is not the regular or accepted experience of women. Whether or not men believe that violence or the threat of violence is generally efficacious, they do find it connected with and sometimes necessary to the establishment of their gender identity. Even men who have no doubts about their identity realize that they may be required to offer proof of it to society. Thus, they prepare themselves to do and suffer violence in a way women do not. Linking manliness to war, then, furnishes a powerful incentive to young men to participate in the military. Mature men are harder to stampede. They have already paid their dues—they have already been initiated. That this is true can be shown by trying to imagine a military composed of men twenty-six and over. It is hard to do. Men who are already husbands and fathers (patriarchs) are not susceptible to demands for proof of their manhood through military service.

## MYTH NUMBER TWO: WARRIORS AND PROTECTORS

Each of us retains summary symbols of the Vietnam War. Some probably would invoke the image of the nude and napalmed child running down a road. Others might select the American soldier's terse statement, "We had to destroy the village to save it." For me the final act was also the summary. In the evacuation of Saigon, an effort was made to salvage something, to do one thing right, to demonstrate that we had, in fact, protected. An American plane was filled with children, "orphans," to bring them to the United States, where they might grow up strong and free and be proof that the war had not been in vain. That plane crashed. What is common to these events is not just the protector's failure to protect. In each case the purported protector was also the *agent* of destruction.

Charlotte Perkins Gilman, perhaps the original little old lady from Pasadena, said it well. She once proposed to go for an evening walk. Her companion (male) announced, "I shall go with you—I am your natural protector." Gilman replied, "And from whom will you protect me?" She amplified, "As a matter of fact, the one thing a woman is most afraid to meet on a dark street is her natural protector."[4]

If warriors and other protectors frequently cannot protect, and worse, if they are sometimes dangers in disguise, why is the myth that warriors are protectors constantly reconstituted? It is, of course, comforting to the warrior, enabling him to find meaning for the sacrifice asked of him. But it is also comforting to the "protected," who are encouraged to focus on "the threat" rather than on the relationship between themselves and their protector(s).*

Since the United States now has a standing army of professional protectors as an integral part of its culture, it is important that citizens, the protected, examine their relationship to them. For the most part, though, citizens are nonchalant. They accept the fact that the military is the government in many countries; that in such countries obtaining a commission is the route to political success; that citizens there are more likely to be killed by their own soldiers than by foreign ones. But Americans are generally both unconcerned and incurious about the relationship between their government and its military. They see law school as the route to power, and they tend not to identify with the victims of governmental violence. All this, it would appear, demonstrates the power of the myth that warriors are protectors.

The myth concerns only the relationship between the protector and the protected; it puts to the side the relationship of each to a third party referred to as "the enemy," or "the threat." I have discussed these relationships in an essay in *Women and Men's Wars*.[5] Let me provide a condensed version of that discussion here. Citizens easily grasp the danger created by their protectors when the context is nuclear weapons. Consider the general case of which this is but one instance.

First, protectors are given a monopoly on the use of legitimate force. In effect, other members of society are unilaterally disarmed. Second, protectors are selected. Enloe has discussed ethnic and cultural selection, but the young, the old, the valuable (Congressmen and farmers),

---

*A special and breathtaking "threat brief" is offered by the Pentagon to legislators and selected groups of citizens that is intended to generate support for the military and its budgets.

the despised (homosexuals), the "dangerous" (Communists), and women (who seem to be variously or simultaneously seen as too valuable, too despised, and too dangerous) are also excluded.[6]

Protectors are chosen, trained, and armed. But they know (better than anyone) that they can effectively protect very little. Indeed, their ability to protect is based principally on lack of challenge. Experts willingly admit that there is no defense against an attacker willing to give up his or her life—and that a ratio of ten to one is necessary to control armed resistance. Indeed, one suspects that terrorism is abhorred not because it is "war on the cheap" (anyone would like to conduct a social contest in the most economical way possible), but because it so effectively displays the ineffectiveness of protectors. Indeed, protectors are limited precisely to the degree that people actually depend upon them, because a successful attack on any dependent is evidence of a protector's failure. Dependents, then, can be a source of pride; they can bestow honor; but they can also be a burden, a liability. Further, dependents can make protection difficult, draining their protectors by being unruly, risk-taking, careless, and uncooperative.

Ironically, then, the role of protector is most desirable when protection is not actually needed. When it *is* needed, it becomes costly. When the protected begin to make claims on the protector, the protector is likely to begin to make claims on them. The protector may demand more resources. Or the protector may try to control the protected for the protected's "own good." A homely and extreme example is the man who maintains his family's honor by imposing purdah on his women relatives. A more general practice, one employed by all governments, is to limit the freedom of citizens in times of "emergency." Put simply, it is easier to restrict your unarmed protectees than it is to control an armed enemy.

Moreover, protectors can actually endanger the protected by attracting notice and even violence through challenging or belligerent behavior. (Some Europeans are concerned that U.S. foreign policy is dangerous to them in this way.) In extreme cases a protector may desert those he is supposed to protect, or even turn on them. The humiliation of certain defeat can lead some protectors to acts that will certainly destroy those they have pledged to protect—and this may be preferred to permitting protectees to survive and witness their protector's failure. The destruction of cities with their leaders when those cities could have been surrendered illustrates this phenomenon.

It is the most thoroughly dependent protectees—those who represent the greatest burden—who seem most likely to trigger a nihilistic response in their protector. Likewise, the safest protectees may be those who need little or no protection. They do not impose a burden, and if a real threat should materialize, they will be able to help their protector.

As protectees, most of us have probably not fully considered the responsibility felt by protectors, but it is real. Women, so often perceived as albatrosses by men, should make an effort to understand the role they play as protectees, whether they finally elect to accept that role or not. (Men may or may not wish to have women share in the use of legitimate force; possibly they will insist on defending women regardless of the vigor with which women reject their protection.)

The insulation of the protected—at least up to the point where protection fails—is worrisome. It results in ignorance about the general realities of war and the specific actions being taken on their behalf, and it permits them to dehumanize the enemy. The protectee can ignore, condone, even support actions done for her that she would never do herself.

One study of military policy making showed that civilian policymakers were more hawkish than military ones. (Once engaged in conflict, however, military personnel were more committed to doing whatever was necessary to complete their assigned task.)[7] This suggests that military leaders understand the limitations of violence better than civilians. Professional warriors know that "surgical" strikes are not; that sand can disable helicopters; that soldiers take drugs and sometimes frag officers. Civilian officials, on the other hand, most strongly feel the onus of the protector role. They see themselves as having been chosen from all the rest to direct the defense of the country and its citizens. Unfortunately, they are often innocent of practicalities. Thus, they may believe that they cannot risk any hint of weakness, indecision, or hesitation and may be relatively naive about the application of force. As a result, they may believe in and direct others to act upon myth rather than reality.

Even if only inadvertently, then, the protectee is essential to legitimate violence. The protectee is its justification. She also implicitly or explicitly endorses, supports, encourages. Because she relates only indirectly to the violence, she is unlikely to consider whether warriors truly are or are not protectors (even of themselves) until an extreme situation develops, until she is confronted with a My Lai massacre or the bombing of a Marine barracks.

## MYTH NUMBER THREE: SOLDIERS ARE SUBSTITUTABLE

If myth number one supports war by getting young men into uniform, and myth number two justifies the warrior while insulating the civilian, myth number three works primarily on men *in* uniform, to entrap some and to relieve most of guilt over their survival.

Myth number three is never explicitly stated. Its functions (entrapment and guilt assuagement) are not ones we ordinarily celebrate. It manifests itself in enthusiasm for uniformity and in the promotion of cohesion. It goes somewhat as follows: We are all in this together. We are all warriors. We are all brave, willing, and valiant. Some few of us will be called to sacrifice our lives. (Some fewer of us will volunteer to do so.) Anyone may be called. Whoever is called is a "poor bastard." It probably won't be me. There are so many of us that the odds are against it. If I am sacrificed, it will be impersonal bad luck. It could have been anyone else. If I survive, I was lucky. Being lucky is not my fault; it is just my fate.

The Marine slogan "Every man a rifleman" glorifies the interchangeability of personnel: the substitutability, the possibility, the equally shared jeopardy of every marine. The Corps is a relatively small service with a low ratio of support personnel and, even during a draft, a high ratio of volunteers—men who wish to be riflemen. There is some truth to the substitutability myth for marines. But most marines do not die. The Marines took more casualties in Vietnam than any other service, but even so only a small percentage of them died. Being a Marine is, basically, safe.

On the other hand, those marines (and others) who are in the wrong place at the wrong time do die. How do they get there? Some have described a process of "progressive entrapment." That is, an individual volunteers or is coerced into combat step by step—enlistment, training, assignment, combat. Until the last step, the odds of death remain low. Still, even in the face of combat, two strong motives impel an individual to do his best. One is survival (John Keegan reminds us that once in battle it is actually safer to participate than to run).[8] The second is avoiding shame—or, to phrase it positively, backing one's "buddy."[9] One might say, then, that the art of leadership is getting people into situations where the only choice left is to fight bravely.

The military's emphasis on disciplined uniformity is very much in line with this myth. Basic training is a shared trial by ordeal; everyone gets the same treatment, and the safest tactic is to be indistinguishable. At the same time, everyone knows that certain kinds of military service are preferable and safer than others. For enlisted personnel the Air Force is the safest, and it finds recruiting easier than the other services. Certain specialties and units are safer than others. The military may try to share the risk by rotating assignments, but service personnel know who has and who has not seen combat. (Their ribbons show it.) Those who have use terms like "cherries" or "virgins" to refer to those who have not. But the difference can be papered over with the assertion (explicit or implied): "*I could have been called*—it's not my fault I was not."

Women in uniform make this myth less believable. Their very presence forces recognition that military personnel are *not* "in this together." Holding noncombat jobs only, uniformed women are a constant reminder that all those in uniform are not equally jeopardized. Further, it could be argued that their presence increases men's risk by making fewer safe jobs available to men.

Here the convergence of women's and men's roles increases tension and resentment. Some men seem to be able to tolerate women's being kept safely at home; others seem willing to have women share equally in effort, responsibility, and risk. What seems hardest for men to accept is having women share in effort, responsibility, and reward but not in risk —especially if their failure to do so increases men's risk.

If women were kept out of uniform, they could do the same jobs most of them now do without violating substitutability, because they would not be in the pool; they would be civilians. Or women could be removed from all military-associated jobs, and uniformed men could fill them. If those men were eligible for combat, even if they were unlikely ever to be assigned to it, the myth could be sustained. Fate could then be held responsible for men's unequal risk.

It seems, then, that the myth of substitutability, like those of manliness and protection, is at odds with the assimilation of enlisted women—at least as long as the combat exclusion is maintained.

These myths may help to explain such apparently strange decisions as the evolution of women's uniforms. For example, the Army has now added pants to women's uniforms. It has also added a stripe (like men's) down the pant leg and has been working to create "unisex" sizing for all uniforms. The myths also give coherence to the Army's integration of basic training in the interest of uniformity *and* its resegregation of that training to make it "manly." The myth of substitutability also explains the Army's juggling of the physical-strength criteria it uses for assigning individuals to jobs so as to include virtually all men.* And it makes comprehensible the current policy of forbidding service personnel to wear religious apparel—in particular, Jewish yarmulke and Sikh turbans.†

CONCLUSION

Men have a stronger sense of the inevitability of violence than women. They know that they must be prepared to absorb it and possibly

---

*See Chapter 6. The new category of "moderately heavy" work, which encompassed all men, enhanced the myth of substitutability. Yet by encompassing one in five women, it diminished the myth of manliness, although the combat exclusion made it possible to segregate these women occupationally.

†The latter policy was supported by a "twenty-star" letter (from five officers with four stars each), and by the Supreme Court in *Golman* v. *Weinberger* (84 U.S. 1097). The decision (by Rehnquist) accorded "deference" to military authorities' efforts to "foster instinctive obedience, unity, commitment and esprit de corps." Congress was considering legislation to overturn this decision in 1988.

to do it. Many of them believe that the way to minimize the violence one may have to absorb is to perfect the violence one *could* do oneself. Men also assume that the purpose of violence is not actually to kill or to be killed, but to establish one's position in a hierarchy that is worth being in—even at the bottom—because so many (for instance, all women) are excluded. Hierarchy provides order and, equally important, an orderly progression—a promise to younger men of a future when the older men will have gone and they themselves will be in charge. Hierarchy offers young men the opportunity to replace the older men while reassuring the older that they will not be displaced.

The last time the United States fought a war at home, it concerned the "peculiar institution" of slavery. Is it imaginable that belief in the legitimacy and inevitability of violence could someday seem as outdated and peculiar as nineteenth-century thinking about slavery? What is the alternative to war's being manly? Its being womanly? Its being gender-less? Its ceasing to exist? Each of these possibilities deserves thought; each represents a radical change. If women are not prepared to make a commitment to nonviolence as a way of life, and to advocate it for others (especially their "protectors") as well, shouldn't they assume their share of responsibility for exercising legitimate violence? Is it fair to leave conscience-burdening dirty work to men? And should the myth of the warrior–protector be supported and sustained? Or is there a new role, something akin to citizen–defender, that would better serve?* Or should the concept of protection be recast to show that *real* protection may lie in shared effort, in trade, in intermarriage, in the exchange of populations, at least as much as in the threat of or capacity for violence?

Would genuine substitutability increase safety by making every citizen liable for service? Would officials exercise more restraint if ordering troops into combat meant sending themselves, their fathers, sisters, mothers, wives, and daughters instead of just sons (men between eighteen and twenty-five)? Would acknowledging the limits of substitutability reduce the cooperation of those slated to be victims and increase the guilt of those sure to be safe? (The opposition to the Vietnam War included an uneasy alliance between the less privileged who were there and college students who were exempt.)

If the myths of manhood, protection, and substitutability are necessary to the enterprise of war, and if their vitality in the face of disproof is evidence of their necessity, efforts to demythologize the military will be futile. The outside observer who believes that these myths are disfunctional for society must, therefore, probe more deeply. We must under-

---

*The analogy is to Rousseau's concept of citizen as simultaneously sovereign and subject. In the same way, a defender would be simultaneously protector and protectee.

stand not just that they are myths, but why they persist. An examination of enlisted women enables these abiding beliefs to emerge—to become explicit. It may be that enlisted women, who have little stake in being manly, who are embarrassed about being protected, and who have not been part of the death lottery that requires a belief in substitutability, are in the best position to discover what truly makes a society secure. It may not be violence; it may not be national boundaries impervious to migration; and it may not be allowing men to hold a monopoly on the means of violence.

# Conclusion

When he retired as chairman of the Joint Chiefs of Staff in 1984, Gen. John W. Vessey, Jr., said, "The greatest change that has come about in the United States Forces in the time I've been in the military service has been the extensive use of women. . . . That is even greater than nuclear weapons, I feel, as far as our own forces are concerned."[1]

Is this credible? Can a handful of young, unprivileged women be more unsettling than nuclear arms? This book began as a story about pioneering women, a tale of bold, independent women prepared to challenge taboos, take risks, and venture where few had gone before. It turned out, of course, that enlisted women are ordinary women, most of whom are just trying to do their job—with dignity. Few of them wish to change the world, and fewer of them think they are doing so. Enlisted women, then, have more in common with Rosa Parks than with Susan B. Anthony. Yet, merely by insisting upon their own validity and impinging on men's consciousness, they create disarray in the world's mightiest military organization.

Much of this volume has been descriptive. The overview, the narrative, the historical account of generational change and backlash, and even the chapters on military and public opinion have sought to present the enlisted woman's experience in context, while emphasizing the variety of that experience.

Enlisted women serve in four services, in many countries, in hundreds of jobs, and under thousands of commanders, who have a substantial amount of discretionary power. Enlisted women's culture is multiracial, but it is relatively homogeneous with regard to education and social class, and it is very age-stratified. Women who enlist make a nontraditional decision. Once in service, though, they encounter the men in our culture who are most devoted to polarized roles for women and men.*

Moreover, since sex integration, these very men have had to lead and command women, including lesbian women. Having to police woman-to-woman relationships has been difficult for some men, and their discomfort may have had the effect of driving what were previously (tacitly)

---

*I believe "polarized" is a far more accurate description than is "traditional" for roles which prescribe distinct and different activities for men and for women.

accepted relationships into the closet, and of disrupting the bonds between straight women and straight and lesbian women. Thus, integration has probably affected the bonds between women as much as it is said to have affected those between men, yet as the military integrated, it did little (at least self-consciously) either to assess this loss or to foster male–female bonding in the enterprise known as "soldiering."

Sociologists may be able to use this volume to examine theories relating to social change, group proportionality, double and conflicting roles, and socially influenced perception. My interest, though, lies with the policies related to women, and especially with the justifications offered for those policies as they have developed through law, research, and bureaucratic decision making.

If one assumes that women are as competent as men to serve in their nation's defense, and that as citizens they are equally obliged to do so, and if one also assumes that the nation can and should be militarily defended, one must conclude that current policies do not make much sense. The tedious sifting of the military's own documents, rationales, and evidence leads to this conclusion, and the chapters on litigation and legislation, research, accessions, and biology and family are the fruit of that labor. The Navy's discomfort with women on ships, the disjunction between Army research findings and the policies pushed by commanders, and the elaborate formulas created by the Air Force for women's accessions suggest that defensiveness rather than sense drives much of the policy on women.

A great deal of military time and effort has been consumed by women's issues during the last fifteen years. In part, the "women problem" may have served as a welcome diversion from the need to reflect on the lessons of Vietnam and the difficulties of maintaining a volunteer, peacetime military with an ambiguous mission. Indeed, women may have been just the right problem—not too large, not too serious—and, in addition, they were new, they rarely made demands, and their congressional and other allies lacked sustained, intense interest.

The solution to the problem, it was often implied, was to get rid of the women. If the goal had been to make women accepted, effective participants in the nation's defense, there are a number of things the military could have done differently, even without removing the chronically irritating combat restriction. First, incentives for enlistment and reenlistment could have included guaranteed day care and joint-spouse assignments. These inducements would be no more "unfair" than currently offered reenlistment bonuses, educational benefits, and guaranteed geographic assignments, even if they did prove more attractive to women than to men.

Second, promotion criteria could be changed to accommodate specialized careers (for both men and women). Third, equipment could be redesigned for easier use by women (and smaller men). Fourth, the military could acknowledge that current "sex-blind" or "gender-free" policies are an experiment and inaugurate a new program of experimentation in which the differing effects of all-female units, all-female MOSs, and 50–50 units would be explored. Speculation would be fruitful, too. What if women were given the Air Force and the other three services were left to men? What if women were given all repair jobs or all supply jobs or all communications jobs?

Fifth, the military's role as a social institution should be recognized, and just as young men are trained and prepared for work in civilian life, young women could be supported as mothers. How to support the successful pregnancies of short-term, unskilled workers is a grave problem for the nation and all employers. A general solution is required—the military cannot be exempt.

Sixth, many of the jobs open to women should probably be reserved for them. This position assumes that the military would benefit from enlisting young people in a ratio approaching their availability. Thus, if men are required for one-third of a service's jobs, two-thirds of the remaining two-thirds could be earmarked for women, giving them slightly less than half of all jobs.

Seventh, the services could give more attention to learning what builds women's morale, what welds women and men into a cohesive team, what is required to lead women, and what is needed to teach men to respect and follow women's leadership.* (The need to reintegrate basic training seems almost self-evident.)

Much research on military women has been directed toward presumed deficiencies: attrition, job migration, pregnancy, single parents, and military couples. Moreover, much has been made of the "opening" of a handful of jobs in a few new fields, while dubious physical standards and equipment design that disqualify thousands of women are ignored. (The Air Force is not the only service that attempts to get the attentive, critical audience to focus on gnats rather than camels.)

If reason *were* to control policy, how might analysis, evidence, and questions differ?† First, one would insist on self-consciousness about the

---

*Much military policy is developed by high-ranking officials who have few or no women peers. It is applied to and by lower-ranking personnel. Both groups seem to assume that servicewomen will continue to be few and young. Mature, seasoned women NCOs do not seem to be part of policy planning—except as supervisors of and role models for women.

†Excellent, systematic and salient research on enlisted women exists, but its audience is limited, it is often narrowly conceived so that hypotheses and theories are left unstated, and results that would tend to undermine existing policy are left implicit. This will

unit of analysis, whether it is the individual, the work unit, a service, or "the military" as opposed to "civilians." Thus, if the problem is that some single parents do not respond promptly to emergencies, to what unit should policy be directed? Should those individuals who fail be dismissed, or should it be some larger category—women single parents, first-term enlisted single parents, or all single parents? And what stance should be taken toward deserting parents (typically men who thereby create women single parents). The children of single military women are likely to have deserting military fathers. Should military attention be directed toward those fathers?

Similarly, should capacity to do work be tested individually or by work unit? Are individuals recruited for "the military," or for particular services? Should the more desirable services be allowed to skim the cream from the recruit pool, or should differently skilled enlisted personnel be equally distributed across the services? For example, if one service is able to require two years of college for enlistment, should it be allowed to do so, or should the military be open not to the *most* able, but to those able *enough*? One needs to be careful to select the appropriate unit for analysis, and equally careful to use the same unit in making one's analysis and in reaching one's conclusions.[2]

Second, questions asked about women should also be asked about men. For example, as we have noted, a wife who does not speak English may impair a man's "readiness" as much as (or more than) a child impairs that of a single mother. If the issue is reenlistment, it may be as economical to provide day care as to provide jobs for civilian wives (or jobs for those wives may be found delivering day care). In examining cohesion, the familiar divisions between racial groups, English-speakers and non-English-speakers, short-termers and careerists, combat soldiers and technicians may turn out to be more salient than those between men and women.* Similarly, although one must not ignore the fact that having dependents makes some enlisted personnel respond slowly to alerts and deployments, attention needs to be directed to remedies and also to other substantial limitations on readiness—for example, lack of transportation or a telephone, school commitments, and even the use of civilians in jobs necessary to mobilization.

Even when questions are well framed, there are problems related to

---

probably continue as long as the military controls access to subjects and provides most of the funding for military research. Still, it should be remembered that policies are themselves predictions (hypotheses) and can be reviewed and tested.

*Since the Army finds that it can promote cohesion by keeping whole units together when it rotates personnel, keeping mere couples together should present no problem at all.

the weighing of evidence. Should "experience" control, even if an officer has had almost no experience commanding women? And does it matter whether "opinion" is well founded? What data should be treated as real—narrow but measurable items like times for a one-mile run? or less measurable but clearly important items like "morale" and "effectiveness"? How should caveats about a real war as opposed to, for instance, field exercises be applied?

The need for a new or additional model for thinking about military personnel seems clear. Planners now use an "economic man" model, even counting enlisted personnel as employed. But Thomas Hobbes, the progenitor of market theory, knew that war was precisely the area in which his model did *not* work. Moreover, men's resistance to women's service, and women's enlistment behavior, which is not related to unemployment rates, disprove the adequacy of the economic man model.

Logic and fact are often violated in discussions of military women, and war's death and destruction are themselves clearly irrational. It is therefore important to try to grasp just what does drive the military as an institution (see Chapter 10: "Myths Necessary to the Pursuit of War"). I hope that readers, too, will give concentrated attention to what is left unsaid as well as what is said in such discussions.

Finally, a reorientation—indeed, a reversal—as to the very subject under discussion may be called for. When a now-retired Air Force colonel, something of an intellectual and even a researcher, is willing (as late as 1981) to pronounce women "an unmitigated disaster," it suggests that the time allocated to rational assessments of women's ability may be misspent.[3] It might be more valuable to reflect on men's disability—their apparent incapacity to assimilate women, or even to accommodate to their presence. I would recommend a shift to the investigation of *men's* limitations and to the study of the military as a male, rather than a human or national, institution. Doing this should make the military more accessible to inquiry. War and the military can still be taken seriously, but need not be seen as inevitable. In fact, to the degree that war is seen as a male initiation rite or a large-scale gang fight, it can be perceived as modifiable and controllable. Thinking of war as a price extracted by old men from young ones, one is better able to ask whether that rite can be made less deadly, or whether women and others could at least gain exemption from its destructiveness.

Consider the fact that men have staked their very gender identity on a social role (that of warrior/protector) at the same time that they have based women's gender identity on biology (motherhood). By doing so they have made women's identity "secure," immutable, but left their own identity chronically open to challenge. Perhaps that is why they have claimed as their role one most people (including men) do not want—killing and dying.*

If, on the other hand, military service is conceptualized as an opportunity rather than as a sacrifice, quite different questions arise. For example, if it creates social mobility, how can it avoid becoming political; and if the military is politicized, how can one be confident that it will not act to pressure or coerce political opponents? How can one be sure it will not, in fact, try to *become* the government?

Feminist scholars, then, are presented with a particular challenge in the study of the military. Once one gets over the incredulity engendered by the services' hypocrisy (e.g., the Air Force's concern that it might be discriminating against men), once one has extracted oneself from the Matina Horner–Carol Gilligan role of *again* pointing out that classical social science studies often do not "work" for female subjects, once one has grasped that patriarchy includes ghastly male–male behavior, one might agree that what is required is attention to "The Man Question."[4]

At root that question is: how has it come to pass that men have presumed to set the intellectual agenda, to label and define social relationships, and even off-handedly to debate how women shall be "utilized"? Is it because they hold a monopoly on legitimate violence? Do they really believe inequity can be efficient in the long run? Do they understand cohesion to derive from shared jeopardies, from shared responsibilities, or do they also believe it to involve shared guilt? (See Freud's *Totem and Taboo*, and the William Calley case.) If young men without dependents or some other social stake are a danger to society, what would it take to force elite men to give them a stake instead of unleashing those men on each other? How should one judge a culture that makes young men so desperate for honor that they resort to self-destruction—either privately or with state complicity—to win respect.

Feminists need to ask themselves what kind of patriarchy tolerates high levels of child abandonment by fathers, and (apparently) leaves men less well connected intergenerationally than women. How is it that allegedly patriarchal men organize themselves by age group in competing organizations, whereas women's informal groups more often cut across age lines, using the extended family as a model?

Do feminists fully understand that most men carry, or believe they carry, or believe they *should* carry, a burden of dependents, while feminists are likely to be talking about independence or interdependence?

Do we fully understand the anxiety of men who see the world in market

---

*The military is a very coercive institution; even so, no state has been willing to try to shape that institution without the psychological bludgeon of offering "manhood" in return for submission. This suggests that participation is reluctant.

terms when they must confront women who have entered that market and thus doubled the competition?

Do we understand that this is intellectual work that *women* must engage in, because men are invisible to most men *qua* men?

General Vessey should be taken seriously. The military is a male institution, and unless its very nature changes, women will continue to be indigestible.* This will be especially true so long as it is possible to pretend that women can be excluded from combat.

And when we have muddled through all the above queries, we must turn to the most fundamental of all questions—"of what is this an instance?"—as it applies to our own, feminist, analysis. We must ask ourselves whether feminist thought, too, is confining because it tends to create dichotomous categories. We must ask whether or how we can think in another way. Perhaps the military is a mere byproduct of polarized thinking and a need to have an external enemy, a distinctive, contrasting "other." Is this need tied to an essential human nature always cognizant of sex? That is, is the centrality of being male or female so firmly imprinted that oppositeness, otherness, controls all our thinking unless we make a supreme effort to enlarge our categories?

In large part we still treat race relations as a problem in majority and minority, or Black and white, yet in many places—my homes, Los Angeles and Miami, in particular—there is no majority and there is no duality, *and* there is as yet no intellectual handle for understanding our pluralistic, rapidly changing culture.

One wonders: How would society be different if people could not be killed—if they either lived forever or died at an appointed age, but never died before or after that age? And how would society be different if men also gave birth and nurtured infants? And would thinking beyond dichotomies be more likely if there were three sexes (or four or five) instead of two?

---

*In the spring of 1988 the military's code of conduct was finally altered so that a woman no longer had to declare "I am an American fighting man" ("Code of Conduct Revised," *Army Times*, 13 April 1988).

# Appendices

# APPENDIX A

## "I am a Veteran . . ."

I am a veteran of the United States Air Force, in which I spent six years from 1974 to 1980. My job was jet engine mechanic, and I had attained the rank of staff sergeant at the time of my discharge. I entered the service in September 1974 shortly after the war in Vietnam ground to a military halt, if not a diplomatic one. The decision to enter the service wasn't really a difficult one; it was one born of desperation.

I had a lot of moral problems (which I quickly shelved) over the idea of joining the military because I had been quite involved in political activities, especially the antiwar movement, when I was in high school.

I graduated high school in June of '72. The school I graduated from was a girl's Catholic high school in a predominantly working-class parish in San Francisco, where I grew up. The neighborhood that I grew up in, which was across town, was mostly Irish and Italian blue-collar workers. San Francisco in the late sixties and early seventies certainly bred in any somewhat alert kid a host of countercultural attitudes, and being against the war in Vietnam was a part of that. My cousin had gone to Vietnam, people in the neighborhood had gone to Vietnam, you would go into any of the high schools in the area and there was a list of kids who had gone and been killed during the previous five or six years. I was very righteous about war.

When I graduated high school my prospects of going on to college were dim. Although I had gotten into San Francisco State, I couldn't afford to register, much less go. My parents were hard-working, but they couldn't have afforded putting the kids through college, and I wasn't about to suggest they try. So I left home, and I went to a vocational school which was primarily for retraining welfare recipients and the chronically unemployed. I learned to be a veterinary technician there and that took about a year. After that I practiced in the city. I guess I worked about six months as a veterinary technician. It was a very exploitative position, and I was young and stupid and didn't know you weren't supposed to put up with being economically exploited because you are female. I mean, I was intellectually aware of the women's movement, but that was something that happened to other people—and San Francisco as a whole was a pretty loose town. I had seen women truck drivers and linemen and everything else; still, it didn't occur to me until I slapped up against it that discrimination could happen to me. When I left that job, I went to a coffeehouse which was in the same neighborhood and met a lot of interesting people. I was really involved at that point in my life with being a typical street freak. I had a lot of friends who came to the coffeehouse; it was almost a community center; there were a lot of artists, musicians, some famous and some not so famous, some just your basic degenerate freak. I played a central role in connecting people to housing and food and lodging and with knowing who was going east and who was coming west and that kind of thing; I really enjoyed it.

After about a half-year I heard about a job in Ashland, Oregon, in another coffeehouse. I quit in San Francisco and went north to take over that job. When I got there the job didn't materialize and I was left hanging. I didn't have any contacts there so I went back to San Francisco via Stockton, where I lived with some old friends from Haight-Ashbury for a while. Then I went back to the city and began pounding the pavements. It was rough because San Francisco is a union town and there weren't a lot of jobs going, and I wasn't a skilled veterinary tech. In the recent past it had been a matter of going to school, getting training, and getting a licensed position, but it wasn't by then.

I was good with my hands and I was a hard worker, so I used to bullshit my way into subcontracting jobs. You know, doing a bit of sheetwork or house painting. I put up some bars and built interiors of bars in the city, worked on some doors that were hung in City Hall—that kind of thing. I was constantly hustling. The only thing that I didn't hustle was my butt. I mean the offer was made to turn tricks, but there was just no way a good Catholic kid could do it. I worked for a while as a restaurant porter in a downtown restaurant at night. It was a kind of red light district, but it was also the hoity toity financial area too—a lot of good restaurants. Finally my unemployment ran out. I was too stupid, I mean I had my pride in the way, to get on the welfare, and that would have taken too long—probably would have starved to death before I got anything, but by this stage I couldn't pay rent. I had the keys to the outer door of an apartment building and I lived on the roof top. After a few weeks I moved to the tool shed in the back of the building which was a little drier and a lot less degenerate, but it was still pretty gross. I suppose that was hitting rock bottom. Never in my life have I been so depressed, so suicidal. Street freaks are not always there when you need them. What goes around doesn't always come around. At that point I decided that I would live, that I wouldn't give in, although I had no idea (I had just turned twenty and had *no* idea) what dreams to even hope for, much less what goals to reach for, or how to get myself out of my situation.

I was not welcome in my parents' home at this time, although I would see my mother occasionally. My father had chucked me out of the house over another whole issue. My brother had actually (he was seventeen) joined the Air Force that summer, and the thought occurred to me that that might be a way out. Then I got sick. I had some kind of bronchial pneumonia or something, and I was deathly ill and in bad shape, but I was still looking for work when I went by a recruiter's office. I stopped in.

Three days later, within *three* days, they had taken me, chauffeured me back and forth to the Oakland induction center, where I had my physical, and I was in. They had told me that they needed women to fulfill this quota for mechanics. I could have cared less. I would have done anything. I would have been a permanent floor-washer. You know, anything for three squares and a cot. They said if I wanted to go in then I had to go as a mechanic or wait six months. I was in no position to wait. I went. My father was tentatively reconciled, and both my parents drove me to the induction center.

I spent the day there, raised my hand, and a very lean, mean marine pledged us all to the cause. I can remember standing in the induction center being sworn in and seeing a whole bunch of guys handcuffed to parole officers. I was really impressed.

We left from the induction center. I was put in charge of the group flying to Lackland Air Force Base, in San Antonio, Texas, which is where all basic training is held for the Air Force. That was the second time I have ever been on an airplane and I was deathly ill. I think I threw up from San Francisco to San Antonio. Of course, that was to the endless amusement of everybody else. "Ha! Ha! going to the Air Force and you are air sick, Ha! Ha!" I didn't think it was too amusing, but anyway, we got to Texas and from that point on it was scream, yell, order, whatever. A lot of it was done for the women's benefit, even though there were only about three of us. We assembled in San Antonio that night, and they drove us straight to the base. When we got there we went to the chow hall. The male TIs (training instructors) invited the women to sit with them at this podium while they yelled and screamed to the guys sitting in the main part of the chow hall. I think it was supposed to impress us, but I was more disgusted than impressed. I was also pretty numb. I mean, I was physically exhausted. I had reached the end of my tether.

For the next few weeks, I was a zombie. They had us marching around getting information about the Uniform Code of Military Justice and putting us in uniforms. We began to make some sort of contact with each other. My flight (or unit) was about 30 percent Black; a good half were southern, Black and white. We had a few nut cases—you know, crazies who talked to themselves and threatened to kill people—who were phased out within a couple of weeks. It wasn't a terrifically tight bunch, but then you can never predict when you get fifty people from all over the country and stick them together. During training recruits are pulled together, which is what a lot of the harassment is about that you get in the Air Force or in any basic training. The point of that kind of harassment and tension and the creating of and asking for impossible tasks is to create teamwork. That is a difficult thing to do. I think it happens (if it happens) because you don't get through it at all unless you pull together.

We went through about four or five TIs because either one or another was on vacation or leave or sick or whatever, so there was a lot of discontinuity. It was tough to take some of the crap, and there were times when I just wanted to slug them. You know, somebody gets in your face and starts yelling at you about some bullshit and you just want to say, "Fuck off!" But you had to swallow it; you had to swallow your pride; you had to shut up; you had to take it—and by taking it you overcame it to some degree. Also, everybody else was in the same boat. I had been in worse situations, but, like I said, at this stage sleeping indoors and eating regular meals was a plus. I mean, I couldn't eat when I first got there because I hadn't been eating, but I put on weight. I got a lot healthier.

Our flight ran the obstacle course, which was a lot of fun, but it was not serious. I mean, they weren't really taking women very seriously at that stage. We were part of the first rush of women into nontraditional jobs, and they had just started trying women out on obstacle courses, firing weapons, all that kind of thing.

I went from basic to Chanute Air Force Base (Illinois) in November of '74. It was cold. I didn't come from snow country, and it was snowing when I first got there. That surprised me; I didn't know quite how to deal with it. That had to be one of the most dismal, depressing places I had ever seen. They put us in a U-shaped compound of three-story concrete barracks that were all-women. Chanute was strictly for maintenance training. (They trained for health care at Sheppard, and other bases in different areas trained for other things.) I arrived at Chanute with a friend from basic training who was a twenty-eight-year-old single mother with a master's degree. That was helpful because we knew each other, but the whole place was very weird, or so I thought.

The second or third day I was there, a woman jumped out of the third floor of one of the barracks. Eventually it came out that there was this heavy dyke trip going on in that barracks, where this group called the "Rat Pack" was going around beating the shit out of people. This girl freaked out and jumped out of the third-story window. I don't know if she was killed or what, but it was all hushed up and she was whisked away in an ambulance. Anyway, that group was a tough, nasty bunch, and shortly after that incident somebody else got beat up who saw two women making out in one of the dayrooms. She was a New Yorker, I mean she could care less, she was just going to do her laundry, and whatever they were doing was their business, but they were paranoid and they beat her up and put her in the hospital. Then everything broke loose.

For the next two or three months, they had an investigation by the Office of Special Investigations, which is sort of the stormtroopers of the Air Force, I guess. These guys were in plain clothes and infiltrated for drugs and homosexuality and all that other sort of stuff. So they began this incredible investigation. I remember that during it the woman that I had come up from Texas with stopped speaking to me. We had been very friendly, and all of a sudden she had nothing to do with me. Then I caught her coming out of an interrogation session. This woman was a tough nut, I mean she was a hard woman, she had had a rough life, but she was nice and she was in tears. They had put her through the wringer. It turned out that she was a lesbian, and although she wasn't making a big issue out of it or putting the make on anybody, she was being harassed. She avoided having any contact with me because she knew that I was straight and didn't want me to be implicated.

The whole situation was just vile. The women were bringing their boyfriends, and the guys were saying, "That doesn't prove anything," and throwing them out. It was automatic discharge, because the women didn't have their 180 days in the service (after that point you are considered relatively permanent). No matter what these women said, these guys were in an incredible situation of power. There was no way to prove that you weren't a homosexual. I assume it was just a matter of somebody's word to prove that you were. In fact, at one stage it was getting pretty hysterical because women were saying, "Do you want to get out of service? Well, here, I'll finger you to the OSI because they know I am a dyke, so I finger you, and you can get out if you give me ten bucks." It was really ridiculous. Women were afraid of being around other women. You were afraid to have anything to do with them for fear of being fingered and chucked out. For a lot of us the military was our last resort. It was what was going to get us out of the ghetto; it was going to get us out of the vicious circle that most of us were in. It was going to get us somewhere. You didn't want to be fingered by some idiot you didn't even know. It was a despicable time.

While all this was happening, I was also studying to be a jet engine mechanic. I was doing a lot of class work. I was on B-shifts—went to school in the afternoons for six hours. I got out of a lot of marching and other stuff because I started a self-help maintenance team. That was because we couldn't get our barracks painted, we couldn't get our lockers fixed, or our doors hung, or whatever. I was into carpentry, so I suggested that plenty of us were capable of doing it ourselves. That one went over really good. I was put in charge, and we did a lot of door hanging and faucet fixing and whatnot, and I didn't have to go and march and put up with a lot of mickey mouse stuff.

I also got to do things like ride around on the garbage truck. That was kind of cute because we used to ride around down by the Illinois highway, and we would pick up the cigarette butts and the garbage and trash along one side of the highway. The state prison farm was on the other side, and they picked up that side. Essentially what we did was pick up trash from our side and chuck it on theirs. They, of course, would pick it up on their side and chuck it on ours, so it was kind of nice make-work. There were funny moments like that—but not too many.

I was in a maintenance field, but I was not issued (male) gloves, combat boots, field jackets, or other mandatory equipment for the job I was doing. So I had to buy them. That was tough on me. I think we were getting $190 every two weeks. It was depressing. It was like, you know, you were there, but the women were ignored a lot.

I suppose the real low point there involved a couple of NCOs that were in my group. They were older guys. Two of them were married, and one of them I was really friendly with. We got to having a coffee or something on occasion. It was very difficult to have a social life because you were so paranoid all the time. The guys were so offensive—but this guy was nice. I figured he was safe. You know, he was married. So one night a bunch of us went down to a hotel in Champaign, Illinois, to watch the Superbowl. I think it was the football finals sort of; there isn't a hell of a lot else to do in that part of Illinois, so mind you this was big excitement. We went down, and I'm pretty naive. I mean it never occurred to me that I was putting myself in an awkward situation. I just thought I was going down with these guys, and there was another couple that I was friendly with, and we would watch this football game. I can't go into all the details because it's just too painful, but it essentially ended up in my being raped. Because he was an NCO, it was my word against his. I had put myself (I realized afterwards) in a very compromising situation. There wasn't anybody who was going to believe me, and of course that was what every WAF was. I mean, we all know the term WAF means "we all fuck." So, if I didn't fuck, then I had to be a dyke. Since there was an OSI investigation, there was no point in my trying to get around that one, so I shut up. I was hurt, I was freaked, I was bitter, and I was shut down for a long time.

Shortly after that I left Chanute. I was one point shy of being an honor student. I was pretty proud of that, since I always figured that kind of thing was beyond me. I went to Grand Forks, North Dakota, in January or February of '75. They had just had a three-day blizzard. I thought there had been a lot of snow in Illinois! I hadn't seen nothing. I mean there was nothing between Grand Forks and Texas but a barbed wire fence. There was snow right up to the third floor of the barracks. It just drifts against anything; it was incredible! And I was coming from California—I mean my God—people pay money for this stuff. I couldn't believe it! I checked in at the base, got settled down, got my gear, and got taken over to my shop, which worked on J57s and TF33s (engines) and KC-135 tankers and B-52 bombers. Grand Forks is Strategic Air Command (SAC), and they are part of this whole strategic triad of bombers, Polaris submarines, and missiles. It was pretty bleak, pretty bleak. They had had three other women in that shop, and all three of them had either gotten pregnant or screwed up or refused to work and were handing out tools in the tool crib or handing out technical orders in the technical order library, but none of them were working in their field. None was actually putting engines together.

I began my on-the-job training, my apprenticeship. After six months I would be considered a mechanic and earn a level. At first I was gungho —I was ready to go. But they put me on stand maintenance, which means I worked on maintaining the stands on which engines and components were being built up. I was supposed to put safety pins in these things or oil them up. I was nowhere near a jet engine. Having just come out of school, I was disappointed. It was really strange. The guys didn't know whether to come on to you or to stand back and let you screw up. It was still a new situation. Some guys were very hostile. There were still a lot of guys who had come into the Air Force to avoid the draft. We also had a group that was being phased out because they worked on a type of aircraft that was no longer being used, and they were just hanging around. The base had a pretty high rate of alcoholism, of drug abuse, and of divorce, too. The base was in the middle of nowhere. It was called a northern tier base, which used to mean that over a certain latitude it was considered an Arctic situation. You were supposed to get extra facilities and movies and have a better PX system. But because it would have taken the major source of income away from the town of Grand Forks twenty miles down the road, they altered the position of the base entrance in such a way that it was just under the northern tier line; so we didn't have a hell of a lot of anything up there.

It was really rough on Blacks. Minot had had a big race riot—the chow hall was taken over. Minot is sixty to seventy miles further west than Grand Forks, but we had a lot of problems, too. There was nothing for Blacks, although there wasn't a lot of discrimination because no one had ever seen any Blacks. But they didn't have any cultural events or music. That was bad for them, but it was for everybody else, too. A lot of times you were snowed in. Or, if you weren't, you didn't have any vehicle or money and couldn't get to town. It was pretty horrendous; a lot of marriages broke up; there were some suicides and whatnot. We used to have sit-down strikes because they had us working six days a week, twelve hours a day. We couldn't get parts and whatnot, and they blamed us for not getting the engines repaired. So we had sit-down strikes or slow-downs. When I first got there, they had just had a sit-down strike, including the NCOs. That's a bad situation, and there was a real shake-up. The slow-downs meant that it would take three hours to get a nut or a bolt, and it would take you another five hours to tighten it up, so even if they made you work twelve hours it didn't mean diddly-squat.

Usually I've found a shitty workplace has a good barracks or a good workplace has shitty barracks. This was the former. I had good people in the barracks. The women in my barracks hung together a lot, went places together, and had a lot of fun, a real nice group. There were lesbians, some Blacks, some whites, some Chicanas; there were some religious types, party types, young, old, you name it, we had it. But people were cooperative; they cared about each other, and that was the beautiful thing about our horrendous situation. It was a shitty place; but it sparked the people there. We went into town and partied a lot together; it was really good.

You had a sense of family in those days because there was still a Women's Air Force. It meant that everybody in the barracks worked all over the base, so you had a lot of contacts in the different shops. Now the situation is different. Women are assigned to the barracks of their work squadron. For example, I was in field maintenance, so I would now be in a coed barracks or in a barracks with other women from field maintenance. In South Dakota, though, we had women from Personnel, from the hospital, from the missile wing, you name it. It really was a central point; we knew what was happening everywhere.

But we were also a target. When generals came to the base, they would call us up. I was really amazed. They would call you up and say, "General So-and-so is having a party, we need some women, send some over." When I first got there, within fifteen minutes of getting on my floor the phone rang. This guy said, "You are Airman So-and-so, your weight is such and such, your height is such and such." It was like he had my file, and he was going through it. There were about 150 women in the barracks, and there were about the same number of married women living in base housing who were military officers. All in all there were about 300 of us on a base of about 7,000 or 8,000 people. Maybe it was that kind of siege mentality that made us all band together, though I certainly had a lot of good relationships with guys, too. Eventually I moved out of the barracks, and I lived in the town—a little dingy town north of the base. I lived with a guy I was really fond of, but, I don't know, it was a pretty strange place.

I think I should get back to the shop and what my work was like. When I started, I was in engine stand maintenance. That included small gas turbine engines, which are in aircraft start carts; it wasn't terribly stimulating. I was pretty bored, but I knew from the start that I wanted to go to the flight line.

There were two parts to the shop. There was in-shop maintenance, which is where the components and the engines come in—say for an inspection—or where a brand-new engine has to be put together. The compressors, turbines, the combustion cans, the inner cases and the outer cases, and the kit or the electrical lines and hoses, and the plumbing and the extra components have to be built up. This takes maybe a week or so, to put together an engine from scratch or to tear one down. It is all shop work, and it was, to my mind, repetitive. I was much more interested in being in the other half of the shop, which was flight line or engine conditioning. This was outside—everybody worked outdoors. To do this job you had to be fairly strong.

They had never had a woman on the flight line when I came and started making noises about it. They weren't about to have one on the flight line, either. It was a really macho group. There aren't a lot of really tough jobs in the Air Force, but bomb loaders and engine mechanics are probably two of the toughest. I was insistent, though, so they moved me from small gas engines to in-shop. We had a lot of problems in the in-shop —I mean people problems. My boss who had been on flight line was very noncommunicative. I would be standing around (by this stage I still hadn't experienced the reality of working on an engine and didn't know one part from another); he wouldn't say anything, absolutely nothing. I mean, literally, he could go all day with maybe three words. It was hard, and when I finished the study course that went with this "hands-on experience," I was really disillusioned.

Finally there was a shake-up, and a new guy came in. Meanwhile I had asked permission to go on the flight line of my shop chief, but he kept ignoring me or smiling nicely and doing nothing. Eventually he took me into his office and said, "You can see there is nobody here, and everything I am going to tell you is strictly between us because there is nobody else here, Air Force Regulation 7-2"—his seven stripes to my two stripes. He said, "The reason I am not putting you on the flight line is (a) I am not going to have any woman on my flight line, (b) you couldn't handle the elements, the cold, heat, and whatnot, (c) if you could handle the elements you would get attacked by every male on the flight line, and (d) if you were to do better than the guys . . . well, there are twenty guys on flight line and one of you, and the mission requires that their priority come first."

Needless to say I was stunned. But he was right—there was no way I could report him, because there was nobody to overhear or witness it, and I had little doubt whose word was gonna be listened to. At least I knew what I was up against. A couple of weeks later, I related this to my new crew chief, and he went and bet this guy a case of beer that I would last on flight line. So in December they put me on flight line. I had no parka, and no parka pants; mind you, in winter in North Dakota it can get to 60 degrees below zero, so it was pretty bloody cold, and they put me out there, and for a week or so I totally lacked the equipment. I lasted, and I stayed there for most of the rest of my time in service. It was rough. We had stepvans, which look like bread trucks, and those stepvans housed six people with their toolboxes and their special equipment and a driver who is usually shift chief. The procedure is that the shift chiefs go out to the flight line and drop off airmen on a particular job. Then he checks on them later. If the aircraft needs to be run to check the engine out, he does so. As I said, we worked on B-52s and KC-135s. A B-52 has eight turbo fan engines, and tankers have four regular jet engines. We took engines off the wing as "on-wing maintenance," but we never broke stuff down. We either removed or replaced components, or removed and replaced engines, or we did maintenance work while the components were on the engine. We checked oil, and we inspected them. There was a phase inspection dock that we worked in. We ran the aircraft, we trimmed it, which is sort of like tuning it up. (After you put a new engine on, it requires adjustment so it will be on line with the rest of the engines and with the parameters set for its operation.) We did essentially everything except taking the plane off the ground. It was hard work. I worked eight hours a day. For a while I worked swing shift, which I liked. That is three to eleven PM. You often get tight with people on your crew, but I had a lot of problems. I wasn't tight with these guys. I mean, most of the conversations revolved around booze, women, and cars. I like cars, but I don't drink and I couldn't talk about women. It was hard to listen when they talked about women—the way they thought about them—but it was either be a tease or be one of the guys, and I figured my options were better if I was one of the guys. So I got tough. I did it by keeping my mouth shut and biting my tongue a lot and putting up with some really insulting behavior. I don't know—sometimes I think I have done myself psychic damage and other times I feel like I have overcome it. I didn't always take it. One bitching cold day we were operating the heater so we wouldn't freeze to death while working on engines. I was standing with my parka open to the back blast area, so I could fill my parka with heat. This guy that I knew, I had worked with for a long time, a sergeant, was standing there. He came up to me and grabbed me by the crotch. It was the last thing in the world I had expected, I was humiliated, I was insulted, I mean all I could do was stutter, and the guy says, "Oh, it's my birthday; I deserve a little snatch"—like it was no big thing, like he could not see why I was upset. Sure we were friendly, sure we were working together, and of course doesn't everybody offer their physical self to be molested or harassed? Well, I mean, it is just a part of the game. I couldn't believe it. I was furious. When I could finally function, I threatened him with a wrench.

I generally tried to remove myself by not being overly friendly and by not having much to do with people's social life. By this time I had moved off base with Dave, and we were living in a nearby town with about fifty people including goats, chickens, dogs, and cats. It was a pretty sparse existence, but it was nice. David was in missiles, so I knew a lot of people in that wing. His best friend's wife was a troop in field maintenance, so I developed a circle of friends outside my shop. As I said, the hardest part of the work was having to deal with the people. The work itself was tough, grinding. I don't think I ever came home without bleeding somewhere —from safety-wire cuts or catching on something or bruises. I gave it a lot of my strength. My toolbox wasn't very heavy; there they had a small kit, maybe 30 pounds. The bomber components were generally heavier. But everything that was over 50 pounds was considered a two-person lift. I didn't see a lot of women that were crew chiefs, but crew chiefs had to handle these huge fire bottles used on aircraft parking stands. Some women were shorter than the fire bottles. They couldn't even move them. I kind of figured that they were setting women up for failure by putting us in work we couldn't do or didn't know how to do. Some women were physically incapable, and the guys would say, "See, we told you women can't hack it." The more I saw of that, the more pissed I got, and the more determined I got to stick it out.

It was also really hard to see that there were some women coming in then (in the spring of '76) with a completely different attitude. For example, one of the new women who was trying out on the flight line was a real tease. I mean, she didn't know how to operate; she couldn't get past her femininity, I guess, and the more she carried on, the more pissed I'd get, because it was kind of degrading. She would tease the guys with all that sexual shit—at work. It wasn't really flagrant, but it was pretty obvious. There was a lot of ass-grabbing kind of stuff, and then in the middle of this whole thing, "I can't carry my toolbox," and of course there would be eight guys breaking their necks to do it for her. In the long run it meant she wasn't doing her job and others were having to do two jobs. It made it much harder for other women; there is just no place for sugar around the flight line. Even those guys who ran for the toolbox resented being pulled into the game, but they thought it was something they had to do. It was a bad situation.

A lot of stuff was beginning to pile up by then. I was getting fed up. I kept putting in for a change of orders, a change of assignment, but it was pretty hopeless. I mean, Grand Forks is one of the places that once they get you there, they are not gonna let you go because it's so damn hard to get you in the first place. I put in for a change once a week, I guess.

Orders finally came through to England. I had put in for an extended overseas tour, which I thought was for three years; it turned out to be four, but I was in ecstasy. You could hear me all the way to Fargo. I was so happy to get out of North Dakota—it was such a pit—and I was so glad to be going to England because I had a friend that was sort of like a father who was from England, and I was going to work on the flight line. It was a bit tough breaking up with Dave. Because he was "missiles," he couldn't go anywhere else, so there was no chance of him coming, and there wasn't any chance of me staying. I guess for about the last month or so I had what they call "short-timer" disease. That was like you get a "who gives a shit" attitude. You get to the last stage of withdrawing. I had just made E-4, so I was going to a new base with some rank, which always helps for women because you have to take a lot less crap the farther up the line you go. So I packed up my stuff and flew to Mildenhall, England.

Mildenhall is the gateway to Europe. All flights stop there, refuel and let passengers off, and then fly on to the continent. It is a big, big airport, and it was really beautiful—all that green after North Dakota's brown and yellow! It was the most beautiful sight I have ever seen. I'm never gonna forget the view I saw from that window. Anyway, we landed. It was a World War II base, so it was kind of rustic, you know, lots of brick and stuff, and this guy who met me—this tall, blond, nice guy—took me to the shop, and everybody in the shop was on a break and lined up out front to see the WAF mechanic. Nobody gets welcomes like that! I was not only the first woman in the shop, but one of the first women in the squadron, so it was a big deal. There I was in my class A uniform (that's something maintenance troops almost never wear, and I hadn't worn a skirt in I don't know how long). I felt like a fool. Nobody said much, everybody was just checking me out, so I talked to the shop chief. I had a lot of flight-line experience, and I would get to stay there. They were going through a big transition then to new engines, and more aircraft. I had more experience than a lot of people on the particular kind of engine we were getting, so I plunged right in. We were changing J57-43s with J57-59s. It was really busy, but it was really good. I mean I was right there, an E-4 working on flight line right from the start, and I didn't give it much thought.

The barracks situation, though, sucked. There weren't enough women for a women's barracks, so we had the third floor of the building that housed the personnel and headquarters squadrons. Mildenhall is a transit base; there are a lot of people coming in and going out, plus there are a lot of temporary troops who come in on short rotations. So all of these big guys were arriving with the C-130 cargo planes from Little Rock, Texas, North Carolina. They were a tough, rowdy bunch, and they were there for a good time, and of course the WAF barracks was right there. One night a guy tried to break into my room. I complained to his first sergeant, but he just laughed and thought it was funny. It was really a pit! Unknown people were constantly staying in the dayrooms. It was very different from the spit and polish of a SAC base.

My roommate was a space case. It was weird. There was no community like there had been in North Dakota. Also, I had been living off the base, and it was hard for me to get used to the barracks again. I felt really alienated. The work situation was good, though; people liked me. (My shop chief personally showed me around. Later I found out that was something he only did for women and that it had caused a problem.)

It was a beautiful base; I loved it; I did a lot of traveling around.

The flight line at Mildenhall was set up differently. It was like a circuit. The taxiway went around the runway, and there were clusters of parking stands off each side of it. It wasn't just lined up wing tip to wing tip. I worked aircraft launch a lot. What happens is they fill the maintenance vans with specialists from each shop, and as the aircraft is getting ready to take off, you monitor it with the radio. If it breaks down, you zoom up to the aircraft and (sort of like Roy Rogers, I guess) put the ladder up to the cockpit to find out what the problem is, then you fix it or determine that the mission has to be scratched. It could take about fifteen minutes to do this, and it was tense. There was a lot of tension, but I liked doing it, running up there with the ground shaking from the power of the engine, and whipping off the engine cowling and looking at it with everybody depending on you and expecting you to make a brilliant decision! Saying, "Hey, it's all right, sir, you can go ahead and fly it," and having to be right. If not, everyone was out of luck! It was a real high to know that engine was or wasn't gonna make it. You've got sixty people on board; you know they are depending on you.

Sometimes I had a problem because a lot of people weren't used to women on flight line and didn't believe in me. Once I had an officer that had a problem. He said he had engine vibration. Vibration in the throttle can be a dangerous situation. So he stopped before he turned around to make his take-off roll, and there were a couple of airplanes right behind him. I hurried out. I was a sergeant. I knew what I was doing, so I went to the airplane with my toolbox, which now was about sixty pounds and hard to run with. I went to the aircraft. He was quite snobby; he showed me the throttle was shaking. I could see it was a mild case of vibration and pretty much, I still think, a case of cable slack. I checked the engine and went back to the pilot and said, "My opinion is cable slack; you can fly this airplane." He said, "What do you know about it! I want to see your supervisor. I want to see a man." So I said, "With all due respect, sir (the prerequisite formula), I don't have to take your shit." I climbed out of the aircraft and got back on the maintenance truck. The guys all went, "What's the matter, what did he say?" I said, "It's just cable slack and he said he wanted a man's opinion."

It was great. My guys called over the radio (you are not supposed to be sarcastic on the radio) and said, "They have to have a man's opinion out here because the pilot isn't going to listen to a broad." The maintenance officer of the day came hurrying out, and I knew him and he respected me for my work, so he went to find the pilot. Well, the guy had shut the airplane down on the runway with other planes behind him and was getting into the crew bus. The maintenance officer stopped him and made him get back in and fly the airplane. I felt really good. It was like a victory, you know; I mean they had to listen to me, and I knew my stuff, and I didn't have to take their shit. After we got back to the shop, one of the senior NCOs demanded we do a vibration check anyway. I was vindicated. They did a vibration check, which takes at least a full shift, and there was nothing wrong with that engine. But that NCO didn't believe me. He was one of the crew bosses, and he should have known. He should have had faith in me. I had a lot of incidents like that where I diagnosed something and somebody overrode me and it turned out that I was right.

Mechanics (who are enlisted) have to take a lot of crap off the pilots (who are officers). Pilots are probably the most dangerous guys I've ever met. They have a little knowledge and they go up there and fly around and scramble their brains and come down and think that they know the answers. The old guys, those from World War II, are usually more adept, because they had to go to aviation ground school, and they know about the aircraft they are flying right down to where every circuit or wire is. But a lot of the young guys, geezus, they are defensive and obnoxious. I've been kept waiting for a maintenance debriefing while these guys drank beer in the officers' club.

I can still remember the first time I saw a woman crew member. She was a navigator. She stepped off a plane from McGuire. We were freaked! I thought that was great, really great. And we had couple of women maintenance officers. But as a rule I didn't see many women. I didn't work with any—no, I did work with one, and she was good. She was about nineteen and from southern California. She was one of the best. She was excellent; she had a lot of talent.

It was hard work. I mean, there is no getting away from the fact that flight line is painful work. My toolbox weighed 60 pounds. A lot of components we put on were a good 40, 50, 60 pounds, or more. The advantage I had was that I have very small hands—I'm also ambidextrous —so I could do things that a lot of people couldn't, and I could get my hands in a lot of places other people couldn't. When I couldn't do something, I had to think up a solution to the problem, a problem the guys could just use a hammer and screwdriver on. A lot of times it was frustrating, and I wasn't always successful. If you had an inch-and-a-half nut to take off of an engine mount, I would get a wrench to put on it, and then I would find an extension to put on the end of the wrench, because the longer the wrench, the easier to break the nut loose. If you are not getting anywhere, and if you fall off the stand or something, it is frustrating. And if you are the only person out there, and if you have a job to do, you're stuck with it. There is nobody around to help. It is your problem.

I had a real sense of obligation, and felt like a failure if I had to ask for help or had to have a guy come break a nut loose or something. I swallowed my pride a lot. There is a tendency to try to be Superwoman or what they used to call me—"Wonder Woman." I guess the fact is there was constant pressure to prove yourself—not just because you were a woman, but then because you were an NCO, or because you were a "flight line ramp rat." I don't know if the pressure was really there or if it was just me believing I always had to be the best.

The turning point was hurting my back. I mean, I really liked my work. There was a joy about flight line work where one gets to be outside in rain and fog and the elements. You see things changing around you, the weather, the scenery. It is purifying in some strange way. Sometimes you had to be out there twelve or sixteen hours a day working on a problem that wasn't getting fixed, and it was pouring rain, and it was 11:00 PM and you couldn't see what you were doing, and you were frozen (I used to have a lot of pain in my knees), and the evenings were cold, and you spent a lot of time there, and you were in it, and it was just too bad if you got wet. There was no quitting, no crying, no saying that you want to go back to the shop.

But I hurt my back. We had been putting up one of those CSDs, and we had been working a good six hours, and we were exhausted. It's very easy to exhaust yourself and just burn out because of the constant heavy labor. It was pouring rain, and the fuel was dissolving tarmac in the parking area where the airplane was. Because we were such a distance from the shop, a truck came around and checked on us, and they asked if we were done. We were doing the safety wire, the last few connections. I started putting stuff together and counting out tools and whatnot, and we knew that if we didn't get our shit together and get on that truck we would be stuck there another hour until the shift changed, so I just yanked up this 90-pound generator, which I normally couldn't move very far, and stuck it in the box. You had to lift it waist high and then drop it into what looks like a sawed-off 55-gallon shipping drum. I felt my back go snap, crackle, and pop, and knew that was it. I had tried for five years to be careful, but I just, I don't know, out it went, and that was it. I was in agony. I couldn't move; but the next day I came back to work, and I was running an airplane. To run an airplane, you have to set the brakes. This means you have to extend your legs and push the pedals down with your toes. You are all stretched out and lifting levers and pushing toggle switches and whatnot. I couldn't do it, I could not do it. My back went out, again. When you are carrying around 60 pounds with your back screwed up, you just physically wear yourself out after a certain point. Most of the guys I worked with were big, beefy guys, and maybe they can handle it—I don't know. I wasn't at a stage where I was willing to admit that maybe not all women can do all jobs, and although I'm strong for a woman, I'm not that big. I guess I was just sort of tired of it, and tired of physically destroying myself. My back was bad, and it would take a month for my hands to heal from a safety wire cut, or from fuel drying them out, or from a scrape or whatever. And it was impossible to get the oil out of my skin so everybody didn't know what I did for a living by looking.

My last year in the Air Force, I went to test cell. After an engine is put together in the shop, it is sent to a test cell, where they have special equipment to see if everything is operating right. You have to hook up all these leads to test the heat, temperature, vibration, oil temperature, fuel-flow ratio, and all that stuff, then send it out to engine conditioning, and finally put it on the airplane which needs an engine. It was less work but it was inside. If you are away from the shop, you are away from some of the mickey mouse bullshit—washing floors, waxing the hangar, and all the kind of crap which I couldn't get behind. We had solved the mickey mouse to some degree in our area because it was ours and we kept it up. There weren't three shifts coming through. We worked really well together, but it was heavy work. You were pushing an 8,000-pound engine around on the stand, off the stand, jacking it up, jacking it down —I probably got out just in time to avoid permanent injury. I did miss flight line. I guess what I missed the most was the fact that when you finished the job on an airplane (they all had their own personalities), you got to see it take off, fly, and, oh, it was beautiful. There was a sense of completion, a sense of totality, I guess. When I worked on an engine in the shop or tested something, it tested out. If it didn't, I would send it back to the shop and then test it again when it came back. It was more inanimate. I don't know if it makes sense, but it did at the time to me.

The test cell was all right. We didn't have a lot of work and spent a lot of time waiting for stuff to come from the shop. We played a lot of cards, piddled around. Eventually we began to build a new test cell, and that took a lot of work. You know, we built everything. In service, you do everything yourself; there is none of that "that is his job and this is my job" stuff. It was everybody's job. It was hard on the hearing, though. We had head sets, and we were supposed to wear earplugs, too. The head set connected you up, just like they do in an aircraft, with the cockpit. Only in this case the test cell cockpit was on the ground to one side of the engine. But if you had earplugs on you couldn't hear, and it's crucial that you hear what somebody is saying—that they are taking the engine up to power, or that they are going to put in water, or are going to make major changes in speed. If you can't hear, you are gonna be in big trouble when the change takes place. They might be telling you there is a fire or something, and you might not hear, so I wouldn't wear the earplugs. But if you don't wear the earplugs and they run the engine for several hours, it feels like you've got an icepick through your ear. It is very fatiguing, all that noise. I don't know why, it makes you feel like jello. Makes you real tired.

I knew there was going to be an end to it with my back the way it was. I knew it wasn't going to be a career for me, so I wasn't as motivated at the test cell as I had been on the flight line. I was a staff sergeant by this time and wasn't worked up about rank anymore. I guess I didn't feel I was going to be a part of it forever. A lot of people wanted me to stay in; a lot of people wanted me to be careered, because women weren't in staff, tech, or master slots, and I had a good chance of making it to the top. But it was frustrating because parts of me weren't being challenged. I was taking night courses in a University of Maryland program, and if I brought heavy books to work, or said anything beyond shit, piss, fuck, and baby barf, it was like I was speaking another language—like I was deliberately putting myself above the guys—and it created hostility. I was also involved in a lot of local political stuff with the women's movement in Cambridge, like pro–abortion rights, and I lived off the base at this stage. I lived off the base for two or two and a half, three years in a village nearby, and I guess I was concentrating on my civilian status.

I was working a lot on cars by this time. Within a year of being there, I had got involved with working on cars with people in my shop, and then I started working part time in an auto-hobby shop, which is like a self-help place on base. You know, you can do tune-ups and work with other people. That freaked a lot of guys out, except the maintenance guys. They thought it was great; they never even blinked. I put together some cars, and I painted a couple, and I really liked that. I liked cars more than airplanes because they were more my size, and I enjoyed it. I mean, it's a major part of my life, but also something was missing —you know, I felt like a kind of schizophrenic. I was going back and forth between the intellectual, political thing, which was sort of female, and the male mechanical, physical hard work, military bullshit. I think we were getting kind of flaky, too. The United States was involved in the Iranian thing. Once the base was on an alert, and we all freaked out. There were a bunch of mysterious helicopters. There were guys in camouflage, you know, Army dudes, which we hardly ever saw. They came and then shortly thereafter there was the Iranian rescue mission. I don't know—I was getting fed up with the whole situation.

I was feeling pretty detached from my feminine side because I wasn't around women that much, and the political contact I had was too schizophrenic. I guess I had the feeling that I had to get to a place where I could be more integrated. So I applied to some schools. I tried to stay in England, but you had to have five years residence to apply for resident alien status, so I knew I had to come back to the States. I went to the base librarian, a school friend of mine, and he showed me some books about different colleges. I had some friends in New Hampshire, and I had been there once, so I applied to go to schools in New England and got accepted to all of them except Harvard. I had thought that it would be kind of neat just to try, but I got accepted to Smith, and got a lot of mail from Smith, so I thought, well, I'll try a little women's community now. I thought it might be good for me as a balance to the total male community I was in. So in August of 1980, I got my discharge at McGuire (New Jersey) for terminal leave, went to Northampton, and started school.

I just utterly freaked. Everybody there looked alike, blond, tan, and rich—perfect hair, perfect teeth, perfect skin, soft hands. The atmosphere was incredibly intellectual, liberal, not at all what I was used to. I talked crude; I still talk that way—a lot of slang and a lot of crude. It wasn't their way. I felt more like I was coming from a foreign country, going to a school like that, than I ever felt going to Turkey or Germany or Italy or anyplace else. It was bizarre. Now I'm getting past the adjustment phase. I feel like I'm just on leave and gonna go back to real life any minute. But people are so naive, so innocent, so righteous and judgmental about people who were in the service. And nobody knows what that means—especially for women. They can't imagine what it was like, why some of us have to go in, and why some of them don't have to. Smith has been an eye-opening experience, and sometimes I'm bitter and uptight about it, and other times I'm mellow.

I've begun to involve myself in the veterans' movement, doing work with women veterans because we are a nearly invisible force. Women come out of the service and get lost. They don't identify as vets; they don't have an organization, and in most groups you don't want to talk about it because you get stereotyped as gay or whore. It's really uncomfortable because it's a discussion you can't have. Nobody knows what you are talking about, or what it meant, or they don't like the idea in the first place, or they don't want to know, or they do want to know but they don't really care. "Oh, what was that like!" and when you start telling, they are not listening. They don't give a shit, they just think they are supposed to ask. One woman, one eighteen-year-old kid, put me down for being a defender of the patriarchy. How the hell do I know what a patriarchy is? I mean, they don't know. Everything is not black and white. It used to be black and white for me too, but you know, you learn to bite the bullet. I guess you learn to be more rational about people's choices and people's lives, about responsibility and discipline. God, civilians are so snobby in a lot of ways. It took me a long time to get used to that. I'm still in the process of getting adjusted, I realize that. It will be a while, because six years is a long time in an enclosed community. It's like the Air Force was most of my adult life. All I knew was the hippie years, the countercultural late sixties and early seventies, and then I was in the military. It's like all of the tremendous change taking place in the country didn't affect me. The apathy, the amnesia about Vietnam, about the whole period, is very strange to me. My parents are glad that I'm out and going to school, but we never discuss the service. I talk to my brother a lot about it because he was in for four years, and we have that in common, but I'm more involved than he is. I was in longer, and it was a different experience for a woman. Maybe this outline of what it was like is interesting. I hope so. There are a lot of women veterans and a lot of women still in service today, and not very many people seem very interested.

# APPENDIX B

## Women
## at Sea

Women have long been taboo at sea. There seems to be a sense that they do not belong there, and even that it is dangerous to have them there. Still, the Women at Sea Program that followed Judge John L. Sirica's decision in the *Owens* case was not completely unprecedented.[1]

During World War I, Navy women who served in France, Puerto Rico, and other overseas locations went there by ship, as did the 10,000 Army nurses who served abroad. Moreover, many of the Navy's 12,500 "yeomanettes" were formally assigned to tugs on the bottom of the Potomac River because regulations then required both that all yeomen be assigned to ships and also that women not be assigned to sea duty.[2]

Two decades later, during World War II, Army officers (including nurses), Army enlisted women, Red Cross women, and stewardesses served on ships, but ironically, except for nurses, Navy women did not. In that war they were restricted by law to service in the United States; later (1944), they were permitted to serve in U.S. territories, particularly Hawaii and Alaska. Yet Navy women were less restricted in their job choices than women in other services. One in four worked in aviation, and one thousand women taught instrument flying. The Navy was apparently happy to have women do nontraditional work; it just did not want them doing it at sea.[3]

Following that war, and in accordance with the restrictions of § 6015 of Title 10, U.S.C., some Navy women saw duty on transport and hospital ships, and one woman line officer was assigned to a ship as an assistant transportation officer.[4] However, as ships ceased to be used to transport dependents, and as hospital ships were decommissioned (the last in 1971), Navy women found themselves high and dry. Almost immediately, though, a new way was found to provide some in-ship opportunities for women. In his Z-Gram 116, then Chief of Naval Operations Adm. Elmo R. Zumwalt, Jr., initiated what would be a three-year pilot program for women on a recommissioned hospital ship, the U.S.S. *Sanctuary.*

Pilot programs are not necessarily good tests, because they are likely both to attract highly motivated participants and to burden those participants with press scrutiny. All the women in the *Sanctuary* program were volunteers, and the ship was not at sea much. In fact, its principal function was to provide medical care as a shore station. During the program's first year, the ship was underway only 42 days; it spent 100 days in upkeep (maintenance) status, 25 in port visits, and 199 in overhaul and renovation. At the end of the first year, only 53 enlisted women were on board (21 in the hospital, 9 as deck hands, 4 in supply, 3 in Operations, 10 in resale, 5 in administration, and 1 in engineering). Ten had been transferred; 2 had been sent to naval hospitals for observation (for alleged homosexual activity ashore) and 4 for treatment; 2 were given changes of station; 1 had deserted; and 1 had swapped her billet. Nine other women had been discharged at the convenience of the government —7 for pregnancy and 2 for unsuitability.[5]

Enlisted women's doubts (really complaints) about the experiment focused on (1) loss of femininity through having to wear male work clothing; (2) being treated like men; (3) vulgarity and gross behavior (by both males and females); (4) poor living conditions; and (5) lack of privacy.*

Official conclusions drawn from the study were (1) that storage space was inadequate for women and (2) that more senior women petty officers were required. Each woman brought aboard a sea bag plus a (recommended) footlocker, several suitcases, and frequently an iron and a hairdryer. Women also required washers and dryers for clothing not up to the perils of the ship's laundry. As for privacy, women's berthing facilities (like the men's) were designed for seventy-five, with bunks three high in an open style. A better design was possible but was not used because the Navy preferred identical arrangements to guarantee that there could be no charges of favoritism.† More petty officers were needed for supervision during nonwork hours. Usually berthing areas include all individuals from a particular work space, and the same supervisors direct work and quarters assignments. The women's berthing area, though, included women from the whole ship who worked for a number of different (often male) petty officers. This meant that there was no clear responsibility for cleaning and maintaining the berthing area.

Reports from the deck crew said that women's physical strength was not a problem, since the crew had always had some small men, but that "menstruation debilitation" put a strain on work relationships and

---

*Submergence in a traditionally male institution may encourage men's traditionalism and masculine traits, but it has two different effects on women. Some become more androgynous; others seek more strongly feminine identities.

†In one 1970s remodeling, the Navy is alleged to have used 1945 bathroom fixtures to ensure that women would not have better facilities than men.

planning. The report also noted that women manipulated supervisors with a "carefully designed technique." Both official reports suggest that male petty officers had not (yet) learned how to supervise women.

The *Sanctuary* summary includes the following observations: women had doubts about sea assignments, but men liked having them on board, although enlisted supervisors liked having them least. The young women were courted with energy, and the ship's inactivity left them with much time to socialize; when at sea, previously discreet behavior became public, and the commander had to declare affectionate acts "contrary to the good order and discipline of the naval service." (As a result, "not as much" hand holding was seen.) Men resented women's ability to get out by getting pregnant, but (authors of the report "strongly believed") none of the women who separated used pregnancy to escape military life. Women stood all watches and fulfilled all duties for which they qualified, including those of pier sentries and shore patrols—and did them well: "women perform their assigned tasks with radiant and inspiring enthusiasm which invites a man to do his best."

The authors of the report drew other conclusions as well:

1. It is desirable to screen enlisted women prior to assignment at sea.
2. Women's berthing must be totally segregated from that of men.
3. Habitability and privacy are more important to women's morale and productivity than to men's.
4. The policy of separating married people must be continued.
5. Commanding officers must have authority to transfer personnel who prove embarrassing.
6. Enlisted women's work uniforms and dress uniform pants are inadequate.
7. Women have fewer personal problems and make fewer special requests than the average married male.

Having demonstrated that "women can perform every shipboard function with equal ease, expertise, and dedication as their male counterparts," the U.S.S. *Sanctuary* experiment was concluded and the ship was decommissioned for the second time. Except for a few women assigned to yard boats and tugboats (beginning in 1975), the "wet" Navy again became all-male.[6]

Only after three more years—only after they had taken the Navy to court and won, and an act of Congress had been passed—were Navy women again assigned to some ships. The Navy's Women at Sea Program began in 1978, immediately after the *Owens* decision. Judge Sirica had not said when, where, or how many women should be allowed to go to sea; much was left to the Navy's discretion. Its response was prompt but cautious: 396 enlisted women and 53 women officers were assigned to ten of the fifty ships for which women were declared eligible.* By 1987 some 5,000 women were serving on sixty-two ships, but 1,200 "female billets" were unfilled. Women were then 55,000 of the Navy's 576,000 uniformed personnel.

The Navy's plans for women remain limited, primarily because of the combat ship exclusion but also because of the Navy's classification of particular ships and their missions. For example, in November 1986 the Navy changed the name of its Mobile Logistics Support Force (MLSF) to the Combat Logistics Force (CLF). A month earlier it had said that women would be permitted to serve in the MLSF. After the name change, it seemed clear they would not. Yet only one month later it was announced that women *would* be eligible for as many as 9,000 CLF slots.[7]

Other policies limit the use of women. Guidelines stipulate that only 25 percent of a ship's crew can be female, that women cannot compose more than 50 percent of the crew at any work site, that a minimum of twenty-five women should be assigned to any ship with women, that 30 percent of the women on board must hold the rank of E-4 and above, and that women officers must be on any ship with enlisted women.†

Until 1987 the Navy could increase the number of women "at sea" by calling some overseas shore duty "sea duty" (for women but not for men). The result was that perhaps 30 percent of Navy women were stationed abroad—many of them in "sea duty" shore billets—and fewer than 10 percent actually held shipboard assignments (most of them in U.S. home ports). In sharp contrast, the Navy has had a difficult time giving its men shore duty even half the time. Its goal is a 36-month sea duty/36-month shore duty rotation, but over 60 percent of distributable billets are for sea duty. The one-to-one goal is made approachable only by assigning most first termers to sea and, when they leave the Navy, filling those slots with more first termers. A particular individual's rotation is also affected by his or her specialty, some of which do not achieve the one-to-one rotation. Those in such specialties cannot help but believe that it is nonseagoing women who create their unfavorable duty ratio, although "civilianization" of shore jobs, using both men and women, has probably had a larger effect.

Nevertheless, letting more women go to sea would let more men come ashore. It would also reassure men that women are doing their full share.

---

*These included auxiliaries like tenders. Later women would be declared eligible for research vessels and aircraft carriers on training missions.

†The requirement limits the pace of assignment, not just because female petty officers are few, but also because even the few available are not well distributed through the sea-going ratings.

Navy policymakers, however, are not trying to use women more exten-sively. Indeed, their goal has been to "man" their soon-to-be 600 ships with 40,000 more sailors without increasing the number of women at all.*

Naval duty is nearly impossible for women, Congressman Don Edwards of San Jose has concluded.[8] The fact that 240 women were on the 1,300-person ship sent to Bahrain to repair the U.S.S. *Stark* in 1987 made news because it was, indeed, unusual. The Navy tradition of pleading legal restrictions continues.

Yet some uniformed U.S. women *do* work at sea without restriction. The uniforms they wear are not those of the Navy, but those of the Coast Guard. These women provide a constant reminder of what is possible. In peacetime they are commanded by the Department of Transportation, and many of them do not relish the possibility that in time of emergency the Navy would take over and perhaps apply its restrictive policies to women who are now very much in command.

*At the same time the Navy has announced that women and men would follow the same sea/shore rotation. This should expand the use of women at sea (Ted Bush, "New Policy for Women Requires More Sea Duty," *Navy Times*, 13 July 1987).

# APPENDIX C

## Data on Enlisted Women

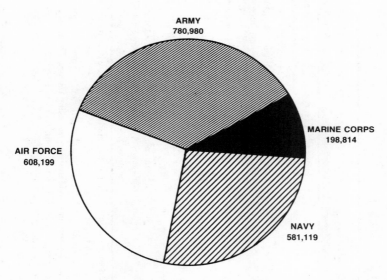

ARMY
780,980

MARINE CORPS
198,814

AIR FORCE
608,199

NAVY
581,119

FIGURE 3.    Active-Duty Military Personnel by Service, Fiscal Year 1986
*Source: Selected Manpower Statistics, Fiscal Year 1986* (Washington, D.C.:
DOD, 1986), p. 37.

TABLE C.1.  Grade Titles of Enlisted Personnel [a]

| Pay Grade | Army | | Navy [b] | Marine Corps | Air Force |
|---|---|---|---|---|---|
| | NCOs | Specialists | | | |
| E-9 | Command Sergeant Major; Sergeant Major | | Master Chief Petty Officer | Sergeant Major; Master Gunnery Sergeant | Chief Master Sergeant |
| E-8 | First Sergeant; Master Sergeant | | Senior Chief Petty Officer | First Sergeant; Master Sergeant | Senior Master Sergeant |
| E-7 | Platoon Sergeant; Sergeant First Class | Specialist 7 | Chief Petty Officer | Gunnery Sergeant | Master Sergeant |
| E-6 | Staff Sergeant | Specialist 6 | Petty Officer, 1st Class | Staff Sergeant | Technical Sergeant |
| E-5 | Sergeant | Specialist 5 | Petty Officer, 2nd Class | Sergeant | Staff Sergeant |
| E-4 | Corporal | Specialist 4 | Petty Officer, 3rd Class | Corporal | Sergeant |
| E-3 | Private First Class | | Seaman [c] | Lance Corporal | Airman First Class |
| E-2 | Private, PV-2 | | Seaman Apprentice [d] | Private First Class | Airman |
| E-1 | Private, PV-1 | | Seaman Recruit [d] | Private | Airman Basic |

[a] Among the services, rank and precedence are determined by pay grade. However, within the Army, for rank and precedence, specialist grades fall between staff sergeant and private first class.

[b] In general, titles for petty officers are according to "rating" (naval skill), such as boatswain, gunner's mate, yeoman, storekeeper, etc. Personnel in pay grades E-3, E-2, and E-1 are not considered as possessing ratings. The titles listed denote the "rate" or pay grade.

[c] E-3 pay grade also includes airman, construction man, dental man, fireman, hospital man, and stewardsman.

[d] E-1 and E-2 pay grades also include recruits and apprentices in the six rates listed in note c.

Source: Selected Manpower Statistics, Fiscal Year 1986, p. 56.

TABLE C.2. Military Personnel on Active Duty by Grade, 30 September 1986

| Rank/Grade | | Total DOD | Army | Navy | Marine Corps | Air Force |
|---|---|---|---|---|---|---|
| General | Admiral | 35 | 11 | 9 | 3 | 12 |
| Lt. General | Vice Admiral | 125 | 46 | 32 | 8 | 39 |
| Maj. General | Rear Admiral | 362 | 144 | 80 | 21 | 117 |
| Brig. General | Rear Admiral (Lower) | 533 | 199 | 130 | 33 | 171 |
| Colonel | Captain | 14,603 | 4,620 | 3,709 | 652 | 5,622 |
| Lieutenant Col. | Commander | 32,740 | 10,777 | 7,765 | 1,654 | 12,544 |
| Major | Lt. Commander | 54,404 | 17,730 | 13,382 | 3,259 | 20,033 |
| Captain | Lieutenant | 104,727 | 34,265 | 22,433 | 5,959 | 42,070 |
| 1st Lieutenant | Lieutenant (junior grade) | 44,398 | 15,160 | 9,687 | 4,549 | 15,002 |
| 2d Lieutenant | Ensign | 39,218 | 11,475 | 11,695 | 2,610 | 13,438 |
| Chief Warrant Officer W-4 | | 3,320 | 2,040 | 1,125 | 155 | — |
| Chief Warrant Officer W-3 | | 4,850 | 3,794 | 810 | 246 | — |
| Chief Warrant Officer W-2 | | 9,508 | 7,701 | 1,194 | 613 | — |
| Warrant Officer W-1 | | 2,232 | 1,795 | — | 437 | — |
| Total Officers | | 311,055 | 109,757 | 72,051 | 20,199 | 109,048 |
| E-9 | | 15,454 | 4,423 | 4,742 | 1,343 | 4,946 |
| E-8 | | 38,973 | 15,208 | 9,949 | 3,962 | 9,854 |
| E-7 | | 133,404 | 51,770 | 32,983 | 9,441 | 39,210 |
| E-6 | | 241,608 | 88,297 | 78,580 | 15,534 | 59,197 |
| E-5 | | 361,106 | 119,623 | 102,821 | 24,616 | 114,046 |
| E-4 | | 443,873 | 187,559 | 106,866 | 34,494 | 114,954 |
| E-3 | | 328,630 | 95,450 | 86,041 | 55,535 | 91,604 |
| E-2 | | 148,710 | 47,202 | 42,463 | 20,780 | 38,265 |
| E-1 | | 132,580 | 57,136 | 39,944 | 12,910 | 22,590 |
| Total Enlisted | | 1,844,338 | 666,668 | 504,389 | 178,615 | 494,666 |
| Cadets and Midshipmen | | 13,719 | 4,555 | 4,679 | — | 4,485 |
| Total | | 2,169,112 | 780,980 | 581,119 | 198,814 | 608,199 |

Source: Selected Manpower Statistics, Fiscal Year 1986, p. 55.

TABLE C.3.    Female Military Personnel on Active Duty by Grade, 30 September 1986

| Rank/Grade | | Total DOD | Army | Navy | Marine Corps | Air Force |
|---|---|---|---|---|---|---|
| General | Admiral | — | — | — | — | — |
| Lt. General | Vice Admiral | — | — | — | — | — |
| Maj. General | Rear Admiral | — | — | — | — | — |
| Brig. General | Rear Admiral (Lower) | 8 | 4 | 1 | 1 | 2 |
| Colonel | Captain | 309 | 101 | 106 | 10 | 92 |
| Lieutenant Col. | Commander | 1,308 | 482 | 383 | 35 | 408 |
| Major | Lt. Commander | 4,072 | 1,371 | 1,292 | 75 | 1,334 |
| Captain | Lieutenant | 13,253 | 4,471 | 2,847 | 233 | 5,702 |
| 1st Lieutenant | Lieutenant (junior grade) | 6,138 | 2,380 | 1,220 | 152 | 2,386 |
| 2d Lieutenant | Ensign | 6,054 | 2,130 | 1,382 | 89 | 2,453 |
| Chief Warrant Officer W-4 | | 9 | — | 6 | 3 | — |
| Chief Warrant Officer W-3 | | 38 | 31 | 3 | 4 | — |
| Chief Warrant Officer W-2 | | 240 | 202 | 20 | 18 | — |
| Warrant Officer W-1 | | 114 | 91 | — | 23 | — |
| Total Officers | | 31,543 | 11,263 | 7,260 | 643 | 12,377 |
| E-9 | | 64 | 17 | 15 | 10 | 22 |
| E-8 | | 459 | 227 | 96 | 50 | 86 |
| E-7 | | 3,731 | 1,800 | 817 | 169 | 945 |
| E-6 | | 15,666 | 6,505 | 4,575 | 594 | 3,992 |
| E-5 | | 42,551 | 14,751 | 10,469 | 1,822 | 15,509 |
| E-4 | | 54,350 | 24,741 | 11,530 | 2,337 | 15,742 |
| E-3 | | 39,202 | 10,829 | 12,009 | 2,634 | 13,730 |
| E-2 | | 17,163 | 4,838 | 4,524 | 1,082 | 6,719 |
| E-1 | | 12,701 | 5,443 | 2,761 | 548 | 3,949 |
| Total Enlisted | | 185,887 | 69,151 | 46,796 | 9,246 | 60,694 |
| Cadets and Midshipmen | | 1,459 | 518 | 408 | — | 533 |
| Total | | 218,889 | 80,932 | 54,464 | 9,889 | 73,604 |

Source: *Selected Manpower Statistics, Fiscal Year 1986*, p. 54.

TABLE C.4.   Minority Women and Men by Service, 1986

|  | Women | Men | Total |
|---|---|---|---|
| **DOD** | | | |
| Black | 30.5% | 18.1% | 21.2% |
| Hispanic | 3.4 | 3.8 | 4.1 |
| Other | 3.5 | 3.8 | 4.2 |
| White | 62.5 | 74.0 | 70.4 |
| **Army** | | | |
| Black | 43.3 | 25.1 | 29.6 |
| Hispanic | 2.6 | 3.7 | 4.0 |
| Other | 4.0 | 3.6 | 4.0 |
| White | 50.1 | 67.6 | 62.4 |
| **Navy** | | | |
| Black | 21.8 | 12.6 | 14.2 |
| Hispanic | 4.7 | 3.7 | 4.1 |
| Other | 2.9 | 5.5 | 5.7 |
| White | 70.6 | 78.2 | 76.0 |
| **Marines** | | | |
| Black | 26.4 | 19.2 | 20.5 |
| Hispanic | 4.2 | 4.9 | 5.2 |
| Other | 3.7 | 2.8 | 2.9 |
| White | 65.7 | 73.1 | 71.4 |
| **Air Force** | | | |
| Black | 22.9 | 14.3 | 17.2 |
| Hispanic | 3.1 | 3.3 | 3.7 |
| Other | 3.3 | 3.0 | 3.4 |
| White | 70.7 | 79.4 | 75.7 |

*Source*: Women's Equity Action League, Project on Women and the Military (Carolyn Becraft, director), *WEAL Facts*, rev. Carol Martinelli and Lisa Zurmuhlen (Washington, D.C.: WEAL, 1987), p. 2.

TABLE C.5.    Monthly Basic Pay Rates as of 1 January 1987

| Pay Grade | Years in Service | | | | | | |
|---|---|---|---|---|---|---|---|
| | Under 2 | 2 | 3 | 4 | 6 | 8 | 10 |
| **Commissioned Officers** | | | | | | | |
| O-10 | 5,378.10 | 5,567.70 | 5,567.70 | 5,567.70 | 5,567.70 | 5,781.00 | 5,781.0( |
| O-9 | 4,766.70 | 4,891.50 | 4,995.60 | 4,995.60 | 4,995.60 | 5,122.50 | 5,122.5( |
| O-8 | 4,317.30 | 4,446.60 | 4,552.20 | 4,552.20 | 4,552.20 | 4,891.50 | 4,891.5( |
| O-7 | 3,587.40 | 3,831.30 | 3,831.30 | 3,831.30 | 4,002.90 | 4,002.90 | 4,235.1( |
| O-6 | 2,658.90 | 2,921.40 | 3,112.50 | 3,112.50 | 3,112.50 | 3,112.50 | 3,112.5( |
| O-5 | 2,126.40 | 2,497.20 | 2,669.70 | 2,669.70 | 2,669.70 | 2,669.70 | 2,750.7( |
| O-4 | 1,792.50 | 2,182.80 | 2,328.30 | 2,328.30 | 2,371.50 | 2,476.20 | 2,645.1( |
| O-3 | 1,665.90 | 1,862.40 | 1,990.80 | 2,202.90 | 2,308.20 | 2,391.30 | 2,520.6( |
| O-2 | 1,452.60 | 1,586.40 | 1,905.60 | 1,969.80 | 2,011.20 | 2,011.20 | 2,011.2( |
| O-1 | 1,260.90 | 1,312.80 | 1,586.40 | 1,586.40 | 1,586.40 | 1,586.40 | 1,586.4( |
| **Commissioned Officers With More Than 4 Years** | | | | | | | |
| **Active Duty as Enlisted or Warrant Officer** | | | | | | | |
| O-3E | 0.00 | 0.00 | 0.00 | 2,202.90 | 2,308.20 | 2,391.30 | 2,520.6( |
| O-2E | 0.00 | 0.00 | 0.00 | 1,969.80 | 2,011.20 | 2,074.80 | 2,182.8( |
| O-1E | 0.00 | 0.00 | 0.00 | 1,586.40 | 1,694.70 | 1,757.10 | 1,820.7( |
| **Warrant Officers** | | | | | | | |
| W-4 | 1,697.10 | 1,820.70 | 1,820.70 | 1,862.40 | 1,947.00 | 2,032.80 | 2,118.3( |
| W-3 | 1,542.30 | 1,673.10 | 1,673.10 | 1,694.70 | 1,714.50 | 1,839.90 | 1,947.0( |
| W-2 | 1,350.90 | 1,461.60 | 1,461.60 | 1,504.20 | 1,586.40 | 1,673.10 | 1,736.7( |
| W-1 | 1,125.60 | 1,290.60 | 1,290.60 | 1,398.30 | 1,461.60 | 1,524.30 | 1,586.4( |
| **Enlisted Members** | | | | | | | |
| E-9 | 0.00 | 0.00 | 0.00 | 0.00 | 0.00 | 0.00 | 1,974.0( |
| E-8 | 0.00 | 0.00 | 0.00 | 0.00 | 0.00 | 1,655.70 | 1,702.8( |
| E-7 | 1,155.90 | 1,247.70 | 1,294.20 | 1,339.20 | 1,385.10 | 1,429.20 | 1,474.8( |
| E-6 | 994.50 | 1,083.90 | 1,129.20 | 1,177.20 | 1,221.00 | 1,265.40 | 1,311.9( |
| E-5 | 872.70 | 950.10 | 996.00 | 1,039.50 | 1,107.60 | 1,152.60 | 1,198.5( |
| E-4 | 814.20 | 859.50 | 909.90 | 980.70 | 1,019.40 | 1,019.40 | 1,019.4( |
| E-3 | 766.80 | 808.80 | 841.50 | 874.80 | 874.80 | 874.80 | 874.8( |
| E-2 | 738.00 | 738.00 | 738.00 | 738.00 | 738.00 | 738.00 | 738.0( |
| E-1* | 658.20 | 658.20 | 658.20 | 658.20 | 658.20 | 658.20 | 658.2( |

Note: Monthly pay of generals and admirals has been capped at $5,900.10 by Level V of the Executive Schedule.

| | | | Years in Service | | | |
|---|---|---|---|---|---|---|
| 12 | 14 | 16 | 18 | 20 | 22 | 26 |
| ,900.10 | 5,900.10 | 5,900.10 | 5,900.10 | 5,900.10 | 5,900.10 | 5,900.10 |
| ,335.80 | 5,335.80 | 5,781.00 | 5,781.00 | 5,900.10 | 5,900.10 | 5,900.10 |
| ,122.50 | 5,122.50 | 5,335.80 | 5,567.70 | 5,781.00 | 5,900.10 | 5,900.10 |
| ,235.10 | 4,446.60 | 4,891.50 | 5,227.80 | 5,227.80 | 5,227.80 | 5,227.80 |
| ,112.50 | 3,218.10 | 3,727.20 | 3,917.70 | 4,002.90 | 4,235.10 | 4,593.30 |
| ,898.30 | 3,092.70 | 3,324.00 | 3,514.80 | 3,621.30 | 3,747.60 | 3,747.60 |
| ,793.90 | 2,921.40 | 3,049.50 | 3,133.80 | 3,133.80 | 3,133.80 | 3,133.80 |
| ,645.10 | 2,710.20 | 2,710.20 | 2,710.20 | 2,710.20 | 2,710.20 | 2,710.20 |
| ,011.20 | 2,011.20 | 2,011.20 | 2,011.20 | 2,011.20 | 2,011.20 | 2,011.20 |
| ,586.40 | 1,586.40 | 1,586.40 | 1,586.40 | 1,586.40 | 1,586.40 | 1,586.40 |
| | | | | | | |
| ,645.10 | 2,750.70 | 2,750.70 | 2,750.70 | 2,750.70 | 2,750.70 | 2,750.70 |
| ,266.20 | 2,328.30 | 2,328.30 | 2,328.30 | 2,328.30 | 2,328.30 | 2,328.30 |
| ,884.00 | 1,969.80 | 1,969.80 | 1,969.80 | 1,969.80 | 1,969.80 | 1,969.80 |
| | | | | | | |
| ,266.20 | 2,371.50 | 2,454.60 | 2,520.60 | 2,601.90 | 2,688.90 | 2,898.30 |
| ,011.20 | 2,074.80 | 2,136.60 | 2,202.90 | 2,288.40 | 2,371.50 | 2,454.60 |
| ,800.30 | 1,862.40 | 1,927.50 | 1,990.80 | 2,053.80 | 2,136.60 | 2,136.60 |
| ,652.10 | 1,714.50 | 1,778.10 | 1,839.90 | 1,905.60 | 1,905.60 | 1,905.60 |
| | | | | | | |
| ,018.70 | 2,064.30 | 2,111.70 | 2,158.80 | 2,200.80 | 2,316.60 | 2,541.90 |
| ,747.50 | 1,793.10 | 1,840.20 | 1,882.80 | 1,929.00 | 2,042.40 | 2,270.10 |
| ,520.70 | 1,589.40 | 1,634.70 | 1,680.30 | 1,702.20 | 1,816.50 | 2,042.40 |
| ,379.40 | 1,422.60 | 1,468.50 | 1,491.00 | 1,491.00 | 1,491.00 | 1,491.00 |
| ,242.60 | 1,265.40 | 1,265.40 | 1,265.40 | 1,265.40 | 1,265.40 | 1,265.40 |
| ,019.40 | 1,019.40 | 1,019.40 | 1,019.40 | 1,019.40 | 1,019.40 | 1,019.40 |
| 874.80 | 874.80 | 874.80 | 874.80 | 874.80 | 874.80 | 874.80 |
| 738.00 | 738.00 | 738.00 | 738.00 | 738.00 | 738.00 | 738.00 |
| 658.20 | 658.20 | 658.20 | 658.20 | 658.20 | 658.20 | 658.20 |

*E-1 with less than 4 months—$608.40
*Source*: *Handbook for Military Families* (Springfield, Va.: Times Journal Corporation, 1987).

TABLE C.6.    Pay Grade by Sex and Service for Enlisted Personnel, 1985

| Pay Grade | Army | | | Navy | | |
|---|---|---|---|---|---|---|
| | M | F | Total | M | F | Total |
| E-1 | 0.6% | 0.2% | 0.6% | 0.6% | 0.0% | 0.6% |
| E-2 | 2.8 | 1.3 | 2.7 | 3.6 | 3.4 | 3.5 |
| E-3 | 15.0 | 12.7 | 14.7 | 17.9 | 25.8 | 18.6 |
| E-4 | 30.7 | 47.3 | 32.3 | 21.9 | 30.5 | 22.7 |
| E-5 | 19.9 | 25.1 | 20.4 | 23.8 | 28.3 | 24.2 |
| E-6 | 15.9 | 9.9 | 15.3 | 19.1 | 9.9 | 18.3 |
| E-7 | 10.5 | 3.1 | 9.8 | 8.7 | 1.8 | 8.1 |
| E-8 | 3.3 | 0.4 | 3.0 | 3.0 | 0.2 | 2.8 |
| E-9 | 1.2 | 0.0 | 1.1 | 1.3 | 0.1 | 1.2 |
| Total | 99.9 | 100.0 | 99.9 | 99.9 | 100.0 | 100.0 |
| Number of cases | 12,347 | 6,852 | 19,199 | 11,634 | 5,650 | 17,284 |
| Total personnel (in thousands) | 502 | 54 | 556 | 380 | 36 | 416 |

Source: *Description of Officers and Enlisted Personnel in the U.S. Armed Forces: 1985* (Arlington Va.: Defense Manpower Data Center, 1986).

TABLE C.7.    Military Occupation by Sex and Service, for Enlisted Personnel

| Military Occupation | Army | | | Navy | | |
|---|---|---|---|---|---|---|
| | M | F | Total | M | F | Total |
| Direct combat | 27.4% | 4.2% | 25.2% | 4.6% | 1.1% | 4.3% |
| Elec. equip. repair | 5.3 | 2.4 | 5.0 | 15.4 | 6.5 | 14.7 |
| Commun. & Intell. | 11.3 | 13.8 | 11.5 | 11.0 | 15.3 | 11.4 |
| Medical & dental | 5.7 | 15.5 | 6.6 | 5.4 | 14.5 | 6.2 |
| Other technical | 3.4 | 2.9 | 3.4 | 1.0 | 2.4 | 1.2 |
| Support & admin. | 16.1 | 41.9 | 18.6 | 9.7 | 30.4 | 11.5 |
| Elec./mech. repair | 15.8 | 6.7 | 15.0 | 30.8 | 7.1 | 28.7 |
| Crafts | 3.0 | 0.5 | 2.7 | 5.7 | 2.1 | 5.4 |
| Service & supply | 11.7 | 11.5 | 11.7 | 5.8 | 5.0 | 5.8 |
| Non-Occupational | 0.3 | 0.5 | 0.3 | 10.5 | 15.5 | 11.0 |
| Total | 100.00 | 100.00 | 100.00 | 100.00 | 100.00 | 100.00 |
| Number of cases | 12,347 | 6,852 | 19,199 | 11,634 | 5,650 | 17,284 |
| Total personnel (in thousands) | 502 | 54 | 556 | 380 | 36 | 416 |

Source: *Description of Officers and Enlisted Personnel in the U.S. Armed Forces: 1985*, p. 3-14.

| Marine Corps | | | Air Force | | | Total DOD | | |
| M | F | Total | M | F | Total | M | F | Total |
|---|---|---|---|---|---|---|---|---|
| 1.0% | 0.2% | 0.9% | 0.1% | 0.1% | 0.1% | 0.5% | 0.1% | 0.5% |
| 6.1 | 3.1 | 6.0 | 3.1 | 3.9 | 3.1 | 3.4 | 2.8 | 3.4 |
| 33.6 | 29.1 | 33.4 | 20.7 | 25.2 | 21.2 | 19.2 | 20.9 | 19.3 |
| 20.8 | 31.7 | 21.4 | 24.0 | 34.3 | 25.2 | 25.5 | 38.0 | 26.7 |
| 16.2 | 25.2 | 16.7 | 24.3 | 28.9 | 24.8 | 21.8 | 27.2 | 22.3 |
| 11.2 | 7.5 | 11.0 | 14.0 | 6.3 | 13.1 | 15.8 | 8.6 | 15.1 |
| 7.0 | 2.0 | 6.8 | 10.1 | 1.2 | 9.1 | 9.6 | 2.1 | 8.9 |
| 3.0 | 0.5 | 2.9 | 2.4 | 0.2 | 2.1 | 2.9 | 0.3 | 2.7 |
| 1.1 | 0.6 | 1.0 | 1.4 | 0.0 | 1.3 | 1.3 | 0.1 | 1.2 |
| 100.0 | 99.9 | 100.1 | 100.1 | 100.1 | 100.0 | 100.0 | 100.1 | 100.1 |
| 2,767 | 1,126 | 13,893 | 12,083 | 7,566 | 19,649 | 48,831 | 21,194 | 70,025 |
| 139 | 7 | 146 | 386 | 49 | 434 | 1,406 | 146 | 1,552 |

| Marine Corps | | | Air Force | | | Total DOD | | |
| M | F | Total | M | F | Total | M | F | Total |
|---|---|---|---|---|---|---|---|---|
| 31.9% | 8.9% | 30.8% | 10.1% | 2.1% | 9.2% | 17.0% | 3.0% | 15.6% |
| 7.5 | 4.2 | 7.4 | 15.5 | 7.3 | 14.5 | 11.0 | 5.2 | 10.5 |
| 7.2 | 9.0 | 7.3 | 7.1 | 10.4 | 7.4 | 9.6 | 12.8 | 9.9 |
| 0.0 | 0.0 | 0.0 | 3.6 | 10.2 | 4.3 | 4.5 | 12.7 | 5.3 |
| 2.3 | 4.3 | 2.4 | 4.0 | 2.7 | 3.9 | 2.8 | 2.8 | 2.8 |
| 18.3 | 49.9 | 19.8 | 19.7 | 43.3 | 22.3 | 15.5 | 39.9 | 17.8 |
| 17.8 | 7.9 | 17.3 | 23.2 | 9.1 | 21.6 | 22.1 | 7.7 | 20.7 |
| 2.1 | 1.4 | 2.0 | 6.1 | 3.4 | 5.8 | 4.5 | 1.9 | 4.2 |
| 11.7 | 12.9 | 11.8 | 9.3 | 10.4 | 9.4 | 9.5 | 9.6 | 9.5 |
| 1.2 | 1.6 | 1.2 | 1.5 | 1.2 | 1.5 | 3.5 | 4.5 | 3.6 |
| 00.00 | 100.00 | 100.00 | 100.00 | 100.00 | 100.00 | 100.00 | 100.00 | 100.00 |
| 2,767 | 1,126 | 13,893 | 12,083 | 7,566 | 19,649 | 48,831 | 21,194 | 70,025 |
| 139 | 7 | 146 | 386 | 49 | 434 | 1,406 | 146 | 1,552 |

TABLE C.8.  Household Composition by Pay Grade, Sex, and Service for Enlisted Personnel

| Pay Grade/ | Army | | | Navy | | |
|---|---|---|---|---|---|---|
| Household Composition | M | F | Total | M | F | Total |
| **E-1–E-3** | | | | | | |
| Unmar. no dep. | 69.2% | 62.6% | 68.7% | 74.8% | 58.5% | 73.0 |
| Unmar. 1 child | 2.8 | 4.9 | 3.0 | 1.7 | 4.6 | 2.0 |
| Unmar. 2–3 children | 0.0 | 0.7 | 0.1 | 0.7 | 0.7 | 0.7 |
| Unmar. 4 + children | 0.0 | 0.0 | 0.0 | 0.0 | 0.0 | 0.0 |
| Unmar. other dep. | 1.7 | 1.1 | 1.7 | 2.3 | 0.5 | 2.1 |
| Mil. spouse no dep. | 1.0 | 16.5 | 2.1 | 0.6 | 13.7 | 2.1 |
| Mil. spouse 1 child | 0.3 | 3.0 | 0.5 | 0.3 | 5.8 | 0.9 |
| Mil. spouse 2–3 chld. | 0.0 | 0.7 | 0.1 | 0.1 | 1.2 | 0.2 |
| Mil. spouse 4 + chld. | 0.0 | 0.0 | 0.0 | 0.0 | 0.0 | 0.0 |
| Mil. spouse other dep. | 0.0 | 0.2 | 0.0 | 0.0 | 0.4 | 0.0 |
| Civ. spouse no dep. | 10.2 | 4.3 | 9.8 | 8.8 | 9.2 | 8.8 |
| Civ. spouse 1 child | 8.6 | 3.5 | 8.2 | 5.8 | 4.1 | 5.6 |
| Civ. spouse 2–3 chld. | 5.1 | 1.8 | 4.8 | 3.5 | 0.7 | 3.2 |
| Civ. spouse 4 + chld. | 0.1 | 0.0 | 0.1 | 0.4 | 0.0 | 0.4 |
| Civ. spouse other dep. | 1.0 | 0.7 | 1.0 | 1.1 | 0.5 | 1.0 |
| Total | 100.0 | 100.0 | 100.0 | 100.0 | 100.0 | 100.0 |
| Number of cases | 1,282 | 453 | 1,735 | 1,562 | 780 | 2,342 |
| Total personnel (in thousands) | 92 | 8 | 100 | 84 | 11 | 94 |
| **E-4–E-5** | | | | | | |
| Unmar. no dep. | 38.5 | 33.0 | 37.7 | 47.0 | 41.7 | 46.5 |
| Unmar. 1 child | 2.4 | 7.7 | 3.1 | 2.1 | 6.9 | 2.6 |
| Unmar. 2–3 children | 0.8 | 2.3 | 1.0 | 1.1 | 1.4 | 1.1 |
| Unmar. 4 + children | 0.0 | 0.1 | 0.0 | 0.0 | 0.0 | 0.0 |
| Unmar. other dep. | 0.9 | 1.0 | 0.9 | 0.7 | 1.0 | 0.8 |
| Mil. spouse no dep. | 2.1 | 15.2 | 3.8 | 1.6 | 15.7 | 3.1 |
| Mil. spouse 1 child | 1.2 | 11.1 | 2.5 | 1.0 | 10.6 | 2.0 |
| Mil. spouse 2–3 chld. | 0.6 | 5.4 | 1.2 | 0.3 | 4.1 | 0.7 |
| Mil. spouse 4 + chld. | 0.1 | 0.5 | 0.2 | 0.0 | 0.1 | 0.0 |
| Mil. spouse other dep. | 0.2 | 0.9 | 0.3 | 0.0 | 0.3 | 0.0 |
| Civ. spouse no dep. | 14.9 | 9.4 | 14.2 | 15.4 | 8.2 | 14.6 |
| Civ. spouse 1 child | 16.9 | 7.8 | 15.7 | 14.6 | 6.3 | 13.7 |
| Civ. spouse 2–3 chld. | 18.5 | 4.4 | 16.6 | 14.1 | 3.0 | 12.9 |
| Civ. spouse 4 + chld. | 1.6 | 0.4 | 1.4 | 1.0 | 0.1 | 0.9 |
| Civ. spouse other dep. | 1.5 | 0.8 | 1.4 | 1.0 | 0.5 | 0.9 |
| Total | 100.0 | 100.0 | 100.0 | 100.0 | 100.0 | 100.0 |
| Number of cases | 5,474 | 4,560 | 10,034 | 4,858 | 3,401 | 8,259 |
| Total personnel (in thousands) | 254 | 39 | 293 | 174 | 21 | 195 |

| Marine Corps | | | Air Force | | | Total DOD | | |
|---|---|---|---|---|---|---|---|---|
| M | F | Total | M | F | Total | M | F | Total |
| 73.7% | 54.9% | 73.0% | 60.2% | 60.2% | 60.2% | 68.9% | 59.9% | 68.0% |
| 1.5 | 2.5 | 1.5 | 1.1 | 1.8 | 1.2 | 1.8 | 3.4 | 2.0 |
| 0.3 | 0.1 | 0.3 | 0.1 | 0.1 | 0.1 | 0.3 | 0.4 | 0.3 |
| 0.0 | 0.0 | 0.0 | 0.0 | 0.0 | 0.0 | 0.0 | 0.0 | 0.0 |
| 1.0 | 0.7 | 1.0 | 0.6 | 0.4 | 0.5 | 1.4 | 0.6 | 1.3 |
| 1.2 | 26.4 | 2.2 | 1.9 | 19.9 | 4.3 | 1.2 | 17.7 | 2.7 |
| 0.1 | 8.0 | 0.4 | 0.6 | 5.2 | 1.2 | 0.3 | 5.1 | 0.8 |
| 0.0 | 0.0 | 0.0 | 0.1 | 0.5 | 0.2 | 0.1 | 0.7 | 0.1 |
| 0.0 | 0.0 | 0.0 | 0.0 | 0.1 | 0.0 | 0.0 | 0.0 | 0.0 |
| 0.0 | 0.0 | 0.0 | 0.1 | 0.2 | 0.1 | 0.0 | 0.2 | 0.0 |
| 11.8 | 3.9 | 11.5 | 18.0 | 8.6 | 16.8 | 12.3 | 7.5 | 11.9 |
| 6.4 | 2.6 | 6.3 | 12.1 | 2.6 | 10.8 | 8.5 | 3.3 | 8.0 |
| 2.9 | 0.8 | 2.8 | 4.4 | 0.3 | 3.9 | 4.1 | 0.8 | 3.8 |
| 0.0 | 0.0 | 0.0 | 0.1 | 0.0 | 0.0 | 0.1 | 0.0 | 0.1 |
| 1.1 | 0.0 | 1.1 | 0.8 | 0.2 | 0.8 | 1.0 | 0.4 | 0.9 |
| 100.0 | 100.0 | 100.0 | 100.0 | 100.0 | 100.0 | 100.0 | 100.0 | 100.0 |
| 2,390 | 157 | 2,547 | 2,002 | 1,292 | 3,294 | 7,236 | 2,682 | 9,918 |
| 56 | 2 | 59 | 92 | 14 | 106 | 325 | 35 | 359 |
| 43.9 | 28.9 | 42.8 | 27.0 | 24.9 | 26.7 | 37.9 | 32.2 | 37.2 |
| 1.8 | 7.9 | 2.2 | 1.9 | 6.3 | 2.5 | 2.1 | 7.1 | 2.7 |
| 0.7 | 1.3 | 0.7 | 1.2 | 2.4 | 1.4 | 1.0 | 2.1 | 1.1 |
| 0.0 | 0.0 | 0.0 | 0.0 | 0.1 | 0.1 | 0.0 | 0.1 | 0.0 |
| 0.7 | 1.1 | 0.8 | 0.3 | 0.6 | 0.4 | 0.7 | 0.8 | 0.7 |
| 1.9 | 17.7 | 3.1 | 3.4 | 19.0 | 5.5 | 2.3 | 16.6 | 4.1 |
| 1.0 | 14.1 | 1.9 | 2.2 | 14.3 | 3.9 | 1.4 | 12.2 | 2.7 |
| 0.3 | 8.0 | 0.9 | 1.9 | 11.4 | 3.2 | 0.8 | 7.2 | 1.6 |
| 0.0 | 0.6 | 0.1 | 0.1 | 0.9 | 0.2 | 0.1 | 0.6 | 0.1 |
| 0.0 | 0.3 | 0.0 | 0.1 | 0.6 | 0.1 | 0.1 | 0.6 | 0.1 |
| 16.5 | 9.4 | 16.0 | 15.3 | 7.8 | 14.2 | 15.3 | 8.6 | 14.4 |
| 16.7 | 6.8 | 16.0 | 18.7 | 6.4 | 17.0 | 16.8 | 7.0 | 15.6 |
| 14.0 | 3.4 | 13.2 | 24.9 | 4.9 | 22.1 | 18.8 | 4.2 | 17.0 |
| 0.9 | 0.1 | 0.8 | 2.1 | 0.2 | 1.9 | 1.5 | 0.2 | 1.4 |
| 1.6 | 0.5 | 1.5 | 0.9 | 0.3 | 0.8 | 1.2 | 0.6 | 1.1 |
| 100.0 | 100.0 | 100.0 | 100.0 | 100.0 | 100.0 | 100.0 | 100.0 | 100.0 |
| 5,019 | 705 | 5,724 | 5,823 | 5,185 | 11,008 | 21,174 | 13,851 | 35,025 |
| 51 | 4 | 56 | 186 | 31 | 217 | 666 | 95 | 761 |

(TABLE C.8 continued on pages 280–81)

TABLE C.8.  Continued

| Pay Grade/ | Army | | | Navy | | |
|---|---|---|---|---|---|---|
| Household Composition | M | F | Total | M | F | Total |
| **E-6 or higher** | | | | | | |
| Unmar. no dep. | 5.3 | 21.4 | 6.0 | 10.5 | 30.5 | 11.2 |
| Unmar. 1 child | 1.8 | 9.4 | 2.1 | 1.7 | 6.8 | 1.9 |
| Unmar. 2–3 children | 1.9 | 3.5 | 2.0 | 2.0 | 2.3 | 2.0 |
| Unmar. 4+ children | 0.2 | 0.0 | 0.2 | 0.2 | 0.1 | 0.2 |
| Unmar. other dep. | 0.2 | 2.5 | 0.3 | 0.4 | 0.8 | 0.4 |
| Mil. spouse no dep. | 1.1 | 10.8 | 1.5 | 0.8 | 12.2 | 1.2 |
| Mil. spouse 1 child | 1.1 | 10.9 | 1.6 | 0.8 | 9.7 | 1.1 |
| Mil. spouse 2–3 chld. | 1.5 | 12.3 | 2.0 | 0.9 | 10.1 | 1.3 |
| Mil. spouse 4+ chld. | 0.1 | 1.0 | 0.2 | 0.2 | 0.9 | 0.2 |
| Mil. spouse other dep. | 0.1 | 1.0 | 0.1 | 0.0 | 0.7 | 0.1 |
| Civ. spouse no dep. | 9.2 | 11.1 | 9.3 | 10.0 | 11.3 | 10.0 |
| Civ. spouse 1 child | 18.2 | 7.0 | 17.7 | 17.2 | 5.8 | 16.8 |
| Civ. spouse 2–3 chld. | 48.5 | 7.2 | 46.7 | 47.4 | 7.7 | 46.0 |
| Civ. spouse 4+ chld. | 8.8 | 0.8 | 8.5 | 6.7 | 0.5 | 6.5 |
| Civ. spouse other dep. | 1.9 | 1.1 | 1.9 | 1.1 | 0.6 | 1.0 |
| Total | 100.0 | 100.0 | 100.0 | 100.0 | 100.0 | 100.0 |
| Number of cases | 5,162 | 1,494 | 6,656 | 4,885 | 1,221 | 6,106 |
| Total personnel (in thousands) | 155 | 7 | 162 | 122 | 4 | 127 |
| **Total** | | | | | | |
| Unmar. no dep. | 34.0 | 35.8 | 34.2 | 41.6 | 45.4 | 41.9 |
| Unmar. 1 child | 2.3 | 7.5 | 2.8 | 1.9 | 6.2 | 2.2 |
| Unmar. 2–3 children | 1.0 | 2.2 | 1.1 | 1.3 | 1.3 | 1.3 |
| Unmar. 4+ children | 0.1 | 0.0 | 0.1 | 0.1 | 0.0 | 0.1 |
| Unmar. other dep. | 0.8 | 1.2 | 0.9 | 1.0 | 0.8 | 1.0 |
| Mil. spouse no dep. | 1.6 | 14.8 | 2.8 | 1.1 | 14.7 | 2.3 |
| Mil. spouse 1 child | 1.0 | 9.9 | 1.8 | 0.8 | 9.1 | 1.5 |
| Mil. spouse 2–3 chld. | 0.7 | 5.6 | 1.2 | 0.4 | 4.0 | 0.7 |
| Mil. spouse 4+ chld. | 0.1 | 0.5 | 0.1 | 0.1 | 0.2 | 0.1 |
| Mil. spouse other dep. | 0.1 | 0.8 | 0.2 | 0.0 | 0.4 | 0.1 |
| Civ. spouse no dep. | 12.3 | 8.9 | 12.0 | 12.2 | 8.9 | 11.9 |
| Civ. spouse 1 child | 15.7 | 7.1 | 14.9 | 13.5 | 5.6 | 12.8 |
| Civ. spouse 2–3 chld. | 25.2 | 4.4 | 23.2 | 22.3 | 2.9 | 20.7 |
| Civ. spouse 4+ chld. | 3.5 | 0.4 | 3.2 | 2.7 | 0.1 | 2.5 |
| Civ. spouse other dep. | 1.5 | 0.9 | 1.5 | 1.0 | 0.5 | 1.0 |
| Total | 100.0 | 100.0 | 100.0 | 100.0 | 100.0 | 100.0 |
| Number of cases | 11,918 | 6,507 | 18,425 | 11,305 | 5,402 | 16,707 |
| Total personnel (in thousands) | 502 | 54 | 556 | 380 | 36 | 416 |

Source: *Description of Officers and Enlisted Personnel in the U.S. Armed Forces: 1985*, pp. 4-58–4-61.

| Marine Corps | | | Air Force | | | Total DOD | | |
|---|---|---|---|---|---|---|---|---|
| M | F | Total | M | F | Total | M | F | Total |
| 6.6 | 31.0 | 7.2 | 4.8 | 15.4 | 5.2 | 6.8 | 22.9 | 7.4 |
| 1.9 | 5.6 | 1.9 | 1.5 | 5.1 | 1.6 | 1.7 | 7.5 | 1.9 |
| 2.6 | 2.0 | 2.6 | 2.7 | 3.8 | 2.7 | 2.2 | 3.2 | 2.2 |
| 0.2 | 0.0 | 0.2 | 0.1 | 0.3 | 0.1 | 0.2 | 0.1 | 0.2 |
| 0.2 | 1.2 | 0.3 | 0.3 | 1.3 | 0.3 | 0.3 | 1.7 | 0.3 |
| 0.9 | 15.0 | 1.3 | 1.1 | 16.9 | 1.6 | 1.0 | 12.8 | 1.4 |
| 1.0 | 12.5 | 1.3 | 1.1 | 14.9 | 1.6 | 1.0 | 11.6 | 1.4 |
| 1.3 | 9.7 | 1.5 | 2.0 | 23.0 | 2.7 | 1.4 | 14.1 | 1.9 |
| 0.3 | 0.8 | 0.3 | 0.2 | 2.3 | 0.3 | 0.2 | 1.3 | 0.2 |
| 0.0 | 0.0 | 0.0 | 0.1 | 0.6 | 0.1 | 0.1 | 0.8 | 0.1 |
| 9.7 | 8.4 | 9.6 | 7.6 | 6.5 | 7.6 | 9.1 | 9.9 | 9.1 |
| 17.2 | 6.4 | 16.9 | 15.2 | 4.3 | 14.9 | 17.1 | 6.0 | 16.7 |
| 48.4 | 6.0 | 47.4 | 54.7 | 5.1 | 53.0 | 49.7 | 6.8 | 48.2 |
| 8.0 | 0.8 | 7.9 | 7.5 | 0.3 | 7.2 | 7.8 | 0.6 | 7.5 |
| 1.6 | 0.4 | 1.6 | 1.1 | 0.3 | 1.1 | 1.4 | 0.8 | 1.4 |
| 100.0 | 100.0 | 100.0 | 100.0 | 100.0 | 100.0 | 100.0 | 100.0 | 100.0 |
| 4,979 | 232 | 5,211 | 3,877 | 766 | 4,643 | 18,903 | 3,713 | 22,616 |
| | | | | | | | | |
| 31 | 1 | 32 | 107 | 4 | 111 | 416 | 16 | 432 |
| | | | | | | | | |
| 47.9 | 37.6 | 47.4 | 28.9 | 34.5 | 29.6 | 36.1 | 37.8 | 36.2 |
| 1.7 | 5.9 | 1.9 | 1.6 | 4.9 | 2.0 | 1.9 | 6.2 | 2.3 |
| 0.9 | 1.0 | 0.9 | 1.3 | 1.9 | 1.4 | 1.2 | 1.8 | 1.2 |
| 0.1 | 0.0 | 0.1 | 0.0 | 0.1 | 0.0 | 0.1 | 0.1 | 0.1 |
| 0.7 | 1.0 | 0.7 | 0.4 | 0.6 | 0.4 | 0.7 | 0.9 | 0.8 |
| 1.4 | 20.3 | 2.3 | 2.4 | 19.1 | 4.2 | 1.7 | 16.5 | 3.0 |
| 0.6 | 11.9 | 1.2 | 1.5 | 11.7 | 2.6 | 1.0 | 10.4 | 1.9 |
| 0.4 | 5.6 | 0.7 | 1.5 | 9.1 | 2.3 | 0.8 | 6.4 | 1.3 |
| 0.1 | 0.4 | 0.1 | 0.1 | 0.8 | 0.2 | 0.1 | 0.5 | 0.1 |
| 0.0 | 0.2 | 0.0 | 0.1 | 0.4 | 0.1 | 0.1 | 0.6 | 0.1 |
| 13.1 | 7.5 | 12.8 | 13.8 | 7.9 | 13.2 | 12.8 | 8.5 | 12.4 |
| 12.6 | 5.4 | 12.3 | 16.1 | 5.1 | 14.9 | 14.9 | 6.0 | 14.1 |
| 17.0 | 2.8 | 16.3 | 28.2 | 3.5 | 25.4 | 24.4 | 3.6 | 22.5 |
| 2.1 | 0.1 | 2.0 | 3.1 | 0.2 | 2.8 | 3.0 | 0.2 | 2.8 |
| 1.4 | 0.3 | 1.3 | 0.9 | 0.3 | 0.8 | 1.2 | 0.6 | 1.2 |
| 100.0 | 100.0 | 100.0 | 100.0 | 100.0 | 100.0 | 100.0 | 100.0 | 100.0 |
| 12,388 | 1,094 | 13,482 | 11,702 | 7,243 | 18,945 | 47,313 | 20,246 | 67,559 |
| | | | | | | | | |
| 139 | 7 | 146 | 386 | 49 | 434 | 1,406 | 146 | 1,552 |

TABLE C.9.    Spouse at Same Base as Member by Sex and Service for Enlisted Personnel, 1985

| Spouse at Same Base as Member | Army | | | Navy | | |
|---|---|---|---|---|---|---|
| | M | F | Total | M | F | Total |
| Yes | 81.7% | 81.8% | 81.7% | 87.0% | 82.8% | 84.8% |
| Spouse will be same | 3.4 | 1.8 | 2.6 | 1.7 | 2.4 | 2.0 |
| Will be same as spouse | 2.8 | 4.5 | 3.7 | 1.5 | 3.2 | 2.4 |
| Can't get same base | 6.8 | 7.1 | 6.9 | 6.0 | 5.9 | 5.9 |
| No, other reasons | 5.3 | 4.9 | 5.1 | 3.9 | 5.8 | 4.9 |
| Total | 100.0 | 100.1 | 100.0 | 100.1 | 100.1 | 100.0 |
| Number of cases | 457 | 2,283 | 2,740 | 300 | 1,624 | 1,924 |
| Total personnel (in thousands) | 17 | 16 | 33 | 9 | 10 | 19 |

Source: Description of Officers and Enlisted Personnel in the U.S. Armed Forces: 1985, p. 4-79.


TABLE C.10.    Plans in Event of Separate Assignments by Sex and Service, for Enlisted Personnel

| Plans | Army | | | Navy | | |
|---|---|---|---|---|---|---|
| | M | F | Total | M | F | Total |
| Accept assignments | 36.2% | 42.8% | 39.5% | 28.7% | 35.5% | 32.3% |
| Will leave service | 25.9 | 51.8 | 38.8 | 32.4 | 55.3 | 44.4 |
| Spouse will leave service | 37.9 | 5.3 | 21.7 | 38.9 | 9.1 | 23.3 |
| Total | 100.0 | 99.9 | 100.0 | 100.0 | 99.9 | 100.0 |
| Number of cases | 306 | 1,604 | 1,910 | 204 | 1,118 | 1,322 |
| Total personnel (in thousands) | 17 | 16 | 33 | 9 | 10 | 19 |

Source: Description of Officers and Enlisted Personnel in the U.S. Armed Forces: 1985, p. 4-81.

| | Marine Corps | | | Air Force | | | Total DOD | |
|---|---|---|---|---|---|---|---|---|
| M | F | Total | M | F | Total | M | F | Total |
| 31.2% | 85.7% | 83.2% | 89.6% | 89.3% | 89.4% | 85.9% | 85.2% | 85.6% |
| 2.7 | 1.3 | 2.1 | 1.5 | 1.3 | 1.4 | 2.2 | 1.7 | 2.0 |
| 3.8 | 2.7 | 3.3 | 2.4 | 2.6 | 2.5 | 2.5 | 3.4 | 2.9 |
| 7.1 | 6.3 | 6.7 | 3.5 | 4.3 | 3.9 | 5.3 | 5.7 | 5.5 |
| 5.1 | 3.9 | 4.6 | 3.1 | 2.4 | 2.8 | 4.1 | 4.0 | 4.1 |
| )9.9 | 99.9 | 99.9 | 100.1 | 99.9 | 100.0 | 100.0 | 100.0 | 100.1 |
| 384 | 431 | 815 | 680 | 3,216 | 3,896 | 1,821 | 7,554 | 9,375 |
| 3 | 3 | 6 | 21 | 19 | 40 | 50 | 48 | 98 |

| | Marine Corps | | | Air Force | | | Total DOD | |
|---|---|---|---|---|---|---|---|---|
| M | F | Total | M | F | Total | M | F | Total |
| 43.3% | 60.3% | 51.3% | 37.1% | 38.7% | 37.9% | 35.7% | 40.6% | 38.1% |
| 29.2 | 38.7 | 33.6 | 27.6 | 54.2 | 40.4 | 28.0 | 52.8 | 40.3 |
| 27.4 | 1.0 | 15.1 | 35.3 | 7.1 | 21.7 | 36.3 | 6.6 | 21.6 |
| )9.9 | 100.0 | 100.0 | 100.0 | 100.0 | 100.0 | 100.0 | 100.0 | 100.0 |
| 252 | 302 | 554 | 494 | 2,383 | 2,877 | 1,256 | 5,407 | 6,663 |
| 3 | 3 | 6 | 21 | 19 | 40 | 50 | 48 | 98 |

# Abbreviations
and
Insignia

# Abbreviations

AFQT     Armed Forces Qualifications test

AFSC     Air Force Specialty Codes (similar to MOS in Army and ratings in Navy)

ARI     Army Research Institute

ASVAB     Armed Services Vocational Aptitude Battery

DACOWITS     Defense Advisory Committee on Women in the Services (An oversight committee that monitors the progress made by women in the services and makes recommendations to further that progress, it was originally established in 1951 as an organization of prominent women committed to assisting the recruitment of women.)

DOD     Department of Defense

MAX WAC     The Army Research Institute's *Women Content in the Units Force Development Tests* study of the effects of different percentages of women on overall company performance

MOS     Military Occupational Specialty (categorization of the jobs available in the Army)

REF WAC     The Army Research Institute's study of the effects of different percentages of women on company performance during ten-day field exercises

TOCAP     Total Objective Plan for Career Personnel (Air Force's manpower goals, including goals for specialties and the number of women to be accessed)

WAC     Women's Army Corps (formed in June 1943 from the earlier Women's Army Auxiliary Corps, WAAC)

WAF     Women in the Air Force

WAVES     Women Accepted for Voluntary Emergency Service (organization established for women who volunteered for service during World War II in the Navy Women's Reserve)

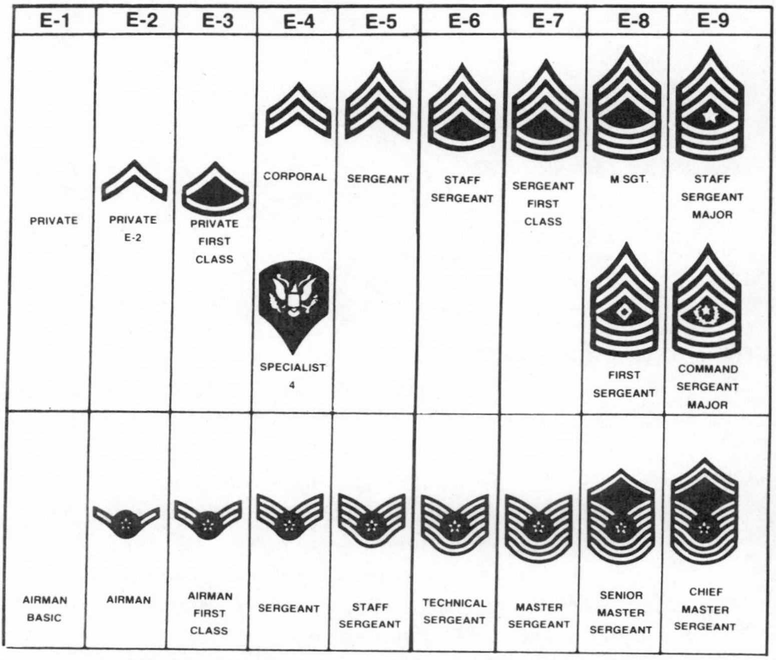

| E-1 | E-2 | E-3 | E-4 | E-5 | E-6 | E-7 | E-8 | E-9 |
|---|---|---|---|---|---|---|---|---|
| PRIVATE | PRIVATE E-2 | PRIVATE FIRST CLASS | CORPORAL / SPECIALIST 4 | SERGEANT | STAFF SERGEANT | SERGEANT FIRST CLASS | M SGT. / FIRST SERGEANT | STAFF SERGEANT MAJOR / COMMAND SERGEANT MAJOR |
| AIRMAN BASIC | AIRMAN | AIRMAN FIRST CLASS | SERGEANT | STAFF SERGEANT | TECHNICAL SERGEANT | MASTER SERGEANT | SENIOR MASTER SERGEANT | CHIEF MASTER SERGEANT |

ARMY & AIR FORCE ENLISTED RANK INSIGNIA

| E-1 | E-2 | E-3 | E-4 | E-5 | E-6 | E-7 | E-8 | E-9 |
|---|---|---|---|---|---|---|---|---|
| PRIVATE | PRIVATE FIRST CLASS | LANCE CORPORAL | CORPORAL | SERGEANT | STAFF SERGEANT | GUNNERY SERGEANT | FIRST SERGEANT / MASTER SERGEANT | SERGEANT MAJOR / MASTER GUNNERY SERGEANT |
| SEAMAN RECRUIT | SEAMAN APPRENTICE | SEAMAN | PETTY OFFICER THIRD CLASS | PETTY OFFICER SECOND CLASS | PETTY OFFICER FIRST CLASS | CHIEF PETTY OFFICER | SENIOR CHIEF PETTY OFFICER | MASTER CHIEF PETTY OFFICER |

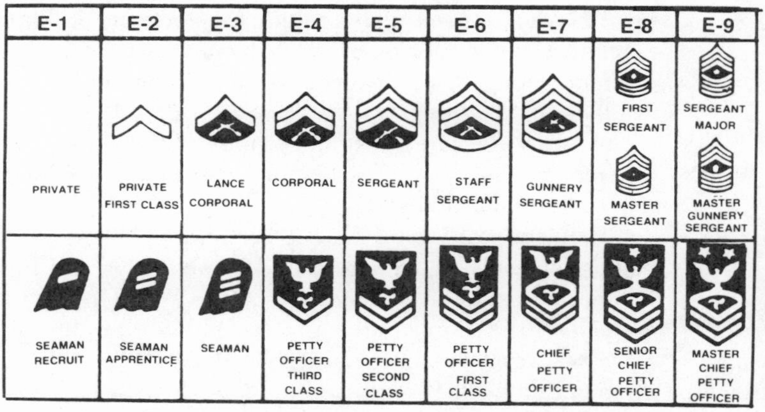

MARINE & NAVY ENLISTED RANK INSIGNIA

FIGURE 4.    Insignia of the U.S. Armed Forces

# Notes, Bibliography, and Index

# Notes

## CHAPTER 1

1. Helen Rogan and Michael Rustad have provided good descriptions of the experiences of Army women. Helen Rogan, *Mixed Company: Women in the Modern Army* (New York: Putnam, 1981); Michael L. Rustad, *Women in Khaki: The American Enlisted Woman* (New York: Praeger, 1982).
2. Linda J. Waite and Sue E. Berryman, *Women in Nontraditional Occupations: Choice and Turnover* (Santa Monica, Calif.: Rand, 1985), pp. 52–53, 73.
3. Mary Wollstonecraft, *A Vindication of the Rights of Women*, ed. Carol H. Poston (New York: Norton, 1975), pp. 23–24.
4. Mattie E. Treadwell, *The U.S. Army in World War II, Special Studies: The Women's Army Corps* (Washington, D.C.: Office of the Chief of Military History, Department of the Army, 1954), pp. 191–218.

## CHAPTER 2

1. For a summary of cohort methodology, see Norvall D. Glenn, *Cohort Analysis* (Beverly Hills, Calif.: Sage, 1977).
2. Unless otherwise noted, numerical data are from *Selected Manpower Statistics, Fiscal Year 1986* (Washington, D.C.: Directorate for Information, Operations and Reports, the Pentagon, 1986), or from a series of tables prepared by T. Wisener for the Office of the Assistant Secretary of Defense, Manpower, Reserve Affairs and Logistics, Research and Data, on 4 April 1981.
3. Gen. Jeanne Holm, USAF (Ret.), *Women in the Military: An Unfinished Revolution* (Novato, Calif.: Presidio Press, 1982), chaps. 10, 11.
4. Ibid., pp. 118, 124–25, 157–58, 184.
5. Ibid., p. 250.
6. U.S. Congress, House Armed Services Personnel Committee, Report by Special Subcommittee on Utilization of Manpower in Military, 92d Cong., 2d Sess., 28 June 1972.
7. Chief Naval Officer Elmo Zumwalt, Z-Gram 116, dated 7 August 1972. For Quigley's memo see Holm, *Women in the Military*, pp. 280–82; the Z-Gram is reproduced as app. 3.
8. Mary Ellen McCalla, Stuart H. Rakoff, and Zahava D. Doering, *Description of Officers and Enlisted Personnel in the U.S. Armed Forces: 1985,*

*Supplementary Tabulations from the 1985 DOD Survey of Officer and Enlisted Personnel* (Arlington, Va.: Defense Manpower Data Center, 1986), pp. 4-45, 49-51, 4-58–4-60.
9. Ibid., p. 4-61.
10. Holm, *Women in the Military*, pp. 106, 136–37, 190, 195–96, 211, 239–40, 270, 300–301.


CHAPTER 3

1. Seth Cropsey, "The Military Manpower Crisis: Women in Combat," *Public Interest*, Fall 1980, pp. 58–73.
2. Defense Advisory Committee on Women in the Services (DACOWITS), *Fall Meeting Minutes* (Washington, D.C.: November 1980), Tab D.
3. DACOWITS, *Fall Meeting Minutes* (Washington, D.C.: October 1979), Tab E.
4. DACOWITS, *Spring Meeting Minutes* (Washington, D.C.: April 1980), table I, pp. 21–22.
5. "Slow Female EM Recruiting," *Air Force Times*, 19 January 1981.
6. "Official Urges Enlistment Slowdown: Women's Impact on Military Questioned," *Colorado Springs Sun*, 20 February 1981.
7. "Pentagon Reassessing Impact of Women in the Armed Forces," *Washington Post*, 13 May 1981.
8. "Army Calls Virtual Halt to Recruiting Women," *Army Times*, 10 August 1981.
9. "General Attacks Pregnancies: Urges Abortions for All First-Term Women Soldiers," *New York Daily News*, 24 June 1981.
10. "Air Force, Navy Chiefs Oppose Registering Women for Draft," *Baltimore Sun*, 6 February 1980.
11. *Selected Manpower Statistics, Fiscal Year 1980* (Washington, D.C.: Directorate for Information, Department of Defense, 1981), p. 73; U.S. Department of Defense, Office of the Assistant Secretary of Defense, Manpower, Reserve Affairs and Logistics, *Women in the Military: Background Review* (Washington, D.C.: Office of the Assistant Secretary of Defense, 1981), p. 103; "Slow Female EM Recruiting."
12. DACOWITS, *Spring Meeting Minutes* (Washington, D.C.: 1981), Tab E.
13. Ibid., Tab F.
14. Ibid., Tab G.
15. Ibid., Tab V.
16. "Air Force Wants Substantial Reduction in Future Recruiting Goals for Women," *Air Force Times*, 27 July 1981.
17. "New Administration Slows Drive to Ease Combat Bars for Women," *Army Times*, 3 August 1981.
18. Both memos were dated 14 January 1982.
19. Memo of 11 January 1982.
20. "Women in the Military: It Is Really a Matter of Human Power," *Government Executive*, February 1982, pp. 22, 24–26.

21. "Women-in-Army Report Delayed," *Army Times*, 15 February 1982.

22. "Women's Role in Military Faces Pentagon Study," *Memphis Press-Scimitar*, 1 February 1982.

23. "Army to End Coed Companies in Basic Training," *Baltimore Sun*, 4 May 1982.

24. "Retired General Defends Women," *Pittsburgh Press*, 17 July 1982.

25. "Women Ask If Army Is Going Off-Limits," *Washington Post*, 4 August 1982.

26. "Top Pentagon EO Officer to Leave Post in August," *Federal Times*, 23 August 1982, p. 17.

27. "Army Studies Limit on Role of Women," *Long Island Newsday*, 20 June 1982.

28. "Women Ask If Army Is Going Off-Limits."

29. "Goals on Recruiting Women Lowered," *Washington Post*, 27 August 1982; "Army to Close Twenty-Three Job Categories to Women," *Los Angeles Times*, 27 August 1982.

30. "Army Study on Women Draws Divided Reaction," *Army Times*, 6 September 1982; "DACOWITS Told Women's Report Will Be 'Positive,'" *Navy Times*, 6 September 1982; and "Clarke Calls Separate BT 'Step Backward,'" *Army Times*, 16 August 1982.

31. "New Administration Slows Drive."

32. "Women Report Delay," *Army Times*, 25 October 1982.

33. "Where Women Will Fit in the New Army," *U.S. News and World Report*, 4 October 1982, p. 53; "Women in the Army—End of a Honeymoon," ibid., pp. 51–53; see also "Focus on Women in Army Recommendations," *Pentagon News*, 24 February 1983.

34. *Women in the Army Policy Review* (Washington, D.C.: Department of the Army, 1982), pp. 4–17.

35. Ibid., pp. 2-37, 2-17, 2-36.

36. Overall DOD reenlistment rates went up for both men and women between 1980 and 1982, with the highest rates for career men, career women, first-term women, and first-term men (in that order). In the Army, the curves for women and first-term women coincided in 1980, but reenlistment of career women fell below even that of first-term men by 1982. See *Military Women in the Department of Defense* (Washington, D.C.: The Pentagon, 1986), 4: 74–75.

37. Maj. Ann Wright, "The Roles of U.S. Army Women in Grenada," *Minerva* 2: 2 (1984): 103–13; Lt. Col. James Brandy, "The Status of Women Marines," *Marine Corps Gazette*, July 1983, p. 25.

38. "Curb on Navy Women Halted by Weinberger," *Los Angeles Times*, 4 February 1987; "Navy Defends Closing Support Ships to Women," *Air Force Times*, 18 May 1987.

## CHAPTER 4

1. Zahava D. Doering and William P. Hutzler, *Description of Officers and Enlisted Personnel in the United States Armed Forces: A Reference for Military*

*Manpower Analysis* (Santa Monica, Calif.: Rand, 1982), tables 475–94, pp. 564–83.

2. Ibid., pp. 587–88, 601–2. These tables include breakdowns by service and status (enlisted personnel and officers). (See tables 4.1 and 4.2 in Chapter 4.)

3. Ibid., pp. 606, 610, 614, 618; Mary Ellen McCalla, Stuart H. Rakoff, and Zahava D. Doering, *Description of Officers and Enlisted Personnel in the U.S. Armed Forces: 1985, Supplementary Tabulations from the 1985 DOD Survey of Officer and Enlisted Personnel*, vol. 4 (Arlington, Va.: Defense Manpower Data Center, 1986).

4. Patricia J. Thomas, *Why Women Enlist: The Navy as an Occupational Choice* (San Diego, Calif.: Navy Personnel Research and Development Center, 1977).

5. Kathleen P. Durning and Sandra J. Mumford, *Differential Perceptions of Organizational Climate Held by Navy Enlisted Women and Men* (San Diego, Calif.: Navy Personnel Research and Development Center, 1976), esp. p. 25; Kathleen P. Durning, "Attitudes of Enlisted Women and Men Toward the Navy," *Armed Forces and Society* 9 (1982): 20–32.

6. Defense Advisory Committee on Women in the Services (DACOWITS), *Spring Meeting Minutes* (Washington, D.C.: 1981), table R.

7. Marcelite C. Jordan, "Utilization of Women in Air Force Industrial Career Fields," final report of the Women in the Army Study Group (Lackland, Tex.: Human Resources Laboratory, 1976).

8. Lois B. DeFleur, "Organizational and Ideological Barriers to Sex Integration in Military Groups" (Pullman: Washington State University, 1981).

9. John H. Batts et al., *The Roles of Women in the Army and Their Impact on Military Operations and Organization* (Carlisle Barracks, Pa.: U.S. Army War College, 1975), esp. pp. 29 and 32–35.

10. Jack M. Hicks, *Army Enlisted MOS· and Sex Role Attitudes: A Male-Female Comparison* (Alexandria, Va.: Army Research Institute, 1975).

11. This literature is reviewed in Kay Deaux, *The Behavior of Women and Men* (Monterey, Calif.: Brooks/Cole, 1976), chaps. 3 and 4.

12. Joel M. Savelle, John C. Woelfel, and Barry Collins, *Attitudes Concerning Job Appropriateness for Women in the Army*, Research Memorandum 75-3 (Alexandria, Va.: Army Research Institute, 1975). These data were also used in an article appearing in *Sex Roles* 5: 1 (1979). The same authors published *Soldiers' Attribution of Contemporary vs. Traditional Sex Role Attitudes to Themselves and to Others*, Research Memorandum 75-7 (Alexandria, Va.: Army Research Institute, 1975).

13. Savelle, Woelfel, and Collins, *Soldiers' Attribution*, p. 2.

14. *Women in the Army Study* (Washington, D.C.: Department of the Army, 1976), chap. 10.

15. Ibid., pp. 10-10–10-14.

16. *Women Content in Units Force Development Test* (MAX WAC) (Alexandria, Va.: Army Research Institute, 1977).

17. Stanley F. Bolin, Lois A. Johns, and John S. Cowings, *Women Soldiers in*

*Korea: Troop Viewpoints*, Research Memorandum 77-16 (Alexandria, Va.: Army Research Institute, 1977), pp. 15, 39, 96–101.

18. *Women Content in the Army—Reforger 77* (REF WAC) (Alexandria, Va.: Army Research Institute, 1978).

19. Ibid., III-17.

20. Ibid., VI-10.

21. Ibid., pp. B-54–B-57.

22. Laurel W. Oliver, *The Effect of Intergroup Contact on Attitudes Toward the Role of Women in the Army* (Alexandria, Va.: Army Research Institute, 1981).

23. Denise F. Polit et al., *Preliminary Tabulation by Rank and Sex of Selected Responses in an Attitude Questionnaire* (Alexandria, Va.: Army Research Institute, 1978).

24. Ibid., p. 4.

25. Army Military Personnel Center, "Report of Results of 9 October 1978 Survey of Women in the Army," Report no. UR 13-78 (Alexandria, Va.: DAPC-MSF-5, 1978).

26. Mark Foley, *Leadership and Women in the Army* (Fort Harrison, Ind.: Army Administration Center, 1978), prepared for Evaluation of Women in the Army.

27. For one example see Hubert J. O'Gorman, "False Consciousness of Kind: Pluralistic Ignorance Among the Aged," *Research on Aging* 2:1 (March 1980): 105–28.

## CHAPTER 5

1. William V. Kennedy, "The Secretary of the Navy and the Women," *Christian Science Monitor*, 28 April 1987.

2. Maj. Gen. Jeanne Holm, USAF (Ret.), *Women in the Military: An Unfinished Revolution* (Novato, Calif.: Presidio Press, 1982), pp. 113–29.

3. James B. Jacobs, "The Impact of Legal Change on the United States Armed Forces Since WWII" (Ph.D. diss., Cornell University, 1977), pp. 1–41. See also Paul Smith, "Chief Judge Sees Broader Role for Military Court," *Air Force Times*, 9 September 1985.

4. Under Article 15, summary (but limited) punishments are awarded by a commander with little attention to procedure.

5. See *O'Callahan* v. *Parker*, 395 U.S. (1969); *Redford* v. *U.S. Disciplinary Commandant*, 401 U.S. 355 (1971); *U.S.* v. *Nicolas J. Larinoff*, 45 U.S.L.W. 4650 (14 June 1977). The last case involved a plaintiff's right to the variable enlistment bonus in effect when he reenlisted.

6. For a discussion, see Jane Mansbridge, *Why We Lost the ERA* (Chicago: University of Chicago, 1986).

7. "The Equal Rights Amendment and the Military," *Yale Law Review* 82 (1973): 1538–39n.

8. Diana A. Steele, "Women and the Military: Substantial Barriers Remain," *ACLU Women's Rights Report* 3 (Winter 1981):1.

9. Harry C. Beans, "Sex Discrimination in the Military," *Military Law Review* 67 (Winter 1975): 58–59; Holm, *Women in the Military*, pp. 272–73.

10. "Equal Rights Amendment and the Military," pp. 1547–52, 1549; see also Chapter 4.

11. Tables compiled by T. Wisener, Office of the Assistant Secretary of Defense, Manpower, Reserve Affairs and Logistics, Research and Data (Washington, D.C., April 1981).

12. Holm, *Women in the Military*, p. 296.

13. Ibid., p. 298.

14. Ibid., p. 299.

15. U.S. Department of Defense, Office of the Assistant Secretary of Defense, Manpower, Reserve Affairs and Logistics, *Women in the Military: Background Review* (Washington, D.C.: Office of the Assistant Secretary of Defense, 1981), p. 104.

16. "Bar on Single-Parent Enlistments Upheld," *Air Force Times*, 8 July 1985.

17. Notes taken by author at spring 1984 DACOWITS meeting.

18. *Owens v. Brown*, plaintiff's cross-motion for summary judgment, No. 76-2086 (D.D.C. 1978), p. 34n.

19. William D. Hoover, "The Disadvantaged Navy Women," *U.S. Naval Institute Proceedings*, July 1977, p. 118.

20. C. W. Duncan, undersecretary of defense to Thomas P. O'Neill, Jr., Speaker of the House of Representatives, 14 February 1978, Washington, D.C.

21. U.S. Congress, House Armed Services Personnel Committee, *Navy Proposal to Amend 10 U.S.C. 6015, Hearings Before the Subcommittee on Military Personnel H.R. 7431*, 95th Cong., 2d sess., 1978, p. 1194.

22. *Owens v. Brown*, 455 F.Supp. 291 (D.D.C. 1978), pp. 308, 310.

23. Cynthia Enloe, *Does Khaki Become You? The Militarization of Women's Lives* (Boston: South End Press, 1983), pp. 18–45.

24. "Korb: Women Needed to Maintain Readiness," *Air Force Times*, 14 May 1984.

25. Judy Mann, "A Lot of Exposure for a Little Exposure," *Washington Post*, 5 March 1980.

26. "Pinup Fears She'll Be Nailed to the Mast," *Los Angeles Times*, 29 February 1980.

27. "Navy Drops Charges Against Playboy Poser," *Navy Times*, 16 February 1981.

28. "Marines Shun Pick-up of Gay Bar's Gift Toys: Donations for 100 Children Stalled," *Los Angeles Times*, 22 December 1983.

29. Charles Leernsen, Mary Lord, and Elaine Shannon, "Our Standards Are Different," *Newsweek*, 12 December 1983, p. 48.

30. "Honorable Discharges Decrease by 27,000," *Air Force Times*, 18 June 1984.

31. "Army, Colleges Battle Gay Question," *Pacific Stars and Stripes*, 28 July 1982.

32. "Military Right to Discharge Homosexuals Upheld," *Los Angeles Times*, 10 December 1983; "Ruling Clears Way for Homosexual's Discharge," *Air Force Times*, 9 January 1984.

33. Colin J. Williams and Martin S. Weinberg, *Homosexuals and the Military* (New York: Harper and Row, 1971), pp. 52, 60.

34. Ibid., chap. 7.

35. "Homosexual Paranoia," *Equal Opportunity Current News*, October 1981, pp. 29–30.

36. Percentages derived from "Homosexuals—a New Battle for the Military," *Los Angeles Times*, 25 September 1980.

37. Ibid.

38. "Military Harassment of Women and Gays Increasing," *National NOW Times*, May 1983, p. 7.

39. Interview with Susan McGreivy, ACLU attorney, Los Angeles, Spring 1983.

40. "Naval Hospital Corpsman Exonerated," *Open Forum*, January 1982, pp. 1, 2.

## CHAPTER 6

1. Nancy H. Loring, ed., *Women in the United States Armed Forces: Progress and Barriers in the 1980s* (Chicago: Inter-University Seminar on Armed Forces and Society, 1984).

2. Joel M. Savelle, Carlos K. Rigby, and Andrew A. Zibikowski, *An Investigation of Lost Time and Utilization in a Sample of First-Term Male and Female Soldiers* (Alexandria, Va.: Army Research Institute, 1982); Patricia J. Thomas, "Attrition Among Navy Enlisted Women," *Defense Management Journal* (2d Quarter 1980): 43–49.

3. Martin Binkin and Mark J. Eitelberg et al., *Blacks and the Military* (Washington, D.C.: Brookings Institution, 1982), p. 87.

4. Patricia J. Thomas, Marilyn J. Monda, Shelly H. Millsand, and Julie A. Mathis, *Navy Women in Traditional and Nontraditional Jobs: A Comparison of Satisfaction, Attrition and Re-enlistment*, Technical Report 82-50 (San Diego, Calif.: Navy Personnel Research and Development Center, 1982).

5. Patricia J. Thomas and Carol S. Greebler, *Men and Women in Ships: Attitudes of Crews After One to Two Years of Integration*, NPRDC TR 84-600 (San Diego, Calif.: Navy Personnel Research and Development Center, 1983).

6. Shirley J. Bach, personal communication, 1976.

7. Jules I. Borack, "Intentions of Women (18–25 Years Old) to Join the Military: Results of a National Survey," Technical Report 78-34 (San Diego, Calif.: Navy Personnel Research and Development Center, 1978).

8. Marsha S. Olson and Susan S. Stumpf, *Pregnancy in the Navy: Impact on Absenteeism, Attrition, and Work Group Morale*, NPRDC TR 78-35 (San Diego, Calif.: Navy Personnel Research and Development Center, 1978).

9. *Women in the Army Study* (Washington, D.C.: Office of the Deputy Chief of Staff for Personnel, 1976), chap. 11.

10. Ibid., chap. 9.

11. Ibid., chap. 7; Bruce N. Baut, "Working Together: The Army's Assault on Sexism," *Soldiers*, October 1980, p. 8.

12. *Women in the Army Study*, chap. 8.

13. Ibid., chap. 10 and app. C.

14. Ibid., chap. 12, 1-A-14, 1-A-10, and 3-3.

15. Ibid., chap. 3, 4, and 5.

16. Ibid., pp. 5-2, 5-3. See also MILPERCEN Final Task Report, *Utilization of Women in the Army* (Washington, D.C.: Military Personnel Center, 1977), p. 2-8; Martin Binkin and Shirley S. Bach, *Women and the Military* (Washington, D.C.: Brookings Institution, 1977), pp. 26–29.

17. *Women in the Army Study*, p. 5-5.

18. Ibid., pp. 5-7–5-10.

19. MILPERCEN, *Utilization of Women in the Army*, pp. ii, v, 2-7, 2-12, and 2-13.

20. *Women Content in Units Force Development Test* (MAX WAC) (Alexandria, Va.: Army Research Institute, 1977).

21. Ibid., p. III-25.

22. Ibid., p. IV-29.

23. Internal memorandum.

24. C. M. Devilbiss, "Gender Integration and Unit Development: A Study of GI Jo," *Armed Forces and Society* 11 (1985): 523–52.

25. *Women Content in the Army—Reforger 77* (REF WAC 77) (Alexandria, Va.: Army Research Institute, 1978), pp. I-2, I-3, IV-7, IV-8, and IV-9.

26. U.S. Department of the Army, Army Administration Center, *Evaluation of Women in the Army* (Washington, D.C.: Office of the Deputy Chief of Staff for Personnel, 1978), p. 1-3.

27. Ibid., pp. 1-19–1-26.

28. Ibid., pp. 1-27, 1-28, 1-30.

29. Ibid., pp. 1-28, 1-29.

30. Ibid., pp. 1-30, 1-31.

31. Women undergraduates were absolutely and relatively few in number.

32. U.S. Department of the Army, Office of the Auditor General, *Women in the Army Policy Review* (Washington, D.C.: Office of the Deputy Chief of Staff for Personnel, 1982), p. A-1.

33. "Army Fails to Prove Its Claim on Women Dropouts," *Washington Post*, 9 November 1982.

34. *Women in the Army Policy Review*, pp. 2-36, 2-17.

35. Ibid., p. 4-2.

36. Ibid., chap. 4.

37. Savelle, Rigby, and Zibikowski, *Lost Time and Utilization*.

38. Glenda Y. Nogami, *Fact Sheet: Soldier Gender on First Tour Attrition* (Alexandria, Va.: Army Research Institute, 1981).

39. U.S. Department of the Army, *Report of Audit: Enlisted Women in the Army, Fort McClellan, Alabama*, Audit Report 50 82-206 (Washington, D.C.: Army Audit Agency, 1982).

40. U.S. Department of the Army, *Report of Audit: Enlisted Women in the Army, III Corps and Fort Hood*, Audit Report SW 82-208 (Washington, D.C.: Army Audit Agency, 1982).

41. U.S. Department of the Army, *Report of Audit: Enlisted Women in the*

*Army*, Audit Report HQ 82-212 (Washington, D.C.: Army Audit Agency, 1982), p. 34F.

42. Ibid., p. 35.

43. Stanley F. Bolin, Lois A. Johns, and John S. Cowings, *Women Soldiers in Korea: Troop Viewpoints*, Research Memorandum 77-16 (Alexandria, Va.: Army Research Institute, 1977), pp. 12, 13.

44. Patricia Cooney Nida, "Women in the Army, Current Issues," After-Action Report on Seminars Held for the Army Chaplains (San Rafael, Calif.: Nita Training and Development Group, n.d. [ca. 1982]).

45. "Female Soldier Fined and Jailed on Sex Charge," *Army Times*, 21 April 1980.

CHAPTER 7

1. Martin Binkin and Shirley J. Bach, *Women and the Military* (Washington, D.C.: Brookings Institution, 1977), pp. 104–5.

2. Ibid., p. 106.

3. "Women in the Air Force: Package 13," HQ AFMPC/MPCX, Randolph Air Force Base, Tex. (1985), p. 7.

4. Martin Binkin and Mark J. Eitelberg, with Alvin J. Schexnider and Marvin M. Smith, *Blacks and the Military* (Washington, D.C.: Brookings Institution, 1982), pp. 65–66.

5. "Women in the Air Force: Package 13."

6. Maj. Gen. Jeanne Holm, USAF (Ret.), *Women in the Military: An Unfinished Revolution* (Novato, Calif.: Presidio Press, 1982), pp. 151–55.

7. Ibid., p. 181.

8. Ibid., p. 250.

9. Ibid., pp. 258, 387.

10. U.S. Department of Defense, Office of the Assistant Secretary of Defense, Manpower, Reserve Affairs and Logistics, *Women in the Military: Background Review* (Washington, D.C.: Office of the Assistant Secretary of Defense, 1981), p. 95.

11. For discussion, see Holm, *Women in the Military*, pp. 255–57.

12. *Women in the Military: Background Review*, pp. 90–91.

13. Ibid., p. 26.

14. Ibid., p. 27.

15. Office of the Assistant Secretary of Defense, U.S. Department of Defense, *Profile of American Youth: 1980 Nationwide Administration of the Armed Services Vocational Aptitude Battery* (Washington, D.C.: Department of Defense, 1982), p. 4.

16. *Profile of American Youth*, p. 25.

17. Ibid., pp. 25, 27.

18. U.S. Department of the Air Force, *DCS/MP Fact Book* (Washington, D.C.: Department of the Air Force, 1980), p. 45.

19. "Thirteen Pct. Picked for E-5," *Air Force Times*, 7 February 1983.

20. "Two-Tier Promotion System May Be Extended," *Air Force Times*, 10

October 1983; "Two-Tier Hike System Continues for NCOs," *Air Force Times*, 30 April 1984. Balance is also sought through the use of voluntary and involuntary retraining. See "AF to Retrain 1100 EM Under Palace Balance," *Air Force Times*, 27 February 1984.

21. *Military Women in the Department of Defense*, vol. 4 (Washington, D.C.: Department of Defense, 1986), pp. 63–65.

22. Marjorie H. Royle, *Factors Affecting Attrition Among Marine Corps Women*, NPRDC TR 86-7 (San Diego, Calif.: Navy Personnel Research and Development Center, 1985).

23. "Honorable Discharges Decrease by 27,000," *Air Force Times*, 18 June 1984. Two other interesting facts were reported about women's attrition. One is that women quit early; in FY 1983 women accounted for 9.9 percent of discharges but 16.7 percent of early separation discharges. Also, women who attrited had the highest AFQT scores (86.35) and men who attrited the lowest (68.81) when male and female veterans, attriters, and individuals who never served were compared. See Michael Borus, Choongsoo Kim, and Kyle Johnson, *Policy Findings Related to Military Service from the Youth Cohort of the National Longitudinal Surveys of Labor Market Experience* (Arlington, Va.: Defense Manpower Data Center, 1985), p. 21.

24. *Military Women*, 4: 78–79.

25. "Women in the Air Force: Package 13," p. 13.

26. Ibid., p. 15.

27. McCalla et al., *Description of Officers and Enlisted Personnel in the U.S. Armed Forces: 1985, Supplementary Tabulations from the 1985 DOD Survey of Officer and Enlisted Personnel*, vol. 1 (Arlington, Va.: Defense Manpower Data Center, 1986), pp. 3–6.

28. Ibid., pp. 3–14. See also Appendix table C-7.

29. Linda J. Waite and Sue E. Berryman, *Women in Nontraditional Occupations: Choice and Turnover* (Santa Monica, Calif.: Rand, 1985).

30. Les Aspin, "Manning the Military: The Female Factor," *Minerva* 2: 2 (1984): 8.

31. John Ginovsky, "Aspin, McCoy Square Off Over AF's Use of Women," *Air Force Times*, 19 March 1984.

32. John Ginovsky, "Women to Fill SP Slots," *Air Force Times*, 1 October 1984.

33. John Ginovsky, "AF Reluctantly Accepts Quotas on Women," *Air Force Times*, 15 October 1984.

34. Robert C. Oaks, "Force Composition Study: An Analysis of the Effects of Varying Male and Female Force Levels," DACOWITS, *Spring Meeting Minutes* (Washington, D.C., 1985), Tab C.

35. Vonda L. Kiplinger et al., *Propensity of Young Women to Enlist in the Military* (Arlington, Va.: Defense Manpower Data Center, 1985), pp. 43–50.

36. Robert M. Bray et al., "Youth Attitude Tracking Study, Fall 1985" (Arlington, Va.: Defense Manpower Data Center, 1986), p. 48.

37. Ibid., pp. 120, 127.

38. Oaks, "Effects," p. C-23.

CHAPTER 8

1. "O'Neill Opposes Drafting Women," *Los Angeles Times*, 1 February 1980.
2. George H. Gallup, *The Gallup Poll: Public Opinion, 1980* (Wilmington, Del.: Scholarly Resources, 1981), pp. 54, 59.
3. See Thomas D. Cook and Laura C. Leviton, "Reviewing the Literature: A Comparison of Traditional Methods with Meta Analysis," *Journal of Personality* 48 (1980): 449–72.
4. James A. Davis, Jennifer Lauby, and Paul B. Sheatsley, *Americans View the Military: Public Opinion in 1982*, NORC Report no. 131 (Chicago: National Opinion Research Center, 1983); James B. Davis and Paul Sheatsley, *Americans View the Military: A 1984 Update*, NORC Report no. 132 (Chicago: National Opinion Research Center, 1985).
5. Davis and Sheatsley, *Update*, p. 23; and Gallup, *Public Opinion, 1980*, pp. 146–50.
6. Davis, Lauby, and Sheatsley, *Americans View the Military*, pp. 32, 34, and B-18.
7. Ibid., pp. 38–39, 48–51, C-1, C-2, and C-3.
8. Ibid., pp. 35–41; quotation on p. 35.
9. George H. Gallup, *The Gallup Poll: Public Opinion, 1935–1971* (Wilmington, Del.: Scholarly Resources, 1972), pp. 253–54, 316, 401.
10. Ibid., pp. 406, 485, 490, 667.
11. Ibid., pp. 1244, 2051, 2180. See also, Gallup, *The Gallup Poll: Public Opinion, 1972–1977* (Wilmington, Del.: Scholarly Resources, 1978), pp. 952–55.
12. George H. Gallup, *The Gallup Poll: Public Opinion, 1979* (Wilmington, Del.: Scholarly Resources, 1980), pp. 150–56; George H. Gallup, *The Gallup Poll: Public Opinion, 1981* (Wilmington, Del.: Scholarly Resources, 1982), pp. 54–59, 146–50.
13. Gallup, *Public Opinion, 1935–1971*, p. 412.
14. *The 1980 Virginia Slims American Women's Opinion Poll* (The Roper Organization, 1980), p. 103.
15. Louis Harris, "ABC News–Harris Poll," press release, 6 December 1978.
16. George Gallup, "Women in Combat Backed," *Colorado Springs Sun*, 21 June 1978; and *The Gallup Poll, 1979*, pp. 150–56.
17. Faye E. Dowdell, "Gender Difference in Orientation Toward Military Service" (manuscript, University of Maryland, Baltimore, 1978), pp. 26–31.
18. "Women and the Draft," *Glamour*, April 1982, pp. 31–32.
19. Marcelo Rodriquez, comp., "Students Oppose Draft Plan," *Daily Californian*, 19 February 1980.
20. Anita Sanchez and Robert Brown, "Women in the Military: An Experiment in Opinion Polls" (seminar paper, University of Southern California, 1980).
21. Elihu Rose, "The Anatomy of Mutiny" (manuscript, 1981).
22. Jane Mansbridge, personal communication.

CHAPTER 9

1. Cynthia Enloe, *Does Khaki Become You? The Militarization of Women's Lives* (Boston: South End Press, 1983), p. 39; Larry H. Ingraham, *The Boys in the Barracks* (Philadelphia: Institute for the Study of Human Issues, 1984), pp. 109–13; Jesse Glenn Gray, *The Warriors: Reflections on Men in Battle* (New York: Harper and Row, 1970).

2. Author's observation, U.S. Army War College, National Security Seminar, 3–7 June 1984.

3. Mattie E. Treadwell, *The U.S. Army in World War II, Special Studies: The Women's Army Corps* (Washington, D.C.: Department of the Army, 1954), pp. 176–77, 580–81, and chap. 31.

4. Ibid., pp. 439–40.

5. Ibid., pp. 608–9.

6. Pat Dalton, "Separations of Overweight Members Up Fourfold," *Air Force Times*, 16 March 1987.

7. See DACOWITS, *Fall Meeting Minutes* (Washington, D.C.: DACOWITS, 1983), Tab F; Ben Yagoda, "The Man Who Shapes Up the Army," *New York Times Magazine*, 28 September 1986, pp. 34f.

8. DACOWITS, *Fall Meeting Minutes*, 1983, Tab H.

9. Judith Stiehm, *Bring Me Men and Women: Mandated Change at the U.S. Air Force Academy* (Berkeley: University of California Press, 1981).

10. David W. Robertson, telephone interview, Navy Personnel and Development Center, San Diego, Calif., August 1984.

11. *Job Opportunities for Women in the Military: Progress and Problems* (Washington, D.C.: Comptroller General of the United States, 1976).

12. U.S. Department of Defense, *Women in the Military: Background Review* (Washington, D.C.: Government Printing Office, 1981), pp. 82–83.

13. Robert Oaks, "Force Composition Study: An Analysis of the Effects of Varying Male and Female Force Levels," DACOWITS, *Spring Meeting Minutes*, 1985, Tab C.

14. David Robertson and T. T. Trent, "Predicting Muscularly Demanding Job Performance in Navy Occupations," paper presented at the meeting of the American Psychological Association, August 1983.

15. Jack J. Sternberg, Frank Greenberg, and Edmund F. Fuchs, *Identifying Army Jobs Suitable for WAC Assignment*, Research Study 58-3 (Washington, D.C.: Army Personnel Research Office, 1958).

16. David G. Myers, Deborah Gebhardt, and Edwin Fleishman, *Development of Physical Performance Standards for Army Jobs: The Job Analysis Methodology*, Technical Report 446 (Alexandra, Va.: Army Research Institute, 1980).

17. U.S. Department of the Army, *Women in the Army Policy Review* (Washington, D.C.: Office of the Deputy Chief of Staff for Personnel, 1982), chaps. 2, 3.

18. Ibid., pp. 2-4–2-16.

19. Thus, many more men displaced women from "light" jobs than vice versa.

20. "Good Morning, America" television log, Washington, D.C., 13 September 1982.

21. *Women in the Army Policy Review*, pp. 2-29, 2-36.

22. Judy Trent Ellis, "Sexual Harassment and Race: A Legal Analysis of Discrimination," *Journal of Legislation* 8: 1 (1981): 30–45.

23. U.S. Congress, Subcommittee on Investigations of the House Committee on Post Office and Civil Service, *Sexual Harassment in the Federal Government*, 30 April 1980.

24. "Army Survey Finds Sexual Harassment of Military Women Overseas," *Baltimore Sun*, 12 February 1980.

25. "Women Say Sexual Harassment Is Driving Them Out of the Army," *Baltimore Sun*, 26 March 1980.

26. "Harassment Makes Ft. Meade a Sentence 'to Hell' for Women," *Baltimore Sun*, 12 February 1980.

27. "Weinberger Spells Out Defense's Sexual Harassment Policy," *Navy Times*, 31 August 1981.

28. Nina Beth Gilder, *Countering Sexual Harassment: Theory and Applications for the Department of Defense* (Washington, D.C.: Department of Defense, 1981).

29. *Army Times*, 28 April 1981.

30. Ingraham, *Boys in the Barracks*, pp. 176, 209, 107, 108, 72, 64–69.

31. Ibid., pp. xvii, 46–52, 108–13.

32. Elizabeth A. Shields, ed., *Highlights in the History of the Army Nurse Corps* (Washington, D.C.: Army Center of Military History, 1981), pp. 28, 36–37.

33. "Fraternization Policy Changed," *Pentagram News*, 30 November 1978; Lt. Gen. Robert H. Elton, Memorandum DAPE-HRL-L, Department of the Army, Washington, D.C., 29 November 1984.

34. "Marine Drummed Out of Corps Over a Romance," *Los Angeles Times*; Grant Willis, "Officer Convicted of Adultery Claims Discrimination," *Air Force Times*, 24 November 1986; Grant Willis, "Adultery Case Witness Disciplined," *Air Force Times*, 15 December 1986.

35. Treadwell, *Women's Army Corps*, p. 421.

36. Ibid., pp. 193, 372, 620.

37. Ibid., pp. 501–3.

38. Ibid., p. 399.

39. Maj. Gen. Jeanne Holm, USAF (Ret.), *Women in the Military: An Unfinished Revolution* (Novato, Calif.: Presidio Press, 1982), p. 300.

40. Oaks, "Force Composition Study," p. 26.

41. "Navy Halts Automatic Discharges for Pregnancy," *Los Angeles Times*, 3 August 1982.

42. Martin Binkin and Mark J. Eitelberg, with Alvin J. Schexnider and Marvin M. Smith, *Blacks and the Military* (Washington, D.C.: Brookings Institution, 1982), p. 171.

43. McCalla et al., *Description of Officers and Enlisted Personnel, 1985*, pp. 185, 209.

44. *Report on Family Issues*, developed by the first Army Family Symposium (Washington, D.C.: Association of the U.S. Army, 1980).

45. "The Navy Family: It Matters," report prepared by Resource Consultants,

Inc., for Family Support Program Branch, Department of the Navy (Washington, D.C.: Department of Defense, 1980).
46. "To Keep Its Sailors, Navy Woos the Wives," *New York Times*, 5 March 1985.
47. Dennis K. Orthner, *Families in Blue: A Study of Married and Single Parent Families in the U.S. Air Force* (Washington, D.C.: Office of the Chief of Chaplains, 1980).
48. Ibid., p. 23.
49. McCalla et al., *Description of Officers and Enlisted Personnel, 1985: Supplementary Tabulations*, vol. 1: 4-61.
50. "AF Plans More Child Care Centers," *Air Force Times*, 25 February 1985.
51. McCalla et al., *Description of Officers and Enlisted Personnel, 1985*, vol. 1: 4-79.
52. Ibid., p. 4-81.
53. Ibid., p. 4-79.
54. Ibid.

CHAPTER 10

1. Philip Wylie, *The Disappearance* (New York: Warner Books, 1951).
2. Cynthia Enloe, "Women—The Reserve Army of Army Labor," *Review of Radical Political Economics* 12: 2 (Summer 1980): 42–52.
3. Simone de Beauvoir, *The Second Sex*, trans. and ed. H. M. Parshley (New York: Knopf, 1971); Nancy Chodorow, *The Reproduction of Mothering: Psychoanalysis and the Sociology of Gender* (Berkeley: University of California Press, 1978); Dorothy Dinnerstein, *The Mermaid and the Minotaur: Sexual Arrangements and Human Malaise* (New York: Harper and Row, 1976).
4. Charlotte Perkins Gilman, *The Living of Charlotte Perkins Gilman* (New York: Harper, 1975), p. 72.
5. Judith Stiehm, "The Protected and the Protector," in *Women and Men's Wars* (Oxford: Pergamon Press, 1983), pp. 4, 5.
6. Ibid., p. 6.
7. Richard Betts, *Soldiers, Statesmen, and Cold War Crises* (Cambridge: Harvard University Press, 1977).
8. John Keegan, *The Face of Battle* (New York: Vintage Books, 1977).
9. Charles C. Moskos, *The American Enlisted Man* (New York: Russell Sage Foundation, 1970), p. 9.

CONCLUSION

1. "General Vessey Sees Women as Biggest Military Change," *Washington Post*, 3 February 1984.
2. Judith Stiehm, "The Unit of Political Analysis: Our Aristotelian Hangover," in Sandra Harding and Merrill B. Hintikka, eds., *Discovering Reality* (Dordrecht, Holland: D. Reidel, 1983).

3. Frank Margiotta, personal communication, 4 September 1981.

4. Judith Stiehm, "The Man Question," in *Women's Views of the Political World of Men* (Ardsley-on-Hudson, N.Y.: Transitional Publishers, 1984), pp. 207–23.


APPENDIX B


1. Linda De Pauw, *Seafaring Women* (Boston: Houghton Mifflin, 1982).

2. Maj. Gen. Jeanne Holm, USAF (Ret.), *Women in the Military: An Unfinished Revolution* (Novato, Calif.: Presidio Press, 1982), p. 12.

3. Mattie E. Treadwell, *The U.S. Army in World War II, Special Studies: The Women's Army Corps* (Washington, D.C.: Office of the Chief of Military History, Department of the Army, 1954), pp. 333–36; Holm, *Women in the Military*, pp. 63–65, 93.

4. Holm, *Women in the Military*, pp. 160, 328.

5. These figures and the discussion that follows are drawn from a report that was widely circulated but not officially released: "Report on the Evaluation of the Assignment of Women to the U.S.S. SANCTUARY (AH-17) October 1972–31 October 1973."

6. John E. Kane, "Women in Non-Traditional Assignments: A Case Study of Navy Tugs," paper presented at 57th Annual Convention of the Western Psychological Association, 20–23 April 1977.

7. Richard Hallovan, "Military Widening Roles of Women," *New York Times*, 27 December 1987; "Fifteen Thousand Seagoing Billets Being Opened to Women," *Navy Times*, 4 January 1988; and "Wanted: More Women for Sea Duty," *Washington Post*, 22 December 1987.

8. Don Edwards, "Naval Duty Nearly Impossible for Women," *Los Angeles Times*, 15 April 1987.

# Bibliography

## BOOKS

Ackley, Charles W. *The Modern Military in American Society*. Philadelphia: Westminster Press, 1972.

Arendt, Hannah. *On Violence*. New York: Harcourt, Brace and World, 1970.

Barnes, Peter. *Pawns: The Plight of the Citizen–Soldier*. New York: Knopf, 1972.

Berkin, Carol R., and Lovett, Clara M., eds. *Women, War and Revolution*. New York: Holmes and Meier, 1980.

Best, Geoffrey. *Humanity in Warfare*. London: Weidenfeld and Nicolson, 1980.

Betts, Richard. *Soldiers, Statesmen, and Cold War Crises*. Cambridge: Harvard University Press, 1977.

Binkin, Martin, and Bach, Shirley J. *Women and the Military*. Washington, D.C.: Brookings Institution, 1977.

Binkin, Martin, and Eitelberg, Mark J., with Alvin J. Schexnider and Marvin M. Smith, *Blacks and the Military*. Washington, D.C.: Brookings Institution, 1982.

Binkin, Martin, and Kyriakopoulos, Irene. *Youth or Experience? Manning the Military*. Washington, D.C.: Brookings Institution, 1979.

Binkin, Martin, and Record, Jeffrey. *Where Does the Marine Corps Go from Here?* Washington, D.C.: Brookings Institution, 1976.

Böll, Heinrich. *And Never Said a Word*. New York: McGraw-Hill, 1978.

Brownmiller, Susan. *Against Our Will: Men, Women and Rape*. New York: Simon & Schuster, 1975.

Buck, James H., and Korb, Lawrence J., eds. *Military Leadership*. Beverly Hills, Calif.: Sage, 1981.

Chapkis, Wendy, ed. *Loaded Questions: Women in the Military*. Amsterdam: Transnational Institute, 1981.

Chodorow, Nancy. *The Reproduction of Mothering: Psychoanalysis and the Sociology of Gender*. Berkeley: University of California Press, 1978.

Cincinnatus. *Self-Destruction*. New York: W. W. Norton, 1981.

Clausewitz, Karl von. *On War*. Middlesex, England: Penguin Books, 1968.

Cortright, David. *Soldiers in Revolt*. Garden City, N.Y.: Anchor Press, 1975.

Crouter, Natalie. *Forbidden Diary*, edited by Lynn Z. Bloom. New York: Burt Franklin, 1980.

Crozier, Frank Percy. *The Men I Killed*. Garden City, N.Y.: Doubleday, Doran, 1938.

Cuncliffe, Marcus. *Soldiers and Civilians: The Martial Spirit in America, 1775–1865*. Boston: Little, Brown, 1968.

Davis, James A.; Lauby, Jennifer; and Sheatsley, Paul B. *Americans View the Military: Public Opinion in 1982*. NORC Report no. 131. Chicago: National Opinion Research Center, 1983.

Davis, James A., and Sheatsley, Paul B. *Americans View the Military: A 1984 Update*. NORC Report no. 132. Chicago: National Opinion Research Center, 1985.

Deaux, Kay. *The Behavior of Women and Men*. Monterey, Calif.: Brooks/Cole, 1976.

Beauvoir, Simone de. *The Second Sex*, trans. and ed. H. M. Parshley. New York: Knopf, 1971.

De Pauw, Linda. *Seafaring Women*. Boston: Houghton Mifflin, 1982.

Dinnerstein, Dorothy. *The Mermaid and the Minotaur: Sexual Arrangements and Human Malaise*. New York: Harper and Row, 1976.

Dixon, Norman. *On the Psychology of Military Incompetence*. New York: Basic Books, 1976.

Edelman, Murray. *Politics and Symbolic Action*. Chicago: Markham, 1971.

Enloe, Cynthia. *Does Khaki Become You? The Militarization of Women's Lives*. Boston: South End Press, 1983.

——. *Ethnic Soldiers*. New York: Pelican Books, 1980.

——. *Police, Military and Ethnicity*. New Brunswick, N.J.: Transaction Books, 1980.

Fried, Morton, et al. *War: The Anthropology of Armed Conflict and Aggression*. Garden City, N.Y.: Natural History Press, 1968.

Fullinwinder, Robert K., ed. *Conscripts and Volunteers: Military Requirements, Social Justice and the All-Volunteer Force*. Totowa, N.J.: Rowman and Allanheld, 1983.

Gabriel, Richard A., and Savage, Paul L. *Crisis in Command*. New York: Hill and Wang, 1978.

Gallup, George H. *The Gallup Poll: Public Opinion, 1935–1971*. Wilmington, Del.: Scholarly Resources, 1972.

——. *The Gallup Poll: Public Opinion, 1972–1977*. Wilmington, Del.: Scholarly Resources, 1978.

——. *The Gallup Poll: Public Opinion, 1979*. Wilmington, Del.: Scholarly Resources, 1980.

——. *The Gallup Poll: Public Opinion, 1980*. Wilmington, Del.: Scholarly Resources, 1981.

Gilman, Charlotte Perkins. *The Living of Charlotte Perkins Gilman*. New York: Harper and Row, 1975.

Glenn, Norvall D. *Cohort Analysis*. Beverly Hills, Calif.: Sage, 1977.

Glick, Edward B. *Soldiers, Scholars and Society: The Social Impact of the American Military*. Pacific Pallisades, Calif.: Goodyear, 1971.

Goldman, Nancy L., ed. *Female Soldiers—Combatants or Noncombatants?* Westport, Conn.: Greenwood Press, 1982.

Goldman, Nancy L., and Segal, David R., eds. *The Social Psychology of Military Service.* Beverly Hills, Calif.: Sage, 1976.

Goldstein, Leslie F. *The Constitutional Rights of Women: Cases in Law and Social Change.* New York: Longman, 1979.

Goode, William J. *The Celebration of Heroes.* Berkeley: University of California Press, 1978.

Gray, Jesse Glen. *The Warriors: Reflections on Men in Battle.* New York: Harper and Row, 1970.

Griffin, Susan. *Rape: The Power of Consciousness.* San Francisco: Harper and Row.

*Handbook and Manual for the Noncommissioned Officer.* Washington, D.C.: Combat Forces Press, 1952.

Hartsock, Nancy C. M. *Money, Sex and Power.* New York: Longman, 1983.

Herr, Michael. *Dispatches.* New York: Avon, 1978.

Hicken, Victor. *The American Fighting Man.* London: Macmillan, 1969.

Holm, Jeanne, Maj. Gen., USAF (Ret.). *Women in the Military: An Unfinished Revolution.* Novato, Calif.: Presidio Press, 1982.

Hosek, James R.; Peterson, Christine E.; and Eden, Rick A. *Educational Expectations and Enlistment Decisions.* Santa Monica, Calif.: Rand, 1986.

Howard, Michael. *War and the Liberal Conscience.* New Brunswick, N.J.: Rutgers University Press, 1978.

Hunter, Edna J. *Families Under the Flag.* New York: Praeger, 1982.

Hunter, Edna J., and Nice, Stephen D. *Military Families.* New York: Praeger, 1978.

Ibuse, Masuji. *Black Rain.* Tokyo: Kodansha, 1978.

Ingraham, Larry H. *The Boys in the Barracks.* Philadelphia: Institute for the Study of Human Issues, 1984.

James, William. "The Moral Equivalent of War." In *Essays on Faith and Morals.* New York: Longmans, Green, 1943.

Janowits, Morris, and Little, Roger. *Sociology and the Military Establishment.* Beverly Hills, Calif.: Sage, 1975.

Kaplan, Fred. *The Wizards of Armageddon.* New York: Simon & Schuster, 1983.

Karsten, Peter. *Soldiers and Society.* Westport, Conn.: Greenwood Press, 1978.

Keegan, John. *The Face of Battle.* New York: Vintage Books, 1977.

Kleinbaum, Abby Wettan. *The War Against the Amazons.* New York: McGraw-Hill, 1983.

Korb, Lawrence. *The Fall and Rise of the Pentagon: American Defense Policies in the 1970's.* Westport, Conn.: Greenwood Press, 1979.

Kovik, Ron. *Born on the Fourth of July.* New York: McGraw-Hill, 1976.

Kuwahara, Yasuo, and Allred, Gordon. *Kamikaze.* New York: Ballantine, 1957.

Levitan, Sar A., and Alderman, Karen Cleary. *Warriors at Work: The Volunteer Armed Force.* Beverly Hills, Calif.: Sage, 1977.

Loory, Stuart. *Defeated: Inside America's Military Machine.* New York: Random House, 1973.

Loring, Nancy H., ed. *Women in the United States Armed Forces: Progress and Barriers in the 1980s.* Chicago: Inter-University Seminar on Armed Forces and Society, 1984.

Lovell, John P., and Stiehm, Judith H. "Military Service and Political Socialization." In *Political Learning in Adulthood, Constancy and Change: A Source Book,* ed. Roberta S. Sigel. Chicago: University of Chicago Press, forthcoming.

McAllister, Pam. *Reweaving the Web of Life: Feminism and Nonviolence.* Philadelphia: New Society, 1982.

McClelland, David C. *Power: The Inner Experience.* New York: Irvington, 1975.

McCubbin, Hamilton; Dahl, Barbara; and Hunter, Edna J., eds. *Families in the Military System.* Beverly Hills, Calif.: Sage, 1976.

McKitrick, Eric L., ed. *Slavery Defended: The Views of the Old South.* Englewood Cliffs, N.J.: Prentice-Hall, 1963.

Mansfield, Sue. *The Gestalts of War.* New York: Dial Press, 1982.

Marshall, S. L. A. *Men Against Fire.* New York: Morrow, 1947.

Martin, Susan. *Breaking and Entering.* Berkeley: University of California Press, 1980.

Masland, John W., and Radway, Lawrence. *Soldiers and Scholars: Military Education and National Policy.* Princeton, N.J.: Princeton University Press, 1975.

Metzger, Deena. *The Woman Who Slept with Men to Take the War Out of Them; and Tree.* Culver City, Calif.: Peace Press, 1981.

Moskos, Charles C. *The American Enlisted Man.* New York: Russell Sage Foundation, 1970.

————, ed. *Public Opinion and the Military Establishment.* Beverly Hills, Calif.: Sage, 1971.

Nida, Patricia Cooney. "Women in the Army, Current Issues." After-Action Report on Seminars Held for the Army Chaplains. San Rafael, Calif.: Nita Training and Development Group, n.d. (ca. 1982).

Nieburg, Harold. *Political Violence.* New York: St. Martin, 1969.

*1980 Virginia Slims American Women's Opinion Poll, The.* The Roper Organization, n.p., 1980.

Omang, Joanne. *A Historical Background to the CIA's Nicaragua Manual.* New York: Vintage Books, 1985.

Partlow, Col. Frank A. *Womanpower for a Superpower: The National Security Implications of Women in the U.S. Army.* Cambridge, Mass.: Center for International Affairs, 1983.

Pennock, J. Rowland, and Chapman, John H., eds. *Coercion. Nomos 14* (Yearbook of the American Society for Political and Legal Philosophy). Chicago: Aldine-Atherton, 1972.

Peristiany, J. G. *Honour and Shame.* London: University of Chicago Press, 1966.

Petrement, Simone. *Simone Weil.* New York: Pantheon, 1976.
Powers, Thomas. *The Man Who Kept the Secrets.* New York: Pocket Books, 1979.
Rapoport, Anatol, ed. *Clausewitz on War.* Middlesex, England: Penguin, 1968.
Reardon, Betty. *Sexism and the War System.* New York: Teachers College Press, 1985.
Reynaud, Emmanuel. *Holy Virility.* London: Pluto Press, 1983.
Richardson, Lewis. *Arms and Insecurity.* Pittsburgh: Boxwood Press, 1960.
Rivkin, Robert S. *The Rights of Servicemen.* New York: Avon, 1972.
Rogan, Helen. *Mixed Company: Women in the Modern Army.* New York: Putnam, 1981.
Rupp, Leila. *Mobilizing Women for War: German and American Propaganda, 1939–1945.* Princeton, N.J.: Princeton University Press, 1978.
Rustad, Michael L. *Women in Khaki: The American Enlisted Woman.* New York: Praeger, 1982.
Sanders, Ralph. *The Politics of Defense Analysis.* New York: Dunellen, 1973.
Saywell, Shelley. *Women in Wars.* Marham, Ontario: Penguin, 1985.
Schneider, Dorothy and Carl J. *Soundoff! American Military Women Speak Out.* New York: Dutton, 1988.
Scowcroft, Lt. Gen. Brent. *Military Service in the United States.* New York: Sixtieth American Assembly, Columbia University, 1981.
Segal, David R., and Sinaiko, H. Wallace. *Life in the Rank and File.* Washington, D.C.: Pergamon-Brassey, 1986.
Sennett, Richard. *Authority.* New York: Knopf, 1980.
Sharff, Lee E., and Gordon, Lt. Col. Sol. *Uniformed Services Almanac.* 24th annual ed. Washington, D.C.: Uniformed Services Almanac, Inc., 1982.
Shibutani, Tamotsu. *The Derelicts of Company K.* Berkeley: University of California Press, 1978.
Singer, J. David, and Small, Melvin. *The Wages of War 1816–1965: A Statistical Handbook.* New York: Wiley and Sons, 1972.
Stiehm, Judith. *Bring Me Men and Women: Mandated Change at the U.S. Air Force Academy.* Berkeley: University of California Press, 1981.
———. "The Man Question." In *Women's Views of the Political World of Men.* Ardsley-on-Hudson, N.Y.: Transitional Publishers, 1984.
———. *Nonviolent Power.* Lexington, Mass.: D. C. Heath, 1972.
———. "The Unit of Political Analysis: Our Aristotelian Hangover." In Sandra Harding and Merrill Hintikka, eds., *Discovering Reality.* Dordrecht, Holland: D. Reidel, 1983.
———. *Women and Men's Wars.* Oxford: Pergamon Press, 1983.
Stiehm, Judith, and Saint-Germain, Michelle. *Men, Women and State Violence: Government and the Military.* Washington, D.C.: American Political Science Association, 1983.
Tauber, Peter. *The Sunshine Soldiers.* New York: Simon and Schuster, 1971.
Taylor, William J.; Olson, Eric T.; and Schrader, Richard A., eds. *Defense Manpower Planning: Issues for the 1980's.* New York: Pergamon Press, 1981.

Toch, Hans. *Violent Men.* Chicago: Aldine, 1969.
Tuchman, Barbara W. *The March of Folly.* New York: Ballantine Books, 1984.
Venti, Steven F. *Wages in the Federal and Private Sectors.* Cambridge, Mass.: National Bureau of Economic Research, 1985.
Wadge, D. Collett, ed. *Women in Uniform.* London: Sampson Low, Marston, 1946.
Waite, Linda J., and Berryman, Sue E. *Women in Nontraditional Occupations: Choice and Turnover.* Santa Monica, Calif.: Rand, 1985.
Walzer, Michael. *Just and Unjust Wars.* New York: Basic Books, 1977.
────── . *Obligations: Essays on Disobedience, War and Citizenship.* Cambridge: Harvard University Press, 1970.
Warner, Marina. *Joan of Arc: The Image of Female Heroism.* New York: Vintage Books, 1982.
Watson, Peter. *War on the Mind.* New York: Basic Books, 1978.
Webb, Kate. *On the Other Side: Twenty-Three Days with the Vietcong.* New York: Quadrangle Books, 1972.
Weigley, Russell. *The American Way of War.* New York: Macmillan, 1973.
Wilder, Anthony. *Man and Woman, War and Peace: The Strategists' Companion.* London and New York: Routledge and Kegan Paul, 1987.
Wilkinson, David. *Deadly Quarrels.* Berkeley: University of California Press, 1980.
Williams, Colin J., and Weinberg, Martin S. *Homosexuals and the Military.* New York: Harper and Row, 1971.
Windrow, Martin, ed. *Women at War, 1939–1945.* London: Osprey, 1980.
Wolfe, Tom. *The Right Stuff.* New York: Farrar, Straus, Giraux, 1979.
Wollstonecraft, Mary. *A Vindication of the Rights of Women*, edited by Carol H. Poston. New York: Norton, 1975.
Wylie, Philip. *The Disappearance.* New York: Warner, 1951.
Yarmolinsky, Adam. *The Military Establishment.* New York: Harper and Row, 1970.
Young, Michael. *The Rise of the Meritocracy.* London: Pelican Books, 1961.
*Youth and the Needs of the Nation.* Washington, D.C.: Committee for the Study of National Service, Potomac Institute, 1979.

## U.S. GOVERNMENT PUBLICATIONS

*America's Volunteers: Report on the All-Volunteer Armed Forces.* Washington, D.C.: Office of the Assistant Secretary of Defense, 1978.
Army Military Personnel Center. "Report of Results of 9 October 1978 Survey of Women in the Army." Report no. UR 13-78. Alexandria, Va.: DAPC-MSF-5, 1978.
Barlow, Esther M. *Annotated Bibliography of the Air Force Human Resources Laboratory Technical Reports—1977.* Brooks Air Force Base, Tex.: Air Force Human Resources Laboratory, 1979.
*A Battalion Commander's Handbook.* Carlisle Barracks, Pa.: U.S. Army War College, 1977.

*Battalion Commanders Speak Out: An Anthology on the Philosophy of Command.* Carlisle Barracks, Pa.: U.S. Army War College, 1977.

Batts, John H., et al. *The Roles of Women in the Army and Their Impact on Military Operations and Organization.* Carlisle Barracks, Pa.: U.S. Army War College, 1975.

*Bibliography of Unclassified Technical Reports, November 1977 through September 1978.* San Diego, Calif.: Navy Personnel Research and Development Center, 1979.

Bolin, Stanley F.; Johns, Lois A.; and Cowings, John S. *Women Soldiers in Korea: Troop Viewpoints.* Research Memorandum 77-16. Alexandria, Va.: Army Research Institute, 1977.

Borack, Jules I. "Intentions of Women (18–25 Years Old) to Join the Military: Results of a National Survey." Technical Report 78-34. San Diego, Calif.: Navy Personnel Research and Development Center, 1978.

Boyd, H. Alton, et al. *Performance of First-Tour WAC Enlisted Women: Data Base for the Performance Orientation of Women's Basic Training.* Arlington, Va.: National Technical Information Service, 1975.

Bray, Robert; McCalla, Mary Ellen; Immerman, Frederick; Guess, L. Lynn; and Dunteman, George H. *Youth Attitude Tracking Study II.* Arlington, Va.: Defense Manpower Data Center, 1984.

Bray, Robert M.; Whelan, Janice L.; and Cavanaugh, Elizabeth. *Youth Attitude Tracking Study II: Supplementary Tabulations.* Arlington, Va.: Defense Manpower Data Center, 1986.

Cook, Sharla J., and Wilkey, David R. *Social Problems of Enlisted Women in United States Air Force Craft Skills.* Air Force Air Institute. Wright-Patterson Air Force Base, Ohio: USAF Air University, 1977.

*The Costs of Defense Manpower: Issues for 1977.* Washington, D.C.: Government Printing Office, 1977.

Defense Advisory Committee on Women in the Services. *Spring and Fall Meeting Minutes.* Washington, D.C., 1979–1986.

Defense Manpower Commission. *Defense Manpower Commission Studies and Supporting Papers.* 5 vols. Washington, D.C.: Government Printing Office, 1976.

"Development of a Pilot Sex Education Program for Enlisted Marines." San Diego, Calif.: Navy Personnel and Development Center, 1980.

Doering, Zahava D.; Grissmer, David W.; Hawes, Jennifer A.; and Hutzler, William P. *1980 DOD Survey of Officers and Enlisted Personnel: User's Manual and Codebook.* Santa Monica, Calif.: Rand, 1981.

Doering, Zahava D.; Grissmer, David W.; and Morse, Jane S. *DOD Survey of Personnel Entering Military Service: Wave 1 User's Manual and Codebook.* Santa Monica, Calif.: Rand, 1980.

———. *1979 DOD Survey: Wave 2 User's Manual and Codebook.* Santa Monica, Calif.: Rand, 1980.

Doering, Zahava D., and Hutzler, William P. *Description of Officers and Enlisted Personnel in the United States Armed Forces: A Reference for Military Manpower Analysis.* Santa Monica, Calif.: Rand, 1982.

Durning, Kathleen P., and Mumford, Sandra J. *Differential Perceptions of*

*Organizational Climate Held by Navy Enlisted Women and Men.* San Diego, Calif.: Navy Personnel Research and Development Center, 1976.

Elton, Lt. Gen. Robert H. Memorandum DAPE-HRL-L. Washington, D.C.: Department of the Army, 29 November 1984.

*Enlisted Women in the Armed Forces.* Washington, D.C.: National Defense University, 1978–79.

Foley, Mark. *Leadership and Women in the Army.* Fort Harrison, Ind.: Army Administration Center, 1978.

Garvey, Charles J. *Analysis of the Changing Role of Women in the United States Army.* Carlisle Barracks, Pa.: U.S. Army War College, 1974.

Gilder, Nina Beth. *Countering Sexual Harassment: Theory and Applications for the Department of Defense.* Washington, D.C.: Department of Defense, 1981.

Goldich, Robert L. *The U.S. Army's New Manning System.* Washington, D.C.: Congressional Research Service, 1983.

―――――. *Women in the Armed Forces: Proceedings of a CRS Seminar Held 2 November 1979.* Washington, D.C.: Congressional Research Service, 1980.

Goldman, Nancy L. *The Utilization of Women in Combat: An Historical and Social Analysis of Twentieth-Century Wartime and Peacetime Experience.* Washington, D.C.: Army Research Institute, 1982.

Graham, Hugh Davis, and Gurr, Ted Robert. *Violence in America: Historical and Comparative Studies.* Washington, D.C.: Government Printing Office, 1969.

Greebler, Carol S.; Thomas, Patricia J.; and Kuczyuski, Judy D. *Men and Women in Ships: Preconceptions of the Crews.* NPRDC TR 82-57. San Diego, Calif.: Navy Personnel Research and Development Center, 1982.

Griffith, Janet D.; Doering, Zahava D.; and Mahoney, Bette S. *Description of Spouses of Officers and Enlisted Personnel in the U.S. Armed Forces: 1985.* Arlington, Va.: Defense Manpower Data Center, 1986.

Hewitt, Linda L. *Women Marines in World War I.* Washington, D.C.: U.S. Marine Corps, 1974.

Hicks, Jack M. *Army Enlisted MOS and Sex Role: A Male-Female Comparison.* Alexandria, Va.: Army Research Institute, 1975.

―――――. *Attitudinal Correlates of Reenlistment Intent Among Women in the Army.* Alexandria, Va.: Army Research Institute, 1977.

Hinsdale, Kristen; Collier, Barbara; and Johnson, J. David. *Navy Enlisted Women in Traditional and Nontraditional Jobs.* Alexandria, Va.: Defense Technical Information Center, 1978.

Hunter, Edna J., and Nice, D. Stephen, eds. *Children of Military Families.* Washington, D.C.: Government Printing Office, 1978.

*Job Opportunities for Women in the Military: Progress and Problems.* Washington, D.C.: Government Printing Office, 1976.

Jordan, Marcelite C. "Utilization of Women in Air Force Industrial Career Fields." Lackland, Tex.: Human Resources Laboratory, 1976.

Kubala, Albert L., and Warnick, William L. *A Review of Selected Literature on Stresses Affecting Soldiers in Combat.* Alexandria, Va.: Army Research Institute, 1978.

McCalla, Mary Ellen; Rakoff, Stuart H.; and Doering, Zahava D. *Description of Officers and Enlisted Personnel in the U.S. Armed Forces: 1985, Supplementary Tabulations from the 1980 DOD Survey of Officer and Enlisted Personnel*. 4 vols. Arlington, Va.: Defense Manpower Data Center, 1986.

————. *Interim Report to the President and Congress*. Washington, D.C.: Defense Manpower Commission, 1975.

Maginnis, Elena B.; Uchima, Ansho; and Smith, Carol. *Establishing Aptitude Requirements for Air Force Jobs*. Brooks Air Force Base, Tex.: Air Force Human Resources Laboratory, 1975.

————. *Nonviolent Power*. Lexington, Mass.: D. C. Heath, 1972.

————. *Nonviolent Power*. Lexington, Mass.: D. C. Heath, 1972.

Military Manpower Task Force. *Report to the President on the Status and Prospects of the All-Volunteer Force*. Washington, D.C.: Government Printing Office, 1982.

*Military Women in the Department of Defense*. Vols. 1–4. Washington, D.C.: Department of Defense, Office of the Secretary of Defense, 1983–86.

*Mobilization: A Selected Bibliography*. Washington, D.C.: The Pentagon, 1982.

Morden, Bettie C. *The Women's Army Corps, 1945–78*. Washington, D.C.: Office of the Chief of Military History, Department of the Army, Publication pending.

Myers, David G.; Gebhardt, Deborah; and Fleishman, Edwin. *Development of Physical Performance Standards for Army Jobs: The Job Analysis Methodology*. Technical Report 446. Alexandria, Va.: Army Research Institute, 1980.

"The Navy Family: It Matters." Report prepared by Resource Consultants, Inc., for Family Support Program Branch, Department of the Navy. Washington, D.C.: Department of Defense, 1980.

Nogami, Glenda Y. *Fact Sheet: Soldier Gender on First Tour Attrition*. Alexandria, Va.: Army Research Institute, 1981.

————. *The Impact of MOS Traditionality and Soldier Gender on First Term Attrition*. Alexandria, Va.: Army Research Institute, 1981.

Oliver, Laurel W. *The Effect of Intergroup Contact on Attitudes Toward the Role of Women in the Army*. Alexandria, Va.: Army Research Institute, 1981.

Olson, Marsha S., and Stumpf, Susan S. *Pregnancy in the Navy: Impact on Absenteeism, Attrition and Work Group Morale*, NPRDC TR 78-35, San Diego, Calif.: Navy Personnel Research and Development Center, 1978.

Orthner, Dennis K. *Families in Blue: A Study of Married and Single Parent Families in the Air Force*. Washington, D.C.: Office of the Chief of Chaplains, 1980.

Overbey, John W. II; Winter, Phillip E.; and Lawrence, Michael T. *The Medical Fitness of American Youth for Military Service*. Alexandria, Va.: Defense Manpower Data Center, 1986.

Polit, Denise F., et al. *Preliminary Tabulation by Rank and Sex of Selected Responses in an Attitude Questionnaire*. Alexandria, Va.: Army Research Institute, 1978.

Polit, Denise F.; Nuttal, Ronald L.; and King, Eleanor. *Utilization of Women in Industrial Career Fields*. Brooks Air Force Base, Tex.: Human Resources Laboratory, 1979.

*Propensity of Young Women to Enlist in the Military*. Report to Congress. Arlington, Va.: Defense Manpower Data Center, 1985.

*Report on Family Issues*. Developed by the first Army Family Symposium. Washington, D.C.: Association of the U.S. Army, 1980.

Richter, Edward A., and Thorp, David A. *A Comparative Analysis of Enlisted Career Progression Systems*. Wright-Patterson Air Force Base, Ohio: Air Force Institute of Technology, 1980.

Royle, Marjorie H. *Factors Affecting Attrition Among Marine Corps Women*, NPRDC TR 86-7. San Diego, Calif.: Navy Personnel Research and Development Center, 1985.

Royle, Marjorie H.; Molof, Martin J.; and Winchell, Jim D. *Development of a Pilot Sex Education Program for Enlisted Marines*. San Diego, Calif.: Navy Personnel Research and Development Center, 1986.

Savelle, Joel M.; Rigby, Carlos K.; and Zibikowski, Andrew A. *An Investigation of Lost Time and Utilization in a Sample of First-Term Male and Female Soldiers*. Alexandria, Va.: Army Research Institute, 1982.

Savelle, Joel M.; Woelfel, John C.; and Collins, Barry. *Attitudes Concerning Job Appropriateness for Women in the Army*. Research Memorandum 75-3. Alexandria, Va.: Army Research Institute, 1975.

Savelle, Joel M.; Woelfel, John C.; and Collins, Barry. *Soldiers, Attribution of Contemporary vs. Traditional Sex Role Attitudes to Themselves and to Others*. Research Memoradum 75-7. Alexandria, Va.: Army Research Institute, 1975.

Seeley, Leonard C. *Survey of Attrition Factors Among WAC Basic Trainees*. Research Study 70-3. Arlington, Va.: Behavior and Systems Research Laboratory, 1970.

Segal, David R. "Civilian Images of the Military." Alexandria, Va.: Army Research Institute, 1975.

*Selected Manpower Statistics*. Washington, D.C.: Directorate for Information, Operations and Reports, the Pentagon, annually.

"Sexual Harassment in the Federal Workplace: Is It a Problem?" Report of the U.S. Merit Systems Protection Board. Washington, D.C.: Merit Systems Protection Board, 1981.

Shaw, Henry I., Jr., and Donnelly, Ralph W. *Blacks in the Marine Corps*. Washington, D.C.: U.S. Marine Corps, 1975.

Shields, Elizabeth A., ed. *Highlights in the History of the Army Nurse Corps*. Washington, D.C.: U.S. Army Center of Military History, 1981.

Sternberg, Jack J.; Greenberg, Frank; and Fuchs, Edmund F. *Identifying Army Jobs Suitable for WAC Assignment*. Research Study 58-3. Washington, D.C.: Army Personnel Research Office, 1958.

Stremlow, Col. Mary V. *A History of the Women Marines, 1946–1977*. Washington, D.C.: History and Museums Division, U.S. Marine Corps, 1986.

Thomas, Patricia J. *Factors Affecting the Management of Navy Women*. San Diego, Calif.: Navy Personnel Research and Development Center, 1980.

―――. "Issues in the Management of Women in the Navy." In *U.S. Navy Yearbook of Manpower, Personnel and Training*. Washington, D.C.: Deputy Chief of Naval Operations, 1980.

―――. *Utilization of Enlisted Women in the Military*. San Diego, Calif.: Navy Personnel Research and Development Center, n.d.

Thomas, Patricia J., and Greebler, Carol S. *Men and Women in Ships: Attitudes of Crews After One to Two Years of Integration*. NPRDC TR 84-6. San Diego, Calif.: Navy Personnel Research and Development Center, 1983.

Thomas, Patricia J.; Monda, Marilyn J.; Millsand, Shelly H.; and Mathis, Julie A. *Navy Women in Traditional and Nontraditional Jobs: A Comparison of Satisfaction, Attrition and Re-enlistment*. Technical Report 82-50. San Diego, Calif.: Navy Personnel Research and Development Center, 1982.

Treadwell, Mattie E. *The U.S. Army in World War II, Special Studies: The Women's Army Corps*. Washington, D.C.: Office of the Chief of Military History, Department of the Army, 1954.

U.S. Congress, House Armed Services Personnel Committee. Report by Special Subcommittee on Utilization of Manpower in Military. 92d Cong., 2d Sess., 28 June 1972.

U.S. Congress, House Armed Services Personnel Committee, *Navy Proposal to Amend 10 U.S.C. 6015, Hearings Before the Subcommittee on Military Personnel H.R. 7431*. 95th Cong., 2d Sess., 1978.

U.S. Congress, Subcommittee on Investigations of the House Committee on Post Office and Civil Service. *Sexual Harassment in the Federal Government, 30 April 1980*.

U.S. Department of the Air Force. *DCS/MP Fact Book*. Washington, D.C.: Department of the Air Force, 1980.

U.S. Department of the Army. *Report of Audit: Enlisted Women in the Army*. Audit Report HQ 82-212. Washington, D.C.: Army Audit Agency, 1982.

U.S. Department of the Army. *Report of Audit: Enlisted Women in the Army, Fort McClellan, Alabama*. Audit Report 50 82-206. Washington, D.C.: Army Audit Agency, 1982.

U.S. Department of the Army. *Report of Audit: Enlisted Women in the Army, III Corps and Fort Hood*. Audit Report SW 82-208. Washington, D.C.: Army Audit Agency, 1982.

U.S. Department of the Army. Office of the Auditor General. *Enlisted Women in the Army*. Fort Hood, Tex.: U.S. Army Audit Agency, 1982.

―――. *Women in the Army Policy Review*. Washington, D.C.: Office of the Deputy Chief of Staff for Personnel, 1982.

U.S. Department of the Army, Army Administration Center. *Evaluation of Women in the Army*. Washington, D.C.: Office of the Deputy Chief of Staff for Personnel, 1978.

U.S. Department of Defense, Office of the Assistant Secretary of Defense. *Profile of American Youth: 1980 Nationwide Administration of the Armed Services Vocational Aptitude Battery*. Washington, D.C.: 1982.

U.S. Department of Defense, Office of the Assistant Secretary of Defense, Manpower, Reserve Affairs and Logistics. *Use of Women in the Military: Background Study*. Washington, D.C.: 1977.

U.S. Department of Defense, Office of the Assistant Secretary of Defense,
Manpower, Reserve Affairs and Logistics. *Women in the Military:
Background Review.* Washington, D.C.: Office of the Assistant Secretary of
Defense, 1981.
*Utilization of Women in the Army.* Washington, D.C.: Military Personnel
Center, 1977.
*Women Content in Units Force Development Test* (MAX WAC). Alexandria, Va.:
Army Research Institute, 1977.
*Women Content in the Army—Reforger 77* (REF WAC). Alexandria, Va.: Army
Research Institute, 1978.
*Women in America's Defense.* Washington, D.C.: Office of the Deputy Assistant
Secretary of Defense for Equal Opportunity and Safety Policy, 1982.
"Women in the Air Force: Package 13." HQ AFMPC/MPCX. Randolph Air
Force Base, Tex., 1985.
*Women in the Army: A Selected Bibliography.* Carlisle Barracks, Pa.: U.S.
Army War College, 1982.
*Women in the Army Study.* Washington, D.C.: Department of the Army, 1976.
*Women in the Military: Bibliography.* Congressional Resource Service.
Washington, D.C.: Library of Congress, 1981.


## JOURNALS AND MAGAZINES

Anderson, Jeffrey W. "Military Heroism: An Occupational Definition." *Armed
Forces and Society* 12 (1986): 591–606.
"Army Focuses on Women in 'Single-Parent' Debate." *WEAL Washington
Report*, February–March, 1982, pp. 1, 2.
Aspin, Les. "Manning the Military: The Female Factor." *Minerva* 2:2 (Summer
1984): 133–51.
Bachman, Jerald G.; Sigelman, Lee; and Diamond, Greg. "Self-Selection,
Socialization, and Distinctive Military Values: Attitudes of High School
Seniors." *Armed Forces and Society* 13: 2 (Winter 1987): 169–87.
Bailey, Mildred C. "Army Women and a Decade of Progress." *Army*, October
1974, p. 14.
Baut, Bruce N. "Working Together: The Army's Assault on Sexism." *Soldiers*,
October 1980, p. 8.
Beans, Harry C. "Sex Discrimination in the Military." *Military Law Review* 67
(Winter 1975): 58–59.
Berube, Allan. "Coming Out Under Fire: The Untold Story of the World War II
Soldiers Who Fought on the Front Lines of Gay and Lesbian Liberation."
*Mother Jones*, February–March 1983, pp. 23–29, 45.
Bey, Douglas R., and Lange, Jean. "Waiting Wives: Women Under Stress."
*American Journal of Psychiatry* 131 (1974): 283–86.
Brandy, Lt. Col. James. "The Status of Women Marines." *Marine Corps
Gazette*, July 1983, p. 25.
Brotz, Howard, and Wilson, Everett. "Characteristics of Military Society."
*American Journal of Sociology* 51 (1946): 371–75.
Cheatham, Harold E. "Integration of Women into the U.S. Military." *Sex Roles*
11: 1 (1984): 141–51.

Cook, Thomas D., and Leviton, Laura C. "Reviewing the Literature: A Comparison of Traditional Methods with Meta Analysis." *Journal of Personality* 48 (1980): 449–72.

Cropsey, Seth. "The Military Manpower Crisis: Women in Combat." *Public Interest*, Fall 1980, pp. 58–73.

DeGrazia, Sebastian. "Political Equality and Military Participation." *Armed Forces and Society* 7 (1981): 181–86.

Devilbiss, C. M. "Gender Integration and Unit Development: A Study of GI Jo." *Armed Forces and Society* 11 (1985): 523–52.

Dobrofsky, Lynne R. "Military Socialization and Masculinity." *Journal of Social Issues* 34 (1978): 151–68.

———. "Women's Power and Authority in the Context of War." *Sex Roles* 3: 2 (April 1977): 141–57.

Durning, Kathleen P. "Attitudes of Enlisted Women and Men Toward the Navy." *Armed Forces and Society* 9 (1982): 20–32.

Ellis, Judy Trent. "Sexual Harassment and Race: A Legal Analysis of Discrimination." *Journal of Legislation* 8:1 (1981): 30–45.

Enloe, Cynthia. "Bananas, Bases, and Patriarchy: Some Feminist Questions About the Militarization of Central America." *Radical America* 19: 4 (1985): 7–23.

———. "Women—The Reserve Army of Army Labor." *Review of Radical Political Economics* 12: 2 (Summer 1980): 42–52.

"The Equal Rights Amendment and the Military." *Yale Law Review* 82 (1973): 1538–39n, 1553n.

Favis, John W. "Economic and Noneconomic Factors of Personnel Recruitment and Retention in the Armed Forces." *Armed Forces and Society* 10 (1984): 251–75.

Forcey, Linda Rennie. "Making of Men in the Military: Perspectives from Mothers." *Women's Studies International Forum* 7 (1984): 477–86.

Gabriel, Maj. Richard A., and Kessler, Maj. Doris H. "Women in Combat? Two Views." *Army*, March 1980, pp. 45–52.

Gilder, George. "The Case Against Women in Combat." *New York Times Magazine*, 28 January 1979, pp. 29–46.

Goldman, Nancy. "The Changing Role of Women in the Armed Forces." *American Journal of Sociology* 78 (1972): 892–911.

Gottlieb, David. "Women Soldiers: On Joining the Army." *Youth and Society* 10: 2 (December 1978): 159–64.

Hanneman, Robert A. "The Military's Role in Political Regimes." *Armed Forces and Society* 12 (1985): 29–51.

Hartsock, Nancy C. M. "Masculinity, Citizenship, and the Making of War." *PS*, Spring 1984, pp. 198–202.

Hollingshead, August B. "Adjustment to Military Life." *American Journal of Sociology* 51 (1946): 439–47.

"Homosexual Paranoia." *Equal Opportunity Current News*, October 1981, pp. 29–30.

Hoover, William D. "The Disadvantaged Navy Women." *U.S. Naval Institute Proceedings*, July 1977, p. 118.

Huston, Nancy. "The Matrix of War: Mothers and Heroes." *Poetics Today* 6: 1/2 (1985): 153–70.

"Is Parity Possible in Female Billets?" *U.S. Naval Institute Proceedings*, September 1980, pp. 103–4.

Jones, Kathleen. "Dividing the Ranks: Women and the Draft." *Women and Politics* 4: 4 (Winter 1984), pp. 75–87.

Leernsen, Charles; Lord, Mary; and Shannon, Elaine. "Our Standards Are Different." *Newsweek*, 12 December 1983, p. 48.

McKain, Jerry Lavin. "Relocation in the Military: Alienation and Family Problems." *Journal of Marriage and the Family* (1973): 205–9.

McKay, Karen. "Army Womanpower: Go Ahead—Exploit Us!" *Army*, April 1972, p. 24.

Marin, Susan E. "Police Women and Policewomen: Occupational Role Dilemmas and Choice of Female Officers." *Journal of Police Science and Administration* 7: 3 (1979): 314–23.

Mazuri, Ali A. "Military Technology and the Masculinity of War: An African Perspective." *Impact of Science on Society* 26: 1/2 (1976).

Meyer, Gen. E. C. *Defense*, February 1982, pp. 2–9.

"Military Harassment of Women and Gays Increasing." *National NOW Times*, May 1983, p. 7.

"Military Women: Recognizing Realities." *Marine Corps Gazette*, March 1985, p. 60.

Nabors, Maj. Robert L. "Women in the Army: Do They Measure Up?" *Military Review* 62: 10 (1982): 51–61.

"Naval Hospital Corpsman Exonerated." *Open Forum*, January 1982, pp. 1, 2.

O'Gorman, Hubert J. "False Consciousness of Kind: Pluralistic Ignorance Among the Aged." *Research on Aging* 2:1 (March 1980): 105–28.

Priest, Robert F.; Prince, Howard T.; and Vitters, Alan G. "The First Coed Class at West Point." *Youth and Society* 10: 2 (December 1978): 205–24.

Quester, George H. "Women in Combat." *International Security*, Spring 1977, pp. 80–91.

Rose, Arnold. "The Social Structure of the Army." *American Journal of Sociology* 51:5 (1946): 361–64.

Safilios-Rothschild, Constantina. "Young Women and Men Aboard the U.S. Coast Guard Barque 'Eagle': An Observation and Interview Study." *Youth and Society* 10: 2 (December 1978): 191–204.

Segal, David R.; Bachman, Jerald G.; and Dowdell, Faye. "Military Service for Female and Black Youth: A Perceived Mobility Opportunity." *Youth and Society* 10:2 (December 1978): 127–33.

Segal, David R., and Blair, John D., eds. *Youth and Society* 10: 1 (September 1978): special issue on youth and the military.

Segal, David R.; Kinzer, Nora Scott; and Woelfel, John C. "The Concept of Citizenship and Attitudes Toward Women in Combat." *Sex Roles* 3 (1977): 469–77.

Segal, Mady Wechsler. "The Military and the Family as Greedy Institutions." *Armed Forces and Society* 13 (1986): 9–38.

————. "Women in the Military: Research and Policy Issues." *Youth and Society* 10: 2 (December 1978): 99–126.

Segal, Mady Wechsler, and Segal, David R. "Social Change and the Participation of Women in the American Military." *Research in Social Movements, Conflicts and Change* 5 (1983): 235–58.

Shover, Michele J. "Roles and Images of Women in World War I Propaganda." *Politics and Society* (1975): 469–86.

Steele, Diana A. "Women and the Military: Substantial Barriers Remain." *ACLU Women's Rights Report* 3 (Winter 1981): 1, 5.

Stiehm, Judith. "Women and the Combat Exemption." *Parameters* (Journal of the U.S. Army War College) 10: 2 (June 1980): 51–59.

"This Is What You Thought About Women and the Draft." *Glamour*, April 1982, p. 31.

Thomas, P. J. "Attrition Among Navy Enlisted Women." *Defense Management Journal*, 2d Quarter 1980, pp. 43–49.

Thomas, Patricia J., and Durning, Kathleen P. "The Young Navy Woman: Her Work and Role Orientation." *Youth and Society* 10: 2 (December 1978): 135–58.

Wamsley, Gary L. "Contrasting Institutions of Air Force Socialization: Happenstance or Bellwether?" *American Journal of Sociology* 78 (1972): 399–417.

Webb, James. "Women Can't Fight." *The Washingtonian*, November 1979, pp. 144–282.

"Where Women Will Fit in the New Army." *U.S. News and World Report*, 4 October 1982, p. 53.

"Women and the Draft." *Glamour*, April 1982, pp. 31–32.

"Women in the Army—End of a Honeymoon," *U.S. News and World Report*, 4 October 1982, pp. 51–53.

"Women in the Military: It Is Really a Matter of Human Power." *Government Executive*, February 1982, pp. 22, 24–26.

Yagoda, Ben. "The Man Who Shapes Up the Army." *New York Times Magazine*, 28 September 1986, pp. 34–44.


NEWSPAPERS

"Adultery Case Witness Disciplined." *Air Force Times*, 15 December 1986.

"Air Force, Navy Chiefs Oppose Registering Women for Draft." *Baltimore Sun*, 6 February 1980.

"Air Force Opposes Recruitment Quotas for Women." *Air Force Times*, 6 May 1985.

"AF Plans More Child Care Centers." *Air Force Times*, 25 February 1985.

"Air Force Reluctantly Accepts Quotas on Women." *Air Force Times*, 15 October 1984.

"AF to Retrain 1100 EM Under Palace Balance." *Air Force Times*, 27 February 1984.

"Air Force Wants Substantial Reduction in Future Recruiting Goals for Women." *Air Force Times*, 27 July 1981.

"A Lot of Exposure for a Little Exposure." *Washington Post*, 5 March 1980.
"ABC News—Harris Poll." Press release, 6 December 1978.
"Army Calls Virtual Halt to Recruiting Women." *Army Times*, 10 August 1981.
"Army, Colleges Battle Gay Question." *Pacific Stars and Stripes*, 28 July 1982.
"Army Dismissed Eight Women on Sex Charges." *New York Times*, 4 October 1986.
"Army Fails to Prove Its Claim on Women Dropouts." *Washington Post*, 9 November 1982.
"Army Studies Limit on Role of Women." *Long Island Newsday*, 20 June 1982.
"Army Study on Women Draws Divided Reaction." *Army Times*, 6 September 1982.
Army Survey Finds Sexual Harassment of Military Women Overseas." *Baltimore Sun*, 12 February 1980.
"Army to Close Twenty-Three Job Categories to Women." *Los Angeles Times*, 27 August 1982.
"Army to End Coed Companies in Basic Training." *Baltimore Sun*, 4 May 1982.
"Aspin, McCoy Square Off Over AF's Use of Women." *Air Force Times*, 19 March 1984.
"Bar on Single-Parent Enlistments Upheld." *Air Force Times*, 8 July 1985.
"Chief Judge Sees Broader Role for Military Court." *Air Force Times*, 9 September 1985.
"Clarke Calls Separate BT 'Step Backward.'" *Army Times*, 16 August 1982.
"Code of Conduct Revised." *Army Times*, 13 April 1988.
"DACOWITS Told Women's Report Will Be 'Positive.'" *Navy Times*, 6 September 1982.
"DOD Wants Weight Rules for Women Recruits Eased." *Air Force Times*, 8 December 1986.
"The Draft of Women: Let's Settle It Now." *Washington Post*, 1 February 1980.
"Female GI Wins Fight; Army Mum." *Colorado Springs Gazette Telegraph*, 10 April 1984.
"Fifteen Thousand Seagoing Billets Being Opened to Women." *Navy Times*, 4 January 1988.
"Focus on Women in Army Recommendations." *Pentagon News*, 24 February 1983.
"Fraternization Policy Changed." *Pentagram News*, 30 November 1978.
"General Attacks Pregnancies: Urges Abortions for All First-Term Women Soldiers." *New York Times*, 24 June 1981.
"General Vessey Sees Women as Biggest Military Change." *Washington Post*, 3 February 1984.
"Goals on Recruiting Women Lowered." *Washington Post*, 27 August 1982.
"Harassment Makes Ft. Meade a Sentence 'to Hell' for Women." *Baltimore Sun*, 12 February 1980.
"Homosexuals—A New Battle for the Military." *Los Angeles Times*, 25 September 1980.
"Honorable Discharges Decrease by 27,000." *Air Force Times*, 18 June 1984.
"House Eases Single Parents' Reserve Signups." *Air Force Times*, 15 September 1986.

"Korb: Women Needed to Maintain Readiness." *Air Force Times*, 14 May 1984.
"Marines Shun Pick-up of Gay Bar's Gift Toys: Donations for a Hundred Children Stalled." *Los Angeles Times*, 22 December 1983.
"Men Will Be Boys." *Air Force Times*, 6 December 1982.
"Military Right to Discharge Homosexuals Upheld." *Los Angeles Times*, 10 December 1983.
"Military Widening Roles of Women." *New York Times*, 27 December 1987.
"Navy Drops Charges Against Playboy Poser." *Navy Times*, 1980.
"Navy Duty Nearly Impossible for Women." *Los Angeles Times*, 15 April 1987.
"Navy Halts Automatic Discharges for Pregnancy." *Los Angeles Times*, 3 August 1982.
"Navy Tightens Size Requirements for Fliers."*Air Force Times*, 4 June 1984.
"Navy to Allow Female Technicians Aboard Submarines for Sea Trials." *Los Angeles Times*, 6 June 1987.
"New Administration Slows Drive to Ease Combat Bars for Women." *Army Times*, 3 August 1981.
"New Policy for Women Requires More Sea Duty." *Navy Times*, 13 July 1987.
"Officer Convicted of Adultery Claims Discrimination." *Air Force Times*, 24 November 1986.
"Official Urges Enlistment Slowdown: Women's Impact on Military Questioned," *Colorado Springs Sun*, 20 February 1981.
"O'Neill Opposes Drafting Women." *Los Angeles Times*, 1 February 1980.
"Pentagon Reassessing Impact of Women in the Armed Forces." *Washington Post*, 13 May 1981.
"Pentagon Unit Finds Sexual Harassment." *Washington Post*, 18 September 1987.
"Pinup Fears She'll Be Nailed to the Mast." *Los Angeles Times*, 29 February 1980.
"Quotas on Recruiting Women to Continue." *Air Force Times*, 3 June 1985.
"Recruiting Aids Favor Army." *Air Force Times*, 8 November 1982.
"Retired General Defends Women." *Pittsburgh Press*, 17 July 1982.
"Ruling Clears Way for Homosexual's Discharge." *Air Force Times*, 9 January 1984.
"Sailors Pregnant to Avoid Rough Duty?" *San Diego Tribune*, 25 February 1988.
"Secretary of the Navy Clears Way for Woman to Go on Sub Trials." *Navy Times*, 29 June 1987.
"Separations of Overweight Members Up Fourfold." *Air Force Times*, 16 March 1987.
"Slow Female EM Recruiting." *Air Force Times*, 19 January 1981.
"Soviets to Accept Women in Military." *Washington Post*, 1 April 1985.
"Students Oppose Draft Plan." *Daily Californian*, 19 February 1980.
"Thirteen Pct. Picked for E-5." *Air Force Times*, 7 February 1983.
"Top Pentagon EO Officer to Leave Post in August." *Federal Times*, 23 August 1982.
"Tougher Size Rules for Navy Fliers Rescinded." *Air Force Times*, 11 June 1984.

"Tradition Shapes Officers, Author Says." *Air Force Times*, 15 December 1986.
"Two-Tier Hike System Continues for NCOs." *Air Force Times*, 30 April 1984.
"Two-Tier Promotion System May Be Extended." *Air Force Times*, 10 October 1983.
"Use of Women in Military Wanes in Last Four Years." *Army Times*, 19 November 1984.
"Wanted: More Women for Sea Duty." *Washington Post*, 22 December 1987.
"Weight Limits Raised for Women." *Air Force Times*, 6 July 1987.
"Weinberger Spells Out Defense's Sexual Harassment Policy." *Navy Times*, 31 August 1981.
"Women Are Cleared for Duty on Atom Missile Launching." *New York Times*, 8 February 1985.
"Women Ask If Army Is Going Off-Limits." *Washington Post*, 4 August 1982.
"Women-in-Army Report Delayed." *Army Times*, 15 February 1982.
"Women in Combat Backed." *Colorado Springs Sun*, 21 June 1978.
"Women Just Aren't Fit for Combat Duty." *Chicago Tribune*, 6 February 1979.
"Women Move Up in the Military, But Many Jobs Remain Off Limits." *Wall Street Journal*, 14 March 1985.
"Women Report Delay." *Army Times*, 25 October 1982.
"Women Say Sexual Harassment Is Driving Them Out of the Army." *Baltimore Sun*, 26 March 1980.
"Women's Role in Military Faces Pentagon Study." *Memphis Press-Scimitar*, 1 February 1982.
"Women Upset Over Non-Combat Role in Grenada Invasion." *Stars and Stripes —Europe*, 14 December 1983.
"Women Who Fought Sex Bias on Job Prove to Be a Varied Group." *Wall Street Journal*, 8 June 1987.


PAPERS AND MANUSCRIPTS

Berryman, Sue E. "The Social Composition of American Enlisted Forces: Nineteenth and Twentieth Century Images and Realities, Political Dynamics, and Questionable Assumptions." Draft for Comment. Prepared for the Ford Foundation. February 1983.
Clarke, Maj. Gen. Mary E. (Ret.). Speech. Women's Week Activities. Fort Bragg, N.C., 25 August 1983.
DeFleur, Lois B. "Organizational and Ideological Barriers to Sex Integration in Military Groups." Pullman, Washington State University, 1981.
Dowdell, Faye E. "Gender Difference in Orientation Toward Military Service." Manuscript, University of Maryland, Baltimore, 1978.
Dupes, Capt. Yvonne M. "U.S. Report on Experiences with Expanded Utilization of Women in the Services." Paper presented at the 1981 Conference of the Committee on Women in the NATO Forces. Brussels, 25–27 May 1981.
Gal, Reuven. "Combat Stress as an Opportunity: The Case of Heroism." Paper presented at the Northeast Regional Conference of the Inter-University Seminar on Armed Forces and Society. Albany, N.Y., 11–13 April 1985.

Holmes, Douglas S. "Leadership and Women in Organizations." Research Paper, Fort Benning, Ga., 1986.

Jacobs, James B. "The Impact of Legal Change on the United States Armed Forces Since WWII." Ph.D. diss., Cornell University, 1977.

Kane, John E. "Women in Non-Traditional Assignments: A Case Study of Navy Tugs." Paper presented at 57th Annual Convention of the Western Psychological Association, 20–23 April 1977.

Mansbridge, Jane J. "A New Way of Doing Normative Political Philosophy." Paper presented at the annual meeting of the American Political Science Association. Denver, 2–5 September 1982.

Moskos, Charles C. "The Enlisted Ranks in the All-Volunteer Army." Paper prepared for the Military in America Society study. White Burkett Miller Center of Public Affairs, University of Virginia, January 1978.

———. "The Modest Method: Participant Observation in Military Sociology." Paper presented at the Workshop on Research on Military Manpower, 21–23 September 1972.

Robertson, David, and Trent, T. T. "Predicting Muscularly Demanding Job Performance in Navy Occupations." Paper presented at the meeting of the American Psychological Association, August 1983.

Rose, Elihu. "The Anatomy of Mutiny." Manuscript, 1981.

Ruddick, Sara. Drafting Women: Pieces of a Puzzle. Working Paper. College Park, Md.: Center for Philosophy and Public Policy, 1982.

Sanchez, Anita, and Brown, Robert. "Women in the Military: An Experiment in Opinion Polls." Paper, University of Southern California, 1980.

Segal, Mady Wechsler. "The Scientific Knowledge Affecting the Utilization of Women in the Services." Paper presented at the 1981 Conference of the Committee on Women in the NATO Forces. Brussels, 25–27 September 1981.

Toupin, Elizabeth Ahn. "When the Serviceman's Battered Wife Is Also Asian." Manuscript. Medford, Mass.

Woefel, John C. "Women in the Army." Paper presented at the Southwest Regional Conference of the Inter-University Seminar on Armed Forces and Society. N.d.

"Women and the Military." A Women's Equity Action League (WEAL) Fund Kit. Washington, D.C., September 1979.

Wood, Sara Loeb. "Integrating Women into Combat Support Occupations: A Study in Cultural and Policy Conflict." Paper presented at the Southwest Regional Conference of the Inter-University Seminar on Armed Forces and Society. Dallas, 27–29 April 1978.

Wright, Maj. Ann. "The Roles of U.S. Army Women in Grenada." Speech. Women's History Week, Fort Bragg, N.C., 7 March 1984.

# Index